ROAMING FREE LIKE A DEER

BUDDHISM AND THE NATURAL WORLD

DANIEL CAPPER

CORNELL UNIVERSITY PRESS
Ithaca and London

First published 2022 by Cornell University Press

Library of Congress Cataloging-in-Publication Data

Names: Capper, Daniel, 1962– author.
Title: Roaming free like a deer : Buddhism and the natural world / Daniel Capper.
Description: Ithaca [New York] : Cornell University Press, 2022. | Includes bibliographical references and index.
Identifiers: LCCN 2021042211 (print) | LCCN 2021042212 (ebook) | ISBN 9781501759574 (hardcover) | ISBN 9781501761966 (paperback) | ISBN 9781501759581 (pdf) | ISBN 9781501759598 (epub)
Subjects: LCSH: Ecology—Religious aspects—Buddhism. | Environmental ethics. | Buddhist ethics.
Classification: LCC BQ4570.E23 C37 2022 (print) | LCC BQ4570.E23 (ebook) | DDC 294.3/5—dc23
LC record available at https://lccn.loc.gov/2021042211
LC ebook record available at https://lccn.loc.gov/2021042212

All photographs are by the author.

Contents

Acknowledgments

I am most grateful to Mr. James Lance, my editor at Cornell University Press, who offered steadiness, guidance, and excellent aid that improved the text while also patiently tolerating my eccentricities. I am appreciative as well for an Aubrey Keith and Ella Ginn Lucas Endowment for Faculty Excellence Award through the University of Southern Mississippi, which generously supported some useful fieldwork and in so doing made the presentation better. Finally, anonymous reviewers for Cornell University Press provided welcome help that improved the text. The errors that remain are mine.

Note on Transliteration

Words that have entered the English language, such as nirvana, karma, samsara, and ahimsa, are treated as English language words. Pāli and Sanskrit terms have been rendered into standard International Alphabet of Sanskrit Transliteration formats. For the sake of coherence and textual beauty, some Buddhist concepts are employed according to context, so that the Pāli-language "Dhamma," or Buddhist religion, of Thailand becomes the Sanskrit-language "Dharma" of Japan. Sinhalese appears in Government of Sri Lanka transliterations whenever possible. The transliteration of Thai follows the Royal Thai General System of Transcription whenever possible. Chinese appears in the Pinyin standard while Japanese manifests in the revised Hepburn standard whenever possible. Tibetan poses a special challenge since the pronunciations of terms in Wylie transliteration are often opaque to nonspeakers of the language despite the literary precision of these terms. Therefore, in the main text I have relied on phonetic transliterations following the Tibetan and Himalayan Library Simplified Phonetic System, while when relevant I also supply the Wylie term either on first usage in the text or in the notes. Exceptions to these rules may be found regarding the self-referred names of Buddhists, to whom I have deferred. Further, I follow the *Oxford English Dictionary* convention of leaving the names of famous people in the forms that they are best known, so that I render Thích Nhất Hạnh's name with the more familiar spelling of Thich Nhat Hanh. Likewise, familiar places whose names remain commonly known without diacritical marks, like Tokyo, appear without diacritical marks.

Introduction

Because of his compassion for nonhuman creatures, the Chinese Buddhist master Zhuhong (1535–1615 CE) regularly practiced and strongly encouraged others to practice the Buddhist ritual of *fangsheng*, or animal release. In this custom, animals otherwise destined for harm lovingly receive liberation into what are thought to be more beneficial conditions. Zhuhong and his followers, for instance, purchased live fish from human food markets and then, while chanting Buddhist scriptures, released them unharmed into rivers rather than eating them. In freeing animals like this, Zhuhong followed a couple of strategies. First, at the market Zhuhong would buy as many captive animals as he could afford. In addition, according to Zhuhong the deed of releasing is more fundamental than the size or number of animals released, preventing attachment to counting the animals freed.[1] Based on these policies, the Buddhist teacher Zhuhong enthusiastically insisted on performing such animal releases because, in his words, "As a human values her or his life, so do animals love theirs."[2]

Zhuhong obviously intended his animal release practices to benefit the animals themselves, thus bringing a greater sense of sustainability to his environment. In today's world such an intention may be most welcome, given the ecological troubles that beset us so vividly that they almost require no recounting. Temperatures across our globe are currently rising problematically, and, as a result, so are water levels from lost glaciers. The air is so polluted in many cities that citizens wear masks over their mouths for this reason alone. Giant patches of nonbiodegradable plastic clog our world's oceans. Along with ills like these, we are losing animal and plant species at alarming rates.

Ecologically concerned as he was, perhaps if the Buddhist master Zhuhong were with us at present he could help us with some of our environmental travails. Certainly he would seem to fit in well with many contemporary animal rights or environmentalist organizations. Sadly, though, problems lurked even in his own ecological world. For instance, a couple of his followers liberated ten thousand eels from harm but did so believing that the accrued virtue helped them pass their civil service exams early. This created suspicion (which can never be proven) that these followers were motivated more by their own economic benefit than they were for the welfare of eels.[3] Also, as I examine more fully in chapter 7 of this book, animal liberation practices like Zhuhong's at times have resulted in struggles with invasive species, such as native turtles in Guangzhou, China, that have nearly gone extinct as an effect of many released Brazil turtles.[4] There also have been mismatches between comfortable habitats and actual release sites, such as with the birds of prey that have strategically waited downstream in order to devour fish that have just been released in a bunch.[5] Further, counterproductive market arrangements have emerged at times, such as hunters who capture wild animals precisely so that they can be sold to animal releasers.[6] Zhuhong's Buddhist example therefore instructs us that even such an apparently innocuous activity as freeing animals from human dinner bowls can produce ecologically troublesome results.

This book is about environmental tensions like the problems that can arise while freeing fish, even if one is compassionately motivated. Today more than ever, we need a robust set of environmental ethics that can steer us in positive directions, and Buddhism, with its practices like Zhuhong's animal release rituals, can provide us with at least some of the moral ecological guidance that we require. Yet, like with all systems of ethics, Buddhist environmental practices like Zhuhong's sometimes do not lead to the most satisfying results. Hence, a synthetic analysis of how Buddhism may help us move forward appropriately in the climate change age as well as a clear-sighted understanding of the limits of Buddhist environmental ethics may provide great ecological value. Over the rest of this book, I pursue precisely such value while I explore a comprehensive, critical, and analytical investigation of the theory, practice, and real-world ecological performance of Buddhist environmental ethics. I begin this examination by turning to some Buddhist environmental ethical voices in order to gain a greater context.

A Critical Examination of Buddhist Environmentalism

Many environmentalists like the motivational factor that religiosity can provide, and therefore there exists plenty of discussion of Buddhism as a religion that supports twenty-first-century ecological initiatives. In fact, because Buddhism describes the universe as dependent arising (in the scriptural language of Pāli: *paṭicca-samuppāda*), or cosmically interconnected across time and space, and emphasizes the importance of compassion for nonhumans in ways unlike some other religions, Buddhism makes a popular choice for religion-based environmentalist discussions.

But, to date, there remain some significant shortcomings within this fertile field of inquiry. First, a great number of environmentalist writings investigate Buddhist approaches to nonhuman nature primarily in terms of the ideals of the tradition, thereby overlooking some rather serious real-world limitations. In addition, many environmentalist works are not set in fruitful critical dialogue nor are they subjected to synthetic analysis, leading to confusion and perhaps limiting beneficial actions. Let me further explore these two shortcomings so that my reader can more clearly see the place of this book.

As for existing environmental literature regarding Buddhist values, it is in no way difficult to find paeans to Buddhist nature-friendliness. A common argument of this literature holds that extending compassion through an interconnected universe, as Buddhism asks one to do, makes Buddhism an intrinsically environmentalist religion, with the occasional rejoinder that simply following the Buddhist path automatically makes one more ecofriendly.[7] Because of this perceived environmentalist potency, Buddhism quite often is acclaimed as the form of religion most likely to aid the pursuit of a more sustainable human future. The scholar of Buddhism Grace G. Burford, for instance, states that the Buddhist precept against intoxicants, when applied metaphorically to intoxicating consumerism, could diminish resource needs in a sustainable way.[8] The ethicists David E. Cooper and Simon P. James argue that Buddhism is an environmentally friendly religion because of the virtues of humility, self-mastery, equanimity, solicitude, nonviolence, and sense of responsibility that Buddhism engenders.[9] Peter Harvey characterizes Buddhism's ideals of relationship with the natural world as embodying "harmonious cooperation," a view echoed by Francis H. Cook with his claim that

Buddhism possesses a "cosmic ecology."[10] The founder of the Deep Ecology movement, the ecophilosopher Arne Naess, lauds Buddhism for its denial of the idea that entities possess abiding and independent essences as well as for its emphasis on the importance of self-realization.[11] Finally, Leslie E. Sponsel and Poranee Natadecha-Sponsel assert that "some of the basic principles of Buddhism parallel those of ecology."[12]

Unfortunately, despite many praises of Buddhist ecofriendliness, Buddhism sometimes fails to deliver in terms of practical realities rather than philosophical ones. When one steps back from Buddhist ideals and examines the material lives of Buddhists, one sometimes finds severe problems in realizing Buddhism's many supportive ecofriendly endorsements. As the scholar of Buddhism Duncan Ryūken Williams states, "When one reviews the history of the interface of Buddhism and environmentalism, the overwhelming tendency has been to define the Buddhist contribution to environmentalism in terms of the most idealized notion of what Buddhism is," while ignoring real-world difficulties.[13] For Buddhists, therefore, "the belief in harmony with nature at the philosophical level is no blueprint for creating and maintaining such harmony on a day-to-day level," as Williams claims.[14]

In the same vein as Williams but with alternative concepts, the environmental ethicist William Edelglass expresses a similar insight in saying, "When environmental philosophy takes place primarily at the level of metaphysics and abdicates the realm of policy to the social and natural sciences, it abandons much of its capacity to contribute to a more sustainable future."[15] Phrasing this outlook in terms of Zhuhong's animal-loving fish releases, attending only to the commendable values of compassion and lovingkindness that drive such releases obscures unintentional negative real-world impacts like introducing invasive species.

In light of the potential empirical-impact limitations of Buddhist environmental philosophies, consider the twelve substantially Buddhist countries studied by Yale University's Center for Environmental Law and Policy (YCELP): Bhutan, Burma (Myanmar), Cambodia, China (Tibet appears as a part of China in these data), Japan, Laos, Mongolia, South Korea, Sri Lanka, Taiwan, Thailand, and Vietnam. According to YCELP, these countries struggle to maintain positive environmental records.[16] In 2020 YCELP ranked 180 countries regarding their ecofriendliness in terms of ecosystems protection and human health issues, using 32 indicators in 11 categories to produce an Environmental Performance Index (EPI) for each country. Of the 12 substantially Buddhist countries, relatively impressive Japan and South Korea scored highest at numbers 12 and 28 in the world, respectively, or in the top 16th percentile of the 180 countries. Surprisingly to some perhaps, among substantially Buddhist nations only Taiwan and Thailand joined Japan and South Korea in performing in the top half of all countries. Burma brought up the Buddhist rear, finishing a miserable 179th out of 180 countries, with Vietnam at 141 out of all countries and Mongolia earning 147th place. The average substantially Buddhist country in these data ranked 102 out of 180 countries, scoring in the bottom 43rd percentile overall, meaning that in terms of environmental difficulties the average substantially Buddhist country appears to be a bit worse than the world's average. While these environmental records could be more dismal, they seem far from justifying many of the environmentalist praises that have been heaped upon Buddhism.

Of course, many factors play a role in creating problematic environmental performances like these and some of these forces have little or nothing to do with Buddhism. Among them, environmental performance is impossible to quantify without subjective elements. Additionally, not all of the people living in the countries YCELP listed are Buddhists. Further, actions with environmental impact in Buddhist realms often stem from social, economic, or political dynamisms rather than religious ones. For example, both Galen Rowell and Liu Jianqiang darkly describe how the massive loss of wildlife on the Tibetan plateau in recent decades has occurred precisely against the protests of some Buddhists.[17]

Despite these limitations, however, significant numbers of Buddhist actors helped create YCELP's unpleasant numbers, which do not appear to support the notion that Buddhism is fundamentally a religion that leads to acceptable twenty-first-century sustainability. Therefore, we need to understand more clearly the empirical, rather than simply ideal, roles that Buddhism can play in shaping the environmental politics, social dynamics, and private practices that may lead to outcomes like those found in YCELP's study. It is worth looking more deeply into the lived world of Buddhism in order to determine exactly what positive and negative roles the Buddhist religion may or may not be playing, along with a host of other factors, in fostering both healthy and harmful ecological situations. Over the rest of this book, therefore, I will maintain a primary focus on the environmental valences of material Buddhist lifeworlds.

Synthetic Analyses

In addition to an inattention to real-world results, as I mentioned, another shortcoming of the literature concerning Buddhism and environmentalism stems from a lack of shared presumptions and conclusions across Buddhist worlds. This situation frequently leaves Buddhist environmentalists talking past each other and inhibits any sense of a critical, comparative Buddhist environmental ethical framework on which either academic scholars or Buddhists from varying pedigrees can agree. For environmental thinkers and actors, there problematically exists a "plurality of views and lack of consensus among scholars working in the area of Buddhist environmental ethics," in the words of the researcher Pragati Sahni.[18]

Let me offer just one example of what I mean. In the excellent collection of essays, *Dharma Rain: Sources of Buddhist Environmentalism*, one finds separate writings from respected Buddhist environmental leaders, including Thich Nhat Hanh from Vietnam, the Fourteenth Dalai Lama from Tibet, and Sivaraksa Sulak from Thailand. Nhat Hanh premises his fine contribution to the volume on the scriptural *Diamond Sūtra* and its collapsing of the distinction between animate and inanimate beings.[19] Yet the Dalai Lama does not collapse distinctions in this way and grounds his presentation instead in Tibetan Buddhist texts in which eliminating this dualism is not a concern.[20] For his part, Sulak produces a searing indictment of consumerism but does so by invoking Thai customs that are not a part of the worlds of Nhat Hanh or the Dalai Lama.[21] Therefore, one finds three intelligent, stimulating, and provocative environmental works in the same volume, yet there is no synergy, resonance, or necessary basis for agreement between their voices.

While this outcome in itself is to be expected, given the acceptable yet disparate Buddhist presumptions of these works, currently we lack a context-providing apparatus that enables environmental ethicists to critically sort through the similarities and differences of works like these. By extension, a critical, comparative basis for Buddhist environmental actions that might influence all Buddhists also appears to be absent, and this latter, practical point is crucial since positive environmental action often mandates concerted, coordinated responses. Human-influenced global warming, for example, cannot be arrested by the green actions of just one person and instead requires relatively coherent counteractions from huge numbers of humans from different nations, races, languages, and cultures—like one finds looking across the Buddhist world. Hence, there exists serious pragmatic value in the warning of the scholar Seth Devere Clippard that "if each individual settles on her own interpretation of what an ecoBuddhist life requires, there is no assurance that any specific environmental problem will be attended to by a large enough population to make a difference."[22] Alternatively, in theory, we realize a more sustainable environment if varied Buddhists can identify their horizons for dialogic agreement as well as disagreement because, as the environmental ethicist Roger S. Gottlieb wrote, "Cooperation among different types of people is often the key to success in environmental struggles."[23]

In response to this set of circumstances, in this book I aim to bring diverse voices together with a critical, comparative approach, so that one can better see how different ecological presumptions and outcomes of varying Buddhists can either be appreciated for being in unison, properly conceived as irreconcilable, or understood in some other relationship, whatever the case may be. By critically and comparatively examining diverse Buddhist environmental viewpoints in a monographic conversation, it becomes easier to separate more universal perspectives and their meanings from more idiosyncratic ones. This allows scholars and Buddhists themselves to advance toward the emergence of a clearer picture of the relationships between varying Buddhist environmental ethics and ecological actions.

Based on the critical orientation of my ethical dialogue, the comparative and synthetic approach employed in this book allows a measure of appreciation for why Buddhist material realities do not always live up to the religion's reputation for engendering a sustainable environment. For instance, as I will explore throughout the book, generally Buddhism encourages the extension of compassion to individual humans and animals. Some American Buddhists, in fact, have chosen to offer compassion even to potential microbes as far away as Mars.[24] This compassion fosters an animal-friendly dynamic within the tradition and Buddhism can provide a relatively solid basis for efforts to improve the welfare of individual animals, especially those that are not used for human food. Such compassion is important in the work of the animal studies scholar Marc Bekoff in undoing "the alienation and fragmentation that currently defines our damaged relationship to the natural world."[25]

However, despite Buddhism's portrayal of a broadly interconnected universe, because of beliefs in reincarnation Buddhists tend to extend this compassion to humans and animals but very rarely also to plants, minerals, and water, these latter being considered unavailable for rebirth. The targeting of Buddhist compassion almost solely to humans and animals in this way results, with exceptions, in a limited biocentric approach to the natural world, meaning that Buddhism ethically values humans and animals but does not substantially value other entities in the natural world similarly. This limited biocentric attitude lacks what a viable environmental ethic demands, which is some sense of an ecocentric orientation, this being an orientation that places substantial ethical value on plants, minerals, and water.[26] In the words of the foundational ecologist Aldo Leopold, a viable environmental ethic must enlarge "the boundaries of the community to include soils, water, plants, and animals, or collectively: the land," and Buddhism often fails to achieve this aside from some welcome attention to animals.[27]

While Buddhism needs a more ecocentric orientation to support a viable environmental ethic, Buddhism itself does not lack some ecocentric voices that extend some ethical value to plants, minerals, and water, as I will show. However, these voices have historically been somewhat marginalized. Additionally, twenty-first-century environmental problems—like the Fukushima nuclear spill that fouled an entire ocean with radioactivity—were not things that ecocentric Buddhists like Japan's Dōgen (1200–1253 CE) had to consider. Through no fault of their own, the voices of many ecocentric Buddhists like Dōgen thereby cannot contend very well with the inevitable issues of choice of what to preserve that arise with contemporary ecological actions and ethics, limiting the potential impacts of their outlooks in the present day. If we must value everything because everything is interconnected, as ecocentric Buddhists like Dōgen appear to assert (see chapter 6), then we must protect ocean radioactivity as well as dolphins, atmospheric carbon as well as parrots, and anthrax as well as human probiotics. Because of this weakness, Buddhism's concepts of an interconnected, dependent arising universe do not, in themselves, provide an environmentalist magic pill despite commonly found portrayals to the contrary. As the environmental philosopher Arne Naess put it, "'All things hang together' is a good slogan, but it does not bring us far if we do not form some notions of *how* things hang together."[28]

Another problem arises regarding Buddhist compassion which, through its focus on individuals, struggles in application to complicated ecosystems in which a multitude of beings rely on constant predation on each other for survival. The scholar of Buddhism Ian Harris emphasizes this point in writing, "Compassion for the fate of individual members of the animal kingdom is not the same as the more general concern for the destiny of species characteristic of much environmentalist literature," so that for Harris, "Buddhism cannot uphold a self-consciously 'environmentalist' ethic."[29] In fact, difficulties in applying ideals of compassion to the complexities of the natural world are one reason why the scholar of Buddhist history Johan Elverskog wrote, "Ecological awareness is not inherent in the Buddhist tradition itself."[30]

Therefore, my analysis throughout this book suggests that the animal-friendly elements that contribute to Buddhist credentials for green living also provide obstacles to the development of full environmental thinking and action from within the tradition itself despite its assertion of an interconnected universe. As my reader will see, Buddhism deserves some of its nature-friendly reputation in terms of providing a nice home for animals that humans do not fancy eating but struggles to establish sustainability when it comes to broader ecosystem welfare and maintenance.

Having briefly surveyed Buddhism's environmental strengths and weaknesses, I must now answer a question: What measure do I use to delineate what is a strength and what is a weakness? After all, what may be perceived as tragic deforestation by one person may be another person's lovely pasture. I answer this question with the concept of a sustainable biosphere.

Sustainable Biosphere

In this book when I describe something as an environmental strength, I mean it operationally fulfills the definition of a "sustainable biosphere" as delineated by the leading environmental ethicist Holmes Rolston. In reflecting concepts found in the work of the foundational ecologist Aldo Leopold, Rolston describes a sustainable biosphere as "a baseline quality of environment" founded on the ecocentric notion of "land as community," this community broadly including organic beings as well as inorganic entities such as stones, rivers, and atmospheric constituents.[31] Holistically, Rolston asserts, "The bottom line, transcultural and nonnegotiable, is a sustainable biosphere . . . [of] the full Earth" since "our integrity is inseparable from Earth integrity."[32] With this statement, Rolston eschews more narrow concepts of sustainable development because with a sustainable biosphere the biospheric environment takes precedence over economics as a concern.[33] The full biosphere, according to Rolston, must be ecocentrically sustainable in terms of meeting the needs of both humans and nonhumans today while not sacrificing their systemic ecological needs of tomorrow.

Given that the standard we use to analyze data colors the outcomes that we perceive, my use of Rolston's sustainable biosphere concept requires some contextualization. In contrast to the often-found goal of sustainable development, for instance, Rolston substantially agrees with the environmental economist E. F. Schumacher, who led a generation of ecologists in emphasizing that sustainable development is itself an unsustainable strategy. The finite resources of a finite planet eventually will run out if development is endless. Hence, Schumacher wrote, we must all "question" "the idea of unlimited economic growth."[34] In reflecting this thread of Schumacher's thought, Rolston claims, "The fundamental flaw in sustainable development is that it typically sees the Earth only as resource."[35]

Additionally, despite its explicit concern with biology, Rolston's sustainable biosphere concept embodies an ecocentric, rather than a strictly biocentric or anthropocentric, circle of ecological concern. With intention and for their own sake, Rolston extends ethical value to abiotic elements of the environment such as gases, water bodies, and stones as part of enhancing total ecosystem health. This outlook is important since the environmental scientist Andrew Balmford, among many others, stresses how positive environmental healing and relative ecological stability can arise by attending foremost to abiotic, rather than animal, realities.[36]

Such ecocentrism appears to be a required weapon within our environmental ethical arsenal for battling global warming since in this struggle we must attend to our ethical valuations, or lack thereof, of atmospheric gases and stones. Climate change results in part from a broken carbon cycle, in which carbon that was underground as a mineral has been quickly released into the atmosphere as a gas instead, so that in the climate change era we must consider the circumspect ecological care not just of animals but also of gases. Finding ethical value for some, but not too much, carbon dioxide in our atmosphere, for instance, must be a part of our global warming moral toolbox.

Moreover, a number of global warming mitigation strategies like those involved with carbon capture attempt to transform atmospheric carbon dioxide into stone formations, so that responsible climate change strategies must attend to the possible ethical value of stones, too. A number of environmental thinkers, such as the geologist Murray Gray, in fact emphasize the interconnected realities of global warming and stony geosystems' health.[37] Reflecting this need to value abiotic entities like stones and gases along with biotic beings, the environmental ethicist Katie McShane states that we need "to learn how to talk about ecosystemic welfare directly" by embracing ecocentrism in fighting climate change.[38] Thus, although other perspectives exist, I employ Rolston's sustainable biosphere concept specifically because it has an ecocentric orientation that the global warming era seems to require at least in part.

I therefore utilize Rolston's sustainable biosphere concept as a standard throughout this book to assess environmental data from the Buddhist world. As statistical researchers know, though, data first must be formatted before it can be analyzed. One cannot randomly throw numbers into statistical software and expect a cogent analysis to result since the computer works with data that are ordered in specific ways. Likewise, in this book I cannot simply start producing random Buddhist stories and see where we go. If we are to get anywhere meaningful, I must order the data. The way that I order the data is distinctive to this book since I follow the innovative method of relational animism. Now, I must briefly describe the method of relational animism, beginning with a vibrant tale that brilliantly illuminates the essence of the method.

Buddhist Relational Animism

We can discover relational animism illustrated in a fascinating story about how the Buddha interacted with trees.[39] During the time of the Buddha around 500 BCE, there were some monks at Ālavī in India who cut down trees to build huts since it was common for the Buddha's disciples, who were instructed to "roam about free as deer," to construct simple housing.[40] Reflecting some beliefs found in ancient India, the resident spirit of one of these trees pleaded with a monk to stop. The monk paid no heed to the tree spirit's request and in fact struck the tree spirit's son with his ax. The tree spirit, now incensed, pondered killing the monk, but eventually decided to seek the counsel of the Buddha. The Buddha compassionately listened to the tree spirit's case and directed the spirit to a vacant tree as a new home.

In the meantime, however, word had spread regarding the monks' actions, with lay people and clerics speaking badly about the monastics. The Buddha responded by chastising the tree-cutting monks for being foolish and making the Buddhist order appear to be uncaring in the eyes of the people. He then issued a new monastic rule, Pācittiya 11, which forbids the unreasonable destruction of plants.[41]

In conversationally expressing concern for its home and family as well as respect for the Buddha, the tree spirit in this story appears as a person, by which I mean, following the anthropologist A. Irving Hallowell, a perceived subject with whom one interacts socially in linguistic, ritual, or other ways, rather than an object.[42] Throughout this book, there will appear many more instances in which animals, plants, and other nonhuman natural beings or, in this case, a spirit who is closely identified with an empirical natural entity, appear as persons in this sense. Although to date the personhood of nonhuman natural beings in the Buddhist world have been little discussed, from this story of a frustrated tree spirit who appears within a set of canonical rules for nuns and monks, one can already appreciate that this is an important topic to consider if one is to understand Buddhism fully.[43]

While the Buddha encountered a tree spirit, elephants as persons aided the Buddha's two chief disciples, Sāriputta and Moggallāna. At one time Sāriputta fell ill with a fever and needed lotus-stalk soup for medication, causing Moggallāna to visit the fabled Mandākinī lotus pond of the Himalayas. There, he asked two elephants for lotus stalks. One of the elephants bounded into the lake, used his trunk to pull up lotus stalks by their roots, then rinsed the mud off the stalks with lake water. These stalks were then reverentially offered by the elephants to Moggallāna, who quickly returned to Sāriputta's side. Moggallāna prepared Sāriputta's medicine, and, having taken it, Sāriputta's health improved.[44] In this way, Sāriputta's recovery intrinsically included a couple of affable pachyderm chemists who piously sought to reduce the suffering of one of the Buddha's disciples, therefore in a sense practicing devotional Buddhism.

Besides faithful elephants, in this story about lotuses and animals one discovers that the monastic precept against unreasonable plant use that I mentioned previously does not prevent all uses of plants. Moreover, in this story the elephants receive treatment as persons but the lotus stalks do not, a point that is instructive in fully comprehending Buddhist approaches to the nonhuman realm. Such differentials in attributed personhood appear in numerous other contexts across the Buddhist world and bear ramifications at least for Buddhist environmental habits, dietary propensities, ethics, notions of the character of the enlightenment experience of nirvana, and philosophical conceptions of the web of relationships that the Buddha claimed make up our phenomenal universe. As such, convergences and divergences in Buddhist attributed personhood form the bedrock of analysis in this book.

Throughout this work I investigate instances in which Buddhists attribute or decline to attribute personhood to nonhuman beings as a grid for organizing and understanding data. On occasions when elephants but not lotus stalks appear as persons, we learn a great deal about some Buddhist environmental attitudes, for the elephants clearly enjoy greater ecological respect than the plants do.

Such differentials in the ascribed personhood of natural beings propel the interdisciplinary method that I use during the course of the book—a new model called relational animism. I describe this method, which arises from insights in animal studies, botany, anthropology, and philosophy, in much greater detail in chapter 2. Put briefly for now, relational animism consists of a form of belief and/or practice in which nonhuman entities are experienced as persons in their own right, with respect accorded to their specific agencies through linguistic, ritual, or other interactions.[45] With relational animism, animals, plants, and even stones and bodies of water receive positive human regard for their perceived subjective agencies.

In this light, many of my readers have had moments in which they verbally treated a pet, an automobile, or a computer not unlike a human person; relational animism extends such experienced personhood, albeit in a manner perhaps more respectful than the unfettered cursing of a recalcitrant computer, to various entities in the nonhuman environment. However, as we have already seen with elephants and lotus stalks, sometimes humans experience relational animism while at other times they do not, and these divergences can teach us a great deal about how humans interact with the nonhuman natural world. Used as a method, relational animism pointedly attends to such differentials in outcomes in terms of respectful personhood (non)attributions and the effects of these attributions and thereby provides outstanding benefits to our understanding of Buddhism and to our environmental ethics.

In terms of Buddhist studies gains, experiences with nonhuman nature like the Buddha and the tree spirit are often called "animism" by scholars. Any visitor to a primarily Buddhist country today almost certainly has encountered such animism within Buddhist realities, from houses for local spirits within Thai Buddhist monasteries to reverence for boulders at some Japanese Buddhist temples. Although some scholars ascribe this nature religion simply to the influences of local traditions, actually things are more complex since everywhere in the Buddhist world one finds local religions thoroughly admixed with, rather than simply coexisting with, Buddhist realities. The religion scholar Geoffrey Samuel describes an instance of this by ably probing how indigenous traditions work in tandem with Buddhist ones to create what Tibetans experience as an integrated religiosity, and there exist many other examples.[46] This blending of Buddhism with other religious forms prompts questioning about how Buddhism may participate from its own side in generating the numerous nature-religious phenomena found not just in Buddhist Asia but in the Buddhist West, too. Therefore, we need to explore nature religion in Buddhist universes more fully, as I do here.

In order to engage in this exploration, I expand the investigative purview beyond the world of humans so that we may appreciate more effectively the roles of nonhumans in Buddhism. In theater terms, I turn up the stage lights so that one may better witness more of the onstage nonhuman actors, not just those human-only actors previously in the spotlight. While I attend as much as I can to economic, political, psychological, and historical contexts so that we may comprehend more clearly the actions of Buddhists, my focus is on Buddhist personhood relationships with nonhumans, or the notable lack of them, in whatever contexts they may appear. In examining representative samples of approaches to nature from India, Sri Lanka, Thailand, China, Japan, Tibet, and the contemporary West, I intentionally look broadly across the Buddhist world to reveal that personhood relationships with nature pervade the tradition and are not just the province of specific Buddhists at specific times and in specific places, although they vary significantly according to conditions. I do this because we can learn much about Buddhist philosophy, practice, and environmental behavior from observing moments when personhood is attributed to nonhuman entities as well as when it is not so attributed.

Following my relational animist method, though, does more than enrich Buddhist studies, for, additionally, it advances crucial discussions in environmental ethics. For instance, the environmental philosopher Eric Katz skillfully describes how personhood-focused ethical discussions like those found here aid the development of healthier environmental outlooks and practices, such as those that may lead to the sustainable biosphere ideal of Holmes Rolston.[47] The political theorist Bruno Latour in fact encourages employing personhood models in battling climate change.[48] Indeed, personhood principles have already been successfully implemented in some environmentalist legal causes such as the preservation of the Whanganui River in New Zealand.[49] Explicitly bringing similar personhood attitudes into the Buddhist fold, the American Buddhist teacher and scholar David R. Loy asserts that ecologically applying personhood principles initiates ecological successes by overcoming social obstacles to action while beneficially resacralizing the landscape.[50]

Thus, in the ways that I have described, the relational animist method used in this book organizes data while it also advances Buddhist studies and empowers environmental ethical decision making. These contributions become visible especially in terms of three themes, which I now delineate.

Three Comparative Ecological Touchpoints

In the course of utilizing relational animism, from within the data three touchpoints for ecological comparison emerge: Buddhist vegetarianism, the alleged practice of religion by animals and other natural beings, and nature mysticism. These ecological touchpoints supply a framework for developing comparative Buddhist environmental ethics conversations by helpfully directing our attention to active and salient issues, so they arise repeatedly throughout the book and deserve some explanation now.

Regarding dietary habits, meat eating is at least somewhat permissible according to the Theravāda Buddhist scriptures, with Theravāda representing one of the three great sects of Buddhism along with Mahāyāna and Vajrayāna. As a result of this allowance, meat consumption commonly persists in predominantly Theravāda countries like Sri Lanka, Burma, Thailand, and Cambodia, although sometimes followers of Theravāda traditions abjure meat for reasons of personal piety. Conversely, there are Buddhist outlooks, especially in the Mahāyāna Buddhism that emerges from China and exists throughout the Buddhist East Asian worlds of Taiwan, Korea, Japan, and Vietnam, in which vegetarianism, and sometimes veganism, exist as fundamental Buddhist commitments. However, meat eating within these lineages is hardly unknown. Thus, in the Buddhist world carnivores may live next door to vegetarians despite the fact that they presumably follow the same teachings on proper diet. Reflecting this complex situation, in the West one commonly finds a cliché that all Buddhists are vegetarians. But while a greater vegetarian sensibility does mark Western Buddhism, as I will describe in chapter 8, this vegetarian stereotype still experiences constant debunking from the existence of numerous carnivorous Buddhists in the West and elsewhere.

Although many factors that I will describe contribute to this complicated situation regarding Buddhist eating habits, one gains traction in understanding if one probes Buddhist relational animism since often (but not always) humans shrink from eating beings that they consider to be persons, such as family pets.[51] As I will explore as one comparative touchpoint throughout the rest of the book, perceptions of which nonhuman beings count as persons and why helps determine whether Buddhists eat or do not eat certain nonhuman entities. For instance, more than do Theravāda scriptures, some Mahāyāna scriptures, such as the Laṅkāvatāra Sūtra, place greater emphasis on not eating animals because animals are perceived as persons, even kin persons like our mothers, and this outlook helps stimulate the more energetic vegetarian impulses that may be found in Mahāyāna worlds.

In addition to this culinary comparative ecological touchpoint, the tale of a tree spirit's reverencing the Buddha that we saw earlier, or, in other words, a nonhuman being as a person practicing religion, represents the second touchpoint for ecological comparison that I will investigate. As this book progresses, at times snakes will venerate the Buddha, a horse will mourn the Buddha's leaving, tigers will show devotion to monks, and plants will realize nirvana, among numerous other examples. These phenomena show that, in Buddhism, nonhuman beings may sometimes express their own personhood through perceived religious agency. Investigating the occurrences in which animals, plants, and even stones and wind are experienced as religious practitioners in their own right enables a new appreciation of the textures of social relationships in the Buddhist world as well as a stirring way of philosophically understanding the interconnected universe that Buddhism portrays.

Enriching the importance of these moments, and perhaps astonishing my reader, scholars such as the religion specialist Donovan O. Schaefer, the cognitive anthropologist Stewart Guthrie, and the chimpanzee expert Jane Goodall each have speculated that animals may be religious in their own, nonhuman, ways.[52] Goodall observed what she considered a possibly religious "dance of awe" among chimpanzees, and primatology offers other intriguing possible incidents of the practice of nonhuman religion. For example, a group of primatologists has observed wild chimpanzees in four separate locations in Western Africa ritually creating apparently functionless piles of stones around trees and have compared this behavior to that of the erection of religious rock cairns, such as the *la tsé* holy stone piles of Tibet, by humans.[53] Even more provocative, the baboon behavior specialist Barbara Smuts observed wild baboons on rare occasions sitting as if, in her words, in quiet Buddhist meditation as they gazed into pools of water for thirty-minute stints.[54] The entire baboon troop, even the youngsters, became uncharacteristically still, noiseless, and solemn, while they appeared to use the spots of water as their objects of focus. Given what to Smuts seemed to be contemplative practices by nonhuman beings, it pays to examine Buddhist examples relevant to scholarly claims of potential religious behavior in animals, and this is what I will do. However, throughout this book, I personally remain descriptive and critical in probing Buddhist contentions regarding nonhuman religiosity, making no claims of my own on this issue.

As for the third comparative ecological touchpoint of this book, nature mysticism, let me first describe what I mean by this phrase. Perhaps the fullest presentation of the theory of nature mysticism belongs to the scholar of religion R. C. Zaehner in his book, *Mysticism Sacred and Profane*. In Zaehner's terms, two diagnostic marks apply to discern nature mysticism. First, there must be a powerful experience of oneness of the human and the nonhuman, a "panenhenic" experience in which "without and within are one" in an altered state of consciousness experience that transcends both time and space.[55] Zaehner further states that the essentially sensual aspect of the experience is "different *in kind* from ordinary sense experience."[56]

Another scholar of mysticism, W. T. Stace, describes nature mysticism as belonging to the "extrovertive" type of mysticism. For him, extrovertive mysticism such as nature mysticism entails experiences of the oneness of the universe while possessing a "feeling of blessedness, joy, happiness, satisfaction, etc."[57] He interestingly contrasts this with the "introvertive" character of Buddhist meditation. In Stace's view, introvertive mysticism enjoins

FIGURE 1. A Tibetan *la tsé* stone cairn.

a consciousness in which "all the multiplicity of sensuous or conceptual or other empirical content has been excluded," a description that is difficult to apply to nature mysticism.[58]

While Zaehner's and Stace's criteria for the most part offer handy academic tools, their emphases on an experience of oneness with nature may offend Buddhist philosophers, who sometimes shy away from notions of oneness in deference to models of interconnection. But if one describes the experience as "nondual with nature" instead, one appears to preserve the meaning of the criteria provided by Zaehner and Stace while also pleasing Buddhists. Integrating these ideas, I will treat nature mysticism as a powerful altered-state-of-consciousness experience of human nonduality specifically with a nonhuman natural entity within a physical human habitat, an experience that significantly lacks dimensions of time and space and has a sensory or emotive quality, although perhaps unlike ordinary senses or emotions.

Armed with this definition of nature mysticism, we can begin to locate the place of nature-mystical practice in Buddhism. Remembering that the Buddha spoke against ancient Indian pre-Buddhist Brahmanic rites, including rites for sacred natural beings, there existed a sense in early Buddhism as portrayed by the scriptures to self-consciously steer away from any practices that might involve nature worship or nature mysticism.[59] This relative resistance against nature worship and nature mysticism thereby exists in the scriptures across all three great sects, so that expressions of it repeat throughout the chapters in this book.

At the same time, some Buddhists have found it difficult to renounce nature-mystical experiences and perspectives. Thus, in chapters to come we still discover some Buddhist nature-mystical practices, especially in the realms affected by Vajrayāna Buddhism, where mountains can become holy mandala residences of Buddhist deities. In these Chinese, Japanese, Korean, Mongolian, and Tibetan alpine practices, traversing a sacred mountain becomes understood as an inner journey of consciousness to nirvana, thus producing Buddhist nature-mystical phenomena.

The rest of the book highlights the presence of attitudes within Buddhism that emphasize treating nonhuman beings like animals as persons as well as examining some of the empirical outcomes of these attitudes. These empirical outcomes from India, Sri Lanka, Thailand, China, Japan, Tibet, and the contemporary West lead to a new understanding that Buddhist environmental ethical strengths in protecting animals fascinatingly often also instigate Buddhism's own weaknesses in dealing with larger ecosystems. By providing a more powerful environmental ethics methodology to uncover previously unappreciated real-world dynamics, this book provides a strong understanding of the multifaceted ways in which Buddhist humans interact with their nonhuman surroundings ecologically for both good and ill.

The next chapter, "Some Methods in Buddhist Environmental Ethics," provides scholars with a description of the relational animist method that I apply throughout the text. It also defines essential Buddhist terms and concepts regarding the character of human and nonhuman environments. While I recommend this material for focused academic researchers, other readers may wish to skip ahead to chapter 2, where they will encounter vibrant personhood relationships in the biography of the founder of the tradition, Gautama Buddha.

CHAPTER 1

Some Methods in Buddhist Environmental Ethics

Given that the population of the constitutional monarchy of Thailand is 95 percent Buddhist, for many Thais if there is a great saint within the nation, it must be the Buddhist king.[1] Thus, the late king, His Majesty King Bhumibol Adulyadej (1927–2016 CE), a one-time monk, remains widely respected as the embodiment of Buddhist principles even after his death. Interacting with such a religious king could have been intimidating, but fortunately ordinary Thai Buddhists received direction on this issue from the king's dog friend Tongdaeng, for whom His Majesty wrote a touching and popular biography, *The Story of Tongdaeng*.[2]

Tongdaeng (1999–2015 CE), whose name means "copper," was a mixed-characteristic Basenji who was adopted as a five-month-old stray on the streets of Bangkok. Because she had the same white spots on her nose and the tip of her tail as Tongdam, the royal male dog at the time, attendants brought her into the palace in a kind of canine arranged marriage. Described in her biography as "a common dog who is uncommon," Tongdaeng and the king enjoyed a special connection from the beginning since on the day that she was brought to the palace, she cried constantly but quickly became quiet and even fell asleep when the king took her into his lap.[3]

As portrayed in her biography, Tongdaeng had a noble bearing well before she became an official royal pooch since she had learned courteous behavior from her mother, Mae Daeng. Thus, according to the king's biography of her, Tongdaeng's behavior can instruct everyone since "one royal attendant mentioned that, if one wanted to know how to sit properly when one had an audience with the King, one should look at Tongdaeng" because her humility would lead her always to sit lower than the king.[4] Like a good subject, Tongdaeng was extremely loyal to the king, to whom she also was remarkably obedient.[5] Further, as a role model she exhibited proper Buddhist gratitude to others and therefore was "not presumptuous at all."[6]

This sweet royal canine tale contains a couple of important elements for scholars of Buddhist environmental ethics. First, the Buddhist king clearly treated Tongdaeng as a respected person who was worthy of emulation as well as her own biography. Additionally, *The Story of Tongdaeng*, given its sculpting by geography, politics, and society, reminds us that cultures crucially influence how we perceive and understand human and nonhuman environments.

Because of cultural personhood themes like these, in the introduction I explained that throughout this book I will utilize the innovative scholarly method of relational animism. With this interdisciplinary method we analyze how nonhuman entities become respectfully treated as persons, or not so treated, in order to understand Buddhist ecological dynamics with the nonhuman natural world. But to comprehend more fully what this means I need to delineate the method of relational animism in terms of its origin and function. Further, because cultures influence our concepts of the roles of humans and nonhumans, like *The Story of Tongdaeng* shows, additionally I must describe how human and nonhuman relational animist persons may or may not interact according to Buddhist cultural notions.

In this chapter, I tackle both of these methodological tasks. First, I delineate the method of relational animism, then I explore some specifically Buddhist concepts of human and nonhuman environments.

Relational Animist Method

By all accounts instances of nature religion, or animism, appear in profusion within Buddhist lifeworlds. However, to date, many scholars of Buddhism have hesitated to apply the concept of animism to Buddhist realities because of the outlines of the idea, which originated with Edward Tylor's encyclopedic two-volume *Primitive Culture* of 1871. Tylor described animism as a form of indigenous belief in "souls of individual creatures, capable of continued existence after the death or destruction of the body," so that in

Tylor's animism, squirrels, oak trees, and other beings in the nonhuman world possess their own independent souls.[7] An influential notion from the beginning, effects from Tylor's concept of animism extended to James George Frazer, author of the book, *The Golden Bough*, which enthralled readers in the early twentieth century. Frazer described animism as the belief that natural beings, especially plants in his presentation, possess souls like humans.[8] With their soul-based notions of animism, both Tylor and Frazer widely shaped scholarship throughout the twentieth and into the twenty-first century, although today some researchers avoid their works due to their implications in colonialist agendas.

The notions of animism of Tylor and Frazer never meshed well with Buddhist philosophical sensibilities despite the profusion of nature religion in the Buddhist world. Buddhist thought famously rejects individual separateness in space or continuity in time, meaning that Buddhism generally discards the idea of a soul, as the Pāli *Brahmajāla Sutta* and other scriptures show.[9] From this, so goes the often-made argument, if in Buddhism nothing has a soul, and animism is defined, following Tylor, as possession of a soul, then animism is impossible within Buddhism proper. Frazer himself proposed this argument, offering a piece of continuing received scholarly wisdom that animism exists in the Buddhist world not from the Buddhist side but only from the effects of local traditions.[10] Following Frazer, other scholars have tended rigidly to hold Buddhism and nature religion conceptually apart ever since.

Further, in his prominent work, *Burmese Supernaturalism*, the anthropologist Melford Spiro offered another reason why Buddhism may tolerate but cannot host animism: karma, or the moral law of cause and effect.[11] In many animist systems, spirits alter human destinies, granting prosperity as a boon or cursing people with problems. But, for Spiro, in Buddhism our fates are controlled by the force of karma as we take responsibility for our own actions rather than being randomly manipulated by capricious spirits. Because of this disjuncture that he perceived between individual karmic responsibility and the sporadic actions of spirits, Spiro kept animism theoretically separate from Buddhism, and many other scholars have followed suit.

However, Spiro's perspective, as well of those of Tylor and Frazer, have been eclipsed by recent scholarship in the field of religion and nature. This research story begins in 1934 when the prominent biologist Jacob von Uexküll forwarded the idea that each animal is a living subject who maintains its own *Umwelt*, or perceptive, active, and temporal world. Uexküll wrote, "We no longer regard animals as mere machines, but as subjects whose essential activity consists of perceiving and action."[12] This pioneering work then became buried for years by the overwrought denials of animal thought and emotion found among many behaviorists.[13] But, as a latter-day incarnation of Uexküll's insights, over the last two decades the academic world has witnessed the emergence of a broad movement, embracing many otherwise disparate disciplines, in which nonhuman beings in the human habitat increasingly receive scientific treatment as methodological subjects, as persons, rather than merely as objects within a human field. In these newer paradigms, nonhuman beings are respected as sources of autonomy and agency in their own right, not just regarded as existents for human use.

As an instance of what I mean, many people consider family pets to be persons; scientific theorists regarding the personhood of natural beings seek to extend this understanding in methodologically potent ways, but without the anthropomorphism that can occur with pet keeping. Scholars in this interdisciplinary movement, in fact, argue strenuously against anthropomorphism, in which nonhuman beings are granted human qualities like you may find in a children's movie. Personhood theorists wish to treat a hawk as a hawk person, not as a human person, through respect for the existential reality of a hawk as an ecological subject. So, for example, while the philosopher Thomas Nagel may have been correct that humans struggle to imagine what it is like to be a bat, this does not mean that bats lack their own lifeworlds. It just means that their lifeworlds are somewhat opaque to human experience.[14] Personhood scholars in animal studies, botany, and other fields recognize this situation as a research challenge and have produced some fine studies in doing so.

The late philosopher Jacques Derrida was part of this natural personhood movement. In his book, *The Animal That Therefore I Am*, Derrida told of a moment in which his cat saw him naked and Derrida felt shame as he would in front of a human person.[15] This incident caused Derrida to reflect on how Western philosophy traditionally has overlooked such moments and excluded a priori any real sense of personhood for animals. Derrida's recognition of nonhuman personhood appears as well in the work of the philosopher Eric Katz, who feels that respecting the subjectivities of natural beings may allow the unification of the sometimes-divergent discourses of environmental ethics and animal rights.[16] The animal studies specialist Marc Bekoff strongly promotes the methodological extension of personhood to a number of species, claiming that without recognizing subjectivity, one cannot understand animal behavior.[17] The nature writer David Abram extends this sense of personhood even to stones since treating natural entities as persons, he argues, is evolutionarily adaptive.[18] Natural personhood approaches exist in religious studies as well, such as with David Haberman's ethnographic study of Hindu tree veneration, *People Trees: Worship of Trees in Northern India*.[19] Haberman found that he most clearly understood the religious lives of his often modern and cosmopolitan informants when he appreciated that they regarded sacred trees as people in their own right in healthy, rather than morbid or childish, ways.

Perhaps most striking, though, in his book *Plants as Persons: A Philosophical Botany*, Matthew Hall, a research botanist at the Royal Botanic Garden Edinburgh, describes the surprising abilities of plants, our distant evolutionary cousins, to chemically enact personhood states that resemble human feeling, communicating, and remembering. Like humans, plants arise as complex systems of internal electrical communications modulated by calcium, sodium, and potassium, enabling plants to manifest states almost as if they had brains. As a result, Hall claims that, "since the early nineteenth century, scientific evidence has steadily accrued which directly contradicts the hierarchy of nature. . . . Plants are increasingly being shown to demonstrate more sophisticated aspects of mentality such as reasoning and choice. . . . Plants and humans share a basic, ontological reality as perceptive, aware, autonomous, self-governed, and intelligent beings."[20] Therefore, along with other botanists, Hall asserts that one can only understand plant lives by recognizing their personhood subjectivities. Together, Uexküll, Derrida, Katz, Bekoff, Haberman, Hall, and many other scholars teach that treating natural beings as subjects or persons, when done correctly and without anthropomorphism, can be good science, not juvenile sentimentalism.

A subset of this scholarly movement to accord personhood to nonhumans is informally called "New Animism," since its thinkers turn to diverse worldviews in order to create an innovative, interactive understanding of animism. New Animists reject Tylor's definition of animism in terms of possession of a soul and instead define animism relationally since animism, for them, means living in a community of persons who are both human and nonhuman and extending respect for the existential agency of those persons.

The scholar of religion Graham Harvey, for example, states that "animists are people who recognize that the world is full of persons, only some of whom are human, and that life is always lived in relationship with others."[21] Harvey makes clear that what is meant is not an anthropomorphic projection onto natural beings but a respectful recognition of relationship with an Other who may be very different. I can courteously treat my human neighbor as a person despite his love of tuba playing, which I do not share.

In the same way, I can treat pine trees or spiders as respected persons while recognizing that our existential worlds vary dramatically. However, such a recognition of nonhuman personhood is not an Edenic world of constant blissful communion because Harvey helpfully informs us that "an 'all-encompassing moral community' need not be a cozy, romantic vision of peace, co-operation, and unity. Not only is enmity relational, but persons can be prey and/or predator."[22]

Based on their redefinition of animism, some New Animists like Harvey seek to create a novel animist ontology, or theory of the nature of existence, for scholarship. Whatever the merits of such an approach, though, I will not follow this lead since I try to restrict my gaze to Buddhist understandings of existence. Nonetheless, by focusing on personhood relationships rather than possession of a soul, New Animists like Harvey provide a useful new method for discussing nature religion in the Buddhist world that is as heuristically effective as it is elegant. Because of this, I will describe relational animism as a form of belief and practice in which nonhuman entities are relationally experienced as persons in their own right, with respect accorded to their specific agency through linguistic, ritual, or other interactions.

Because the concept of a soul is irrelevant to this relational concept of animism, this revised understanding does not create the Buddhist discomfort engendered by Tylor's soul-based notion. In fact, animism understood relationally dovetails nicely with Buddhist portrayals of an interdependent universe. This relational understanding also responds to Spiro's rejection of Buddhist animism on karmic grounds because Buddhism has long recognized the roles of persons as emissaries through which the mechanisms of karma work. You hurt me in a previous life, so in this life I hurt you; in this life I am your karmic emissary, the person who delivers your karmic due.

Likewise, with a relational understanding of animism that recognizes natural beings as karmic persons, prosperity or demise occurs not through the random activities of nature spirits, as Spiro proposed, but rather through the actions of nonhuman animist persons as karmic emissaries. With nonhuman persons as karmic actors, instead of subverting the karmic ethic of personal responsibility, relational animist persons help supply the system through which karma shapes the world. Indeed, a relational concept of animism emphasizes the traditional Buddhist understanding that not just humans but also nonhumans may participate in the workings of karma. By employing a relational animist approach within Buddhist studies, the dynamics of karma appear to be more coherent and vivid as well as more inclusive since a relational animist approach better recognizes the nonhuman karmic actors that Buddhism has always said were involved.

In the Pāli scriptures, the Buddha demonstrates an understanding of just this relational animist karmic perspective. At one time the Buddha was staying at the Jeta Grove monastery when some merchants came to him, seeking a blessing for their travel. Respectfully, the merchants pledged to follow the Five Precepts, which are fundamental ethical injunctions, incumbent on lay and monastic alike, against harming living beings (the ahimsa precept), taking what is not given, engaging in uncompassionate sexual behavior, issuing false speech, and consuming intoxicants. After embracing these precepts, the merchants set out. Before long, they found themselves lost in a trackless forest and, bewildered, they ran out of supplies. Then the merchants discovered a tree that glistened as if it was wet and they reasoned that the tree must be full of life-giving water. The merchants cut off a branch and out poured clear, satisfying liquid. Wondering what else the tree might hold, they removed another large branch, and from the resulting hole in the tree all manner of delicious foods appeared, satiating the starved travelers. The merchants lopped off yet another branch and, from the tree wound, friendly women appeared. Cutting one more branch caused treasures of all types to flow forth. The fortunate merchants then gleefully loaded up their carts and managed to return home. Afterward, they respectfully offered some of their treasure to the Buddha but were careful to credit the deity of the tree for making the offering possible. When the merchants had finished their story, the Buddha did not credit the tree deity and instead pointed to the men's karma as the source of their good fortune: "This treasure you have received for your moderation and because you have not given yourselves to the power of desire."[23] In this story, an animist spirit offers a prosperity boon, precisely the behavior that Spiro claimed shipwrecks karma. But the Buddha makes it clear that karma is working as expected, and the tree spirit merely acts as the karmic emissary for the merchants. In this story from the Pāli scriptures, there is no conflict between Buddhism and animism regarding karma when animism is understood relationally.

A relational animist approach accentuates how natural beings may participate in karmic processes as interconnected entities, fostering a richer and more sophisticated portrait of the dynamics of the Buddhist tradition than previously seen. Because of the artificial separation between Buddhism and nature religion created by Tylor, Frazer, and Spiro, for 150 years scholars of Buddhism from various disciplines have struggled to understand the nature religion that appears rife in Buddhist worlds, with numerous studies producing analyses of Buddhist interactions with nonhumans that are unsatisfying in the eyes of many.

For instance, despite the fact that *Bodhi pūjā* reverential rituals for holy trees occur every day in the Buddhist world, analyses of the ritual have flustered some researchers, who in their etic or outsider position typically if uncomfortably wish to deem the ritual not Buddhist. These scholars often diverge from emic insiders and their perspectives since many on-the-ground Buddhists experience Bodhi pūjā tree rituals as undeniably and unambiguously Buddhist. Reflecting the outlook of these local Buddhists, Bodhi pūjā rituals make sense if one comprehends them following a personhood approach, given that the Buddha realized nirvana under a tree, making tree persons ideal stand-ins for the person of the Buddha himself, as I will describe further in chapters 3, 4, and 5.

A personhood approach thus helps one appreciate that Bodhi pūjās represent synergistic outgrowths from thoroughly combining, not layering as veneer, genuinely Buddhist nature religion with local nature religious elements. This admixture of genuinely Buddhist nature religious impulses with local religious forms then results in a hybrid nature religion with both Buddhist and regional flavors. As a result, a relational animist approach allows one to appreciate those many moments, heretofore neglected, in which Buddhism, rather than simply coexisting with local nature religion, itself produces nature religious phenomena, permitting us to speak of specifically Buddhist animism or Buddhist nature religion.

In this book, I highlight the fact that applying the model of relational animism to a variety of Buddhist universes allows an awareness of the effectiveness of the model within specific Buddhist worlds as well as comparatively across them. While I include some of my own original field research from India, Thailand, Tibet, and the United States, my central effort is to synthesize existing materials as I demonstrate that a relational animist approach, based on the personhoods of nonhumans, contributes a fruitful methodological framework for understanding Buddhist relationships with nonhumans that the study of Buddhism has heretofore lacked.

This personhood approach spurs a word of warning for my reader, however, that the narrative of this book diverges in some ways from other treatments in Buddhist studies. Typically, scholars of Buddhism create insightful works that trace economic, political, psychological, or historical threads through various Buddhist phenomena. Such approaches are now, and will continue to be, quite helpful. Not only have I written books of this kind before, I express my gratitude in saying that I could not have written this book without the aid of many capable works of this genre.[24] However, issues in economics, politics, psychology, and history are generally human-oriented issues, putting humans in the spotlight and leaving nonhumans mostly in the shadows. Yet one cannot fully understand Buddhism without taking into account the presence of nonhuman entities, whether nonhuman beings like termites or ivy share the economic and political preoccupations of humans or not. This is why the anthropologist Barbara Noske and the philosopher Mary Midgley, among many others, have asserted that concepts of social action that exclude relevant nonhumans distort our knowledge of the world, even including our knowledge of purely human life.[25] In the same vein, the ecofeminist philosopher Val Plumwood insists that one cannot effectively comprehend human relationships until one exerts the effort to "situate nonhumans ethically."[26] Or, put differently by the animal studies expert Paul Waldau, focusing analyses purely on humans while excluding relevant nonhumans engenders errors in both ethical and critical thinking.[27]

But what do we mean by "human" or "nonhuman" beings in a Buddhist context, anyway? Are not environmental concepts culturally constructed? Let us now probe some Buddhist scriptures and philosophical notions in order to clarify the roles of humans and nonhumans within Buddhist environments.

Buddhism's Natural World

Unsurprisingly, one cannot speak of ecological issues without employing the word *nature*, as I have already done, despite this being a notoriously slippery term across cultures and historical periods. Even just in contemporary English, the word *nature* takes diverse meanings, referencing as it does things like "essence," "character," or "ordinary" along with "nonhuman." The use of concepts of the word *nature*, one may suspect, is culturally shaped, and no study of Buddhism and the nonhuman environment can proceed without understanding what "nature" may mean in different Buddhist cultural worlds.

In grappling with this word *nature*, the anthropologist Tim Ingold offers some useful assistance. He says that a recognition of the cultural construction of the concept of nature, while common among scholars, does not reach the heart of the issue, since he startlingly tells us that the idea that nature is culturally constructed is "incoherent."[28] Having studied hunter-gatherers extensively, he often found that hunter-gatherers make no dualistic distinction between "human" and "nature," rendering it impossible to have "nature" as a culturally constructed reality separate from the "human."

According to Ingold, the hunter-gatherers he studied "do not see themselves as mindful subjects having to contend with an alien world of physical objects; indeed, the separation of mind and nature has no place in their thought and practice."[29] Given this insight, for cross-cultural research he calls on scholars to develop an "ontology of dwelling" that begins with a focus on people's immersions in their relational environments, in their relational "dwelling," not with simply presuming a divide between the human and the natural worlds. He instructs that doing so is "not a matter of construction but of engagement, not of building but of dwelling, not of making a view of the world but of taking up a view in it."[30]

Following Ingold's cue, I begin dwelling in the Buddhist world by recognizing that Buddhism fundamentally regards the universe as profoundly interconnected, as paṭicca-samuppāda in the canonical language of Pāli, or dependent arising. A classic example of dependent arising consists of three sticks placed relatively vertically so that they lean on each other to make a tripod. Take one stick away and the other two fall; the tripod dependently arises from the interconnected reality of the sticks and lacks independent existence because it emerges only in interrelation with its causes. In this way, Buddhism teaches that the phenomenal universe, including the human and nonhuman natural worlds, lacks independent things since everything, like the tripod, appears only in dependence on causes.

The Pāli scriptures memorably offer a plantain tree as an example of this idea.[31] Plantain trees do not have heartwood; instead, they consist of folds of vegetable fibers. If one pulls away the brown and green stalks of fibers, one finds nothing, no essence, in the center. A plantain tree exists only conditionally as a result of its leafy causes. There are of course numerous other ways to understand dependent arising, as one will see throughout this book.[32]

Sometimes in works of Western Buddhist ecology one finds models of dependent arising utilized without reference to Buddhism's system of rebirth. Yet this usage is not consistent with the scriptures since they almost always presume the inseparability of the doctrines of dependent arising and rebirth. I am not arguing here that the concepts of dependent arising and reincarnation cannot be separated at all, but I do argue that they have not been separated traditionally. Historically speaking, notions of dependent arising describe the universe of rebirth and the universe of rebirth dependently arises. Thus, across Buddhisms, with some consistency one finds models of five or six *gatis*, or realms of rebirth, allied with notions of dependent arising, with the collection of these rebirths being called samsara. From the top of the five-tiered model, these realms of reincarnation include gods, humans, animals, ghosts, and hell beings.[33] Sometimes the god realm is subdivided into *asura*, lesser gods, and *dēva*, high gods, thus giving six realms of rebirth as seen artistically in the well-known Tibetan Wheel of Life.[34]

The inclusion of the god realms provides Buddhism with a special character, shared with some other religions from India, which diverges from other forms of religion which teach that humans are qualitatively the best of all creations. Buddhist gods live incredibly satisfying lives and may possess powers of which humans can only dream. Thus, it is easy to argue that in Buddhism, the gods, not humans, are the best creatures, thereby diminishing some claims to human superiority in the universe.

A human rebirth is the most desirable, though, even if it lacks the utopian spark of the god realm. Only a human can join the monastic community, as I will discuss later. But even more, outside of marginal tales, Buddhism generally teaches that only humans can realize nirvana, or liberative enlightenment. Gods busy themselves with pleasure too much to undertake spiritual practice, while animals and lower rebirths lack what is called in Pāli *paññā* (Sanksrit: *prajña*), the capacity for wisdom that is required to realize nirvana.

As for an instance of the general reservation of liberation for humans only, in the scriptural *Suttanipāta* some laypersons ask the Buddha whether one becomes a Brahmin (a spiritually advanced human being) by birth or by action. In his response the Buddha describes the nonhuman natural world by distinguishing entities according to birth within species, saying, "Consider the grass and trees. Although they do not profess any difference, their distinguishing mark arises from their species."[35] He continues to apply the same logic to insects, animals, snakes, fish, and birds. But when he describes humans, the Buddha says that a Brahmin is not one who is born into that state, a Brahmin is one who accomplishes the realization of nirvana. The Buddha said, "Whoever indeed, having cut every fetter, does not tremble, gone beyond attachment, unfettered, him I call a brahmin."[36] Thus, in this passage, the Buddha defined nonhumans by birth and humans by the capacity to realize nirvanic liberation. This division is a common Buddhist approach, so I use it as a measuring stick for delineating the human realm, while I also mention that in this book there appear several instructive crossers of this usually true boundary.

With their capacity for liberation, humans are not just better than animals, they are better than any other being in the universe of rebirth, thus providing one clear expression of human superiority to other entities that extends across forms of the religion. The *Vinaya* code of conduct for monastics in the Pāli scriptures also demonstrates, with qualifications, this point about the superiority of Buddhist humans. Violation of the precept of celibacy with either a human or an animal is a *pārājika* offense, the most serious kind of breach, meaning that the perpetrator is expelled from the monastic community. With this rule, animals and humans are equal. But it is a similar-category pārājika offense to kill a human being, while killing an animal is a lower, *pācittiya* offense, requiring only confession as a punishment.[37] In this way, the rules for monastics treasure human life more than animal life, and although the prohibition against killing animals is relatively animal-friendly compared to strictures found in some other religions, still animals do not realize equality on this issue. Moreover, in the *Vinaya* monastics should not dig in the earth, make use of water that is known to contain living beings, or spit on, urinate on, or unreasonably injure plants or seeds. Yet, as the *Vinaya* is primarily interpreted within the Theravāda Buddhist world, meat eating is allowed even for monastics, as long as the animal was not seen, heard, or suspected to have been killed for the monastic's sake.[38] Therefore, in the scriptural rules for nuns and monks, you find a complex blend of both restrictions on and permissibility toward using and possibly harming nonhuman natural entities.

As I briefly mentioned previously, one more monastic stipulation retains strong influence on Buddhist relationships with nature: only humans can join the monastic community, or sangha.[39] Indeed, monastic rules counsel the ordained against even reciting the monastic code in the presence of animals or imitating animal behaviors.[40] From the earliest tradition, Buddhist nuns and monks have embodied the highest vocation in which any being of any type can participate because it is monastics who are most energetic in their pursuit of spiritual progress. But this most respected of lifestyles is by definition denied to any entity but a human one, instantly rendering all nonhuman natural beings second-class citizens, if they are considered as citizens at all.

Of course, nonordained humans share with nonhuman entities this same hierarchical distinction from the monastics. Nonetheless, with the closing of the monastic sangha to nonhumans, Buddhism explicitly displays an attitude of human superiority to the natural world. This sense of Buddhist human superiority may surprise some readers. It is a commonplace of Buddhist environmental literature to gloss over this fact and instead attack attitudes of human superiority to the natural world that occur among the Abrahamic religions. Certainly, biblical and Qur'anic notions of dominant human stewardship, uses of Aristotle's Great Chain of Being, and denials of animal souls by Augustine, Aquinas, and Descartes appear to support attitudes of human superiority to the natural world in the West, and these elements are relatively lacking from traditional Buddhist worldviews. But Buddhism can lack Western attitudes of human superiority while still retaining its own senses of human ascendance, like the denials of monastic spiritual opportunity to nonhumans reveal, and there appear to be many more Buddhist assertions of human superiority to nonhumans across the tradition, as I will show the rest of this book.

Given this understanding of dependent arising and rebirth, we may "dwell" in Buddhism with some much-needed definitions. Buddhism posits a dimension of reality known as the *sattvaloka*, or realm of living beings such as humans and animals, which is synonymous with samsara, or the five- or six-tiered universe of rebirth. Alternatively, the *bhājanaloka*, or receptacle realm, consists of nontransmigrating entities, such as plants, minerals, and water, which provide a relatively spiritually inert backdrop for the realms of rebirth through which sentient beings transmigrate. In this presentation I reflect this Buddhist usage in designating the samsaric sattvaloka realm of reincarnating beings as "animate" and the nonreincarnating bhājanaloka receptacle realm as "inanimate." "Nature" and "natural world" combine the sattvaloka realm of animate transmigrating beings together with their usually inanimate bhājanaloka container.[41] By "human," I mean an entity whose species within the natural world lends the potential to realize nirvana in this life or to join the monastic sangha community.

With this last definition I employ the word *species* with some trepidation. While the Buddha clearly understood "species" in the broadest way—he not only could tell the difference between a goat and a tiger, he used such discernment to rhetorical effect in sermons—it is doubtful that the Buddha used any of the words in his vocabulary with the scientific connotations that "species" carries for most readers of this book. Moreover, Western biologists still actively debate what a species is, with some questioning whether "species" exist at all.[42] Therefore, it is difficult to find an English term that is at once faithful to the Buddha's context, intelligible to readers of contemporary English, and acceptable to all biologists. But I must provide some sort of grounding, so I employ "species" to mean types of entities as portrayed within the Buddhist scriptures or by Buddhists themselves.

In this book, "animals" are those beings recognized as such by Buddhist systems of rebirth. Animal rebirths are just one notch lower on the ladder of rebirth than human rebirths and afterlife passages between the two realms is common. The differences between humans and animals are temporary and not final, thereby creating a kind of fluid moral community that encompasses both human and animal realms and sometimes instigates extensions of personhood. Therefore, in Buddhism one cannot draw a definitive, inflexible ethical line between humans and animals as some other forms of religion do. At the same time, a human rebirth is clearly superior, for humans not only possess the capacity for liberation, they also suffer less than animals. In an idea that goes back at least to the Indian Upaniṣads, Buddhism explicitly describes animal rebirths as beset with terrible woe as well as a lack of freedom.[43] The ghost and hell realm beings exist even lower, so that the bottom three rebirths of animals, ghosts, and hells are generally considered to be evil rebirths to be avoided, although a few animal-friendly stories mitigate this fact somewhat.[44]

What the round of samsaric rebirths is missing, however, are significant places for the plants, minerals, and water of the bhājanaloka receptacle realm. Although plants, minerals, and water exist in all realms, even heavens and hells, they generally are not available for rebirth and thus usually represent the overlooked furniture of Buddhist existence.[45] Regarding the exclusion specifically of plants, the Buddhism scholar Lambert Schmithausen's research reveals that, in the earliest days of the religion, plants were ambiguous beings in terms of treatment, given the influences of other religions as well as practicality.[46]

Regarding plants, on one hand, religions like Jainism and Hinduism that influenced nascent Buddhism taught that plants are one-sensed beings that make up parts of the rounds of rebirth. Jainism, for instance, generally describes an ecocentric universe in which all existents possess a *jīva*, or soul, so that supposedly inanimate entities like stones or bodies of water actually appear as living, animate beings. All such beings exist on a continuum in terms of possession of from one to five senses, and thus most entities cannot practice religion and pursue enlightenment. Nonetheless, Jainism's ecocentrism challenged early Buddhism to retain its own broad sense of the environment, and Jainism's treatment of all entities as vague persons capable of sensory experience may have shaped early Buddhism's own sense of the relational animist personhoods of nonhumans.[47]

On the other hand, there existed within Buddhism a concern for pragmatic living for the monastics and especially for lay people. With wood, plants used as food, and other plant-based products representing essential commodities in the daily lives of the Buddha and his contemporaries, practicality perhaps dictated little concern for the possible spiritual lives of plants.

Faced with a dilemma regarding the place and value of plants, Schmithausen avers that the early community thereby left the question of plant sentience and reincarnation unanswered through neglect.[48]

In the Pāli canon, there appear to be no explicit declarations either way regarding plant sentience and reincarnation, although equivocal passages exist, such as one from the *Sotāpattisaṃyutta*. In this passage, the Buddha seems to indicate that plants lack the capacity for wisdom (paññā) necessary for nirvana when he says, "Even if these great *sāl* trees could understand what is well spoken and what is badly spoken, then I would declare these great *sāl* trees to be stream-enterers, no longer bound to the nether world, fixed in destiny, with enlightenment as their destination."[49] Likewise, in the *Aṅguttara Nikāya* the Buddha says, "If these great *sāl* trees would be converted toward the abandoning of unwholesome qualities and the acquisition of wholesome qualities, that would lead to the welfare and happiness even of these great *sāl* trees for a long time, if they could choose."[50]

Alternatively, in the *Suttanipāta*, one of the oldest of Buddhist scriptures, one finds the exhortation to extend ahimsa, or nonharm, to all beings, "both those which are still and those which move," thus seemingly exhibiting spiritual respect for plants.[51] Nonetheless, through the rest of the Pāli canon, the same formula is commonly applied as nonharm "for all living beings" or "for all sentient beings," using the Pāli word *pāṇa*, which almost always indicates humans and animals but not plants.[52] Moreover, Pāli texts use *jīvitā voropeti*, "to deprive of life," for humans and animals but not for plants, forming an ontological distinction with humans and animals on one side and plants on the other.[53]

On the issue of the possible rebirths of plants, it seems telling that in the 547 previous lives of the Buddha as recounted in the Pāli *jātaka* rebirth tales, plus other stories found sprinkled around the scriptures, the Buddha never once was reborn as a plant. He was a deity that resided in a tree in several previous births but never a tree. Further, the Pāli scriptures are full of predictions, made by the Buddha and others, of the future lives of various characters. In my research I found that in none of these numerous predictions is a future rebirth as a plant prognosticated. This dearth of plant rebirth stories may result from the ways that the early tradition distinguished itself from Hinduism and Jainism since such a plant-excluding ethic can be more lay-friendly, especially for agriculturalists.

As the years passed, Indian Buddhist texts appeared that more clearly rejected plant sentience and rebirth.[54] By the time of the Pāli *Milindapañha*, written as a semicanonical text around the lifetime of Jesus, plants had been explicitly and fully denied any notion of rebirth.[55] Moreover, among early Mahāyāna scriptures, the *Vimalakīrti Sūtra* asserts that plants, trees, and the earth "lack understanding"; the *Mahāratnakūta Sūtra* explains that "grasses and trees have no awareness"; and in one often-overlooked passage, the *Lotus Sūtra* appears to deny plant sentience.[56] The *Nirvāṇa Sūtra* relates that a medicine tree gives without discrimination, which is a Buddhist virtue, but does so because it has no thoughts of its own.[57] The *Ugraparipṛcchā* enjoins non-harm to "any living beings" but excludes plants from this formulation since, in that text, they represent mere property.[58]

Given these contrary streams of thought that result in a general, if largely tacit, rejection of plants from rebirth, in this book I define plants as organic beings who do not transmigrate through samsaric rebirths, unlike humans and animals who are organic beings who do transmigrate. I also define minerals as nontransmigrating solid inorganic entities and water as a nontransmigrating fluid inorganic entity. As for these latter elements of nature, if one excludes detachable spirits that reside in natural entities, Buddhists in the scriptures almost always consider mineral and water worlds to be lifeless, insentient givens of experience, so the texts pay little attention to delineating these realms. In those moments when the scriptures do attend to water, the *Milindapañha* explicitly denies water life, sentience, or a soul, as does the Mahāyāna text *Śikṣāsamuccaya*.[59] These denials seem unsurprising since water and minerals in themselves, outside of specific appearances like sacred rivers or mountains, were not much venerated in the earlier Indian Vedic texts so, for early Buddhists, there was not the same established cultural regard for inorganic entities as there was for organic ones.[60] But because plants, minerals, and water are not reborn but animals are, personhood attitudes toward animals far outnumber personhood attitudes toward other nonhuman entities across the tradition, as my reader will see throughout this book.

Like the varying voices regarding plants within the tradition, over the rest of the book multiple and contesting voices bloom regarding Buddhist relationships with the wider natural world. Thus, during the course of the book, I will happily indicate exceptions to the general definitions that I established in this chapter as befits the multitude of approaches to nature found in Buddhist worlds.

This chapter's concepts and definitions help us understand how one time a tree spirit became intoxicated by a sermon offered by the Buddha's disciple Sister Sukkā. Like the nuns in attendance, the tree spirit found that

Sukkā's inspiring words appeared as if she were "giving them sweet mead to drink and sprinkling them with ambrosia." The tree spirit thereafter left the nunnery and roamed the streets of Rājagaha, all the while chastising the "idle" townspeople for not attending the enlightening session. Moved by the tree spirit, "excited" residents of the city then attended Sukkā's preaching and "listened attentively."[61] What Sukkā offered them was the words of her teacher, Gautama Buddha, thereby inspiring this investigation to look more closely into his life and teachings in the next chapter.

CHAPTER 2

The Buddha's Nature

If you attempt to place yourself into the sandals of the Buddha (born circa 500 BCE), however imperfectly, and attend to his South Asian natural world, you immediately are confronted by the fascinating presence of the most remarkable beings: *nāgas*. A nāga is a special Indian serpentlike being who can possess both special powers and notable sacredness. In Indian literature the *Ṛg Veda* speaks of holy serpents and in the *Śatapatha Brāhmaṇa* there appears the first mention specifically of a nāga, an entity who is at once a snake, a shape-shifter with a standard snake form, and a powerful spirit.[1] Potent nāgas can shape-shift even into human form, but they embody their default serpent forms during sex and relaxed sleep.[2] This shape-shifting power allows nāgas to be known for their godlike instrumental music despite their native lack of hands and feet.[3] Understood to be humanlike in many ways, in Buddhist art some nāgas appear with human faces on serpent bodies. Although Westerners often consider snakes to be just secular pests or demonic tempters, meaningful only for their perceived threatening character, in the world of ancient Indian Buddhism nāgas appeared as sometimes-benevolent holy people, and they emerge as revered pious citizens in other Buddhist traditions, too.

In ancient Hinduism, nāgas were worshipped as leaders of all serpents, being the empowered royalty of the snake world, so that you could fend off a snake bite by venerating the *nāgarāja*, or divine king of the snakes. The religious studies scholar Laurie Cozad tells us that Buddhists later developed their own, alternative understanding of these sacred snakes since in the Hindu *Mahābhārata*, nāgas fear fire, whereas in the early Buddhist texts they emit fire, not unlike the fire-breathing dragons of Western lore. Buddhist snakes also may purify the earth, and in Indian Buddhist texts nāgas often act more like the spirits of the earth instead of there being a separate earth spirit. Because of their ownership of the earth, in ancient India nāgas were propitiated in rituals concerning the laying of the foundation stone in a house being built, with nāgas thereafter guarding the house and its occupants.[4] This guardian function even extended to Buddhist sacred monuments; Robert Decaroli highlights that, at the notable ancient cave temple complex at Ajaṇṭā, there were artistic portrayals of nāgas who worshipped devotedly, and nāgas in turn were venerated at an on-site shrine. Decaroli avers that all of this occurred perhaps out of respect for the great nāga king who resided there when the caves were carved and painted.[5]

The Buddha's multifaceted interactions with nāgas provide a useful template for understanding the overall roles of natural beings in the Buddha's

FIGURE 2. A stylized horned *nāga* protects the entrance to the main hall at Wat Phra Sing monastery, Chiang Mai, Thailand.

life, the subject of this chapter. Just as nāgas expressed their personhood in a variety of colorful ways, even when they were threatening, so the Buddha enjoyed vivid personhood relationships with an expansive array of natural beings. Among other appearances, the Buddha sacrificed himself for tigers and intimately longed for a lost swan friend. Natural beings missed him, too, including one very sad horse. The earth, along with cows, served the Buddha as witnesses to his enlightenment, much like a human might. These dynamic experiences of the Buddha of the personhood of diverse nonhumans helps inject the tradition with impulses toward developing and expressing respectful personhood relationships with nature. In this way, the Buddha's life supplies precedents for emulation, and these precedents later manifest themselves in numerous different relational animist forms in Buddhist lands, as the other chapters in this book reveal.

Nāgas articulate their personhood by practicing Buddhism in sometimes surprising ways, and the Buddha's biography contains tales of other natural beings, even plants, who practice religion. Such appearances include human-like expressions of devotion to the Buddha by trees, cobras, bulls, and birds. The Buddha instructed parrots in religion as he would a human. Mundane trees and animals adored the Buddha, but he also was revered by offbeat cryptozoological *supaṇṇas*, or mythical spirit-birds like the well-known Garuda, and *kinnaras*, or divine musicians who appear as half-human and either half-horse or half-bird.[6] Birds, nāgas, and tree spirits anticipated the Buddha's enlightenment more accurately than did his human colleagues, demonstrating spiritual insight superior to that of humans, like Balaam's ass did in the Bible. The Buddha even gave teachings to a grumpy elephant, who then became a pious pacifist.

But, of course, the Buddha's personhood relationships with nonhumans, as vibrant as they sometimes were, arose with ambivalence. The Buddha sometimes excluded entities from personhood, engaged in some negative interactions with nonhumans, and allowed human uses of beings that some may consider to be persons. Such uses appear to include animals consumed for food, and the Buddha's scriptural example persists without clarity on this account. The Buddha's personhood relationships also did not evidence much nature mysticism, as I will describe.

In order to more clearly understand these complex relationships of the Buddha with his natural world, in this chapter we will explore the life of the Buddha from his prior incarnations through his final lifetime and on to his passing. Before undertaking this journey, though, first I must provide the Buddha with some ecological context.

The Indian World of the Buddha

According to Irfan Habib in *Man and Environment*,[7] India was one of the first places where modern *Homo sapiens* settled after leaving Africa, as they entered the subcontinent about 75,000 years ago (17). These early Indians encountered large wild populations of elephants, buffaloes, aurochs (ancestors of domesticated cattle), crocodiles, rhinoceroses, tigers, lions, cheetahs, and numerous species of snakes (13). Yet, by the time of the Buddha around 500 BCE, India was highly agricultural since domesticated varieties of wheat, barley, and cotton had appeared by 4,000 BCE, with domesticated rice arriving from China around 3,000 BCE. Goats, sheep, donkeys, zebu cattle, horses, some buffaloes, and some elephants had already been domesticated long before the Buddha's era (27–56). The resulting expansion of farmland and pastureland led to deforestation problems already during the lifetime of the Buddha, in part prompting the later Buddhist emperor Aśoka (304–232 BCE) to plant many new trees intentionally (60).

As I will discuss more fully later, the largely agrarian India of the Buddha's era, unlike today's India, commonly included meat eating. Vedic cattle sacrifices and their attendant beef feasts were ordinary enough for the Buddha to repeatedly speak against them, and even outside of sacrifices beef played a central role in the Indian diet (65). The hunted meat of deer and gazelle also provided familiar meals, as one sees in the Pāli Buddhist scriptures. In these ways, meat eating within its larger agricultural context provided some of the ecological and cultural background to the life of the Buddha. As we will see, these circumstances led to controversies regarding Buddhist vegetarianism as well as a subtle preference for, or at least general acceptance of, an agricultural lifestyle for laypeople in the Buddhist scriptures.

Part of Indian farming, then and sometimes still now, involved propitiating snakes as owners of the fields. It is no surprise, therefore, that nāgas, the leaders of the serpents of the rice paddy, shaped the agricultural world of the Buddha and the early tradition. Hence, we learn more about the Buddha by appreciating the role of nāgas in the Buddha's life more fully.

Buddhist *Nāgas*

Snakelike nāgas play frequent and visible roles in stories of the Buddha's life, not least because of their sublime ability, perhaps above all other animals, to practice religion like humans. For example, the *Saṃyutta Nikāya* of the Pāli canon contains a series of scriptures describing the spiritual relevance of nāgas, supaṇṇas (spirit-birds), *gandhabbas* (celestial musicians who, in this case, appear in plants), and cloud gods. Of these entities, the texts mention only nāgas as being capable of practicing religion, because nāgas observe the *uposatha* fortnightly fast so that they can improve their merit and be reborn as humans.[8] The *Lotus Sūtra* goes further since it tells a story of a sacred were-serpent who realized enlightenment.[9] The Buddha himself reflected the religiosity of nāgas, because in the *Campeyya Jātaka* the Buddha was born in a prior life as a snake charmer's cobra who intentionally practiced non-harm by refusing to eat frogs fed to him by his handler.[10]

Besides observing the fortnightly fast, nāgas also practice religion by serving the Buddha in various ways. In the Buddha's previous birth as Prince Paduma, nāgas saved his life and then sheltered him when he was falsely accused of sexual misconduct.[11] At his final birth, rain-bringing nāgas created a shower to cleanse both the Buddha and his mother. Later, when the Buddha was an adult, a pious human king built one bridge across the Ganges River for the use of the Buddha and his followers, and then a group called the Licchavis, out of adoration for the Buddha, built a second bridge for him to use. At this, the nāgas felt shamed by their limited offerings to the Buddha and resolved also to build a bridge for him. The cobras spread out their hoods and laid down their bodies, forming a flat bridge over which the Buddha and his attendant, Ānanda, walked.[12] Thus, Cozad relates that nāgas are "portrayed as recognizing the dharma [the Buddhist tradition], proclaiming the dharma, being like the dharma, and even instructing on the subject of dharma."[13] Perhaps their potency in affecting human lives leads snakes to be so revered, as the biologist Edward O. Wilson theorized.[14] But, for whatever reason, Buddhist nāgas cannot be regarded simply as legless troublemakers, since they may serve as respected Buddhist practitioners and preachers, at least at times.

Nāgas additionally may undergo the essential Buddhist ritual of taking refuge in the Buddha, his teachings, and his community. The Buddha himself did so in a previous life when he was born as a nāga in the era of the Buddha Sumana. In another tale, during his final lifetime there were two great nāga kings, Gautama and Krishna, who wanted to hear the Buddha preaching in Sūrpāraka, so they set out to hear the teachings with a retinue of five hundred sacred snakes. The Buddha foresaw the arrival of the pious snakes and sought to bar them from the city, fearing that they would bite humans, so the Buddha and his disciple Moggallāna ventured outside the city gates to meet the serpentine royals. The Buddha beseeched the snakes to avoid entering the city, sharing his concerns, at which point the gentle snakes asserted their nonviolent intentions. The Buddha listened, offered a discourse on spiritual living, and then administered the ritual of refuge to the snakes, who also adopted the Buddhist Five Precepts of avoidance of harming, stealing, lying, sexual misconduct, and intoxicants.[15] In taking refuge and the Five Precepts, these devoted nāgas practiced religion very much like humans did. Nevertheless, by the Buddha's command the serpents still did not enter the city.

Despite their religious regard for these serpent persons, though, the Buddha and his followers were no fools about physical snakes, as this last story shows. Thousands of humans die in India every year from snakebites—not just from cobras but also from kraits, Russell's vipers, and other serpents. In light of this reality, in the time of the Buddha recluses were encouraged to establish their hermitages in snake-free areas and instructed to respect but avoid snakes. They were also taught to use *metta*, lovingkindness, as a shield against serpentine dangers, with the *Milindapañha* instructing that it is the active feeling of love that is effective in quelling snake dangers, not just having a loving personality.[16] The *Vinaya*, *suttas*, and jātakas of the Pāli canon, and Mahāyāna scriptures such as Śāntideva's *Śikṣāsamuccaya*, even contain spells for deterring snakes with lovingkindness.[17]

A distancing from worldly snakes went hand in hand with a religious distancing; Cozad informs us that the reluctance, and even hostility, with which early Buddhism treated extant Indian nature worship led early Buddhists to ensure that nāgas, despite their spiritual potency, were kept in religious places too low to usurp the importance of the Buddha and his teachings. Several jātaka tales denigrate snake worship and depict snakes as incapable of delivering on promised religious rewards, for instance.[18] Texts subordinating the supposed power of the serpent to the Buddha further mention how the Buddha and his disciples took from nāgas the power to create or withhold rain.[19] Even in the scriptural *Mahāvastu*, where powerful nāgas are held in high esteem, they are peaceful only because the Buddha negated their ability to work harm.[20] Serpents in the life of the Buddha thereby generate discussion regarding the Buddhist value of nonharm, which was developed by the Buddha through successive lives.

Previous Lives of Our Buddha

According to the scriptures, the Buddha subjugated snakes by developing the capacity for nonharm over many lifetimes. Our Buddha, Gautama Buddha, who was born in what is now Nepal, was just one of many Buddhas who have appeared and will appear across diverse planets and times. For instance, an earlier Buddha, Paduma, was reverenced across species by our Buddha, Gautama, in a previous lifetime. As the Buddha described their encounter,

"I at that time was a lion, overlord of wild creatures. I saw the Conqueror in the forest increasing detachment. I reverenced his feet with my head, circumambulated him, roared loudly three times, and attended on the Conqueror for a week."[21]

The story of the lion-Buddha's reverencing Paduma Buddha appears in the *Buddhavaṃsa* in the Pāli scriptures. Many similar stories of the Buddha's previous lifetimes, called jātakas, are collected together into 547 tales in the *Khuddaka Nikāya* section of the Pāli canon or into 34 stories in Āryaśūra's Sanskrit work *Jātakamālā*, which is influential in the Mahāyāna world. Unique in world literature in the way that they trace the development of one personage, the Buddha, over many lifetimes, through their clear, didactic tones the jātaka tales are often used in the Buddhist world to educate children and adults about the religion, much like Bible or Qur'an stories may be used in the West. But these tales were not written just as children's literature since they serve spiritual purposes for adults, too, having been integrated into practice traditions from Buddhism's early days. For instance, throughout the stories and especially in the last ten in the Pāli canon, the Buddha develops ten *pāramīs* or spiritual perfections for adults: generosity (*dāna*), ethical behavior (*sīla*), renunciation (*nekkhama*), wisdom (*paññā*), effort (*viriya*), patience (*khanti*), honesty (*sacca*), resolve (*adhiṭṭhāma*), lovingkindness (*mettā*), and equanimity (*upekkhā*).[22]

In the jātaka tales, natural beings are treated as persons in several ways, like animals having their own names. Animals possess their own communities and community leaders. Like humans, they take care of their elders. At the same time, many of these senses of personhood in the jātakas arise from rather coarse anthropomorphizing of natural beings rather than respect for their real existential agencies. On this note, the philosopher Simon P. James says that Buddhist descriptions of nature have much more to do with liberating humans and much less to do with respecting natural beings by describing them accurately.[23] Therefore, for just one example, the *Sigāla Jātaka* falsely portrays male lions as hunters and female lions as homemakers. In this light, the scholar of Buddhism Reiko Ohnuma relates that in the Pāli jātakas, "Human violence toward animals is pervasive, omnipresent, and graphic," thereby emphasizing the human-centeredness of these stories.[24]

The scholar of Buddhism Florin Deleanu states that understanding animals as animals was not a concern of the framers of the Pāli canon, since they focused instead on shaping a spiritual path for humans. Scripture writers often remained unclear about species, offering just "deer" rather than "red deer," "barking deer," or some other more specific way of talking about the animals themselves.[25] As an extension of this attitude, sometimes writers focused so much on symbolic negative animal behavior that they missed opportunities for positive appreciation. For instance, jackals were demeaned for being poor hunters, although this very quality would make them better at practicing nonharm, which is a fundamental Buddhist virtue! As Ohnuma argues, animal appearances in the jātaka stories may have little to do with empirical animals because the animals may symbolize humans and their aspirations.[26] The scriptures are just that, religious scriptures, not biology or environmental science textbooks.

The widespread use of animals as symbols that is found throughout the Buddhist scriptures has led to a recent Buddhist studies theory that, when animals appear within jātaka stories, they do so merely as "allegorical human beings" and lack any reference to real animals.[27] This theory seems to me partly sensible, yet it is also limited in scope as well as overly reductionist. To be sure, the theory correctly highlights that Buddhist scriptural animals frequently symbolize the human world, as I have already indicated and will continue to do so. But there are many appearances of nonhuman beings that are found not in literary sources but rather in lived realities, as I recount throughout this book, which cannot adequately be explained by a theory that animals only serve as stand-ins for humans. In addition, the theory that animals are nothing but symbolic humans receives challenge from the many nonanimal, and sometimes even abiotic, agents that appear in the Buddhist world because it seems difficult to view nonanimal appearances like grains of sand simply as figurative avatars of human beings. Finally, if we are to properly understand Buddhist semiotics even just of scriptural animals, we need to recognize that stories and symbols consist of many cultural layers. It is therefore possible for an animal manifestation to symbolize a human state and at the same time to alternatively serve as a locus for perspectives about real animals. As the philosopher Mary Midgley taught us, just because animals are employed in a given context as symbols for humans does not necessarily mean that they are nothing but symbols for humans.[28]

Granting this multilayered comprehension of animal symbols in Buddhism, we can better understand that, as both symbolic and real animals, through many lifetimes Siddhartha Gautama incarnated in numerous different forms. Among domesticated animals he was a dog, bull, ox, horse, rooster, chicken, goat, and pig. In bird form he was a pigeon, quail, mallard, parrot, peacock or peahen, vulture, *singila* bird, goose, crow, and woodpecker. He took wild mammal form as a buffalo, monkey, antelope, elephant, rat, rabbit, jackal, lion, and deer. Additionally, he was a lizard, iguana, frog, snake or nāga, and fish. He also manifested other forms that are not found in most Western zoology textbooks, such as a flying horse, unusually golden deer, unusually golden antelope, golden peacock, golden goose, and supaṇṇa spirit-bird. Of relevance to the limited biocentric aspect of Buddhism that separates humans and animals from the rest of the natural world, in the jātakas the Buddha never incarnated as a plant, physical body of water, or mineral, although several times he was the invisible *yakkha* spirit who resided in trees, grasses, mountains, or bodies of water.[29] Regardless of his incarnation in a specific lifetime, though, over the ages the Buddha-to-be cultivated many virtues, as I will now describe.

Developing Nonharm

His lives before he became the Buddha of our era served as a bit of a rehearsal for Siddhartha Gautama since, during long expanses of time, he developed many qualities of a Buddha through some trial and error. Thus, while the Buddha is justly famous for teaching nonharm, he did not have this quality fully from the beginning, like you see in one of his prior lives when he was the king of Benares. One day, while he was visiting the side of the lake in his royal park, surrounded by musicians and dancers, the fish and turtles in the water swarmed to the shore of the lake near him. When the Buddha-as-king asked his adviser about why the animals behaved as they did, he was told that they were there to serve their king joyfully. Delighted by this, the Buddha-as-king ordered that the fish henceforth be fed rice. However, as the mandated feedings progressed, a problem arose since not all of the fish appeared at the right place and time, so food was wasted. Because of this, the fish feeder began to sound a drum to announce a feeding. This strategy worked to bring the fish together at the right time, much to the ecstasy of a local crocodile, who took advantage of fish feedings to gorge himself on the collected fish. In response, the Buddha-as-king ordered that the crocodile be harpooned and killed, and this was done, thus implicating the Buddha, long ago, in the killing of an animal.[30]

Although the Buddha may have participated in killing in a previous life, eventually he learned to fully embrace ahimsa, or nonharm, directed not just to large and familiar animals but also to microscopic or dangerous beings.[31] Found in some form in all religions stemming from India, especially Jainism, and perhaps predating even the Vedas, ahimsa, the "absence of the desire to kill or harm," counsels refraining from hurting any living being in any way, for "to all animals no one is dearer than self."[32] Nonharm includes the act of physical nonviolence, of course, but also includes emotional or verbal nonviolence. Because of the significance of nonharm, Buddhist religious monarchs are respected because they protect "beasts and birds" since, karmically, killing living beings leads to lower rebirths.[33] Unsurprisingly, therefore, many Buddhist scriptures emphasize ahimsa, and numerous Buddhist animal rights activists give ahimsa a central place in their systems regarding how Buddhists should interact with the natural world.

Of course, this ahimsa attitude is not inviolate and on occasion compromises are made. For instance, sometimes it is clear that Buddhists develop ahimsa more for their own spiritual growth or to avoid their own bad karma than for the benefit of a nonhuman being itself, thus eroding the other-regarding character of nonharm. Among many other instances, a clear example of this comes from the *Divyāvadāna*, which encourages Buddhists to extend positive feelings even to a burnt stump, obviously for the sake of human development rather than for the sake of the dead stump itself.[34] Similarly, Śāntideva's *Śikṣāsamuccaya* encourages nonharm to animals because otherwise one will be reborn as one, thus protecting animals and denigrating them at the same time.[35]

Moreover, full ahimsa remains difficult in practical reality. If one never participates directly or indirectly in the harm of animals, plants, water, and minerals, one quickly dies. Simply eating lettuce for dinner harms at least the head of lettuce and the small organisms who live in and under it. The inevitability of compromise in this situation provides one practical reason why Buddhism strongly encourages ahimsa toward nonhuman animals but not as much toward plants, water, or minerals, since these latter are required for human survival but eating meat often is not.

Sometimes a sense of ahimsa even can go astray; the scholar of Buddhism Lambert Schmithausen describes a group of Thai Buddhist fishers who, because they practice ahimsa, do not club their catches into an instantaneous death. Instead, the fishers leave the fish to suffocate.[36] Although such suffocation is perceived by the fishers as a less active form of harm and thus more in the spirit of ahimsa, we may feel sorry for the fish who die slowly and painfully rather than quickly.

On a related issue, there is the sticky problem of euthanasia, because inflexible ahimsa can prevent Buddhists from killing suffering animals, leaving Buddhists without clear support for situations in which euthanasia may be the most compassionate choice.[37] In compromising nonharm by misdirecting it or not understanding its full ramifications, establishing Holmes

Rolston's sustainable biosphere, as I described in the introduction, can be inhibited by following some examples found in the Buddha's life story and teachings.

Problems with enacting ahimsa notwithstanding, lifetime after lifetime the Buddha advanced in virtue and spiritual state, so that in many previous lifetimes he already was a teacher of wisdom for others. For instance, it seems that at one time a rabbit, otter, jackal, and monkey lived together peacefully in a forest on the Ganges River. These animals openly practiced religion; the rabbit was their spiritual leader and often imparted teachings regarding the need to be generous to those who ask for aid. The friends spent their days hunting according to their species preferences and then returned to the same spot in the evening to renew their friendships. One day the otter went to the banks of the Ganges, where he found some fish that a fisherman had buried and left, intending to return. Finding no owner, the otter happily took the fish back to his forest home. The jackal came across a jungle hut that appeared to be deserted other than a lizard and some milk curd cooking over a fire. Finding no owner, the jackal joyfully took the lizard and curd and returned home. For his part, the monkey found some mangoes, which he brought back with anticipation.

The rabbit fared differently. Although he was able to find plenty of grass, he realized that no one who visited would be as interested in grass as he, so he had no food to offer others if they asked. Thus, he vowed, "If someone asks for food, I will give my own self as an offering." Sakka, the king of the gods, overheard this vow and decided to put the rabbit to the test.[38] Disguised as a holy human beggar, Sakka asked the otter, the jackal, and the monkey for food, and each in turn offered food to Sakka. Then Sakka came to the rabbit and asked for food. Realizing that a grass offering was futile in this situation and keeping his vow, the rabbit encouraged Sakka to kindle a fire, and when the flames were large enough, the rabbit jumped in, intending to sacrifice himself as a roast. But, miraculously, the fire did not burn the rabbit at all, impressing Sakka all the more with the bunny's self-sacrificing virtue. Sakka removed the uninjured rabbit from the flames and gently placed the hero bunny on a bed of grass. Then, wanting to honor the rabbit's valor, Sakka daubed the moon with the rabbit's image, which is one reason why Buddhist cultures generally describe a rabbit in the moon rather than the human face in the moon that Euro-Americans typically see.[39]

Naturally, in this story that emphasizes mercy toward nonhumans who practice religious generosity, the Buddha was that noble rabbit. In this way, the self-sacrificing compassion of the Buddha-as-rabbit served as a teaching to animals and a god regarding the importance of lovingkindness and compassion, thereby exhibiting a brilliant sense of the relational animist manifestations that pervade the Buddha's multiple-life biography.

Our Buddha, the Compassionate Prince

Learning from his previous life experiences, the Buddha thereby fully realized the qualities of lovingkindness and compassion when it was time for his last birth, as our Buddha, Gautama. The Buddha was born under a tree, just as he realized enlightenment, taught his first sermon, and died under trees. In the grove of Lumbinī in southern Nepal, his mother felt no pain as she gave birth standing up while a *sāl* tree, out of devotion to the Buddha, lowered a branch so that she could anchor herself.[40] This was no normal birth nor was it a normal baby: "With his lustre and steadfastness he appeared like the young sun come down to earth, and, despite his dazzling brilliance, when gazed at, he held all eyes like the moon."[41] Reverential nāga serpents sent rain to cleanse both mother and newborn since nāgas are strongly connected symbolically with water and rain, while other nāgas fanned him and showered him with flowers. Baby Gautama then took seven steps, with lotus flowers growing under his feet at each step, before he roared like a lion: "I am the foremost in the world and this is my last rebirth."[42] The natural world became placid in recognition of his birth, as "noxious creatures consorted together and did each other no hurt . . . the birds and deer did not call aloud and the rivers flowed with calm waters."[43]

Having arrived in the world under a sāl tree (*Shorea robusta*), the Buddha's close connection with trees commenced from birth, and when we remember that the Buddha always had special connections with trees, we can appreciate an important but often-overlooked story from his early childhood. One day he went with his father the ruler, as well as the royal retinue, to a village for the Ploughing Festival agricultural ritual. While the adults were busy with their pomp, the youthful Buddha found solitude under a *jambū*, or rose-apple, tree (*Eugenia jumbolana*), that cast its shade on the Buddha no matter where the sun was in the sky. There, the Buddha fell into a deep meditative state as he traversed the *jhānas*, or levels of meditative concentration.[44] Later in life the Buddha would remember this experience as representing the path to awakening and, with that memory, he would take food and head to his place of enlightenment under the Bodhi Tree.[45]

In Buddhism the wisdom gained from such deep meditative states is developed along with compassion for humans and animals, and the Buddha displayed such compassion while he was still young. One morning the Buddha was sitting in the courtyard of his royal palace, when before him a swan fell from the sky, an arrow piercing one of its wings. Tenderly the Buddha picked up the swan, which he caressed with his hands and voice while he removed the arrow. Just then Devadatta, the Buddha's cousin and antagonist over many lives, loudly rushed up, demanding that the swan be given to him. He had shot the swan, Devadatta reasoned, so he owned the game. The Buddha responded that the swan was his because he had healed it. When their argument reached a crescendo, the Buddha and Devadatta agreed to have the case settled by the council of elders. The elders decided that if life had value, then the one who healed the swan had a greater claim since he had protected the swan's life. Thus receiving caretakership of the swan, the Buddha continued to nurture it until it was well enough to depart on its own, leaving him in despair over the loss of his avian friend.[46]

The boy Buddha's interaction with the swan exposes two crucial interfaces of Buddhism with nature with which we are already familiar, the attitudes of lovingkindness and compassion. The Buddha taught his followers to develop within themselves and extend to all living beings four states of mind known as *brahmavihāras* ("divine abodes"): lovingkindness (*mettā*),

FIGURE 3.   Compassionately feeding fish at Wat Traphang Thong monastery, Sukhothai, Thailand.

compassion (*karunā*), appreciative joy (*mudiṭā*), and equanimity (*upekkhā*). These interior states are to be developed without limit, hence they are often referred to in English as the Four Immeasurables. Although this practice cannot on its own lead to nirvana, at least not as portrayed in the Pāli canon, the Buddha emphasized the importance of the Four Immeasurables for helping develop states of mind that do lead to liberation as well as just being the right things to do.[47] The Buddha himself modeled these states of mind, like we have already seen in several stories, so Buddhists often follow his lead in encouraging relationships with the natural world based on lovingkindness and compassion.

Leaving Home

Eventually, in his late twenties, the Buddha memorably renounced his patrimonial kingdom and set out to wander in the forest like other Indian holy people did at the time. It was not just his human family and friends who opposed his departure from home; the natural beings in his town of Kapilavatthu also expressed their sadness, given that "The birds did not sing. The lotuses withered. The trees bore no fruit."[48] His leaving appeared to have affected his trusted horse Kaṇṭaka, who was born on the same day as the Buddha, especially deeply. The pure white Kaṇṭaka neighed loudly, hoping to wake up humans to stop the Buddha while he was sneaking out of the palace early in the morning.[49] Later, as the Buddha renounced his royal finery in the forest, Kaṇṭaka licked the Buddha's feet. After the Buddha was gone, Kaṇṭaka shed tears (unusual behavior indeed for a horse!) and then refused all food, eventually starving himself to death in his grief. He received a lovely funeral and then was reborn in the pleasurable Heaven of the Thirty-Three.[50]

According to the *Buddhacarita*, an authoritative Mahāyāna biography, when the Buddha left Kaṇṭaka and arrived at his forest hermitage to find deer and birds living peacefully, he felt refreshed and emboldened to seek the ultimate realization.[51] The Buddha studied meditation with two teachers, Āḷāra Kālāma and Uddaka, and, while he mastered their techniques, he found that they brought him no closer to his goal, which was a state that lacked *dukkha*, meaning something like suffering or imperfection. Left without a way forward, he remembered his powerful experience as a child under the rose-apple tree and decided that it must contain the secret of enlightenment. He fortified himself with food, leaving five fellow renouncers with whom he practiced fasting to abandon him as a failure. Now completely on his own, he then began, as the scriptures say, roaming free like a deer through the forests of the Ganges River valley.[52]

The Tree of Enlightenment

We will likely never know about many of the trees under which the Buddha stayed during his travels. Eventually, however, near Uruvelā he discovered a delightful grove of trees on the gently sloping banks of a clear river, with a village not far away so that he could beg for alms. In that grove, he came to an impressive *pipal* fig tree (*Ficus religiosa*), a tree that was preordained to provide the seat of his enlightenment. Every Buddha has a specific enlightenment tree. The Buddha Vipassī gained enlightenment under a trumpet-flower tree, Sikhī under a white mango tree, Vessabhū under a sāl tree, the Buddha Kakusandha under an acacia, Konāgamana under a pipal tree, and the Buddha Kassapa sat under a banyan tree.[53] Siddhartha's own enlightenment pipal tree had been designated by the previous Buddha Dīpankara and, in a previous life, the Buddha's attendant Ānanda had venerated this same tree with a sacred festival.[54] After Siddhartha reverenced the tree with circumambulations, thus performing an act of nature worship like he otherwise might decry, Siddhartha sat down under the tree that, for the gods, is a wish-granting tree.[55]

This tree, the Bodhi Tree, has been venerated by many in history and still receives enthusiastic adoration today. During the Buddha's lifetime, for instance, a Bodhi Tree seed was planted in the Jetavana Grove, one of the first Buddhist retreat centers, so that nearby lay disciples of the Buddha would have something to reverence in the Buddha's stead when he went on teaching tours.[56] Thus, the Bodhi Tree was an early doppelgänger for the Buddha himself, a function that it still serves. At present a giant tree with limbs so heavy that they require supports, the Bodhi Tree has died and been replaced several times since the Buddha's lifetime. A Bodhi Tree cutting was transplanted to the Anurādhapura monastery in Sri Lanka in the third century BCE and the Indian tree has been transplanted back from Anurādhapura's tree.

Set beside the Mahabodhi Temple amid beautiful grounds in the Indian town of Bodh Gaya, the Bodhi Tree marks the most sacred location for Buddhists since it daily receives visitors from all over the world. Typically, pilgrims will circumambulate the tree in clockwise fashion, bow to honor it, perform prostrations in front of it, or meditate at its side. Of interest, the scholar of religion David Haberman describes Sri Lankan and Thai pilgrims,

FIGURE 4.   The Bodhi Tree in Bodh Gaya, India, including vertical supports for its heavy branches.

imbued with practices of venerating trees in their local environments, who wrap the Bodhi Tree in cloth of the same color as a monk's robe, temporarily making the tree a symbolic Buddhist monk.[57] We will see a major Thai tree-ordaining movement like this in chapter 4.

As the Buddha sat under the Bodhi Tree, many natural beings reverenced him. A large flock of birds circumambulated him, as did a blind nāga serpent, and other trees bent toward the Bodhi Tree out of respect, an act of religious devotion by plants that is relatively rare in the scriptures.[58] The four deities of the tree—Veṇu, Valgu, Sumanas, and Ojopati—shaped the tree to be perfect for the sitting Buddha while they also made it beautiful, befitting the Buddha's coming accomplishment. The local nāga king even brought a multitude of pious snakes who offered flowers to the Buddha.[59] But, after the sacred preliminaries were finished, the beings of the woodland showed compassion for the Buddha by becoming silent for his meditation. The biographical *Buddhacarita* says, "Then, heavenly beings felt unparalleled joy, the birds and the throngs of beasts made no noise, the forest trees did not rustle though shaken by the wind, when the Lord took up his posture firm in his resolve."[60] Here, one sees that many beings in the natural world may be spiritually sensitive since they anticipated the

Buddha's enlightenment much more perceptively than did his five human fasting colleagues who denounced him as inauthentic. This element of the Buddha's life story turns the perception that humans are more spiritual than nonhumans on its head.

But natural beings did not just anticipate the Buddha's enlightenment experience; they participated somewhat. When Māra, the malign tempter of early Buddhist mythology, came to sway the Buddha from his enlightenment experience, Māra arrived with a threatening army of disfigured, ferocious animals. In many texts, on the Buddha's behalf some nāga serpents hissed at Māra, although in the Pāli text *Nidānakathā* even the king of the nāgas slithered away in cowardly fear of the tempter's power. Māra challenged the legitimacy of the Buddha's experience by saying that there was no witness of it, at which point the Buddha indicated his witness by famously touching his finger to the earth, which at that moment trembled.

By touching the earth in this way, the Buddha perhaps reflected a tradition, albeit in subdued form, of earth goddess veneration that existed in his religious environment. The Buddha replied to Māra, "This earth supports all beings; she is impartial and unbiased toward all, whether moving or still. She is my witness that I speak no lies, so may she bear my witness." Then the Buddha added, "Water and fire and wind are my witnesses, and so are Brahmā, the lord of beings, the moon, the sun, and the stars." Even local cows recognized the truth of his experience since for a period they gave clarified butter from their bodies rather than milk.[61] Thus, the Buddha did not appeal to the earth so much as a great goddess but rather as an authoritative witness among other witnesses, like one may do in a court of law. The earth here clearly remains a feminine person but perhaps is not particularly divine. Later Buddhist traditions, however, often ascribe divinity to an earth goddess, as several other chapters of this book will show.

Once enlightenment was realized, the natural world celebrated his accomplishment: "Throughout the universe flowering trees put forth their blossoms and fruit-bearing trees were loaded with clusters of fruit; the trunks and branches of trees, and even the creepers, were covered with bloom; lotus wreaths hung from the sky; and lilies by sevens sprang, one above another, even from the very rocks. . . . The sea became sweet water down to its profoundest depths, and the rivers were stayed in their course."[62]

Afterward, the Buddha wandered to other trees, resting for a rainy week under a tree where the large cobra king Mucalinda gave protection by spreading his hood, thus beneficially shielding the newly minted Buddha from precipitation and mosquitoes. Then the Buddha moved to a *rājāyatana* tree (*Budhanania latifolia*), under which he had a crucial religious experience.

As described in the Pāli *Vinaya*, up to this point the Buddha was enjoying his enlightenment experience but was not contemplating sharing it with others. He thought that his self-discovered path was too subtle to be understood and he feared that others' lack of comprehension would cause them to misuse his teachings. But while he sat under the rājāyatana tree, the deity Brahmā implored him to teach. In response, the Buddha reflected botanically. He saw that just as there are three types of pond-growing lotus plants—those that never grow high enough to break the surface of the pond, those that just reach the surface of the pond, and those tall ones that rise magnificently above the water line—so humans appear in three capacities. The Buddha then resolved to teach for the benefit of the third, superior capacity, the tall lotuses among humans, and his career as the founder of a religion began.[63] Seeking the five colleagues who had previously rejected him, he ambled to the Deer Park forest near modern day Sarnath, where he delivered his first sermon under a tree. According to Tenzin Chögyel's Tibetan version of the Buddha's biography, several golden deer from the forest attended this sermon.[64]

The Buddha in Nature

These stories of the Buddha's enlightenment make clear the affinity, even affection, that the Buddha had for trees, who notably participated in the major events of his life. As the story of the Buddha's healing of the swan shows, however, the Buddha also enjoyed intimate personhood relationships with many other nonhuman beings. Among the many animal friends of the Buddha, for instance, elephants were perhaps his favorites. Some of these elephants were religious; in the *Suttanipāta* we read about Erāvaṇa, an elephant who took teachings from the Buddha and pronounced them to be "good," and the *Chaddanta Jātaka* intriguingly states that elephants may practice ritual burial cremation.[65] Moreover, in many places the Pāli canon favorably compares the Buddha to an elephant, repeatedly referring to him as "the Immaculate Tusker," with the *Theragāthā* relating that all Buddhist saints are like elephants in their nobility.[66] Also, all Buddhas are said to have the "elephant look," in which they move their whole body, rather than just their heads, when turning to look at something.[67] Thus, the *Majjhima Nikāya* declares that because of his elegance, forbearance, and other fine qualities, the Buddha was like a grand royal elephant.[68]

Further, the Buddha himself stressed his similarities with a male elephant since they typically seek solitude. It seems that at one time the Buddha was in Kosambi and felt frustrated by his numerous responsibilities to his monastic and lay followers. Always a lover of seclusion, the Buddha left the assembly without warning one day and secretly went to Pālileyyaka by himself, setting up a temporary hermitage beneath an auspicious sāl tree at the edge of a pond.

At the same time, a bull elephant found himself in a bind. He lived among a mixed herd of cows and calves, with the latter voraciously chewing off the delicious new plant growth. His drinking water was disturbed by others and his bathing place was intolerably crowded. Feeling claustrophobic amid the mass of trunks, tails, and fanlike ears, the bull elephant left his herd and arrived at the same spot to which the Buddha had repaired. There, the elephant helpfully trampled grasses and retrieved water for the Buddha, showing devotion to an enlightened being.

The Buddha thrived in that serene, solitary hermitage and came to appreciate having left behind the humdrum of humanity, thinking, "I live pleasantly and in ease." At that same moment, the elephant reflected on how grateful he was to be free from the chaotic herd and alone in the forest, thinking of his solitude, "I live pleasantly and in ease." Since the Buddha could read the elephant's mind, knowing that he and the elephant were thinking the same thing underscored for the Buddha his similarity with a majestic elephant person.[69]

Just as human people can work good or ill, though, so do elephant people in the scriptures; the most notable miscreant elephant in the Pāli scriptures was Nālāgiri, a known killer of humans. The Buddha's inimical cousin Devadatta, he who had shot down the swan that the Buddha had healed earlier in life, as an adult nursed such a grudge against the Buddha that Devadatta conspired to kill him. Devadatta went to the mahouts who cared for the ferocious elephant Nālāgiri and promised them royal appointments if they used the pachyderm as a murder weapon against the Buddha, and the mahouts agreed. Then, as the Buddha entered Rājāgaha on the carriage road, the mahouts turned Nālāgiri loose, and the elephant charged the Buddha with ears and tail raised in anticipation of a fight. The Buddha's disciples begged him to get out of the way, but the Buddha assured them that a Buddha cannot be killed through an act of aggression. Townspeople who witnessed the event took wagers on the Buddha and the elephant, with some prognosticating the Buddha's death and others predicting the miraculous escape of the "elephant among humanity." Then the Buddha occupied the center of the road and stood his ground as he radiated mettā lovingkindness toward the elephant. Sensing this loving energy and thereby subdued by it, Nālāgiri changed his course of action. He slowed and then stopped in front of the Buddha, fully tamed, and allowed the Buddha to pet his forehead. The Buddha gave him a short lecture on the importance of nonharm, after which Nālāgiri reverentially used his trunk to wipe the dust from the feet of the Buddha. After this, Nālāgiri returned to his stable a changed pacifist.[70] The Buddha taught that even the worst people may be reformed, and here we see that teaching extended to an elephant who is treated as a spiritual person, too.

In this story Nālāgiri learns religious virtues as a human may do despite the fact that Buddhism generally considers the practice of religion to be a human-only affair. However, there exist many other exceptions to this rule against animal religion in the scriptures. We have already seen several examples, such as trees who bow in reverence to the Buddha's enlightenment experience and nāgas who follow the Five Precepts and even find enlightenment. Moreover, in the *Pañcūposatha Jātaka* a pigeon, snake, jackal, and bear observe the Buddhist fast, and in the Pāli canon cows, peacocks, tree spirits, and other animals venerate the Buddha.

Despite his teaching that animals lack the wisdom required for the pursuit of nirvana, the Buddha preached to and converted animals for their benefit in future lifetimes. The *Buddhacarita* tells us that the Buddha preached to birds, like Francis of Assisi did, and in the *Divyāvadāna* his attendant Ānanda instructed parrots in religion.[71] The Buddha also intentionally delivered teachings to two parrot chicks who, while being seized and eaten by a cat, cried out, "Praise to the Buddha! Praise to the Dharma! Praise to the Community!" By having such devoted minds at death, the two parrots were reborn in heaven.[72]

Nonetheless, perhaps no animal had greater innate faith in the Buddha than a lucky bull found in the *Divyāvadāna*. At one time in Vesālī, a butcher took a large bull out for slaughter, surrounded by impatient customers looking to buy meat. As the bull was led to the place of slaughter, the bull knew what the humans had planned and, in a panic, looked for an escape. Just then the Buddha entered Vesālī seeking alms. When the bull saw the Buddha approaching, he immediately became filled with faith, much as in Indian tradition you should be spiritually overwhelmed by the sight, or *darśan*, of your spiritual teacher. Thinking that the Buddha would save him, the bull snapped his bonds and ran to the Buddha, bowing down before him and licking his feet, with the butcher in pursuit with a sword. The Buddha then asked the butcher to spare the bull's life since no living being wants to die, but the butcher refused, saying that he could not afford to lose his financial investment in the bull. At that point the Buddha mentally communicated with Sakka, king of the gods, who arrived bearing money amounting to three times the bull's worth. The Buddha gave this money to the happy butcher, thus liberating the bull from human dinner bowls. The bull, now filled with even more faith, circumambulated the Buddha three times, just as a human might do, and the Buddha smiled.[73] Such freeing of animals from death then became a basis for various later Buddhist animal release practices, as later chapters of this book explore.

In spite of these examples of nonhumans who practice religion, the teachings of the Buddha nonetheless retained a sense of human superiority and power over nature. Indeed, in the *Sīlavīmaṁsana Jātaka* the Buddha makes clear that being a human is better than being an animal, in that case a cobra.[74] The *Suttanipāta* reinforces this understanding of superiority, calling the human Buddha the "overlord of animals," and the *Milindapañha* describes him as a kind of Master of Animals, a figure who controls all animal behavior.[75]

The Buddha expressed this power over nature both physically and spiritually. For instance, within the list of supernormal powers of the Buddha as described in the Pāli *Mahāsīhanāda Sutta*, one finds that a Buddha can manifest multiple bodies, appear and then vanish, move through walls and mountains, move in and out of the earth as if it were water, walk on water, fly, and touch the moon and the sun with his hand.[76] The Buddha magically transformed bad water into clean water more than once. Additionally, he bit off a small section from a willow tree branch and planted it, and the resulting tree grew to be seven feet tall and no bigger. Then, when jealous rivals of the Buddha cut the tree down, it miraculously came right back.[77] Further, one time the Buddha sent lovingkindness to some blind men who recovered their eyesight and stuck their staffs into the ground in celebration. These staffs then grew into a grove of trees.[78] Another time, the Buddha's attendant, Ānanda, was meditating in a cave when an evil spirit appeared as a vulture and blocked the cave mouth to frighten him. In response, the Buddha reached through the solid rock and patted Ānanda's shoulder to reassure him.[79] The Buddha was even able to spread lovingkindness among supaṇṇa spirit birds and nāga serpents, causing them in his presence to temporarily suspend the eternal enmity between snakes and the birds of prey who hunt them.[80] Perhaps more surprisingly, the early fifth-century CE Chinese pilgrim Faxian tells us of an Indian community that possessed a robe of the Buddha. When drought hit, they made offerings to the Buddha's robe and rain fell immediately, maybe because the scriptures compare the Buddha to a rain-bringing nāga.[81]

Such a sense of the Buddha's control over nonhumans is not surprising given that, as the scholar of Buddhism Ian Harris said, "The sage is under no obligation to submit to the laws of nature."[82] The Buddha's religion teaches that, at the higher levels of meditation, one gains control over the physical constituents of earth, air, fire, and water. Buddhist saints therefore commonly have power over nature, and as such they also reflect the folklore of other religions, which typically include tales of similar saints.[83] Such stories in the Buddhist world simultaneously cut both ways since they often exhibit a sense of intimate interactions between the Buddha and the natural world, but they also firmly establish a human being as supreme over the natural world, with the implication that other humans may share such superiority.

In the Pāli scriptures, this human superiority to and power over the non-human realm provides license to employ nonhuman resources for human ends. As an example, in the *Divyāvadāna* a yakkha forest deity, out of devotion to the Buddha, allowed a forest to be cut.[84] The Chinese pilgrim Xuanzang relates a story in which a nāga was used for the terraforming of a lake.[85] The Pāli *Vinaya* is straightforward about monks using timber to build huts, provide storage, and create spots for drying wet clothes. The Buddha himself supervised the use of timber in the construction of assembly halls for his new community. According to the translations in *The Book of the Discipline*, he allowed the use of wood, bricks, and stones in the construction of buildings for humans and approved the use of tiles, stones, plaster, grasses, and leaves for roofing (2200).[86] Robes could be made of linen, cotton, silk, wool, hemp, or canvas (1823). The use of animal hides for clothing was forbidden for monks living in the Ganges River valley but acceptable for monks in border regions, such as at higher and cooler Himalayan altitudes (1678). Most plant foods and roots, as well as minerals, were acceptable for use, as were a variety of fruits and fruit juices (1756). In the Pāli scriptures, monastics could eat meat and fish but could not beg specifically for them unless they were ill and could not accept them if they saw, heard, or suspected that the animals died specifically for their sake. However, for various reasons including decorum, the Buddha prohibited outright eating the meat of elephants, horses, dogs, lions, tigers, hyenas, snakes, and humans (1713–15, 1741–42). Interestingly, perhaps seeking not to offend the Brahmanical sense of purity, in the Pāli *Vinaya* garlic and onions were forbidden, highlighting the culturally shaped character of some of these prohibitions (2178) The biospheric sustainability of many of these resource uses, such as cutting wood and building monasteries, remains open to debate, as does the role of meat eating in the Buddha's teachings.

Vegetarian Controversies

The Buddha taught that all phenomenal things decay including him, and just as natural beings were part of the Buddha's birth and enlightenment, so they were at the time of his death. He took as his last meal *sūkara-maddava* or "pig's delight," which many scholars think was a pork dish. Other interpreters, though, consider it a vegetarian "food of pigs," meaning perhaps truffles, so the exact content of that meal is open to question. Hence, the heated controversy arises regarding whether or not the Buddha ate meat, with both those who affirm a carnivorous Buddha, as well as those who argue that the Buddha eschewed meat, often claiming his last meal as evidence for their point of view.

I will not resolve this controversy here, for the issue in many ways comes down to a matter of faith. If one places faith in the Pāli scriptures of Theravāda Buddhism, it is unsurprising if one concludes that the Buddha ate meat. In a number of passages the Buddha was straightforward about meat eating since carnivory was common in his cultural milieu in contradistinction to today's more vegetarian India. Deryck O. Lodrick, an expert on Hindu cattle veneration, states that, during the time of the Buddha, it was common in India to sacrifice bulls and even priests ate the resulting beef, leading to a broad acceptance of meat eating. It was not until the time of the *Purāṇas* in the early centuries CE, hundreds of years after the Buddha was gone, that Indian religious attitudes shifted firmly toward a greater stress on vegetarianism, especially as a mark of high-caste status.[87]

Thus, in several stories in the Pāli scriptures, the Buddha's disciples ate meat and he personally recommended "meat broth" to them.[88] As for the Buddha himself, on one occasion the Buddha happily accepted a pork offering from Ugga of Vesālī, and another time when the Buddha was absent, the Buddha received a meat offering from a follower and it was described as "pleasing" by the Buddha's attendant.[89] In the *Jīvaka Sutta*, the Buddha was assailed for eating illicit meat, and the Buddha's response was not that he did not eat meat, but that in this particular case the meat had been proper since the animal had not been killed expressly for him.[90] Further, over several verses the early text *Suttanipāta* denounces a series of vices for being worse than meat eating, such as with the line, "If any persons here are completely unrestrained in respect of living creatures, taking others' property, intent on injury, of bad moral conduct and cruel, harsh, disrespectful—this is tainted fare, not the eating of flesh."[91] Perhaps most tellingly, the Buddha's antagonist cousin Devadatta at one time was a Buddhist monk. He instigated a mutiny against the Buddha by issuing several demands, including one that all monks be vegetarians. The Buddha refused Devadatta's request and allowed monks to dine as they felt best.[92] From the point of view of this story, to insist on Buddhist vegetarianism is to side with a great Buddhist heretic.

Conversely, if one places faith in certain Mahāyāna Sanskrit scriptures, one may fairly conclude that the Buddha was a vegetarian. In the *Laṅkāvatāra Sūtra*, the Buddha indicates that Theravāda Buddhists who follow the Pāli scriptures may be given to eating meat, but he forbids meat for true aspirants since the slaughtering of "innocent victim" animals arises from pride and leads to arrogance.[93] As part of a strong argument for vegetarianism, the *Nirvāṇa Sūtra* teaches that the Buddha allowed meat eating while he was alive but forbade it as a deathbed injunction.[94] The Buddha of the *Śūraṅgama Sūtra* was arguably vegan, forbidding not just meat but also milk, cream, butter, and the wearing of garments made from animals or animal products like silk.[95] Further, and interestingly, the *Śikṣāsamuccaya* argues against meat eating because animals are our kin, thereby displaying brilliant relational animism that leads to ethical and dietary norms.[96] Given the vegetarian ideals found in these texts, followers of these Mahāyāna scriptures generally dismiss any notion that the Buddha's last meal could have been pork and describe the Buddha's diet as thoroughgoing vegetarian. These differences of opinion between Pāli and Sanskrit scriptures about the Buddha and meat help inspire the variety of Buddhist dietary habits that we will encounter in future chapters.

Whatever the Buddha's final meal was, it made him very ill. At a place called Kusinārā, he finally stopped the wandering that had occupied him for nearly fifty years and lay down under a pair of sāl trees to greet his earthly end by resting "on his right side, like a lion."[97] When it was clear that the Buddha would soon die, forest spirits cried out in despair.[98] Surrounded by his disciples, the Buddha uttered his final words, "All conditioned things are of a nature to decay—strive on untiringly!"[99] Then he centered his mind meditatively and was done. As he passed into final *parinibbāna*, winds blew briskly, lightning and thunder appeared, and fire broke out. The moon dimmed. The earth announced the demise of the *"nāga* of *nāgas"* with a "terrible and hair-raising earthquake."[100] The sāl trees under which the Buddha rested bent over and, out of season, rained flower blossoms over his body. Distraught nāgas stood by, "their eyes reddened with grief."[101] Afterward, the Buddha's cremated relics were divided and placed within eight *stūpa* reliquary memorials.

Themes in the Buddha's Biography

This death scene of the Buddha seems most intriguing since it contains rare instances of the practice of religion not just by humans and possibly by animals but also by a wide variety of natural entities, including plants as well as some beings who are commonly regarded as inanimate, such as winds, the moon, and the earth. Here, the relational animist personhood of nonhumans gains expression through their practice of forms of religion, such as devotional mourning, that are often reserved for humans alone. The Buddha's death thereby exemplifies the theme of this chapter that even nonhumans may practice religion within the Buddha's dynamic and multivalent personhood relationships with natural beings.

If we take a step back from the Buddha's death and focus on his full life, other forms of dynamic relational animism typify the biography of the Buddha, such as the personhood of natural beings in the jātakas; the sadness of birds, lotuses, trees, and a lonely horse at the Buddha's great departure from home; and the similarities and friendships with the Buddha among nāgas, trees, and elephants. Natural beings, mostly animals, evidence this animist personhood by practicing Buddhism, such as with the generous and self-sacrificing rabbit in the moon or at the Buddha's birth, enlightenment, first preaching, and passing away. Nāga persons especially express religious realization.

The Buddha's teachings and example demonstrate the importance of maintaining respectful personhood friendships with nonhuman natural beings and many later Buddhists follow this example. Because of the scriptural Buddha's own enjoyment of fascinating personhood friendships with numerous different natural beings, the Buddha's life sets precedents regarding not just the acceptability, but also the desirability, of developing respectful personhood relationships with a multitude of nonhumans. This dynamic then provides a model for later Buddhists to emulate regarding their own region-specific nonhuman persons. From this emulation, throughout the Buddhist world one finds vibrant Buddha-inspired relational animist expressions, some of which roughly match the Buddha's experiences while others gain their unique locally tinted inspirations from the life story of the ultimate Buddhist teacher. In this way, the lively experiences of the Buddha with his nonhuman comrades help provide impetus for the later tradition to develop and express Buddhist nature religion in a myriad of ways, both canonical and noncanonical. Hence, deriving in part from the Buddha's life story, both a profusion and a multihued diversity of Buddhist nature religious experiences will arise in later chapters of this book.

However, whereas one finds robust relational animism like this in the biography of the Buddha, sometimes the Buddha's attitudes carry a negative valence when it comes to establishing Rolston's sustainable biosphere. For instance, the Buddha's relational animism does not promote a unitary vision regarding the issue of Buddhist vegetarianism, while it allows the human employment of natural resources in ways that are occasionally questionable in terms of ecofriendliness.

Likewise, the touchpoint for comparison of nature mysticism is notably lacking. Before sitting at the foot of the Bodhi Tree, the Buddha first reverenced the woody giant, but nothing in the story indicates a nondual experience. The Buddha and an elephant thought the same thing at the same time but did so as a charismatic coincidence among individuals, not a pure nondual experience. That is, from the evidence of this chapter it is difficult to describe the Buddha as a nature mystic. On this note, as the scholar of Buddhism John J. Holder relates, "The Buddha did not celebrate nature as a window on the divine or as a glory that nourishes our souls and liberates our spirits."[102]

In this chapter, Buddhists displayed their respect for nāgas, and the seventh-century Chinese pilgrim to India, Xuanzang, described a parallel manifestation of Buddhist personhood respect, in this case for crocodiles. Xuanzang related that, in the Deer Park in Sarnath where the Buddha gave his first sermon, there were three ponds in which the Buddha had bathed, washed his alms bowl, and cleaned his robe. Xuanzang stated that the crocodiles who lived in the ponds were peaceful if approached with respect, but one would "usually be harmed" if one approached them with "a mind of arrogance."[103] Equally dramatic expressions of respectful personhood attitudes, such as with these crocodiles, persist to the south across the Buddhism of Sri Lanka, but in different forms and with some outcomes that are different from those of the Buddha's India. Now let us turn to the Buddhism of Sri Lanka to explore these similarities and contrasts.

CHAPTER 3

The Clever Bee of Sri Lanka

In many places in the Buddhist world, religious leaders instruct Buddhists by verbally telling jātaka stories of the previous lives of the Buddha. Commonly, teachers will not read the sacred texts word for word in relating such stories since, like storytellers everywhere, they speak from memory while adapting tales to be more vivid and powerful for their audiences. One of these oral jātakas comes to us from Sri Lanka, the subject of this chapter. It seems that, long ago, a barber who happened to be of low moral repute and a pious Buddhist layperson embarked together on a sea voyage. In mid-ocean their boat failed and split apart, and the two only managed to arrive on a small island by clinging to the wreckage. Once on land, the barber began killing birds for food, while the layperson chose to recommit himself to the Dhamma and prayed for help based on his merit. Given this prayer, an ocean nāga serpent transformed himself into a boat. The deity of the sea climbed aboard the nāga-as-boat, becoming its pilot, and invited the layperson to board the boat and return to India. However, the sea deity refused entry to the barber, given his poor ethical qualities, until the layperson voluntarily offered to donate his own merit to the barber. With this, both men boarded the boat, which sailed through the ocean and then up the Ganges River to Benares. Upon their arrival, the sea deity gave teachings about the importance of keeping the right companionship, saying, "It is always good to seek the company of the wise. If this barber had not been in

63

the company of this devoted disciple, he would have been drowned there, in mid-ocean." In later lives, the sea deity would become our Buddha, while the nāga-as-boat became the Buddha's disciple Sāriputta.[1]

This interesting tale, besides highlighting the religious value of keeping virtuous comradeship, possesses several other dimensions that are worthy of consideration. First, despite lacking any monotheistic creator figures such as the God of Abrahamic religious worlds, Buddhist cultural lifeworlds still possess a multitude of deities or spirits, like the spirit of the sea, who are often more powerful than humans yet are at least in part immaterial. Although puissant, they represent unenlightened beings who remain trapped in samsara. Such spirits have been a part of Buddhism from the beginning, as we saw in previous chapters when the Buddha himself incarnated as such beings in past lives and interacted with a variety of similar beings in his life as a religious founder.

Both Buddhists and scholars of Buddhism have discussed these spirits in many different ways, but many people underappreciate the roles that these deities, when appearing in the nonhuman natural world, play in shaping the tradition itself. Frequently, gods of nature are thought to be Buddhist practitioners themselves, for instance, and are recognized as members of the broader sangha community of Buddhists. Further, the story of the shipwrecked men emphasizes that humans express religiosity variously, given that the barber is not moral or pious while the layperson is, and the two interact with spirits differently. Such differences in approaches to spirits may interpenetrate to produce fascinating or unexpected phenomena in Buddhist worlds.

Adding to this situation, as Buddhism has traveled from its original Indian home it has interacted with a vast array of other religious forms, and these interactions have produced some surprising outcomes. For example, as we move through this chapter we will find Buddhist agricultural rituals, especially for rice, done in the names of spirits that are not Buddhist in origin; veneration of sacred spots, such as mountains or rivers; and perhaps most astoundingly for some readers, the practice of animal sacrifice as a Buddhist act, or at least as an act performed by some Buddhists. None of these practices is prescribed by the mainline scriptures, and in fact the Buddha specifically spoke against animal sacrifice. Yet we cannot understand the real lives of Buddhists, or the shape of the Buddhist tradition itself, without comprehending the sometimes important places of these practices in Buddhist lifeworlds.

This chapter investigates the roles of nature spirits and their practices in the Buddhist world of Sri Lanka. In this South Asian Buddhist homeland, we find that nature spirits inspire a number of vibrant relational animist appearances, including the practice of religion by elephants, nāgas, and even trees. Yet, interestingly, little nature mysticism arises, even among forest monastics, and despite some calls for personhood-based vegetarianism, Buddhist meat eating on occasion becomes allied with the practice of animal sacrifice. Further, we discover some of the underlying attitudes toward nonhuman nature that drive such outcomes in terms of the implanting of Buddhism in Sri Lanka, popular religious practices, the careers of monastics who dwell in the forest, and contemporary efforts to enact black magic. The place to begin this journey is with an assessment of the Lankan landscape.

The Lankan World

Both the influence of spirits on relationships with nature and the surprising results of religious intermixing can be found in the Buddhist world of Sri Lanka. The teardrop-shaped island of Lanka, described by Marco Polo as "better than any other island in the world," is about the same size as Lithuania and rests in the Indian Ocean only about forty kilometers (twenty-five miles) from India.[2] The island shares a great deal of its flora and fauna with India, from which Lanka separated about twelve million years ago. But the island also possesses its own unique species since 25 percent of its flowering plant types can only be found in Lanka.[3] Consisting primarily of coastal lowlands, the island of Lanka, home to the modern nation known as Sri Lanka, enjoys two tropical climates, because the southwest tends to be wetter than the northeast, with both climates allowing two rice-growing seasons a year instead of just one. Ancient Lankan kings adapted to this reality, creating a remarkable irrigation network in the dry zone that was a marvel to many visitors.

Because of its warm equatorial climate, especially in the wet coastal areas, Lanka can, or could at one time, boast of being one of the most biodiverse locales in all of Asia.[4] In its grasslands roam, or used to roam, herds of spotted deer (*Cervus axis*), sambar deer (*Cervus unicolor*), wild pigs, monkeys, rabbits, and large rodents. The trails used by wild elephants (*Elephantus maximus*), now almost extinct, and wild buffaloes (*Bubalus bubalis*) criss-crossed mountainsides.[5] Preying on some of these creatures were Lankan leopards (*Panthera pardus kotiya*), which are also now endangered, there being fewer than one thousand left in the wild. The Lankan leopard, however, has survived longer than the Lankan wild cow (*Bos gaurus*), which met extinction sometime between the seventeenth and nineteenth centuries.[6]

In terms of human habitation, archaeologists claim that anatomically modern human hunter-gatherers came from what is now India to reside on the island by around 35,000 BCE, establishing what is called the Balangoda culture. Early human numbers were few, given the difficulties of hunting and gathering in a tropical rainforest, where most of the resources are high in the forest's canopy rather than on its floor. Both iron and rice agriculture arrived from India around the beginning of the first millennium BCE, spawning the practice of *chena* slash-and-burn agriculture that still exists on the island. This practice caught on, so they say, like wildfire, so that by the middle of the first millennium BCE, much of the original forest in lowland areas of the island had already disappeared.[7] Floral and faunal biodiversity declined as the primary forest did, although slash-and-burn practices created the conditions for malaria-carrying mosquitoes to thrive.[8] Then, in the nineteenth century, both British colonials and Lankan natives went to work felling the trees that remained in the highlands, denuding mountains and removing much more forest cover, often in the name of growing tea.[9]

Because of such actions, today less than 31 percent of the original forest cover is left, helping cause a variety of problems, including air pollution that persists in part because of a relative dearth of plants to clean the air.[10] The loss of plants has involved not just trees but also medicinal plants, some of which are "very rare or confined to a few restricted locations."[11] Wetland plants like mangroves and other water entities are also disappearing because of drainage for agriculture, poor fishery management, and coral mining, among other reasons.[12]

Beginning sometime around the fifth century BCE, a new breed of human, the northern Indian Indo-Aryan that was imbued with the culture of the Vedas and their scriptural successors, began appearing on the island, thus changing its culture forever. Displacing the Väddas, or the relatively indigenous inhabitants of the island, these Indo-Aryans may be seen as the forerunners to the Sinhalese, who today ethnically dominate the island, as does the Sinhalese common religion, Theravāda Buddhism. Although, today, Väddas are hard to find in a pure, culturally unmixed state, Vädda populations still exist in small numbers in the dry zone and, as I will indicate, perhaps have left lasting imprints on Lankan Buddhist cultures.[13]

The island has also witnessed centuries of influx not just from north Indian Buddhists but also from Hindus of Tamil south India, so that now Tamils make up about 25 percent of the island's overall population. Some of these Tamils are recent immigrants, while others represent families that have lived on the island for generations. The ongoing antagonisms between Sinhalese and Tamils mark a tragic chapter of the island's modern history, especially through the three decades of civil warfare that began in the 1980s. Even though populations blend almost everywhere, the Sinhalese tend to be concentrated in the southern and western wet areas, whereas Tamils and the remaining Väddas are more often found in the drier east and north. Adding to the population stew, Muslims have lived on the island for centuries, providing an Islamic ambience, and as a result of Portuguese, Dutch, and British colonization, many Sri Lankans today call themselves Christians.

The mixing of these peoples, their religious practices, and their favorite deities has led to the creation of a Sinhalese Buddhist pantheon of divinities that is enormous in its sheer number of spirits and complex in terms of relationships between them. Making things even more complicated, various Buddhists may offer dramatically different accounts of this pantheon, revealing that, in fact, there are many fluid pantheons, not just one. Generally, the Buddha is the leader of the collective pantheons. He is ambiguously placed because his full enlightenment means that he is no longer of this world, yet he leads spirits who clearly are worldly. Below the Buddha, a significant role is played by the four powerful *dēva* spirits that represent Lankan versions of the classic Buddhist deities of the four directions, although agreement on which four Lankan gods fill this niche is lacking.[14] Typically, this group contains Nātha, also known as the Buddha of the future named Metteyya in Pāli, who was a primary protector of rulers of the Kandyan kingdom that lasted from 1594 to 1815 CE. The great divine rider of the spirit-bird Garuda, the god Viṣṇu from India, protects the Sinhalese Buddhist tradition, which many Lankans believe represents the ultimate repository of the Buddha's wisdom. The goddess Pattinī is now mostly forgotten in her Tamil homelands in India, but in Sri Lanka she quite visibly remains as a benevolent, wise, and moral Buddhist goddess who heals sickness and ends droughts. But several scholars tell us that by far the most popular of these four gods today is Kataragama, a former low spirit with a peacock for a mount who has been reformed and thus risen nearly to the top of the pantheon. Pilgrimage to Kataragama's shrine in southern Sri Lanka may be the most popular of all current Sri Lankan Buddhist practices since Kataragama helps with things like passing school examinations and getting ahead in business. During the two-week pilgrimage, Buddhists make offerings to the Buddha, Kataragama, and other spirits while also engaging in practices such as fire walking.[15] I will return to a discussion of Kataragama later, because he retains some connections to both mountain veneration and hunting rituals, with hunting representing a continuing occupation among some Buddhists in Sri Lanka.

Trees, *Nāga*s, and Elephants Implant Buddhism

Spirits from the natural world like Kataragama have always held places within the Lankan pantheon, according to the semicanonical Buddhist historical chronicles of the island, the *Dīpavaṃsa*, *Mahāvaṃsa*, and *Cūḷavaṃsa*. Written sometime around the fourth or fifth century CE, the oldest of these is the *Dīpavaṃsa*, which relates that, at the time of our Buddha, the island of Lanka was uninhabited by humans, being peopled only by nāgas, yakkha cannibal demons, and *piśāca* monsters. Nonetheless, the Buddha wished to make the island the headquarters for his religion, so not long after his enlightenment he visited the island to make preparations and subdue the island's inhabitants.

In this diplomacy the Buddha was remarkably aided by Samiddhi, the deity of a tree, identified by the *Mahāvaṃsa* as a rājāyatana tree that grew in the Jetavana Grove monastery in India.[16] Exhibiting tremendous religious personhood, Samiddhi did not just relocate himself to Lanka, he brought his tree dwelling, roots and all, with him. After the Buddha gave teachings and the ritual of refuge to the now-placid nāgas, he encouraged them, in a manner uncharacteristic of the Buddha of chapter 2, to venerate Samiddhi in his transplanted tree home.[17] Here, we see nāgas worshipping a tree spirit who served the Buddha out of devotion, thus revealing a profusion of natural beings who practice religion like humans do.

An implication of Sri Lanka's chronicles is that if the Buddha were to establish his religion on the island, pious nāgas and trees were not enough, and humans were needed, albeit humans of the were-lion variety. According to the *Mahāvaṃsa*, a lustful Indian princess once took a lion as her mate, then gave birth to a son, Sīhabāhu, and a daughter, Sīhasavali. Eventually, Sīhabāhu became a king and the two were-lion children mated with each other. Their eldest child, the crown prince Vijaya, was so violent that the populace clamored against him, leading King Sīhabāhu to exile Vijaya by setting him afloat on the ocean. Seemingly by chance, Vijaya landed on the island of Lanka on the very day that the Buddha passed away, with the omniscient Buddha having already entrusted Vijaya with the establishment of his teachings. Since Vijaya's father enjoyed the nickname "Sīhala," indicating the qualities of a lion, so the descendants of Vijaya are the "Sihalese," or Sinhalese, who adorn their national flag with a lion emblem just as Vijaya did.[18] It is easy to see how this story blurs the line between Lankan Buddhist humans and lions.

However, the scholar James John Stewart intriguingly claims that lions supply only one side of the Sri Lankan national character, the forceful side, whereas cattle represent the obverse, pacifist side of Sri Lankan minds. Stewart informs us that cattle are the most revered of all animals on this island, reflecting some measure of Indian influence. Stewart says, "The cow is a protected animal, more so, perhaps, than the widely respected elephant. Indeed, an entire movement has developed around the defense of the cow. For many Sinhala Buddhists, the cow represents the nurturing and love expressed by one's own mother."[19] Exhibiting this respect in Buddhist form, the All Ceylon Buddhist Congress calls for cattle protection, as does the Organization for the Preservation of Life, which is run by a Buddhist monk, the Venerable Kosgoda.[20] As we will see, however, this respect for bovines does not compel all Lankan laypeople or monks to avoid meat eating.

According to the *Mahāvaṃsa*, once humans were thriving on the island, the Buddhist Dhamma could be received. King Aśoka of India arranged to have his son Mahinda and daughter Saṅghamittā sent as missionaries to the island.[21] They flew and landed near Anurādhapura on the sacred Missaka Pabbata peak, now the pilgrimage site known as Mihintale, where they were helped by the deity of that mountain. Knowing that the Lankan king Devānampiyatissa (250–210 BCE) was hunting nearby, the mountain deity transformed himself into a sambar deer and tempted the king to pursue him. When on the hunt the king reached the mountain, he found not the deer but the Buddhist elders there. After some discussion, the king invited the two Buddhist elders to spread their doctrine in Lanka, so that Sri Lankan Buddhism was born with the help of a mountain god who appeared as a sambar deer.

In the chapter 2, I mentioned that the current Bodhi Tree in India has been transplanted back from a tree in Sri Lanka, and, along with the ministrations of the divine sambar deer, the planting of this Lankan tree helps mark part of the story of the advent of Buddhism on the island. The appearance of a cutting of the Indian Bodhi Tree in Sri Lanka in 288 BCE also makes for an instructive tale in the study of religion and nature, because in the *Mahāvaṃsa* the Bodhi Tree exhibited first-rate spiritual abilities. The Indian emperor Aśoka wanted to send the Bodhi Tree along with the rest of his transmission of Buddhism to Sri Lanka, so the Bodhi Tree severed its own branch and rooted it, making a new tree. The tree then flew by itself for a week-long spiritual retreat in the Himalayas. Returning to the capital after its retreat, the tree then boarded a ship and set sail with a retinue for Lanka. Arriving at its anointed place in the Mahāmēgha Grove in Anuradhapura, the immigrant Bodhi Tree's roots overflowed its bowl as it planted itself in glory. Humans, assembled for the occasion, offered the tree copious gifts, and the Mahāvihāra monastery was established nearby. Then, on its own initiative, a remarkable royal elephant indicated the spot for Lanka's first nunnery, while another royal elephant highlighted the spot for the Thūpārāma, Sri Lanka's first stūpa reliquary monument.[22] In this tale, the Bodhi Tree performs noteworthy spiritual feats much like a human, although it does so perhaps more because of human-centered anthropomorphism and less from belief in the innate capacities of trees for spiritual progress. The same may be said for the elephants who founded holy places.

Tree Veneration

The religion-implanting bodhi tree of Anurādhapura, known respectfully as Śrī Mahā Bodhiya, continues to attract pilgrims today, and it remains chief of all of the many bodhi trees, also known as bo trees, that dot Sri Lanka. Bodhi trees (*Ficus religiosa*), called *esathu* in Sinhalese, tend to be large, with many branches spreading to form a kind of umbrella, so they offer welcome shade in a hot climate. Moreover, in an enduring belief from pre-Buddhist Sri Lanka, banyan, palmyra palm, *nā* (ironwood), and bodhi trees are thought to provide residences for deities, from minor local *dēvatās* to the great and powerful *dēva* gods, so bodhi and ironwood trees are protected from harm by custom.[23] If such a tree absolutely must be cut, woodcutters may inform its tree spirit a day in advance and perhaps decorate another tree, thus inviting the spirit to a new home.[24]

In the Buddhist world of ancient India, the canonical Pāli text *Apadāna* describes reverence for such sacred trees as a sign of devotion to the seat of the Buddha.[25] Moreover, as mentioned in chapter 2, a bodhi tree was planted during the Buddha's lifetime at the Jetavana Grove to allow reverence for the Buddha in his absence. Additionally, artistic representations at the ancient Indian Buddhist monuments of Bhārhut and Sāñcī employed bodhi tree images as stand-in replacements for the person of the Buddha.[26] Emerging from this historical context in which bodhi trees serve as doppelgängers for the person of the Buddha, temple bodhi trees in Sri Lanka are venerated before any religious activity in order to gain the Buddha's permission.[27] As such, interactions with bodhi trees symbolize interactions with the Buddha himself.

Reflecting the blending of primordial Lankan customs of tree veneration with these Buddhist elements, a common practice of Sinhalese Buddhists is Bodhi pūjā, or ritual interactions with sacred bodhi trees, a practice recommended even by rationalist Buddhist modernists like Anagārika Dharmapāla (1864–1933 CE).[28] A multitude of gifts—such as money, spices, betel or areca leaves, incense, flowers, and butter lamps—may be offered, along with the chanting of scriptural verses and a merit-making watering of the tree. Petitioners may chant, "I worship this bo tree, seated under which the Lord Buddha attained enlightenment by overcoming all inimical forces. I worship this great bodhi tree, which was honored by the Buddha, the leader of the world.

My homage to thee, O King Bodhi."[29] The gifts are not commonly offered to the tree itself, but to the deities resident in the tree, with the Buddhist love and compassion of the gifting making merit for the spirits of the tree. These grateful spirits then grant boons to the sincerely faithful. Such offerings may be made for many different reasons, such as for healing, overcoming a run of bad luck, or receiving a bad astrological horoscope. Bodhi pūjās may also be done, interestingly, as a form of love magic.[30]

Although, traditionally, such veneration of bodhi trees has been largely an individual venture, bodhi tree worship has become much more popular in collective, group rituals since the 1970s in part through the activities of Pānadurē Ariyadhamma, a former forest-dwelling monk who offered lively and large outdoor preaching sessions near bodhi trees.[31] Among adolescent Buddhists, collective Bodhi pūjās remain popular since the events provide human social communion along with interaction with the sacred tree.[32] Collective Bodhi pūjās additionally have been performed for the health and welfare of the whole country. During the social turbulence of the last few decades, Bodhi pūjās have also been enacted to create peace since monks have accentuated the rituals with meditations on lovingkindness. Bodhi tree rituals have even been performed by Sri Lankan expatriots in London.[33] Part of this recent movement, "something of a national ritual for Sinhala Buddhists," involves resurrecting nearly forgotten practices, such as bathing tree roots in water or milk that is scented with sandalwood or saffron.[34]

Mountain Deities

Sri Lankan Buddhists are notable for their enthusiasm for holy trees and the spirits who live in them but they further extend religious respect to holy mountains. For example, we have already seen that in the *Mahāvaṃsa* the missionary monk Mahinda alighted on the island on the sacred peak of Mihintale and was aided by the god of that peak, a deity who was also a god of the hunt. In addition, the prominent god Kataragama supplies another example of a sacred mountain god who, like many mountain gods around the world, serves as a Master of Animals or a god who controls hunting.[35]

According to some popular beliefs as well as the scholarly work of C. G. and Brenda Z. Seligmann, the quite well-loved Kataragama, who today grants a variety of worldly boons, got his start as a local mountain hunting god. To make this point, the Seligmanns turned to the beliefs and practices of the relatively indigenous Vädda people, across whom beliefs are fluid. Among many Väddas, Kataragama may spiritually possess a human being, a function he still performs daily at his shrine crowded with Sinhalese

Buddhists. Further, a fairly universal Vädda deity is Kande Yaka, *kande* indicating the word for "mountain." Kande Yaka is both a mountain deity and a deity of the hunt because he controls both the mountain and the game near it. As the controller of animals, Kande Yaka must be propitiated before any hunt and his required offering is meat or the hunt will fail.

The Seligmanns show that the Hindu god Skanda merged with the figure Kande Yaka in southern Lanka, resulting in Kataragama, who has the mythological biography of Skanda but weapons of the hunt, such as spears, in his iconography.[36] Kataragama's present temple, in fact, may have previously been a shrine for Kande Yaka, and even today the mountain and hunting god Kataragama, as the controller of fauna, may send animals to attack Buddhist shrine pilgrims with whom he is displeased.[37] Interestingly, although the Lankan scholar Swarna Wickremeratne tells us that pilgrims to the Kataragama shrine should practice vegetarianism, Kataragama still sometimes receives offerings of venison, just as any respected Lankan hunting god might get.[38]

Another mountain, the imposing Śrī Pāda, is the most holy of all Lankan peaks. Like Mihintale's mountain, Śrī Pāda helped facilitate the introduction of Buddhism to Lanka, perhaps indicating the lasting power of some Lankan mountain veneration. The *Mahāvaṃsa* relates that when the Buddha flew to Lanka, he landed on top of Śrī Pāda, leaving his footprint in stone as an enduring pilgrimage magnet. At the time, this mountain was inhabited by the "king of the gods," Mahāsumana, whom the *Mahāvaṃsa* describes as a stream enterer, or an advanced Buddhist practitioner. The deferential Mahāsumana asked the Buddha for something to worship, and the Buddha offered him a handful of his hair, this hair forming part of the catalog of relics of the Buddha that remain on the island. Mahāsumana then made another request for an object of devotion, and in response the Buddha left his footprint in the rock at the top of Mahāsumana's montane abode.[39]

The god Mahāsumana, now known more commonly by the Sinhalese name Saman, is one of the most important of Sinhalese Buddhist deities, often joining the group of powerful dēva gods of the four directions that I mentioned previously. As with Kataragama and the deity of the Mihintale peak, in Buddhist liturgies Saman is described not just as a mountain god but more fully as a hunting god.[40] His home is Śrī Pāda, which is so sacred a mountain that it is known by many names, including Siripāda (Illustrious Footprint), Sumanakūṭa (Sumana's Mountain), Samanalakanda (Saman's Mountain or Mountain of the Butterflies), and Adam's Peak.[41] This mountain, located in the south-center of the island near Kandy (Nuwara), rises sharply to an altitude of 2,243 meters (7,359 feet), making it visible from the sea off the southern and western coasts of the island. The apparent footprint in the rock at the summit was made by Adam after his expulsion from Eden in Lankan Muslim and Christian belief, by the god Śiva in Hindu belief, and of course by the Buddha to Buddhists. Moreover, the four main rivers of the island begin at Śrī Pāda, making its reputation for granting prosperity materially vivid. Therefore, the mountain is revered across Lankan religions, adding to its perceived sanctity as well as its popularity as a pilgrimage spot. Sri Lankan tradition holds that the footprint at the summit was discovered by Vaṭṭagāmaṇī Abhaya (ca. 89–77 BCE), but the earliest physical evidence for footprint veneration occurs in inscriptions from the reign of King Vijayabāhu I (1055–1110 CE).[42] Śrī Pāda may have served as the reputed location for the Buddha's preaching as recounted within the Laṅkāvatāra Sūtra, thus connecting the mountain not just with South Asian Theravāda Buddhism but also with East Asian Mahāyāna Buddhism as well.[43]

The steepness of the slope of Śrī Pāda challenges pilgrims, so the path is lined with chains to provide stability for climbers. Nonetheless, at least in the past the ascent could be so treacherous as to be inadvisable during the wind and rain of the monsoon season, so that the pilgrimage season occurs during the milder months of December to April. Typically, pilgrims begin their climb in the dark hours of the very early morning in order to summit in time to catch the often-spectacular sunrise. Pilgrims may be awakened from drowsiness by the necessary purificatory washing of the face in a flowing cold water stream near the beginning of the trail. At this point, Buddhist pilgrims also will begin a conscious observance of the Five Precepts.

In addition, more often than at other Lankan Buddhist pilgrimage locations such as the Temple of the Tooth in Kandy, pilgrims to Śrī Pāda typically chant "karuṇāva yi," a chant for compassion, as devotees appeal not to the Buddha, but for the compassion of Saman, the deity of the mountain.[44] Wickremeratne says, "Those who visit this place of worship do so with reverence and devotion, constantly mindful of Saman. . . . Devotees have tremendous faith that if a vow is made here, it will be granted, provided that it is made with devotion."[45] In this light, Buddhist pilgrims, besides chanting for compassion, may also utter this chant:

> To worship our Buddha, may god Saman help us.
> God Saman, lord of this demise,
> As upwards we trek to worship our Buddha
> Grant us the grace of your compassion.[46]

Thus, pilgrimages to Śrī Pāda operate like Buddhist devotions to the bodhi tree in that the devotee strikes a kind of bargain with the deity. The devotee offers a positive Buddhist inner state, such as lovingkindness or compassion, to the god, who is approached as a person within the natural world and who in turn recompenses the devotee with some kind of boon. In this way, devotional practices directed toward natural beings become integrated into the Buddhist repertoire of practices by embracing elements such as compassion and mindfulness despite perhaps lacking direct canonical support.

Intriguingly, pilgrimages to holy mountains also influence Buddhist dietary choices; Wickremeratne—providing one example—states that pilgrims should abstain from meat for one week before the pilgrimage climb.[47] This marks a departure from customary practices for many Sri Lankan Buddhists, who commonly consume land meats and/or marine animals. Although meat typically is not offered to the Buddha in Sri Lanka, it is commonly offered to monastics since many laypeople feel that they must give to monks what they perceive as the best food.[48] Indeed, like one finds elsewhere in the Buddhist world, Sri Lankan Buddhists may value their Muslim and Christian neighbors for serving as butchers, thus allowing Buddhists to eat meat without directly violating the precept against killing. Because of this, in following a holy period of pilgrimage vegetarianism specifically for the sake of the mountain god of Śrī Pāda, some of these normally carnivorous people temporarily alter their Buddhist approaches to the question of diet. If abjuring meat promotes a more sustainable biosphere, then these Buddhist holy mountain pilgrimage practices may represent Buddhist ecofriendly actions, with energetic alpine relational animism supplying the motive force.

Buddhist Agricultural Resources

When Saman is not mentioned as one of the four high dēva gods, probably the goddess Pattinī, a deity of purity, healing, and fertility, is. In Sri Lanka, Pattinī is a true Buddhist, an advanced practitioner who guards Buddhists through her love and compassion. A goddess of fire, Pattinī is traditionally thought to cure smallpox and other diseases, like Śītalā does in India. With her home shrine at Navagamuva, she was a patron goddess of the Kandyan kingdom.

Existing largely in the world's rice bowl, Buddhist cultures have adapted or developed a number of agricultural rituals for growing rice, and in Sri Lanka Pattinī is an important figure in the rites that govern the plowing, planting, and harvesting of grain. Like in Theravāda Thailand in the next chapter, the first plowing of the season marks an important ritual that, of old, notably included the king. These days, the first plowing rites are more subdued, but the ritual may still be observed. Typically, farmers will leave a patch of a wet rice field unplowed so that lotuses may appear in honor of the Buddha. Likewise, the communal area of the village may remain unmolested so as to provide a home for birds.[49] At planting time, farmers may visit a monk in a temple, asking him to chant *pirit* (*paritta* protective chants derived from scriptural verses) in order to wish them a good, simple planting that is unobstructed by spirits: "Whatever bad portent, and what is inauspicious, whatever unpleasant noise of a bird, whatever evil planet and dream unpleasant, let them all come to naught through the power of the Buddha. May the paddy grow well!"[50]

Harvest time occasions the great *gammaḍuva* holiday celebrations throughout the island villages. A circular area is ritually created, typically with a post at the center, and freshly cut sheaves of rice are laid out on this floor. A shrine is created at the edge of this area, and on this shrine offerings appear, such as flowers and butter lamps, in honor of the Buddha, Pattinī, and other spirits. The light from the lamps is not allowed to dwindle until the ritual is complete. First buffaloes, working in the sacred clockwise direction, stamp on the rice to sever grain from the stalks, then humans finish this activity before winnowing the grain from its chaff. Part of the crop will then be offered to a local spirit, Pattinī, Kataragama, and/or the Buddha. Once the harvested and processed rice is stored, a Buddhist monk is called again to chant pirit over the harvest. Reenacting a part of Pattinī's myth, at this time villagers also commonly play a game called *an keliya*, in which two community teams compete in a tug of war, with the goal of ensuring that in the next season Pattinī will bring plenty of rain and create a good harvest.[51] In these ways, folk Buddhist personhood regard for natural spirits in Lanka may function to create a psychological appreciation of the concept of sustainability.

Buddhaghoṣa

Although practices such as venerating a bodhi tree, climbing Śrī Pāda, and calling the rice goddess may be both old and popular, they were not much recommended by perhaps the greatest Sri Lankan Buddhist saint, the fifth-century scholar monk Buddhaghoṣa, who is still regarded by many throughout the Theravāda world as kind of a second Buddha. Although his masterpiece, *Visuddhimagga* or *The Path of Purification*, offers copious bits of systematized advice for realizing liberation, in it he promotes sitting meditation far more than mountain pilgrimages, homages to rice spirits, and other nature devotional practices. Nonetheless, his guidelines for embodying the lifestyle of a forest monastic rest at the pinnacle of Theravāda orthodoxy, so that Buddhaghoṣa's influence regarding forest practice reverberates not just later in this chapter but also in the next chapter in Thailand's forest monastic movement.[52]

Not much certain is known about Buddhaghoṣa's life. The Sri Lankan chronicle *Cūḷavaṃsa* states that he was a Hindu Brahmin religious teacher in northern India. Although skilled in debate, apparently he lost a contest to a Buddhist elder Revata, causing him to convert to Buddhism and take Revata as his teacher. Prompted by Revata, he traveled to Lanka to find texts lost in India and translate them from Sinhalese to Pāli. During a considerable period of time spent in Lanka, however, he more than translated a few books because he contributed his own original works, which are still respected today.[53]

According to *The Path of Purification*,[54] like many Buddhists, Buddhaghoṣa assented to the notion of the presence of this-worldly nature spirits as he unself-consciously mentions spirits of rocks, trees, and the earth. Yet, for him, such spirits may have some power but they are not close to enlightenment, leaving no reason to venerate them. For Buddhaghoṣa, liberation is won through the union in meditation of concentration and insight and in no other way, so while he does not dismiss spirits, he does not promote their worship either. Therefore, the *Visuddhimagga* generally avoids nature devotions and was clearly written for humans alone to travel the spiritual path, following the mainstream Buddhist belief that only humans can realize liberation. While there are some nonhuman-friendly, biospherically sustaining elements within the *Visuddhimagga*, as I will discuss, the work as a whole thus dramatically expresses attitudes of human superiority to the nonhuman world. Examples of human superiority to nonhumans in the *Visuddhimagga* include the elder Mahā Anula's changing a river of water into a flow of clarified butter as well as the belief that a spiritually advanced human can magically create a pond with fish or take on an animal appearance (392, 399, 401).

Buddhaghoṣa leaves no room for the veneration of nonhuman animals; he explicitly describes them as lower than humans (423). According to Buddhaghoṣa, the Buddha taught religion to animals not for their spiritual welfare in this animal life but for future human lives (204). However, Buddhaghoṣa still intriguingly opens the door for humans to learn spiritual lessons from animals. For example, he tells of a frog who listened, enthralled, to a sermon of the Buddha. During the sermon, the frog was accidentally killed, but his holy mental state at the moment of death led the frog to be reborn in the wonderful *Tāvatiṃsa* heaven, a lesson in devotion for us all (204). Further, echoing a passage from the *Milindapañha*, for Buddhaghoṣa the proper seeker pursues enlightenment as a leopard stalks its prey (263). Moreover, the Buddha taught us to take the middle path between extremes, and Buddhaghoṣa's properly clever bee memorably shows us how to embrace this advice: "When a too clever bee learns that a flower on a tree is blooming, it sets out hurriedly, overshoots the mark, turns back, and arrives when the pollen is finished; and another, not clever enough bee, who sets out with too slow a speed, arrives when the pollen is finished, too; but a clever bee sets out with balanced speed, arrives with ease at the cluster of flowers, takes as much pollen as it pleases, and enjoys the honey-dew" (134).

Additionally, for Buddhaghoṣa, animals can serve as meditation teachers; he told of an elder who tested a meditator by having the practitioner vibrantly conjure a mental image of an enraged elephant about to trample him. When the meditator became anxious about the conjured elephant, the elder counseled him that for those who have destroyed all spiritual afflictions, there is nothing left to fear from any animal (658). In another Buddhaghoṣa tale, there once was a parrot who had been taken in by nuns. The abbess of the nunnery, not wanting any slackers about, taught the parrot to meditate on the decomposition and impermanence of the body, using the word *bones* to focus the meditation. Then one day the parrot was sunning and meditating when he was snatched away by a hungry eagle. While in the grasp of the eagle's talons, the parrot reflected that "a cage of bones is carrying a cage of bones," and thus remained serene rather than panicking. Eventually, the eagle dropped the parrot, who was able to relay his account to the nuns.[55] In another story from Buddhaghoṣa, translated in *The Path to Purification*, a hunter's spear once failed to injure a cow, for at that moment the cow was protected by the intense mettā lovingkindness that she felt for her calf, showing how important lovingkindness is (306).

The story of the loving cow highlights Buddhaghoṣa's recommended approach to nonhumans: an ethic of ahimsa nonharm combined with an attitude of mettā lovingkindness. For Buddhaghoṣa, ahimsa means abstaining from harming "living things" (10, 535). Personhood attitudes toward animals play a role in this extension of ahimsa since Buddhaghoṣa follows the *Saṃyutta Nikāya*'s call to care for animals due to their being our parents from previous lives.[56] In addition, for Buddhaghoṣa, mettā lovingkindness should be extended to pāṇa, "breathing things," meaning animals both human and not (302). Since, for Buddhaghoṣa, mettā makes one "dear to nonhuman beings," the first step in any meditative session should be to develop an attitude of lovingkindness (97–98, 304). In this light, Buddhaghoṣa counsels forest-dwelling seekers to protect themselves from harm by employing ahimsa and lovingkindness. Later in this book, we will discover some fascinating outcomes when monastics take Buddhaghoṣa's advice on the subject.

While animals should receive lovingkindness and compassion, other entities fare more poorly in Buddhaghoṣa's perspective. Reflecting orthodox strands of the Theravāda tradition and in fact within the Buddhist tradition as a whole, Buddhaghoṣa creates an implicit ontological distinction between animals and the rest of the natural world, thus resulting in an element of limited biocentrism along with his erstwhile anthropocentrism. He explicitly states that water, earth, fire, and other elements are insentient, being completely lacking in even the constrained religious sensitivities of animals (349, 356, 364). Plants are insentient as well and therefore are incapable of entertaining spiritual states. Thus, they do not receive the same ahimsa and mettā from Buddhaghoṣa that animals do (349). As an example, in a tale about cutting trees, Buddhaghoṣa's concern is with the noise of tree chopping, because this creates a distraction from meditation, not with the fates of the trees (120). But his unconcerned attitude toward plants perhaps is best found in what may be his most famous literary flourish, where he compares the Buddhist path to liberation with cutting through a heavy thicket of bamboo. To cut through the tangle of bamboo, one needs a knife, the knife of meditative insight. This knife must be sharp to slice through plant materials, and concentration is the sharpening stone. By wielding the knife of insight, a person could "disentangle, cut away, and demolish all the tangle of craving that had overgrown his own life's continuity," thus making the one who has deforested all the inner bamboo "worthy of the highest offerings in the world" (7).

For learning these lessons and cutting through what he considers to be a bamboo thicket of desires, Buddhaghoṣa offers several lifestyle recommendations, such as the thirteen *dhutaṅga* Buddhist ascetic practices that Buddhaghoṣa delineated and organized. Prior to Buddhaghoṣa, various ascetic practices appeared in the Pāli canon, sometimes receiving official approval and sometimes not. By the time the *Milindapañha* was written, around the time of Jesus, however, ascetic practices by Buddhists seem to have been more the norm. A list of thirteen dhutaṅgas appeared in the Parivāra section of the Pāli *Vinaya* and these thirteen practices were later discussed in a work, *Vimuttimagga*, or *The Path of Freedom*, which emerged before Buddhaghoṣa's time.[57] The *Vimuttimagga*'s list is similar to Buddhaghoṣa's own, differing only in small details.[58] Extending the presentations of the scriptures and the *Vimuttimagga*, in the *Visuddhimagga* Buddhaghoṣa dedicated an entire chapter to the organization and systematization of dhutaṅga practices, thus influencing generations of Theravāda renouncers.

According to Buddhaghoṣa in *The Path of Purification*, the first of these renouncer dhutaṅga practices is rag-robe wearing, in which one's clothing consists of stitched-together discards from refuse heaps, the street, or cremation grounds. The second dhutaṅga involves not wearing more clothing than the three robes (shoulder robe, upper garment, and waistcloth) that are canonically described. The alms-food dhutaṅga means eating only food that is offered to one, and the house-to-house dhutaṅga prohibits skipping over houses to beg for food from the ones with the greatest expected alms bounty. A one-sessioner dhutaṅga requires eating all at once only one time a day, a bowl-food dhutaṅga requires eating from just one vessel, and a later-food-refuser dhutaṅga mandates eating only what is first available, whatever that may be. An any-bed-user sleeps in the first available slot, wherever that may be, while a sitter dhutaṅga practitioner never lies down (59–60).

In terms of living space, the forest-dweller dhutaṅga means living in the forest at least five hundred bow lengths from a village, so that one meets the dawn there. Buddhaghosa recommends this dhutaṅga for the quiet, peaceful ambience that it lends to meditation. The tree-root-dwelling dhutaṅga means that one lives at the foot of a tree, a place with no roof. The spiritual benefit of this practice for Buddhaghosa is that one lives closer to deities, with the implication being that there are more deities in the forest. Moreover, in the forest one can learn the truth of change since, according to Buddhaghosa, "the perception of impermanence is aroused through seeing the continual alteration of young leaves" (73). Forest-dweller and tree-root dhutaṅga practices are also good for dispelling hate (80). Two more dwelling dhutaṅgas concern the open-air dweller, who lives not even under a tree, and the cremation-ground dweller, who, besides living among the dead, should renounce eating meat (74–75). It should be noted that, according to Buddhaghosa, nuns should avoid these dwelling dhutaṅgas, because either their vows or practicalities inhibit them from realizing the solitude necessary to gain benefit from these practices (81). He says, however, that for those who lack attachments and inner defilements, "everywhere is a forest dwelling" (92).

Forest Practice

Because of his admiration for forest living as well as his respected descriptions of dhutaṅga forest practices, Buddhaghosa's *Visuddhimagga* has long informed forest-dwelling monastics throughout the Theravāda world, not just in Sri Lanka, although on the island it has played a special role in the relatively recent renaissance of the Sri Lankan forest monastic tradition.

The Lankan forest tradition is hardly new, given that a few Lankan monastics have, for centuries, sought forest solitude. For instance, the forest monastic residence caves at Dambulla, many of which are still in use, date at least from the first century BCE. We know that forest monks were active in the ninth century, and the forest hermitage at Dimbulāgala, also still in use, dates from at least the twelfth century CE.[59] However, the contemporary forest monk movement was stimulated not so much by these precedents but by the restoration of monastic lineages that occurred with the nineteenth-century establishment of the Rāmañña Nikāya monastic order, and from it, the development of a present-day forest monk movement, especially after the modern nation of Sri Lanka gained its independence from the United Kingdom in 1948.

This contemporary Sri Lankan forest tradition diverges in origin and methods from the forest tradition in Thailand that the next chapter examines. Nineteenth-century Thai forest practices largely emerged from among elite Thammayut Buddhists, even if they were disenchanted with centers of power, whereas the Sri Lankan movement arose in part as a lower-caste reaction against the Buddhism of the elites, thus indicating that forest monastics and their motivations are not all alike. What joins the Sri Lankan and Thai movements, though, is the sense that forest living, like that in which the Buddha and his disciples engaged, represents a fundamentally purer form of practice.

In this light, the anthropologist Michael Carrithers, in *The Forest Monks of Sri Lanka*,[60] tells us that part of the attraction to forest monastic life stems from the perception of forest practice as more moral and more spiritually powerful, with these perceptions being driven somewhat by the *Visuddhimagga*. Much of Sri Lankan nonforest Buddhism is based on the jātaka rebirth stories, such as are found in the fourteenth century Sri Lankan jātaka collection *Pansiya Paṇas Jātaka Pota*, which is primarily concerned with settled, agrarian lifestyles. In contradistinction, Buddhaghoṣa's *Visuddhimagga* provides direction for those who wish to imitate the Buddha's sylvan renouncer lifestyle in search of liberation. Carrithers pointedly states that forest life is not about nature mysticism, or "pantheism," but rather a search for deeper wisdom that can only be found in solitude, like Buddhaghoṣa described (41).

In seeking such solitude, the monk Puvakdaṇḍāve Paññānanda, born in 1817 CE, revived Lankan forest living efforts, in so doing describing the forest lifestyle as unfamiliar to laypersons at the time (70, 75). Concerned by what he perceived as lax discipline, weak meditation practices, and pointless disputes among monks, the forest-practice-adoring Paññānanda at one time or another performed all thirteen of Buddhaghoṣa's dhutaṅga regimens before he traveled to Burma to receive a noncaste, ostensibly more pure, *upasampadā* higher ordination. Upon his return to Lanka, he founded a new

monastic fraternity, the Rāmañña Nikāya. Being quite successful at revital-
izing Lanka's forest monasticism, Paññānanda left behind more than five
hundred disciples at the forest hermitages of Baṭuviṭa and Kirinda that he
founded (69–84). After Sri Lankan independence in 1948, both Paññānanda's
forest-loving example and his Rāmañña Nikāya monastic fraternity helped
energize more recent luminaries in the forest monk tradition, such as
Asmaṇḍalē Ratanapāla and Kaḍavädduvē Jinavaṃsa.

Of course, the monastics do not move to the forest for play but for the
serious work of meditation, meaning the imposition of rigorous lifestyles
such as that reported by Paññānanda's chief disciple, Raṃsāgoḍa Sumana. At
four in the morning Sumana would rise, chant pirit (protective verses derived
from the scriptures), and clean his residence. Then he would meditate, either
sitting or walking, until 8 a.m., at which time he would gather food alms.
After returning to his hut, he would offer his food to the Buddha before eating it himself. Afterward, he would clean the shrine and then briefly rest.
More meditation, and perhaps some reading, occupied his time until 4 p.m.
when he would again clean the grounds of his residence before meditating
for a period. At 6 o'clock he would chant more pirit, honor the Buddha, and
give merit to the gods, after which he would return to meditation and reading until bedtime at 10 p.m. (77).

Living away from human habitation, forest monastics can face a variety
of nonhuman threats like dangerous animals and problematic diseases that
are little known to villagers. Indeed, some forest dwellers welcome such haz-
ards, because they may dissuade casual human visitors who could interrupt
the desired solitude (284). The example of the Buddha's taming of the violent elephant Nālāgiri, in as well as the teachings of Buddhaghoṣa's *Visuddhimagga*, instruct monastics on how to respond to such dangers with mettā
lovingkindness. A recent forest monk from the hermitage of Kuḍumbigala,
Tāmbugala Ānandasiri, offers insight into the workings of such mettā. He
asks us to consider bears since, to him, a bear is "one mass of suffering,"
because a bear is "hungry, it is thirsty, it wanders around all day and night
looking for water." Further, a bear fears anything that might move. Moreover,
"its fur is filled with ticks, some the size of a thumbnail, and however much
it scratches, it will never be rid of them." Hence, to Ānandasiri, bears, like all
other animals, are fellow sufferers with humans, being victims of the same
forms of dukkha dissatisfaction that plague *Homo sapiens*. Although animals
like bears have different temperaments and must be respected at times as
given to rage or fear, according to Ānandasiri, since they are much like us, we
should respond to them with neither fear nor aggressiveness but with lovingkindness. This neither-fearful-nor-aggressive-but-loving response, derived in

part from Buddhaghoṣa, is a hallmark of Buddhist forest-dwelling monks throughout this book. Moreover, Ānandasiri recommends active concern for animals; monks at his hermitage have cared for orphaned squirrels and bear cubs. A follower of his further describes monastics' freeing tadpoles from evaporating ponds; as Ānandasiri states, "When we recognize this suffering, whether in humans or animals, we should try to fend it off or at least to diminish it, and therefore practice Buddhism in the purest sense" (291–92).

Besides bears, Sri Lankan forest monks may encounter many snakes, including dangerous cobras and *polangas* (Russell's vipers), and the Buddha himself prepared them for just such encounters. As the scriptural *Aṅguttara Nikāya* relates, at one time the Buddha was staying at the Jeta Grove when one of the monks was bitten by a poisonous snake and died. The Buddha counseled his flock that if the brother had been radiating mettā to the "four royal families of snakes," meaning all venomous snakes understood collectively, then he would not have been bitten. Thus, for nonviolent snakebite avoidance, the Buddha encouraged monastics to eliminate fear and to focus as much mettā as possible on serpents, or other dangerous animals, while reciting these protective verses:

> I have lovingkindness for footless creatures;
> For those with two feet I have lovingkindness.
> I have lovingkindness for those with four feet;
> For those with many feet I have lovingkindness.
>
> May footless beings not harm me;
> May no harm come to me from those with two feet;
> May four-footed beings not harm me;
> May no harm come to me from those with many feet.[61]

Conjuring Red Spirits

Away from serpentine forest dangers, in nonforest religious worlds the Buddha extended ahimsa, like with the forest monks, to the practice of animal sacrifice, deeming it both cruel and pointless. Because of this, many Sinhalese Buddhists shrink in horror from the very thought of practicing animal sacrifice since antisacrifice teachings are scripturally purveyed and orally taught through texts such as the *Matakabhatta Jātaka*. This scripture tells us that there once was a priest in India who readied a goat for sacrifice. The goat at first began to laugh at what was clearly his impending execution but then the goat began to weep. When the priest inquired about the goat's reaction, the goat told him that the goat himself had once been a priest who had sacrificed a goat. For that one sacrifice, the goat-as-priest had been karmi-cally condemned to be decapitated for five hundred lives as a penance. The goat said that he laughed at his imminent demise at first since this would be the last of his five hundred decapitations. But then he began to cry, the goat explained, as he thought of the negative karma the priest would have to endure from the sacrifice. Upset by the goat's tale, the priest thereafter freed the goat from sacrifice. As witnessed by the Buddha, who was born as a tree spirit in that lifetime, a lightning bolt then struck a nearby rock, send-ing a shard flying which decapitated the goat, thus releasing the goat from his long penance. This story, taught by the scriptural Buddha in firm tones, enjoins Buddhists to avoid animal sacrifice.[62]

For reasons such as this, animal sacrifice does not occur through much of the Buddhist world, perhaps leaving some readers surprised to discover that Buddhist animal sacrifice practices exist in many places, including in Sri Lanka, although they can be quite controversial. Naturally, an understanding of context is essential in comprehending how this situation can arise. Tamil Hindu religion includes animal sacrifices, especially to the goddess Kali, so that the long history of Tamils on the island includes incidents of animal sac-rifice. Lankan Muslims annually sacrifice animals for the Id al-Adha holiday that marks the end of the Hajj season as well, adding to the Tamil precedent.

Further, the demands of social life in contemporary Sri Lanka appear to enhance the attraction of animal sacrifice even among devout Sinhalese Bud-dhists. Lankan Buddhists must respond to a variety of social and cultural stressors: interethnic discord, forces of globalization and development, caste prohibitions within a democratic society of theoretical equals, urbanization and loss of traditional agricultural ways, a growing gap between the rich and the poor, and the uncertain anomie of mass society. Many anthropolo-gists tell us that, in response to such pressures, accusations of sorcery have dramatically increased in recent years since someone within the complex Lankan web of actors must be to blame when things go wrong. Although many Sinhalese Buddhists widely understand sorcery to be regrettably non-Buddhist, the tensions of life still may cause them to seek magical retribution for a perceived injustice.[63]

To enact revenge for a slight, traditional Sri Lankan culture offers a variety of local means for ensorcelling others as well as removing black magic spells. However, improved transportation along with a loss of village cultures has led to a centralization of sorcery and countersorcery activities within the Hindu shrine of Badrakali at the major temple complex of Munneśvaram near Chilaw. The temple complex, named for a form of the Hindu god Śiva, houses an important shrine for Pattinī, the great Sri Lankan Buddhist goddess of healing, fertility, and purity, known at Munneśvaram as Ambal, the goddess born of a golden mango. Activities in this shrine are in many ways little different than at any other Pattinī *dēvālē*, or shrine, found around Sri Lanka. But along with Pattinī's shrine, Munneśvaram also provides a home for a major temple to Badrakali, "Good Kali," a goddess known for her multivalent power yet lack of Buddhist attainment. Apparently, this Kali came from India to Lanka, where she sought to eat Pattinī. Pattinī was able to protect herself, so Kali began eating the humans in the area. Pattinī stopped and subjugated her, forbidding Kali to eat human flesh but allowing her to eat animals.[64] Thus, it is a common belief at the Badrakali temple that the goddess must receive animal sacrifices like Kali still may receive in India. Without literal blood sacrifices, some believe, the angry goddess will cause a great deal of suffering.

Animal sacrifices at Munneśvaram are connected to beliefs in sorcery and countersorcery. Feeling that the ambiguously moral goddess will do anything for her followers, it has been a custom in recent years to pursue black magic through animal offerings at the temple. A gift of a chicken causes illness or other problems to the victims of one's sorcery while the gift of a goat brings the death of the other. At Munneśvaram, there are other ways, too, of ensorcelling foes, such as breaking a coconut, using a yam as an effigy, or writing the name of the person to be afflicted on an egg.[65] But it is thought that, given Kali's nature, blood sacrifices provide the most efficient and effective method.[66]

To be fair, some animals are given to Kali as live offerings and they typically later are sold live to benefit the temple. Further, many Hindu pilgrims offer animals to Kali as traditional, pious gifts to the goddess, without any ill intent toward another. But for those humans who are ardent in seeking to harm another, sorcery will be their purpose, and they may insist that the priest give the goddess the blood that she desires. Like in India, these sacrifices to Kali generally involve decapitation with a sharp blade. After the meat has been offered to Kali, it is then eaten by humans, who participate in the grace of the goddess by consuming food first offered to her.

It is reasonable to believe that such sacrifices occurred out in the open in the past, but a Sri Lankan law of 1979 forbids cruelty to animals, which is thought by some to include animal sacrifice, and thus has caused changes in Munneśvaram practices. As recent adaptive responses to this law that retain the theology that Kali must receive blood, animals have been sacrificed in back sheds, away from the public eye. Sacrificed meat also has been sold with the pretense that the temple is engaging in commercial butchery, not animal sacrifice. Moreover, animals have been sacrificed at night, when few people are in the temple.

Such adaptations of practice reveal the alternative Buddhist attitudes toward animals at work in the situation. On one hand, many Sinhalese Buddhists strictly oppose animal sacrifice, resulting in the law ostensibly against the practice. However, some Sinhalese Buddhists continue to patronize the shrine because of their own personal needs and desires, and the anthropologist Rohan Bastin indicates that some of these pilgrims have been the very Buddhist politicians who pushed to pass the law against animal cruelty in the first place.[67] These latter politicians want to appear to be animal-friendly Buddhists in public but employ animal sacrifice sorcery to their own advantage in private, therefore spotlighting the powerful draw of the practice for some Buddhists. But it is not just politicians; the anthropologists Richard Gombrich and Gananath Obeyesekere describe seeing ordinary, seemingly earnest Buddhist pilgrims, dressed in the all-white clothing of devout Buddhist laypersons and lodged in a local Buddhist temple, who bring with them the chickens they intend to sacrifice.[68]

The ebb and flow since 1979 of temple openness about animal sacrifice has reached the courtrooms in recent years. In 2011 a court order prevented animal sacrifice at the temple, citing the 1979 law. However, in July 2014 the Sri Lankan Supreme Court responded ambiguously, only partly upholding this ban. Since animal sacrifice remains a virtual requirement for Hindu followers of Kali as well as the Muslims who live on the island, for the sake of religious freedom the Supreme Court has allowed animal sacrifice as long as it complies with the Butchers' Ordinance and the Cruelty to Animals Ordinance. Thus, in terms of current Sri Lankan law, as long as animal sacrifices are performed with perceived humaneness and under the watchful eye of the Public Health Department, the sacrifices can continue for religious purposes. However, anyone engaging in animal sacrifice must now be a licensed butcher, a provision that sacrificers may see as difficult to comply with for religious, social, or economic reasons.[69]

As later chapters in this book show, animal sacrifices such as these appear in several places in the Buddhist world, not just in Sri Lanka, and exist on the margins of the tradition, not at its center. These Buddhist animal sacrifices do not occur without dispute, since large numbers of Buddhists from across different sects remain appalled at the thought of sacrificing an animal for Buddhist reasons. Many of the Buddhists who oppose these animal sacrifices are motivated by the ideals of ahimsa, personhood considerations, and/or ecofriendly ideologies such as animal rights discourse.

Lankan Buddhists and Nature

This discussion of Lankan animal sacrifice allows us to make some sense of the relationships between Lankan Buddhists and nonhuman natural beings. As we have seen, vibrant instances of relational animism abound in the Lankan world, where human persons exist not separate from lion persons in terms of mythical descent. Venerating the personal deities of sacred mountains and bodhi trees may result in a variety of boons, including romantic love. The Buddha and his helper goddess Pattinī are entreated as essential spirits of the rice crop, while forest monks send lovingkindness to snake and bear persons because, like human persons, animal persons need and respond to positive interpersonal energy.

Among these relational animist phenomena, nonhuman natural beings in Lanka sometimes even exhibit personhood so brightly that they practice religion. A sea deity and a serpent reverently aid a sincere Buddhist in the story that opens this chapter, a mountain god appearing as a sambar deer facilitates the transmission of Buddhism to the island, and elephants indicate the proper locations for the first nunnery and stūpa. Nāgas venerate holy trees. Perhaps most notably, Samiddhi, the holy rājāyatana tree spirit, exhibits strong religious agency in helping the Buddha pacify the island, while a cutting of the Bodhi Tree retains such extreme religious agency that it goes to the mountains for a spiritual retreat, much like humans do. Of course, such appearances, which can be highly anthropomorphic, do not always counteract the mainstream perspective, provided by Buddhaghoṣa, that nonhumans cannot truly practice religion.

In terms of relational animism and diet, Sri Lanka remains complex. Some Buddhists extend a sense of maternal personhood to cattle and, from this, join the Lankan Buddhist reformer Dharmapāla in calling for Buddhist vegetarianism.[70] The fact that the Buddha usually does not receive meat offerings also implicitly appears to hint at vegetarianism as an ideal; one finds this principle manifest in the purity-providing vegetarianism of the Śrī Pāda pilgrimage. Despite these influences, though, eating animals remains a standard practice for large numbers of Lankan Buddhists. A treasuring of meat, in fact, leads to common meat offerings to monks as well as to popular deities like Kataragama and plays a role in animal sacrifices performed for Buddhists, who may not perceive or find compelling the personhood of their slain animal offerings. Many will argue that these practices inhibit the realization of a sustainable biosphere.

Along with the sacrificing of animals, other limitations in Lankan approaches to nature persist. For example, Sri Lankan Buddhism appears to evince little nature mysticism. While Lankan Buddhism features numerous vivid interactions with nature, these are of a more relational animist variety and appear to lack the nondual emphasis of nature mysticism. In fact, the scholar of forest monks Michael Carrithers takes pains to highlight a lack of nature mystical motivations on the parts of forest renouncers.

Besides its own success, Lanka also spread Buddhism to Burma, whose *Glass Palace Chronicle* offers a window into the interactions of Buddhist kings with nature, in one case regarding royal intimacy with a puppy. It seems that, long ago, there was a monk whom a puppy constantly followed in a devoted way. One day the puppy died, and the monk respectfully placed its bones in a pile. Over time, a tree grew up through the pile of bones and knocked against the bones when a strong breeze blew. Later, in the eleventh century, the puppy-loving monk was reborn as the monk Shin Arahan, a great motive force behind the establishment of Theravāda Buddhism in Burma. At the same time, the puppy itself was reborn as the revered Burmese Buddhist king, Htihlaingshin Kyanzittha, who suffered from terrible headaches that would not end. Having insight into the rebirth situation, Shin Arahan advised the king to rebury the bones of the puppy away from the trunk of the tree so that the tree would not hit them. This the king did, thereby eliminating his own headaches and allowing him to continue his work of implanting Burmese Buddhism.[71] Across the border from Burma in Thailand, other Buddhist kings, featuring their own relationships with nature as well as their own headaches, similarly impacted the establishment and maintenance of the tradition. Thus, we will now turn to Buddhism in Thailand in the next chapter.

CHAPTER 4

Beautiful Thai Buffaloes

One day a wild male elephant threateningly approached Achan Lee Dhammadharo, a reclusive Thai forest monk, as he meditated in his isolated jungle hut.[1] The fluid from the eyes of the pachyderm made it clear that he was in musth, a temporary period of readiness for procreation during which even otherwise gentle male elephants may become unpredictably aggressive and violent. As the visibly hostile elephant came near the solitary monk, Achan Lee panicked and quickly jumped up to climb a nearby tree. Partly up the climb, however, he stopped. His training as a monk had taught him to fear nothing, recognize that dangers are produced purely in the mind, and confront his anxieties. Thereby thinking to himself, "You're not true," he returned to his contemplation spot, where he began meditating on and radiating mettā lovingkindness. Eventually, the menacing elephant decided to leave on its own, thus ending the danger.[2]

This humorous and instructive story exhibits some of the numerous, and sometimes conflicting, approaches to nonhuman nature in the Thai Buddhist world. When confronted with a pachyderm threat, Achan Lee's first response was of purely human self-centered concern, no matter how understandable his tree climbing may have been. Similarly, throughout the Thai universe there are many human-centered perspectives regarding the natural world. While Achan Lee's tree climbing seems innocent enough, some of these human self-concerns appear to be not very nature-friendly in terms of leading to a sustainable biosphere, as I will describe. But, at the same time, Achan Lee's Buddhist training encouraged him to adopt an attitude of respectful personhood that was extended to the passion-filled elephant, and such relational animist personhood experiences of respect for nonhumans are also rife in the Dhamma of Thailand. Achan Lee's story thus inspires us to probe a variety of Thai interactions with nature, and this diversity can be fruitfully explored by studying Thai Buddhism and its forest monastics like Achan Lee.

In this chapter we will discover that Thai renouncers like Achan Lee, while living in the wilds apart from humans, still evidence little Buddhist nature mysticism, just like much of the rest of the Thai universe. Also, despite the dynamic relational animism that permeates the Thai religious world, personhood arguments for Buddhist vegetarianism exist but do not predominate. Nonetheless, the energized personhoods of nonhumans still inform numerous instances in which beings such as the spirits of places, tigers, and elephants are said to practice Buddhism. We gain traction in understanding these outcomes if we first tour Thailand's human and nonhuman environments.

The Thai World

Achan Lee belonged to the Thai forest monk tradition. Although some writers erroneously claim that the Thai forest tradition originated in the nineteenth century, actually forest-dwelling monastics are as old as the Thai Buddhist tradition itself, according to the anthropologist J. L. Taylor.[3] A sense of Thai identity, as well as nascent Thai Buddhism, emerged with the Lan Na kingdom that was centered in Chiang Mai beginning around the thirteenth century. The Sri Lankan Buddhist missionaries who helped implant this Buddhism already had a forest tradition that was backed by the *Visuddhimagga*, as described in chapter 3, and this forest tradition became a part of the Buddhist package that the Lan Na kingdom received.[4] Early Thai forest practitioners appear to have been few but still are attested to within sources from the Sukhothai kingdom, the successor to Lan Na and the first great central Thai kingdom.[5] In their efforts to implant Buddhism more deeply, Sukhothai's rulers not only provided doctrinal resources for forest seekers but they also created a blueprint for what would become normative Thai Buddhist attitudes toward the natural world. The *Trai Phum Phra Ruang*, or *Three Worlds according to King Ruang*, offers the most lasting expression of this blueprint, for it remains a staple text for many Thai Buddhists today.

Called "the first true literary work written by a Thai author," the *Three Worlds according to King Ruang* was composed around 1348 by Phaya Litai, who later would become the king of the Sukhothai-Srisachanalai kingdom.[6] Based on the Pāli canon and reflecting Theravāda orthodoxy, the text represents an attempt by the Sukhothai royalty to make Buddhism more accessible and appealing for a lay audience, with Phaya Litai, who piously planted numerous bodhi trees, styling himself as a devoted Buddhist king.

In portraying what is in many ways a standard Theravāda cosmology, the *Three Worlds according to King Ruang* describes a universe consisting of three realms: those of sensual desires, remnant material factors, and no material factors. The physical universe, with six levels of rebirth, rests in the realm of sensual desires, so that the *Three Worlds* has much to say about interactions between different natural forms, including within hells. Like many monastery murals such as at Wat Rakhang in Bangkok attest, the hell realms in the *Three Worlds* are truly gruesome since, for instance, they include a hell in which one is eaten by vultures and crows again and again.[7] According to *Three Worlds according to King Ruang*,[8] killing an animal leads to such a hell rebirth. There is even a special hell for the killers of fish, perhaps leading to the unfortunate Thai habit, described by several writers, in which fish are not quickly clubbed by Buddhist fishers, an active form of killing, but instead are left to suffocate to death slowly and painfully (64, 76). The *Three Worlds* denounces hunting as an evil activity, so that a hunter becomes a *pret*, or hungry ghost, in future lives (101, 103).

Despite these prohibitions regarding hunting, the *Three Worlds according to King Ruang* insists that an animal rebirth is a lower, regrettable rebirth, although not without some ambiguity. For example, in the *Three Worlds* humans who try to speak like animals find a hell rebirth awaiting them (71). Most animals cannot understand true religion, but some do, just as most animals are evil, but lions are good (86). Eating meat is not condemned in the *Three Worlds*, only eating forbidden meat is, although the utopian religious paradise of Uttarakuru is completely vegetarian (133).

Interestingly, blending Pāli scriptural and Thai ideas, the *Three Worlds* not only describes classic deities of the four directions but it also recognizes indigenous *phi* nature spirits that live in mountains, trees, or in the earth, equating them somewhat with the yakkha spirits of Indian lore. Tree spirits in the *Three Worlds*, for example, have their own invisible castles in the tops of big trees (218). Like animals, some of these spirits can understand and practice religion, but most do not, although, setting their resident spirits aside, nonanimal physical entities like mountains and trees themselves utterly lack the capacity for Buddhist wisdom (275). When a phi nature spirit dies, it becomes reborn as an insect, bird, or mammal (96).

Reflecting Phaya Litai's aspirations, in the *Three Worlds according to King Ruang* a noble country is led by a *cakkavatti*, or great Buddhist king.

FIGURE 5. Communing with and compassionately feeding birds at Wat Rakhang monastery, Bangkok, Thailand.

Cakkavattis are not ordinary rulers but instead possess astounding religious charisma due to merit stored up over many past lives. They use this merit to direct the country to more pious outcomes. As the *Three Worlds* says, "Any or all words or orders that such a person says or utters, or anything he enforces, is generally in accordance with the Dhamma" (136). Because of the power of this ruler, he or she is surrounded by some amazing natural beings. Erāvaṇa, or Erawan, the magical multiheaded elephant of the Hindu deity Indra, belongs to the cakkavatti, who cares for him. The great monarch also possesses Valāhaka, the "horse king," who, like Erawan, has the ability to fly, and Maṇiratana, a gem that is "the king of the other 84,000 kinds of gems" (163). This gem lives on the holy Vipulapabbata Mountain, where it tends to its followers (164). The possessor of these treasures, the great Buddhist ruler, receives reverence from both nature spirits and animals, who also serve to feed and entertain the religious monarch (173, 175).

Elephant Saints and Mountain Veneration

One of the Buddhist monarchs who reflects this *Three Worlds* tradition notably, if somewhat inadvertently, stimulated the golden age of the Thai forest monastic movement. In the mid-nineteenth century, King Mongkut sought to purify Thai Buddhism from what he perceived as superstitious accretions, and thus began a new, stricter religious monastic order, the Thammayut. Thammayut monks, for instance, place greater stress on *Vinaya* rules regarding eating only before noon than do the more numerous monastics of the rival Mahanikai sect, and Thammayut monks also dress more modestly by draping robes over both shoulders. In trying to engage a fundamentalist return to the Pāli scriptures in this way, King Mongkut also ended up highlighting early Buddhist elements such as Buddhaghoṣa's dhutaṇga rituals that we saw in Sri Lanka, thus enshrining them as a purer form of practice.[9] This gave many monks who were influenced by the Thammayut, especially those in the northeast, the encouragement that they needed to leave settled monasteries and instead seek places of solitude within what was, in the nineteenth century, a vast expanse of relatively uninhabited wild jungle. The golden age of Thai forest practice had begun.

The early generations of forest monks during this golden age taught complex attitudes toward the natural world. On one hand, being Thammayut Buddhist purists, sometimes these monks encouraged villagers to relinquish the veneration of nature spirits. But some monks emphasized practices that lead to Buddhist liberation, which in the Thammayut perspective nature spirits cannot grant. It is important to recognize that, from this point of view, the veneration of nature spirits is not regarded as non-Buddhist so much as it is understood as not leading to goals worthy of Buddhists. As the anthropologist Barend Jan Terwiel indicates, some monks shrink from participation in forms of nature veneration, not because they do not believe in the spirits, but because nature spirits, as unenlightened persons, are not creditable professional colleagues for spiritually superior monks.[10]

On the other hand, different forest monks—cultural products of the types of supposed superstition that Thammayut monks were expected to fight—sometimes embraced the nature veneration that so spectacularly appears in Thai religion. Indeed, nature religion from Dai, Mon, Khmer, and Brahmanic cultures, as well as from Buddhism, closely interweave and interpenetrate in Thailand, like the study of Thai sacred mountains demonstrates.

The Dai people, whose influx a millennium ago from China into the area now called Thailand helped create the population and culture of the contemporary country, appear to have brought with them a tradition of hill and mountain veneration, according to the ethnobotanist Pei Sheng-ji. For the Dai, places of altitude serve as residences for gods as well as the Euhemerist spirits of deceased great human leaders. All the plants and animals on Dai holy hills are thought to be companions, pets, or food for these resident deities, and so are forbidden in terms of hunting or picking, including the removal of firewood. Hence, a Dai sacred hill "is a kind of natural conservation area founded with the help of the gods, and all animals, plants, land, and sources of water within it are inviolable."[11] Breaches of this taboo incur divine punishments that include diseases, floods, fires, earthquakes, and attacks by animals. As a result of such sacred respect for places of altitude, these holy hills retain the potential to remain relatively stable zones of ecological balance and richness, thereby in the ideal encouraging biospheric sustainability. At least once a year, the Dai will venerate a holy hill through ritual offerings of pork, beef, chicken, rice, fruits, flowers, wine, spices, or candles, and some Thais today behave similarly.

Perhaps reflecting this Dai influence, Thai forest monks often intentionally practiced on or near a number of peaks that had been venerated by locals likely long before Buddhism took hold; the early Buddhist kingdom of Sukhothai already enjoyed the protection of a hill spirit, Phra Kha Phung Phi, according to a pillar left by King Ram Khamhaeng (1239?–1298 CE).[12] Such high-altitude power places are reputed to be the dwelling spots of a variety of gods, demons, and other spirits, and tales abound regarding forest monks who specifically sought out wild spots inhabited by demons so that the malevolent entities could be tamed and turned into good Buddhists. In this way, the boundaries between Buddhism and ancient local nature traditions became blurred since revered spirits of nature, understood as persons, were pacified so they could enter the practice of Dhamma while the Dhamma interacted with nature spirits.

The sacred peak of Doi Suthep, which rises 1,600 meters (5,250 feet) above the bustling city of Chiang Mai, provides one example of such a taming and blurring process. As the scholar of Buddhism Donald Swearer indicates in *Sacred Mountains of Northern Thailand and Their Legends*,[13] *tamnan* historical chronicles describe a pre-Buddhist reverence for Doi Suthep as a spiritual power spot and home for the *phi* nature spirits Pu Sae and Ya Sae, who still reside on the mountain (32). The mountain itself takes its name from the legendary son of these two spirits, the hermit sage Wasuthep, whose mountainside lodging serves as a pilgrimage site (32). When the Buddha visited the mountain, as Thai chronicles describe, he was able to tame the two dangerous *phi* spirits of the mountain by forbidding them human flesh as food, instead allowing them only animal flesh. The two mountain spirits still receive this animal flesh during the annual sacrifice of a water buffalo on the full moon of the seventh month, providing one of several examples in this book in which Buddhist actors engage in animal sacrifice.

Beyond the presence of these nature spirits, Swearer tells us, the Buddha sacralized the mountain further by his mythical visit. In one story, once the mountain spirits had become good Buddhists, the Buddha offered one of his hairs to Ya Sae, instructing her to enshrine it on that "auspicious mountain" (72). This relic of the Buddha then spontaneously divided itself into two pieces in the fourteenth century. One of these pieces is preserved within the *chedi* (stūpa reliquary monument) at Wat Suan Dok monastery at the base of the peak.

The other piece of the Buddha's relic, intriguingly, was entrusted to a nonhuman animal. In 1371 Buddhists placed the relic on the back of a white elephant, Kocha Woramongkul, who was set loose in Chiang Mai so that he might indicate a holy location. Many times, onlookers thought that Kocha Woramongkul would stop, yet the elephant continued to roam to find the perfect location. Eventually, the white elephant reached the summit of Doi Suthep, trumpeted three times, circumambulated three times, and knelt down, thus choosing the location for the esteemed Wat Phra That monastery, which now houses the relic (79). Exhausted by his task of founding a major Buddhist monastery, Kocha Woramongkul died and was buried there, with the monastery's chedi reliquary monument resting on the grave of the insightful pachyderm.

In this remarkable story, one discovers clear Buddhist relational animism, because Kocha Woramongkul acts as a Buddhist person who perhaps is respected above humans for his spiritual sensitivities, just like the elephants that appeared indicating holy spots in Sri Lanka. Since founding a monastery is one of the most meritorious things that a Thai layperson can do, Kocha Woramongkul even practiced Buddhism like a human. Moreover, with the relic of the Buddha enshrined on the holy mountain, the mountain itself acts, according to Swearer, as a conduit through which Buddhists can contact the living presence of the Buddha, somewhat like encounters with the Buddha through the medium of bodhi trees (82). Thus, at Doi Suthep, age-old reverence for elephants and mountains blends with Buddhism to reveal

FIGURE 6. The *chedi* monument that marks the grave of the monastery-founding elephant, Kocha Woramongkul. Wat Phra That monastery, Chiang Mai, Thailand.

indigenous nature spirits who are Buddhist persons, with the Buddha himself experienced as a holy mountain person.

Rice and Religion

In Thailand holy entities do not just reside on mountains like Doi Suthep; spirits also live in agricultural fields. Each plot of soil retains the protection of its resident nāga spirit, who determines the direction of plowing. At the time of plowing, each plot nāga has its head in the west and tail in the east, so one must plow in this west-to-east direction, for one does not want to break one's plow or harm the nāga by going against the grain of the nāga's scales.[14] Each plot further retains the protection of Phra Thorani or Mae Thorani, the indigenous Thai earth goddess who is said to have witnessed the Buddha's enlightenment experience.[15] This goddess looms large in love magic but must be placated whenever she is polluted, such as with the birth of a child or when threatening omens and unlucky events occur. She receives ritual satisfaction through the *thorani san* ceremony, during which monks chant to bless water, which then is used to cleanse the polluted person or place.[16] Additionally, rice fields and fruit orchards possess their own *phum* spirits of place, and the favor of these deities must be sought if the farmer is to have a successful harvest. But perhaps the most important of these local spirits is the rice goddess, Mae Phosob, whom every Thai farmer hopes to call a warm friend since rice grains are her children.[17]

Reverence for the rice goddess begins at the start of the agricultural year. Thai kings of old were famed for their "First Plowing Ceremony," and, for their part, at the first plowing ordinary farmers may erect a post in a corner of the rice field, placing offerings for spirits on top of the post. Showing how mainstream such rice-growing ritualism can be, the Thai government has at times supported rituals for the mass blessing of rice seed and then distributed blessed rice seed through district offices, so that farmers across the country can mix blessed seed into what they plant.[18] Moreover, farmers offer important gifts to the rice goddess's seedbed before germinating as well as to the earth goddess at planting. At threshing time, supplicatory materials for the rice goddess are placed at the center of the threshing floor, and the rice goddess is invited to leave the fields and allow her children to be threshed.[19]

Afterward, when the harvest is stored, the soul of the rice is called to complete the agricultural year. To understand the background to this ritual, consider that in common Thai belief humans have two souls. The first of these is the *winjan*, a philological counterpart to the consciousness element called *viññāṇa* in Pāli Buddhist texts. At death, this soul leaves the body and provides a link in the rebirth process. The second soul, called the *khwan*, consists of thirty-two parts. In common belief, not just humans have khwans but animals like water buffaloes do, too. The khwan soul may be lost during experiences of fright, accident, or being lured by a forest animal, and if not returned to the body, the loss of this soul may cause illness or even death.[20]

Because of the threat of a lost soul, there exists the "calling the soul," or *su khwan*, ritual, in order to retrieve this lost or fragmented soul. In this ritual complex, the dispersion or fragmentation of the khwan soul happens because of the wear and tear of life, so that the soul-calling ritual ideally results in a sense of integration and renewal. Humans may wish to have their souls recalled in case of illness like I have described, but also as a part of marriage ceremonies, as a part of pregnancy, when starting or ending a major undertaking, or when dispelling a run of bad luck. Of relevance here, Buddhist monks remain principal transmitters of the su khwan liturgical texts and may participate in soul-calling rituals.[21] However, monks do not ordinarily lead these rituals. Instead, they are led by lay specialists known by terms such as *paahm* or *mau khwan*. Typically, such officiants are former monks or leaders within local Buddhist congregations. Although meat offerings to the Buddha are common in Thailand, unlike the customary practice in Sri Lanka, su khwan offerings tend to be vegetarian.[22]

In order to restore and invigorate the khwan souls of the fresh rice crop, Mae Phosob, and the buffaloes who helped make the harvest possible, soul-calling rituals may be performed for buffaloes and rice after the grain is stored.[23] Thus, in gratitude and hope Mae Phosob, a Buddhist herself, enjoys a soul-calling ritual renewal, and in this way, the rice goddess receives respectful treatment as a Buddhist person, as a kind of bodhisattva who sacrifices herself for others.

Village Spirits

In the complex and ever-shifting pantheon of spirits in Thailand, spirits of the rice fields may be considered as members of groups of greater village protector spirits whose help agriculturalists also seek. A typical Thai community enjoys the protection of at least two local, communal deities, although sometimes they may be understood as a single deity with different attributes.[24] One of these deities is the owner of local lands and often the ancestor of the local population, and as such receives oblations at a communal shrine or, in larger locales, a shared pillar monument. Such beliefs result in the spirit houses that one finds throughout Thailand since spirits "need a house and proper worship, otherwise they might cause damage."[25] Often, activities such as cutting wood or gardening are forbidden near this shared ancestral shrine.

Another frequently occurring communal spirit is the protector of the monastery, who receives gifts at its own spirit house, which often is found in the rear of a monastery property near a revered bodhi or banyan tree. Usually, the monastery's protector spirit outlaws urination, harming animals, or picking fruits on monastery grounds, and the permission of this spirit must

FIGURE 7.   A house for a monastery's resident spirit next to the monastery's holy bodhi tree. Wat Phra Khao monastery, Chiang Mai, Thailand.

be gained before merit-making ceremonies. This deity of the monastery possesses different culinary tastes than the village ancestral deity. The ancestral spirit receives offerings of meat and strong spices, whereas offerings to the Buddhist monastery's protector tend to be milder and vegetarian. Before plowing commences the agricultural season and again after harvest, the ancestral and monastic spirits, often having some power over the spirits of the fields, are placated with communal offerings, so that Thais may bargain with the two communal spirits with gratitude for the past harvest and as insurance regarding future rice yields.

Sometimes joining these corporate spirits in village protection are a variety of spirits of mountains, rivers, and other natural features. The anthropologist Stanley Tambiah supplies an example of one of these spirits, the spirit of the Byng Chuan swamp, who provides protection not just for a village, but for an entire region, and therefore is venerated by numerous farmers who seek rain and fine harvests. A sacred type of turtle lives in this swamp, with village ancestral deities forbidding the use of its flesh as food. Like many Thai nature spirits, the spirit of the swamp prefers meat offerings that are distributed in a three-year cycle. The swamp spirit is always given cooked chicken before plowing, and after the harvest the swamp spirit receives a similar gift for two years. On the third year, a buffalo is sacrificed instead, with its flesh cooked and ritually consumed by community members. The annual festival of Bunbangfai also celebrates the swamp spirit during the postharvest free time, for this ritual is thought to encourage the swamp spirit to bring plenty of rain in the coming year. Showing how the local pantheon of nature spirits can be knit together, the Bunbangfai festival is communally celebrated at the shrines of both village protectors as well as at the swamp.[26] In this way, relational animism involving ancestral, monastic, and natural deities blurs the boundaries between Buddhism and other traditions, given that all three spirits are typically considered to be Buddhists. Indeed, Michael R. Rhum states that sometimes animal sacrifices occur at some remove from a nature spirit's shrine since the spirit is a Buddhist.[27]

Forest Monastics and Nature Religion

Given the plethora of nature spirits in Thai religiosity like those of the rice field and the monastery, wandering Thai monastics of the early twentieth century sometimes led rituals for local nature deities, while other monks eschewed them, lending a sense of the cultural tensions that affected the lives of the saints of the golden age of Thai forest monastics from the late nineteenth century to the middle of the twentieth century. Their lives thus offer brilliant expressions of sacred closeness to natural persons but not without ambiguity.

Take, for instance, the life of perhaps the most famous Thai forest monk of all, Phra Achan Man Phurithatto (1870–1949). Like many *thudong* (solitary forest wanderer) monks of the early twentieth century, Achan Man came from rural roots in northeastern Thailand. Fully ordained at age twenty-two, Achan Man began to practice insight meditation but found that he made little progress until one night he had a prophetic dream that vividly employed natural symbolism. In the dream, he wandered out of his village through a very dense jungle until he reached a vast meadow on the other side. In the meadow, he walked on a rotting log, reminding him of the Buddhist truth of impermanence. Then, a great white horse arrived and he mounted it, with the two traversing the huge meadow afterward. At the end of the meadow, Achan Man came across a magnificent white glass case that held a copy of the Pāli scriptures. Before Achan Man could open the case, however, he woke up. Interpreting the jungle as the household life to be discarded and the meadow as meditative practice, his dream told him that he would ride the white horse of meditation to enlightenment, although since he did not open the case with the scriptures, he would never be an academic monk.

Refreshed by his dream, he redoubled his practice efforts and commenced wandering the forest in search of liberation.[28]

Forest monks often believed that local spirits disguised themselves as animals to test meditators, so that animals did not just help Achan Man reach liberation in his dream, they also aided him in waking life as religious teachers. Tigers especially performed this role. Besides fasting, sleeplessness, and long bouts of meditation, Achan Man's spiritual practice included intentionally meditating in dangerous places, such as in the middle of a path used by tigers or at the mouth of a cave where a tiger resided. Achan Man taught, "Let what you are afraid of be your trainer and teacher," so "if you are terrified of tigers, be where tigers are, and make friends with them."[29] Another forest monk and disciple of Achan Man, Achan Thet, explains how this tiger practice worked for him:

> I heard the tiger roar and my whole body started shivering and shaking, as if I had a malarial fever. It was then that I realized that this was all due to my fear of the tiger's roar. I sat up and established mindfulness, settling the mind in stillness on a single object and ready to sacrifice my life. Hadn't I already accepted death? Wasn't that the reason for my coming to live here? Aren't tiger and human both a fabrication of the same four elements? After death won't both end in the same condition? Who eats who—who is the one that dies and who is the one that doesn't die? When I was willing to relinquish and investigate in this dauntless, single-minded way, I could no longer hear the noise of the tiger.[30]

Saints across religions, such as the Christian Francis of Assisi, the Hindu Caitanya, or the Muslim Ibrahim Ibn Adham, enjoy repute for using spiritual charisma in order to tame potentially dangerous animals like tigers, and Achan Man and his Buddhist companions were no different. For example, once in rural Laos, Achan Man was meditating with a fellow monk, Phra Sitha, when a tiger approached. Nightly, the tiger would watch from a respectful distance while Achan Man meditated. One night the tiger sat very near to where Phra Sitha was practicing walking meditation. Phra Sitha compassionately encouraged the tiger to go away and find some food for itself, at which the tiger roared loudly in resistance because apparently the tiger preferred to guard the monks. However, when the monastics awoke the next morning, the tiger had departed.[31]

On one occasion Achan Man, whom even nāgas took as a spiritual teacher, was able to tame the smallpox virus in an entire village through the power of his charisma.[32] Achan Man also showed his ability to tame tree spirits in a famous encounter at the Sarika cave in the Khao Yai mountains. When Achan Man first set out for the cave, the locals discouraged him, saying that several monks had stayed there and gotten sick because of the cave's resident demon, with four of these monks dying. Undeterred, Achan Man took up domicile in the cave. Soon he developed a stomach illness that was more acute than any he had suffered before. He tried herbal remedies to no effect and so resolved to heal himself through Dhamma alone, thereafter entering a very deep meditative state. As he came back to everyday consciousness when finished, he noticed that not only was he healed of his illness but he was also glowing, and the light emanating from him illuminated a dark, shadowy figure, who was the demon of the cave. Achan Man confronted the demon, making him admit that the Buddha was more powerful and providing moral arguments that it is better to help than to harm others. Eventually, the demon broke down, admitted that he was the chief of the tree spirits, repented his harmful ways, and became a lay disciple of Achan Man.[33]

Animal Encounters

Achan Man may have tamed tigers and tree spirit kings, but forest monks were beset by other natural dangers, particularly those posed by snakes. Thailand is home to a number of serpents, including pythons, a variety of cobras, kraits, vipers, and coral snakes that can pose serious threats to humans. Interestingly, one forest monk, Achan Butda, discovered that serpent dangers can be avoided by practicing the virtue of generosity. As he sat meditating with his eyes closed in a narrow cave, Achan Butda smelled a pungent odor and thought that a threat must be near. Fear, not mindfulness, filled his consciousness. Reasoning that he had no way out of the cave apart from facing the danger, he opened his eyes and froze, for a giant snake was virtually on top of him. Achan Butda said, "Its head was as big as a coconut. Red eyes. It kept sticking its tongue out!" Pondering how to respond, he decided to give his body willingly as food for the snake, and when he did this, he found his mind free from fear. Focusing his mind on the word *Buddho*, he abandoned attachment to his body. The snake, sensing the gesture, retreated out of the cave. Achan Butda thereby pacified a snake with selfless generosity, in so doing initiating sustainability toward the serpent (who presumably found other food) and himself alike.[34]

Besides tigers and snakes, forest monks also faced danger from wild elephants, like in the story of Achan Lee Dhammadharo that began this chapter. Forest monks frequently encountered pachyderms and so developed a number of methods for safely interacting with them. Because elephants are intelligent, one method involved reasoning and the extension of personhood respect, like the forest master Achan Khao demonstrated. Once, Achan Khao was wandering on a jungle trail along with Achan Man and Maha Thaung-suk when they found a giant elephant completely blocking the path while it was eating. Achan Khao respectfully addressed the elephant by saying, "Big brother! I'd like to talk to you. We monks are powerless and so are afraid of you. We'd be grateful if you would let us pass." The elephant stepped forward, allowing the monks to walk past in single file. When they were through, Achan Khao again addressed the elephant as a reasonable kin person in saying, "My big brother, we have already passed. Now you are free to go on with your eating." The elephant then returned to its grazing and the monks continued their journey.[35]

Achan Khao treated an elephant as a reasonable and intelligent person another time, although on this occasion Achan Khao took things further. One night a wild elephant visited Achan Khao as he was meditating in his hut. He felt the animal's breath as the elephant's trunk entered the window of his hut and sniffed around the meditator's mosquito netting. Then the elephant began to pilfer some tamarind fruits, used by monks to polish their bowls, that were hanging from a tree. Achan Khao decided that he did not want to lose his tamarinds and chose to reason with the fruit taker. Respectfully addressing the large threat as "older brother," Achan Khao described the travails of an elephant's existence: "When you don't follow their commands, humans might hit you on the head or even kill you." Achan Khao explained that if the elephant embraced virtuous actions, then in the future the elephant could be reborn into a more auspicious form, such as that of a human or god, with Achan Khao anthropocentrically saying, "It's better than being reborn as an animal, only to be a vehicle like a horse or a beast of burden like an elephant." Achan Khao encouraged the elephant to practice the Five Precepts, especially in this case highlighting the precept against theft. The elephant stood and listened to the monk throughout the entire sermon. Then Achan Khao asked the elephant to forage elsewhere and leave him alone, which the elephant did.[36] By giving the Five Precepts to the elephant in this way, Achan Khao expected this elephant to practice Buddhism like a human, thus providing a brilliant example of dynamic Thai relational animism and its support for perspectives in which nonhumans practice religion.

It is not every day that elephants listen to sermons on the Five Precepts, but perhaps the most remarkable approach to taming jungle elephants comes from monks who studied the *Khotchasatra*, a collection of holy palm-leaf manuscripts that provides information regarding elephant personalities, habitats, training, and medical care.[37] For taming elephants, the texts describe an unusual meditation practice that converts classic Buddhist concentration meditation into a novel method for pachyderm pacification. Only through concentration meditation, centered on the repetition of the word *Buddho*, can one focus enough to see the spirit of the elephant, this spirit receiving the meditator's full attention, not the physical elephant itself. After one can see the spirit of the elephant, one is able to then effectively radiate taming mettā lovingkindness to it. As the instructions say, "To subdue an elephant that is on a rampage, you must first visualize the deity who is guarding the wild elephant. Then you radiate mettā to the deity. Once the deity receives the mettā radiated by you, the deity will convey this to the elephant and then guide the animal away from you so that it will not harm you." The instructions insist that it is most important to focus on the deity alone, not the animal itself, since "an elephant in musth is unable to receive *mettā*."[38] This meditation method worked well for a monk named Charan: "When I was walking in the forest one day, a huge elephant spotted me and came charging head on, ears cocked, trunk up, screaming with rage, intending to trample over me. I immediately focused my mind in *kasina* meditation as Luang Pho Doem had taught me. From the mind unified in a single point, I radiated *mettā* to the deity who guarded the elephant. Just before he reached me, the big bull halted and turned away."[39]

As we can see here, stories of saints who spiritually tame animals, like the Buddhists recounted here did, cut both ways. First, they obviously show a sense of human harmony with natural beings. Taming often occurs by extending lovingkindness and a measure of personhood respect. However, the stories also indicate a degree of human superiority, because it is the human saint who has the most spiritual power, not the tiger, snake, or elephant involved.

Such a sense of human superiority clearly manifests in another example of a monk who pacified an elephant. One night, while meditating in a secluded hut, a monk named Juan heard the thunder of a herd of elephants approaching his residence. First in the deep dark of the forest and later close by Juan's hut, a giant bull, whom Juan took to be the elephant leader, began trumpeting loudly, tearing up brush, and pawing the earth. Absolutely terrified, Juan began trembling, feeling dizzy, and sweating profusely. But then Juan collected himself by thinking, "You are a human being and superior, and you're also a monk. The elephant is an animal and it's not afraid of you. If you're afraid, you're worse than an elephant." Buoyed by these thoughts, Juan began meditating on death. When he was done with his deep contemplation, he recounted, "I was no longer afraid of elephants or death." He then thought about the elephant "with compassion and pity," at which point the bull elephant left, along with the rest of the herd. After that, Juan was no longer bothered by elephants.[40] It is questionable whether such an attitude of superiority toward animals can lead to the inherent respect found within Rolston's concept of a sustainable biosphere.

Despite Juan's assertion of human superiority, there also exist instances of genuine peer comradeship between animals and forest monks, in which, like the elephant who listened to the Five Precepts, animals appear to exhibit spiritual prowess on their own. Take, for instance, a bodhisattva elephant who saved the celebrated monk Achan Pan. Once, Achan Pan and his disciples settled for the night in a meadow at the edge of a forest, not far from a village. Some villagers came to offer sustenance to the monks as well as to ask them to move closer to the settlement because wild elephants frequented the pasture and had attacked monks before. The fearless Achan Pan would not leave the meadow and instead instructed his monastic charges to begin mettā lovingkindness meditation. Around 10 p.m., a herd of wild elephants approached, and in the clear, full-moon light, the monks could easily see each elephant. Most of the herd walked unceremoniously past the monks, each of whom meditated under an umbrella that supported mosquito netting. However, one troublesome elephant, who went by the name of Twist, wished for more drama and charged Achan Pan as the monk sat in meditation. Although his disciples were worried, Achan Pan remained calm. The lead bull of the herd, seeing what was happening, came to Achan Pan's rescue by neutralizing the rogue elephant. First the bull slapped Twist with his trunk, but this did not stop the charge, so the bull eventually grabbed Twist trunk-to-trunk, knocking Twist to the ground. The mischievous Twist got up and then thundered away across the meadow. The valiant bull elephant surveyed the scene to make sure that the disturbance had ended, and thereafter bowed low with his trunk raised before Achan Pan, thus showing devotion to the monk like a human might. The saintly elephant then rejoined his herd.[41]

(Non)vegetarianism

Extensions of respectful personhood to animals like those appearing in this chapter, however, often did not deter Thai forest monks from eating meat. As my reader already knows, there are a variety of Buddhist attitudes toward the eating of meat, and, remarkably, the nature-loving forest monks likewise exhibited diverse attitudes regarding the proper Buddhist diet. For instance, because many forest dwellers were Thammayut monks and thus were expected to adhere closely to the dietary guidelines of the Pāli canon, many of them hesitated to eat meat from animals that had been hunted, for the Theravāda scriptures as well as the *Three Worlds according to King Ruang* discourage hunting. One gets a sense of this attitude against eating hunted animals, rather than domestic animals, when one considers the passing of Achan Man. Close to death in a remote jungle, Achan Man insisted that his disciples take him to a nearby village to die, reasoning that it would be better to have domestic animals killed for his funeral feast than it would to have forest animals slaughtered for this purpose.[42]

Monks nonetheless sometimes ate hunted meat. Tiyavanich Kamala, for instance, relates a story of a forest monk named Khian who wandered into a small village. With monks a rare sight there, a woman came rushing out of her house toward Khian. Her husband had killed a barking deer for food and she feared the negative karma that his act of hunting would bring on the household. She implored Khian to share in the venison so as to make merit to counteract the demerit of hunting, and Khian accepted, much to the woman's relief.[43]

When it came to eating domestic animals, the forest monks were much less hesitant, as Achan Man's funeral demonstrated. After all, meat from farm animals is offered to the Buddha in Thailand, unlike in some other Buddhist worlds. Kamala relates an incident in which monks refused chicken that had been offered to them by laypeople, not because of the meat content but because they were Thammayut monks who are not allowed to eat after noon.[44]

Indeed, the famous forest master Achan Cha argues specifically for eating meat, despite his own encouragement of nonharm even for ants.[45] To this end, Achan Cha offers a story of an unnamed monk who insisted on being a vegetarian until he found out that it is difficult to be a vegetarian monk, so he disrobed and became a folk religious specialist. But he eventually gave up even this latter career and ended up losing everything. Achan Cha ascribes the man's bad fortune to his attachment to vegetarianism, considering the case as an example of an antinirvanic defilement at work. Achan Cha said, "Did the Buddha go and eat leaves and grass like a cow? Sure, if you want to eat like that go ahead, if that's all you can manage; but don't go around criticizing others."[46] Achan Cha suggests that some forms of ahimsa nonharm, including vegetarianism, can be attachments.[47]

Conversely, another forest monk, Achan Thet, expressed clear vegetarian sentiments. At one point, conditions during a summer rains retreat forced him to embrace a vegetarian diet for a period, and when he tried to return to meat eating, he was dismayed. He said, "As soon as the rains retreat was over, I resumed eating some meat and fish again. But oh! How foul they now smelled. We humans consume their meat and make it into our own flesh. It's just as if we snatch away and steal something foul and then eat it."[48] But it was not just tactile experiences that drove Achan Thet away from eating meat; personhood Buddhist notions of rebirth did as well. Achan Thet stated, "The Lord Buddha recounted how human beings and animals born into this world have, one and all, been mothers and fathers, sisters and brothers, husbands and wives. . . . Perhaps even the poultry and pork that we eat might be the flesh of our father and mother from a previous birth."[49] Exhibiting strong relational animism, this argument by Achan Thet against meat eating because of personhood kinship shared between humans and animals will reappear in the next chapter, which examines a similar argument within the Mahāyāna *Laṅkāvatāra Sūtra*.

Greening Thai Buddhism: Buddhadāsa

Whether they expressed positive intimacy with natural persons or reacted negatively to them, starting in the later twentieth century the forest monks eventually saw their heyday eroding due to a variety of factors. Improved transportation and communication infrastructures made it easier for Bangkok residents, and other Thais, to seek out forest renunciants as revered embodiments of Buddhist holiness. Following a commonly found pattern, the more the forest monks renounced the world, the more the world sought them out, bringing potentially troublesome influences such as large gifts. Because one of the best things that a layperson in Thailand can do to improve merit is to build a monastery, as expressions of devotion new residences were constructed around acclaimed forest monastics, so that previously simple, ascetic, and wandering monks found themselves settled in one place that perhaps sported an ornate new ordination hall but few of the previous rustic elements.

The massive loss of forest in Thailand provided another reason for the disappearance of the golden age of forest monastics. In the year 1900, around 80 percent of the country was covered by forest, but by 2000 the forest cover had receded to less than 20 percent. Because of this, today monastics often find that their monasteries are the only spots of forest on an otherwise denuded landscape of paddy fields and failed plots. This inhibits monastic forest wandering in many places where it used to be common, because there is no forest nearby in which to wander.[50] Moreover, hunters and timber cutters sometimes encroach even on monastic properties, so that temple residents sometimes must not wander in order to defend their premises from unwanted and illegal ecological raiding.

Paradoxically, the forest saints contributed to this deforestation since, in teaching villagers not to fear forest spirits, they also reduced deterrents to chopping down trees in the jungle.[51] Moreover, deforestation was often supported, especially in the towns and cities, by development monks who understood a shift from hunting and gathering lifestyles to farming to represent the civilizing influence of Buddhism. The world of the Pāli scriptures is an agricultural one, so that for some monks, embracing agriculture and adhering to the Dhamma were viewed as a singular movement. Therefore, for religious reasons some urban monastic writers, such as Somdet Uan and even forest wanderers like Achan Thet, supported in some measure the clear-cutting of jungle to replace it with rice fields.[52]

This environmental devastation, which helped end the golden age of Thai forest monks, has drawn a number of responses from Buddhists. Several of these responses turn philosophically to the work of the popular monastic writer Buddhadāsa Bhikkhu (1936–1993 CE). Although not an environmental activist himself, late in his life Buddhadāsa turned to discussing ecological issues in his writings as part of his call for Buddhists to reorient themselves more toward social action in the ordinary world, seeking to "integrate the *lokuttara* concern with salvation with the *lokiya* emphasis on world-involvement."[53]

Rejecting the cosmology of *Three Worlds according to King Ruang*, Buddhadāsa preaches a demythologized, psychological, and lay-friendly form of Buddhism that reflects Buddhist modernist trends.[54] Although he does not deny the idea of realms of rebirth in an absolute sense, he prefers instead to focus on them as inner states within this life, reflecting one's own defilements, rather than as external afterlife destinies. He writes, "Heaven is in one's breast, hell is in one's mind."[55] So, for instance, Buddhadāsa frequently discusses the animal realm as arising within humans whenever we engage in "stupidity or bestiality," thus blocking our own spiritual progress.[56] When we are excited with sense desire, we are in hell; when lustful, we are hungry ghosts; when fearful, we are demons; and when foolish, we are animals.[57]

This shift in emphasis enables a number of innovations in Buddhist thought for Buddhadāsa, especially regarding human relationships with the natural world. Buddhadāsa teaches that there are three levels of nirvana and rather surprisingly grants phenomenal animals the capacity to realize the first level of nirvana, albeit only as long as those animals are "thoroughly trained" from a human point of view.[58] With this granting of animal spirituality, Buddhadāsa's symbolic understanding of rebirth therefore leads him to a position of some respect regarding animals. According to Buddhadāsa, humans are technically higher in terms of rebirth but cause themselves suffering greater than that which pertains to the world of physical nonhuman animals.[59]

Reflecting a view commonly argued by Buddhist environmentalists, Buddhadāsa teaches that our environmental struggles stem from selfishness, including selfishness engendered by capitalist competition. "Self-centeredness is the basic cause of suffering," he said.[60] Instead of engaging in selfishness, Buddhadāsa states, humans should follow the way of nature, for the way of nature is to take only what one needs, not to hoard for the future. In nature, the "true socialist" reality, politics can find its authentic model for cooperation based on needs rather than the destruction that arises from out-of-control desires. For Buddhadāsa, nature is perfect just as it is and, like a true socialist reality, includes all beings.[61] Thus, because, for him, nature is real Dhamma as well as the basis of a proper social order, humans should learn from natural beings, and "it is only by being in nature that the trees, rocks, earth, sand, animals, birds, and insects can teach us."[62] Buddhadāsa continues: "Trees, rocks, sand, even dirt and insects can speak. . . . If we reside in nature near trees and rocks, we'll discover feelings and thoughts arising that are truly out of the ordinary. At first we'll feel a sense of peace and serenity which may eventually move beyond that feeling to a transcendence of self. . . . The lessons nature teaches us lead to a new birth beyond the suffering that results from attachment to self."[63]

By encouraging us to listen to trees and rocks in this way, Buddhadāsa's teachings display vibrant personhood relational animism as he attempts to stimulate attitudes that lead to a sustainable biosphere.

Buffalo Beauties and Tree Monks

Reflecting themes found in Buddhadāsa's thought, sustainability efforts combined with relational animism spectacularly emerge in the monastic creation of beauty contests for water buffaloes. As the anthropologist Susan M. Darlington tells it in *The Ordination of a Tree*,[64] it seems that there was a rich man who was told by medics that he suffered from an incurable illness. For help he turned to a fortune-teller, who, reflecting the animal release practices found in chapter 7 in this book, informed him that he would be healed if he freed a buffalo that was destined for slaughter and gave it to a Buddhist monk. So he purchased a slaughterhouse buffalo, presented it to the monk Luang Pu Phuttapoj, and soon thereafter recovered from his illness (126). As news of this healing spread, other wealthy donors also began giving buffaloes to Phuttapoj, who at first housed them at his monastery, Wat

Pa Dharabhirom in Mae Rim. The monk accepted the buffaloes despite their disruption of the monastic lifestyle both to save the animals and to allow donors to make merit (126).

As it turns out, Luang Pu Phuttapoj, who died in 2008, was no ordinary monk but a respected development monk. Thinking that empty bellies make for poor Buddhists, Phuttapoj sought to integrate economic development and Buddhism through the Foundation for Education and Development in Rural Areas, or FEDRA, the NGO that he founded in the 1970s that seeks agricultural, financial, and social improvements. Where others witnessed a monastery overrun by buffaloes, the ingenious Phuttapoj envisioned an opportunity. He began giving away buffaloes to poor farmers who otherwise would have to rent buffaloes at rice harvest time. Although the tractor and the mechanized "iron buffalo" have increased in use in Thailand, Phuttapoj saw buffaloes as a better choice for poor farmers since buffaloes did not produce emissions like gasoline-run vehicles or need replacement parts. Recipients of buffaloes promised to treat them well and to donate the first-born calf back to FEDRA. Phuttapoj soon found many people who were happy to participate in this buffalo bank program, because either giving or receiving a buffalo was perceived by participants as tantamount to obtaining a strong blessing from Luang Pu Phuttapoj.

Phuttapoj added to this sense of blessing by ritualizing both the giving and receiving of buffaloes, especially through his buffalo beauty contests at Wat Pa Dharabhirom. Buffaloes that were returned to the program by prior buffalo bank recipients were cleaned up and gaily decorated so that they could look their best for an annual competition since there was a keen if good-natured rivalry to see who could add the finest-looking buffalo to the bank. Through his buffalo bank program and beauty contests, the sustainability conscious Luang Pu Phuttapoj simultaneously saved buffaloes from slaughter, helped poor farmers, created regard for buffaloes as Buddhist persons, and opened a place for buffaloes in Buddhist monasteries, although not as practicing Buddhists.

However, while beauty contests for buffaloes represent a provocative form of Buddhist environmental concern, the most visible and famous current form of environmentalist Buddhist animism in Thailand includes the cultural craze for ordaining trees as Buddhist monks. These tree ordinations emanated from the energetic and innovative monk Phrakhru Manas Nathiphitak. In 1986 the Chiangrai logging company entered the forest of Mae Chai district, intending to legally haul away as much lumber as possible from an already highly deforested area. Along with locals and the district officer, this action concerned Phrakhru Manas, who feared there would be no forest left when the company was done. Phrakhru Manas then helped create the Mae Chai Forest Lovers Group, which opposed the logging through petitions and by blocking roads used by the loggers. However, with a development versus conservation controversy heightening in intensity and in light of a drought year, Phrakhru Manas felt that more creative and powerful action was required, and he came up with what would become known as tree ordination ceremonies.

As Susan Darlington notes in *The Ordination of a Tree*, although bodhi trees and Bodhi pūjās for them exist in Thailand like we saw in Sri Lanka, Phrakhru Manas took things further than this common Theravāda Buddhist ritual; he adapted a liturgical text that was used to consecrate Buddha images and revised it to consecrate trees and forests. In Phrakhru Manas's ritual, a shrine with a Buddha image was set up at the foot of an imposing tree. Tree seedlings were arranged at the foot of the Buddha statue so that they could be sanctified. When the consecration ceremony was finished, laypeople planted the seedlings, nurturing and refusing to cut them because they were so sacralized. They called the saplings "ordained trees" (*ton mai thi buat lao*), thus originating the name of the rite. Over time, more monastic accoutrements were added, such as tying cloth resembling a monk's robe around the main tree in the rite, as has traditionally been done with holy trees that reside in Thai monasteries. However, leaders of the rituals insist that the trees are only symbolically, not literally, ordained since only humans can join the monastic sangha community (61).

In creating the rite, Phrakhru Manas sought not to turn trees into monks but to change people's perceptions of the forest. Rather than regarding forests merely instrumentally, with concern only for the forest's economic value for humans, Phrakhru Manas sought to communicate a respectful and sustainable understanding of human interdependence with the forest (65). As Darlington put it, "Tree ordinations, in short, are a form of *upaya*, or expedient means, used to wake people up, not to spiritual realization but to the immediate causes of suffering and ways of relieving it" (53).

Although at first tree ordinations were criticized by some people for being un-Buddhist and an activity unbecoming of monastics, the movement quickly spread among environmentally minded monks from neighboring provinces. A recurrent theme among these tree-ordaining monks involves the effort to impart a sense of humanity's place within a larger moral community. Environmental monks often counter anthropocentric attitudes by emphasizing, at least at times, human equality with other natural beings, the point being that the world does not revolve around humans; instead, humans remain interdependent in a broad sense with the rest of the universe, including its animals, plants, and so on. Combining folk wisdom and some-times anthropomorphism with Buddhist notions of interrelation, these monks inspire others to extend Buddhist compassion and lovingkindness to elements of the ecological habitat in order to arrive at a more sustainable way of living for humans, animals, and trees alike. In so doing, they follow a form of environmental philosophy that is different from typical Western ones since they presume a holistic and integrative view of humans and the natural world rather than starting with a distinction between humans and the rest of the environment (8).

To be fair, a cynic may highlight some self-serving motivations for these forest environmentalist actions. Over time, the influence of the monastic community in Thailand has waned, given the currents of Buddhist modern-ism, secularism, and globalization. In response, besides protecting forests, the tree ordination movement provides monks with a chance to play more visible and potent roles in Thai society in order to stem the decline in the importance of the sangha (123).

Whatever the motivations of the monastics involved, though, Darlington assures us that the effect on the laity of tree ordination rites is significant. She says, "As the monks chanted, people closed their eyes, their hands held together, and their bodies occasionally rocking to the rhythm of the sound. Afterward, people scrambled to receive some of the sacred water sprinkled by the monks. . . . Their behavior toward trees wrapped in orange robes is similar to the respect they show monks" (64).

Because of this enthusiastic lay response, the movement has exploded from its humble beginnings in the late 1980s. In so doing, however, the ritual has become routinized. Now tree ordination ceremonies are so common, laypeople often expect monks who may have no interest in the rites to per-form them. In addition, the national government has done what it can to coopt the popularity of the ritual, such as the effort to ordain trees en masse as part of the king's Golden Jubilee celebration of 1996–97. Exhibiting fur-ther routinization, in 2010 a tree ordination served as a thematic backdrop for a human beauty contest. As Isager and Ivarsson assert regarding the social redeployment of tree ordinations, "Several political, economic, and social interests are reflected in the performance of and participation in tree ordina-tion rituals. . . . Performance of the ritual might therefore constitute an act of resistance against government territorialization or it might be part of a pragmatic process of land-use change."[65]

As such, tree ordinations have lost their original environmentalist punch, having been routinized into social and political events rather than incidents that necessarily raise and capitalize on environmental awareness.[66] In this

respect, they reflect the contemporary Thai hybridization of various religious voices with consumerism and commodification as described by the
anthropologist Kitiarsa Pattana.[67] Of this decline in meaning in tree ordinations, Darlington says, "The contexts for the rituals have changed. Rather
than pushing people to question modern, consumerist values as causes of
environmental destruction and human suffering, such rituals are increasingly
used to support national agendas and to undermine the power of the rural
people whom environmental monks aim to help."[68] However, the impact of
the tree ordination movement persists in the National Environmental Quality Protection and Enhancement Act of 1992, which was in part inspired by
the activities of ecological monks like Phrakhru Manas.[69]

Thai Buddhists in Nature

The complex tale of tree ordinations allows stock-taking regarding human
Buddhist interactions with nonhuman nature in Thailand. Since Thailand
has long been known to scholars as a place with vigorous nature religion, it
is no surprise that a plethora of rich animist relationships with nonhuman
nature emerge in this chapter. These relationships lead to some quite instructive lessons since the Thai people repeatedly interact with natural beings as
respected persons, thereby highlighting relational animist processes within
Buddhism itself. For instance, *The Three Worlds according to King Ruang*, while
generally anthropocentric, allows that some natural beings, even fabulous
stones like the Maniratana, are persons. Buddhist monks participate in the
calling of the soul of rice, who is not just any person, but a Buddhist maternal one. Other natural spirits lead their own Buddhist lives even if they may
be spiritually undeveloped. As superior beings, monks are able to tame dangerous animals but do so sometimes by approaching animals as peer persons.
One even finds a Buddhist concentration meditation practice for controlling
the personal spirits of elephants. Finally, buffaloes and trees receive treatment as respected persons in contemporary rituals that benefit humans and
natural beings alike.

With examples like these, Thai religiosity, viewed through the lens of
relational animism, collapses the old distinction between Buddhism and animism because Buddhism in Thailand fosters its own relational animist forms
that are not simply admixtures from local religiosity. The most poignant
outcome of this fact may be the practice of Buddhism by a variety of natural
forms. Nonhuman spirits of mountains, bodies of water, forests, and agricultural fields practice Buddhism on their own, following their own karmic
stores. Like a human, an insightful elephant founds Wat Phra That on the top

of a mountain that is thought to embody the presence of the Buddha. Animals like tigers and elephants who may be dangerous to humans also serve to teach proper meditation techniques to forest monks. Further, humans interact with some nature spirits like they do revered human Buddhist leaders, adding a political dimension to the experience of the spirits of nature as religious teachers. Finally, a saintly elephant saves a monk from disaster, much as a devout human might do, thus reflecting the call of the respected monk Buddhadāsa to learn religious lessons from the nonhuman world.

Natural beings as persons also condition Buddhist dietary habits in Thailand with some astonishing effects. Being primarily Theravāda Buddhist, quite a few Thais eat meat as an unself-conscious matter of course. Perhaps reflecting this reality, we have seen that the forest monk Achan Cha, who shrank from killing ants because of their perceived personhood, nonetheless openly calls for a diet of meat since many Theravāda monks remain carnivorous. Cha, in fact, speaks against vegetarianism as an un-Buddhist attachment that does not follow what he perceives as the Buddha's example. But his fellow forest monk, Achan Thet, argues differently. In his complex approach to the natural world, Achan Thet favors clear-cutting forests to create farms but decries eating animals, whom he considers to be our kin persons. Thus, personhood relationships lead Achan Thet to vegetarianism but not forest protection, yet similar personhood relationships do not dissuade Achan Cha from eating meat. This multivalence appears reflected in the pantheon of spirits, too, for some spirits demand meat sacrifices, while others, such as the guardian of the village Buddhist temple, request vegetarian fare. Hence, it is no surprise to discover multivalence in Thai attempts to establish something like Rolston's sustainable biosphere.

Within these plural Thai attitudes toward nature, there is a noticeable lack of Buddhist nature mysticism. While Thai Buddhists vibrantly encounter nature, I could find no tales of numinous experiences of nonduality specifically with nonhumans. Indeed, I primarily found expressions of the unworthiness of natural beings as specific subjects for human religious experience, as one can see in the lack of monastic leadership in some nature religion rituals. For his part, Buddhadāsa mentioned the "transcendence of self" in nature, but he did not elaborate more specifically. Moreover, Thai rice field religious practices might be ripe for agricultural nature mysticism, as one finds among the Maya of Central America, but I have not located articulations of such.[70]

In this chapter, Thailand has exhibited a number of religious influences from India, not just that of Buddhism, since Brahmanic notions from India predate organized Theravāda Buddhism in Southeast Asia. Preah Go, the sacred cow statue of Cambodia, provides an example of this ancient Brahamic cattle-venerating influence across the peninsula. Stuffed with sacred scriptures, the statue of Preah Go was a bovine talisman for Hindu kings during the Cambodian Angkor period, given that a part of her blessings included supporting education. When Angkor fell in 1431, the invading Thais spirited Preah Go away to Ayutthaya, the Thai capital at the time, with the loss of Preah Go thus symbolizing both the faded glories of Angkor and the expansion of Buddhism in Cambodia.[71] Across the continent in India, special cattle helped shape a different form of Buddhism in China by influencing India's Mahāyāna scriptures and eventually inspiring mandated vegetarianism for Chinese monastics. My investigation will now turn to China.

CHAPTER 5

Eating the Enlightened Plants of China

The long-lived Chinese Chan school monk Xuyun (1840–1959 CE; name pronounced approximately like "Shooyoon"), whose rich life is acclaimed as "the story of the modern Chinese Buddhist revival," one day met a wild tiger face-to-face.[1] At the Buddhist patriarch Hui Neng's monastery of Nanhua and during a ceremony that Xuyun led to confer the bodhisattva precepts, a tiger entered the main hall "as if to receive the precepts." A large crowd of dignitaries who had assembled for the rites trembled in collective fear before the big cat. Undaunted, the gentle Xuyun performed a Buddhist refuge ceremony for the tiger, who was "receptive, became tame, and went its way."[2]

Of course, turning tigers into good Buddhists like this does not happen every day, not even for masters like Xuyun. But given the general Chinese cultural acceptance of the immanence of the immediately accessible sacred in nonhuman nature, as one sees in diverse strands of Chinese religiosity, it is not surprising that natural beings may become loci for sacredness, such as Xuyun's tiger who practices Buddhism. The mutually symbiotic interactions in China of the Three Doctrines (*sanjiao*) of Confucianism, Daoism, and Buddhism, combined in addition with omnipresent folk religiosity, engender a sense of natural immanence that runs across Chinese religions. As I will investigate in this chapter, this immanence then sparks personhood attitudes toward natural beings which help instigate the nature mysticism which is distinctive of Chinese Buddhism, as one finds within Shaolin martial arts forms. Personhood attitudes also strongly shape the hallmark vegetarian ethos of Chinese Buddhism while they inform the practice of religion of many nonhumans, like Xuyun's tiger, a duck, a raven, a rooster, and, most notably in the Chinese universe, the religious experiences of plants. But first, an examination of these nonhuman personhood relationships within Chinese Buddhism requires some contextualization of Buddhism within Chinese culture.

Chinese Immanent Religiosity

To understand the relationships between the Three Doctrines of Buddhism, Confucianism, and Daoism, one must consider that these religious elements do not stand alone in China as exclusive entities. Each of the three deeply interpenetrates the other two in teachings and ritual, so that approaching Buddhism in China means approaching Confucianism and Daoism, with their sometimes-immanent theologies, as well. But this is not all; Chinese popular or folk religions, with their frequent expressions of the immanence of the sacred, likewise imperceptibly blend with the Three Doctrines in the everyday religious experiences of most Chinese citizens throughout history. The resulting dynamism in differing senses of holy immanence inhibits any attempt to draw a purely Buddhist thread from the overall religious fabric of China, so I will not try to. Instead, in this chapter I will focus my presentation within this mix on the perspectives of self-consciously Buddhist texts, such as the *Lotus Sūtra*, as well as of Buddhists themselves, like the tiger-taming master Xuyun.

Reflecting Chinese ideas of the presence of sacred immanence within nonhumans, once Xuyun was at Gushan monastery when "an unusual gander" entered the main hall and "gazed at" the Buddha statue "all day." Because of this piety, the gander was cremated at death like a human and unlike a typical animal.[3] On another occasion, a mean-spirited rooster was roaming the Yingxiang temple and causing problems. Xuyun administered the refuge formula to the fowl and taught him to recite the Buddha's name, resulting over time in the rooster's crow changing to the sound of "Fo, Fo, Fo" ("Buddha, Buddha, Buddha"). The now-pious rooster would also follow monks to their services and return to his tree when the rituals were finished. Additionally, he renounced eating insects and began consuming only grains instead. Out of a genuine admiration for this rooster who practiced vegetarian Buddhism in such a humanlike way, Xuyun ends his story by questioning, "Where did this being differ from the Buddha?"[4] Indeed, Xuyun went so far as to identify the natural world with the Buddha himself when he wrote, "Mountains, rivers, and the great earth are but the Tathāgata."[5]

These tales from Xuyun's life highlight the blurring of existents across forms and species that represents a fundamental aspect of Chinese Buddhist attitudes toward nonhuman nature. As the scholar of China Roel Sterckx stated, "The classic Chinese perception of the world did not insist on a categorical demarcation of the boundaries between animals, human beings, and other creatures such as ghosts and spirits."[6] Chinese intimacy with nature, like Xuyun showed with the tiger, duck, and rooster, in fact often propels a cultural movement that muddles the boundaries between humans and nature, especially animals.[7] Early examples of such blurring derive in part from the writings of the Daoist sage Zhuangzi, who on one occasion was not sure whether he was a butterfly or not. Another time, he claimed to understand, through seeming empathy, the happiness of fish.[8]

Despite this blurring process, however, at times Chinese intimacy with nature engenders an alternative mindset that involves a sense of human empowerment at the expense of the nonhuman natural world. For instance, Xuyun relates a story regarding a raven he once met. Having been given to the local Buddhist Association for compassionate release, the raven, "a good mimic," learned the refuge formula as well as how to recite the Buddha's name, so that "all day long it never stopped calling Amitābha and Avalokiteśvara Bodhisattva." The resulting growth in Buddhist piety led the raven to abjure meat and become a vegetarian. Then one day an eagle swooped in and captured the raven as a meal, yet the raven continued to call out the Buddha's name despite the terror of its plight, thus serving as an inspiration for mindfulness for all Buddhists, human or not.[9] Xuyun, nonetheless, evinces a clear sense of human superiority in concluding his telling of the tale by saying, "How then can we human beings allow ourselves to be inferior to a bird?"[10] In this story, we find that, although Xuyun was clearly willing to accord a measure of humanlike religious agency to natural beings, his worldview was not without boundaries between humans and nonhumans, including an attitude of human superiority.

Therefore, in the life of Xuyun one discovers human intimacy with the nonhuman natural world that leads to a sense of human peer comradeship with nature as well as human ascendancy over and exploitation of the natural world—a pattern that one finds, in varying permutations, rife within the wider world of Chinese religions, including Buddhism. The Chinese cultural realm consists of a diversity of attitudes toward and approaches to the natural world, from Xuyun's recognition of Buddha-nature in a rooster to the Confucian writer Mencius's claim that a gentle human "is benevolent towards humans but is merely sparing with living creatures."[11] Xuyun's life helps us begin to appreciate this diversity, in which images from nature, besides revealing a sense of closeness, are often also used to delineate human morality more than they are used to represent and educate regarding phenomenal nonhuman existents.[12] In this way, as we will see, while some Chinese Buddhist forms are conducive to developing a sustainable biosphere, other outcomes diminish this effect.

The Chinese World

The Chinese dialectic between companionship with and exploitation of the natural world is far older than Chinese nationhood because China was one of the first places to develop agriculture, and, as I will describe, a number of problematic long-term effects emerged from the advent of farming. Archaeological studies undertaken at the Diaotonghuan cave in China have shown that wild varieties of rice, or *Oryza rufipogen*, made up a significant portion of human diets in the Yangzi River valley already by around 12,000 BCE. By no later than around 7500 BCE, domesticated varieties of rice, *Oryza sativa*, appeared at Diaotonghuan, and by about 6500 BCE at Diaotonghuan, wild varieties disappeared from diets in favor of complete dependence on domesticated varieties.[13] Domesticated strains might have been favored for their larger grains, synchronized germination, or wait-for-the-harvester approach to ripening, but for whatever reason, rice appears to have been domesticated in China prior to India and Southeast Asia. Soon rice was on its way to becoming the most important grain consumed by humans, with China leading the world in both rice production and consumption.[14]

Over time, growing rice for a burgeoning population meant claiming ever-larger areas of forest for farmland, and the terraforming that derived from this way of thinking dramatically altered China's ecosystem over time. While many different species from the interrelated natural world can reveal these historical effects, the environmental historian Mark Elvin helpfully utilizes wild elephants as a measuring stick for delineating Chinese ecological struggles. Elvin tells us that, around 2000 BCE, wild elephants could be found throughout most of China, including the northern region of present-day Beijing. By 1000 BCE, elephants rarely wintered above the Huai River, often taken to divide northern and southern China. By roughly 1000 CE, elephants appeared only in southern China, and, after 1500 CE, they were confined to the southwest. Today, the merely two hundred wild elephants that remain live in small sanctuaries tucked against the border with Burma.[15] Elvin tells us that this spatial and historical loss of elephant territory represents the reverse image of the north to south "expansion and intensi-fication of Chinese settlement" since an agricultural "protracted war" of humans against elephants unfolded through elephant habitat destruction, the protection of fields from pachyderm raids, and the reduction of elephant numbers through commercial killings or domestication. In the end, Elvin says, the war proved that "Chinese farmers and elephants do not mix."[16] Other species disappeared, too; deer, parrots, peacocks, and tigers largely vanished from China's wilds by around the seventeenth century.[17]

Concomitant with the loss of elephants as both cause and effect, the deforestation of China can be detected as early as the Bronze Age. Elvin claims that the process accelerated until it nearly ran out of control, with irreversible effects manifesting especially in the eighteenth and nineteenth centuries. Thus, the reserves of wood in today's China are ten cubic meters per inhabitant, which is about one-eighth of the world's average.[18]

Notably, this massive deforestation unfolded within a strong cultural tra-dition in China of reverence and respect for individual trees. As an example, in the third-century BCE collection of poetry known as the *Songs of the South* (*Chuci*), one finds spiritual paeans to trees of many different types, and indi-vidual trees could symbolize a number of important political and social ide-als.[19] But, as Elvin indicates, this same reverence for individual trees was not extended to forests as collections of trees. In ancient China, there were "no distinctive gods or goddesses of the forest." Forests instead were typically considered with fear as abodes of demons, leaving Chinese culture "as hos-tile to forests as it was fond of individual trees."[20] Armed with this cultural deprecation of forests, the landscape became denuded of much of its bio-diversity before the mid-twentieth century since "more than any premod-ern northwestern Europeans, the Chinese were driven by a desire for the rational mastery of the world."[21] Environmentally unfriendly actors include Buddhists, the Sinologist Henrik H. Sørensen claims, because many Chinese Buddhists extended respect to natural entities "not because of the nature of the resources *per se*, but because the lives and institutions of the practitio-ners depended on them."[22] As a result, numerous contemporary travelers tell eerie stories of being in the Chinese wilds, where mammal, bird, and insect sounds should be abundant, yet there is no noise, only an unsettling silence. Like we see with historical elephant and deforestation patterns, this situa-tion, reflecting an unsustainable biosphere, does not arise merely from the recent negative effects of communism or Western influences, as some have maintained, but has deep historical roots.[23]

This environmental record should pause some of the praise for nature-friendliness that has been heaped on Chinese culture. Numerous writers have described the Chinese people simply as deeply nature-loving models for emulation, these writers being perhaps stirred by Chinese nature poetry; landscape painting; Daoist notions of naturalness since "the Dao is nature"; traditional beliefs in a trinity of Heaven, Earth, and Human; or rhetorical elements of Chinese nationalism.[24] While there is a Chinese cultural strand of intimacy with nature as I have described, this simplistic perspective on Chinese realities is skewed and incomplete because the concerns and realities of a farmer or hunter may dramatically diverge from those of a poet or meditator, resulting in multiple and sometimes conflicting approaches to the natural world. The China specialist Roel Sterckx describes this situation as a tension between, on the one hand, "the assertion that humans have a degree of control over the animal world" and, on the other hand, "the recurrent idea that humans should strive to harmonize the workings of human society with the rhythms and patterns of the animal world."[25] This tension in Chinese approaches to nature invites attitudes that remain much more complex than beautiful waterfall scenes painted on vases may reveal because human needs and desires have literally intruded to change the landscape of China. Indeed, according to the beloved novel *Journey to the West*, dominance of the natural world is in fact what makes us human. Regarding the Buddhist monkey Sun Wukong, a spirit from the planet Venus asks, "Now that he has the power to subdue dragons and tame tigers, how is he different from a human being?"[26]

Fengshui

Perhaps the varying degrees of (non)sustainability within Chinese Buddhist attitudes toward the nonhuman world may be better understood by exploring fengshui, a Chinese practice in which Buddhists commonly participate when building or furnishing a house or constructing a grave for an ancestor. According to the specialist Ole Bruun, fengshui, meaning "wind and water," enjoys a long history in China, although it was not formalized into schools until the Tang dynasty (618–907 CE) and only came into full flower in late imperial times.[27] The practice takes many forms across time and space. Today's fengshui in China is not the same as it was a century ago or as it is commonly packaged in the West. Moreover, differing practitioners in the same town may not agree on a common method, so that there is little standardization across regions of China. For instance, sometimes fengshui professionals, referred to as *yinyang duangong* (yin yang practitioner) or *fengshui xiansheng* (fengshui master), call souls of humans like the soul calling that we saw in Thailand, while others do not. Because of its individualized practices and diffused nature, fengshui escaped the attacks against spiritualities during the Cultural Revolution from 1966 to 1976, eventuating in a position of prominence in the current religiosity of China.[28]

Fengshui arises from the notion that landmasses, bodies of water, buildings, and furnishings can catch, repel, or redirect the cosmic energy of qi and its two flavors, yin and yang. Proper manipulation of the flow of qi energy maximizes health, happiness, and prosperity, whereas improper or incomplete qi flow may result in disharmony or disaster. As the geographer of China Chris Coggins states, "Good *fengshui* optimizes the flow of beneficial *qi*; mitigates destructive *qi*; draws in and retains wealth, health, and longevity; and confers blessings upon the ancestors, the living, and generations of descendants."[29] In this way, fengshui applies to the proper siting of both the yang dwellings of living humans as well as the yin graves of the dead. Graves receive fengshui treatment because if they are uncomfortable or disrespected, Chinese ancestors can incite a lot of mischief among the living, so their afterlife needs remain important.

For a home, ideal fengshui siting includes an open front that faces south, the direction of the sun and hence life and prosperity. This open front, symbolized by the Red Phoenix, serves to capture qi. The rear of the building, symbolized by the Black Turtle, should be blocked, whether by a mountain, line of tall trees, or similar feature, to stop the flow of qi. Near the Black Turtle should be a source of running water to move qi within the site. If one stands at the entrance to the plot and faces the building, to the left (ideally in the west) there should be a tall feature, such as a hill, representing the yang balancing energy of the Green Dragon. On the opposite side, there should be a similar barrier, but shorter, embodying the yin energy of the White Tiger. As for tombs, the dead should be buried near the top of a rise, in a kind of "armchair position," with an open front but hills on either side and behind the tomb.[30]

Fengshui specialists use intuition, their own experience, the traditional calendar, and an instrument called a *luopan* that includes a compass. Around the compass is a flat disk that is inscribed with the Eight Characters that are based on the Eight Trigrams of the classic text *Yijing*. The specialist appropriately aligns the compass needle, the relevant character, and local topographic features to maximize and balance the flow of qi of a domicile or grave. In so doing, care must be taken not to cause conflicts among neighbors that may arise from redirected or stolen qi. Then, typically, a chicken is sacrificed, and its blood is scattered over the plot in order to drive away negative forces. Some of the many Buddhists who engage in fengshui in China provide additional examples in which Buddhist actors engage in animal sacrifice.

Commonly, Chinese Buddhists will consult fengshui specialists when needed for moving or for burying their loved ones, even though the Buddha himself never taught the practice of fengshui. Monastics engage in fengshui, too, perhaps most famously at Longchang monastery. This temple once served as the most respected place for ordaining monks in central China and enjoyed fame as a *Vinaya* study center. Many of the monks, however, also began specializing in fengshui practice, which they performed as part of their public ministry. Then, when the nearby village of Liujiabie soured on the monastery and refused to let its monks enter, the monastics turned to fengshui geomancy to enact their revenge. Noticing that the village looked like a two-masted sailing ship when viewed from above, on a promontory the monks constructed an eight-sided pagoda that was shaped like an anchor. Intended to stop the sailing of the qi of the village, the monument worked to halt the energy flow of the village, which then went into decline.[31]

As one can see, the practice of fengshui expresses a sense of human intimacy with the natural world. Human happiness arises from living in harmony with the spiritual natural forces that surround us, and one should take care to orient oneself and one's ancestors toward conditions that emerge organically from a locality and its band of spirits. Only by communing with these spirits does one clearly understand how to navigate decisions with powerful ramifications; fengshui teaches that, in some measure, nature shapes human affairs. Because of this feature, especially in the West some people tout fengshui as a form of green religion that offers viable solutions to current environmental problems. For instance, E. N. Anderson wrote that fengshui "is a matter of sound ecological principles" that constrain "ecologically unwise" actions.[32] In this light, Chris Coggins has indicated that village fengshui forests may helpfully direct wind and water while also aiding erosion control.[33]

Unfortunately, such ecological perspectives on fengshui overlook a fundamental characteristic of the practice: its human-focused anthropocentrism. While fengshui may teach one to realize a deep harmony with the immanent sacredness of one's natural surroundings, a question remains regarding the uses to which this harmony will be put, and in fengshui those uses are almost always human-centered, like we saw with the Longchang monastery monks who ruined a village. One does not orient one's house to local mountains and rivers for the sake of those mountains and rivers but for the sake of the human residents of the house. Benefits for the mountains and rivers involved may accrue but do not do so by design as does human benefit. Graves are not oriented necessarily to enhance hills or trees but to shelter the beloved human dead who are contained within them. Therefore, despite fengshui's rich sense of harmony and intimacy with nature, this intimacy becomes a tool primarily for realizing human dominance and welfare. Anthropocentrism inherently marks fengshui's goals, as the presence of animal sacrifices seems to indicate.

Moreover, while occurrences of this anthropocentrism may sometimes appear benign, there are no real blocks within fengshui to manifesting serious environmental harm. For instance, you may become rich by clearing a large forest, and other humans then may envy your prosperous, positive fengshui. In other words, fengshui may be employed to help or hinder a sustainable biosphere; its ultimately human-oriented aims can be put to unsustainable usages. Hence, the fengshui specialist Ole Bruun claims, "There is no straight path from Chinese popular religion to ecology."[34]

Holy Mountains

Whatever the approach to fengshui, central to its theory and practice are places of altitude such as sacred mountains, which have received respect and veneration throughout recorded Chinese history. Early Shang dynasty (ca. 1700–1000 BCE) oracle bone inscriptions included appeals to mountain deities who were thought to control rain and other water sources.[35] The third-century BCE *Songs of the South* contained passages regarding mountain veneration, which also fill many pages of the fourth-century BCE *Guideways through Mountains and Seas (Shanhaijing)*, including descriptions of the fabulous eastern mountain of Penglai, the possessor of the elixir of life within its gold and silver palaces.[36] Balancing Mount Penglai in the west, according to the *Guideways through Mountains and Seas*, is the famous Kunlun Mountain, the earthly capital of the supreme deity Di and legendary source of the Yellow River that flows through the ancient cradle of Chinese civilization. Home of the Queen Mother of the West goddess, Kunlun receives the protection of the mountain deity Luwu, who has a human face with a tiger's body that includes nine tails.[37] The *Guideways through Mountains and Seas* recognizes a wide variety of other mountain protector spirits, including appearances in the form of a leopard, a bee, an alligator, a human holding two snakes, and a tiger who also controls the weather, much like mountain gods in Sri Lanka may control weather, as we have seen.[38]

Out of the plethora of sacred mountains that were extolled through oral tradition as well as through sources such as the *Guideways through Mountains and Seas*, over time Daoists came to consider five mountains to be especially holy: Taishan in the east, Hengshannan in the south, Huashan in the west,

Hengshanbei in the north, and Songshan in the center. This latter mountain remains holy to Buddhists, too, because Songshan provides the location for the Shaolin monastery that I will explore later. Nonetheless, Buddhists developed their own canon of four extraordinarily holy mountains: Putuoshan in the east, the base of the bodhisattva Guanyin, a Chinese form of the bodhisattva of compassion, Avalokiteśvara; Jiuhushan in the south, home of the bodhisattva Kṣitigarbha; Emeishan in the west, residence of the bodhisattva Samantabhadra and frequent haunt of the Chan master Xuyun; and the greatest of them all, Wutaishan in the north, the abode and living mandala, or representation of a spiritual utopia, of Mañjuśrī (Chinese: Wenshu Pusa), the Mahāyāna bodhisattva of wisdom.[39]

Wutaishan, "the most ancient and most prominent pan-Asiatic Buddhist sacred site in China," rests a few hundred kilometers west of Beijing.[40] It is actually not just one mountain, but a collection of five peaks that, remarkably, are roughly situated at the four cardinal points with one peak at the center. This topography makes it easy to perceive Wutaishan as a living mandala with numerological significance regarding the number five, and in fact the five peaks give Wutai its name, "Five Terraced." Due to its multiple summits, Wutaishan occupies an area of about 250 square miles. All five summits rise above the tree line, making Wutaishan a cold and snowy place in the winter, which limits many pilgrimages to the summer months. The northernmost of the peaks is also the highest mountain in northern China at 3,058 meters (10,033 feet).[41]

Archaeological studies indicate that humans have lived on or near Wutaishan since Neolithic times, and Daoists started to regard it as holy no later than the first century BCE.[42] An ancient site in Buddhist terms as well, Wutaishan's most important monastery, Xiantong Si, claims to be the second oldest Buddhist monastery in China. By the fourth century, Buddhists had already begun to consider Wutaishan to be the abode of the bodhisattva Mañjuśrī.[43] Then, it was during the Tang dynasty (618–907 CE) that Wutaishan perhaps saw its heyday, as it had over three hundred monasteries and temples and was already an international Buddhist pilgrim destination. Moreover, the Buddhist leader Amoghavajra was able to persuade the emperor Daizong to elevate Wutaishan's patron deity, Mañjuśrī, to national patron deity around 770 CE.[44]

The "Mecca of Chinese Buddhism," Wutaishan for centuries has drawn hordes of Buddhist pilgrims from all over the world, a function that it still serves today; it is still "one of the most active and vibrant centers of Buddhism in China."[45] Indeed, an interesting aspect of Wutaishan is that, for centuries, it has provided a meeting place for Chinese, Mongolian, and Tibetan

Buddhists to mingle and practice together since Buddhism in all these lands includes devotional respect for Wutaishan.

For centuries, Buddhist pilgrims have flocked to Wutaishan because it is the home and natural mandala of Mañjuśrī, the ubiquitous Mahāyāna Buddhist bodhisattva of wisdom. The *Avataṃsaka Sūtra* informs us that, on Clear Cool Mountain to the east (Indian version) or northeast (Chinese version) of the Ganges River valley, Mañjuśrī constantly teaches crowds of deities and bodhisattvas.[46] Clear Cool Mountain then became identified by Chinese Buddhists as Wutaishan.[47] On Wutaishan Mañjuśrī rides a blue lion with a green mane, with the roar of his lion awakening the spiritually lazy, and pilgrims to the mountain visit the spot where Mañjuśrī subdued five hundred poisonous dragons.[48] At Wutaishan Mañjuśrī therefore acts as a master of the dragons who inhabit the mountain and thus, by extension, the master of the rain and agriculture that dragons abet.[49] In this way, at Wutaishan Mañjuśrī is not just the bodhisattva of wisdom, he is a mountain god who is a master of animals, plants, and weather. As the master of animals, Mañjuśrī may shapeshift to protect sincere pilgrims; he frequently emanates as a fox or a deer, so that Buddhists sometimes protect animals on the mountain.[50] Mañjuśrī also famously appears as floating fireballs of "Buddha lights" (*foguang*), or luminous apparitions that drift through the mountain air, as Xuyun himself claimed to witness.[51]

Because it is a five-pointed living mandala, or representation of the enlightened world of Mañjuśrī, pilgrimage to Wutaishan is understood sometimes rather literally like physically traversing a mandala, a notion that will arise again in terms of nature mysticism in the chapters on Japan and Tibet of this book. While remaining Mañjuśrī's home, over time each peak further became identified as the residence of one of the five Mahāyāna Buddha families. Amoghasiddhi Buddha occupies the north peak with Akṣobhya in the east, Ratnasambhava in the south, Amitābha in the west, and Vairocana in the center.[52] With the landscape thoroughly sacralized in this way, natural features provide subpilgrimage locations and the earth and water become natural holy souvenirs. There are over twenty lakes and streams on Wutaishan, and pilgrims will bring some of this water home because drinking it is thought to confer wisdom. Pilgrims will also collect soil, herbs, stones, or mushrooms since they are believed to contain medicinal or spiritual properties.[53] In these ways, Wutaishan appears as a benevolent and compassionate divine person within Chinese Buddhism.

Despite this glory, over time Wutaishan suffered from environmental if not spiritual neglect, so that by 1580 CE its once thickly vegetated slopes were deforested and its wild animals had disappeared. So thorough was the denuding of trees that the inclines did not renew their forest cover until the Communist leader Mao Zedong sponsored an intentional tree planting effort in the mid-twentieth century.[54] Monasteries on Wutaishan were largely razed during the violence of the Cultural Revolution, but now some rebuilding and revitalization is occurring, like what is happening throughout much of the Chinese Buddhist world. Nonetheless, the history of holy Wutaishan includes real struggles to maintain something like Rolston's sustainable biosphere, despite its sacredness as a vibrant manifestation of Chinese religiosity's immanent spirit.

Plants as Buddhas

Like at Wutaishan, throughout this chapter Chinese Buddhism reveals a dynamic in which intimate human relationships with the natural world lead to a sense of human partnership with nature along with human ascendancy over nonhuman realms. The way this dynamic has appeared in China in terms of the place of plants marks a distinctive feature of the interface between Chinese Buddhism and nature. On one side, some Chinese Buddhists have accorded humanlike, or nearly humanlike, spiritual capacities to plants, even going so far as to declare plants to be Buddhas. Conversely, diverse currents resulted in a greater stress on vegetarianism within Chinese Buddhism as compared to Theravāda and Vajrayāna forms of the religion, with the development of these vegetarian sentiments later importantly influencing Buddhists in Korea, Japan, and Vietnam. An aspect of this vegetarianism involves the insistence on and general promotion of eating plants, which aids the sustainability of many animals but not necessarily of plants or plant habitats. Thus, in the complex Chinese world, movements both to respect plants as Buddhas as well as to consume more plants burgeoned, even during the same time periods. No final consensus on the place of plants in Chinese Buddhism has yet been reached despite the ramifications for both plants and animals.

As I described in chapter 2 of this book, Indian Buddhism as found in the Pāli scriptures was vague and ambivalent about the sentience of plants, and therefore the ability of plants to realize nirvana, until the *Milindapañha*, around the time of Jesus, definitively announced that plants were insentient.[55] In the Pāli jātakas, the Buddha never once incarnated as a plant, although he did appear as a spirit residing in a plant. Additionally, the Indian Mahāyāna scripture *Mahāratnakūṭa Sūtra*, respected among Chinese Buddhists, explains that "grasses and trees have no awareness."[56] Among other Mahāyāna scriptures, the *Nirvāṇa Sūtra* relates that a medicine tree gives without discrimination, which is a Buddhist virtue, but does so because it has no thoughts of its own. This scripture specifically states that insentient existents lack Buddha-nature, or the capacity for enlightenment.[57] The *Ugraparipṛcchā* enjoins nonharm to "any living beings," but excludes plants from this formulation, for they are mere property.[58] The *Śūraṅgama Sūtra* portrays the belief that plants are sentient as an obstacle for aspiring meditators.[59] In the *Sūtra on Contemplation of Amitāyus*, a Pure Land text, trees expound "the wonderful Dharma," but these natural teachers are apparitions within a Pure Land, not phenomenal trees.[60] They are made of jewels, not wood, so that trees in a Pure Land do not reflect on the reality of earthly trees.[61] Further, regarding the insentience of plants, the Chinese Buddhist monk Zhen Luan presented an anti-Daoist argument to Emperor Wu of the Northern Zhou in 570 CE in which Zhen, on behalf of Buddhism, ridiculed some Daoist magic that presupposed the sentience of trees, thus highlighting the low places that may be accorded to plants in Chinese Buddhism.[62]

With the rise of Mahāyāna Buddhism in China, however, a recognition of the possible enlightenment of plants emerged, reflecting universalizing tendencies in Chinese Buddhism. Indian scriptures were sometimes read in China to spotlight the idea of one religious form for all sentient beings while accrediting the capacity for enlightenment to as many beings as possible. This effort was inspired in part by Mahāyāna *tathāgata-garbha* philosophical teachings, which assert that sentient beings possess Buddha-nature, or the capacity for liberation.[63] Perhaps even more influential universalizing tendencies derived from the great role of and sincere admiration for the *Lotus Sūtra*, an Indian Mahāyāna scripture, with this admiration apparent especially within Chinese Tiantai Buddhism. The *Lotus Sūtra* emphasizes the universality of the message brought by the Buddha, who in the *Lotus Sūtra* taught one unified message for the benefit of all sentient beings everywhere. There really are not different sects such as Theravāda and Mahāyāna, claims the *Lotus Sūtra*. Instead, there is one religion, one Ekayāna or "One Vehicle," that is taught through a variety of expedient means so that all sentient beings may understand in their own ways. Notably, the *Lotus Sūtra*'s chapter on "The Parable of the Plants" uses the analogy of one rain falling on plants, nurturing each plant in its own way, to represent how the Buddha rains one religious teaching everywhere:

I [the Buddha] appear in the world
like a great cloud
that showers moisture upon
all the dry and withered living beings,
so that all are able to escape suffering.

What falls from the cloud
is water of a single flavor,
but the plants and trees, thickets and groves,
each accept the moisture that is appropriate to its portion.

All the various trees,
whether superior, middling, or inferior,
take what is fitting for large or small
and each is enabled to sprout and grow.[64]

For many Buddhists, this analogy of the Buddha as a cloud who rains on plants is just that, simply an analogy. Reflecting this perspective, within the same chapter of the *Lotus Sūtra* the Buddha implies that actual plants are insentient when he speaks of "those plants and trees, thickets and groves, and medicinal herbs which do not themselves know whether they are superior, middling, or inferior."[65] The possible Buddha-nature of supposed insentient beings (the insentience of plants will be challenged by some botanists in the next chapter) is an active point of contention for some East Asian Mahāyāna Buddhists.

These doubts notwithstanding, beginning in China and continuing into Japan, some Mahāyāna adherents of the *Lotus Sūtra* began to read the Dharma rain passage more narrowly and literally, taking it to indicate that plants have the capacity, in their own ways, to realize enlightenment. One of the first of such readers of the *Lotus Sūtra* was Jizang (549–623 CE), a member of the Sanlun school and master of Mādhyamaka philosophy, who was the first to use the phrase, "the attainment of Buddhahood by plants and trees."[66] Along with the more literal reading of the *Lotus Sūtra*, the *Vimalakīrti Sūtra* also influenced Jizang. The *Vimalakīrti Sūtra* states that when the Buddha of the future Maitreya awakens, all sentient beings will be liberated. Jizang included plants in this group, despite the fact that the *Vimalakīrti Sūtra* baldly states that plants, trees, tiles, and pebbles remain "without understanding."[67] Writing theoretically, Jizang reasoned that plants are essentially like mammalian sentient beings and therefore hypothetically may realize Buddhahood, using the phrase *caomu chengfo* or "plants become Buddhas."[68] Jizang, however, spoke only in terms of theory and did not apply his discussion to practical questions regarding actual plant spirituality.[69]

Another Chinese master, Zhanran (711–782 CE), was more daring in his claims regarding plants.[70] Zhanran was the ninth patriarch of the Tiantai school, which, perhaps more than other sects of Chinese Buddhism, insists on and explores the *Lotus Sūtra*'s universalism. Zhanran, taking the universalistic claims of the *Lotus Sūtra* rather seriously, proposed that Buddha-nature exists in all things, sentient and insentient, not just human beings, because of the nondualism between sentient beings and their environments. He argued, "Why should the substance of the *Bhūtatathatā* [Suchness or Thusness] pertain exclusively to 'us' [humans] rather than to others [nonhumans]?"[71] Zhanran thus extends notions of Buddha-nature to all existents, from rabbits to elms to stones, so that his ethic embraces more than just plants. Applying this thinking to plants, Zhanran reasoned that, possessing similar Buddha-nature, plants may realize enlightenment like humans. He wrote, "Within the Assembly of the Lotus, all are present without division. In the case of grass, trees, and the soil, what difference is there between their four types of atoms? Whether they merely lift their feet or energetically traverse the path, they will all reach the Precious Island [of nirvana]."[72] However, Zhanran based his views on universalistic theory, so he did not enter deeply into the contentious issues of whether plants are sentient and religious agents in their own right, issues that appear with greater clarity in the next chapter in the Japanese Buddhist philosophies of Ryōgen, Annen, Kūkai, and others.

Buddhist Vegetarianism

Jizang's and Zhanran's views regarding the Buddha-nature and Buddhahood of plants influenced the later Chinese tradition, especially within Tiantai circles. Overall, the greater spiritual valuation of plants by thinkers such as Jizang and Zhanran has created a more plant-friendly ethos for East Asian Mahāyāna Buddhism than that found in other Buddhist realms.[73] But while such plant-friendly approaches were developing, countervailing tendencies also appeared that led to perceiving plants solely as food sources for the practice of vegetarianism, with vegetarianism, like the enlightenment of plants, marking a distinctive thematic element within Chinese Buddhism. Therefore, in order to understand Chinese Buddhism, one must probe the contours of Chinese Buddhist vegetarianism, which includes examining Daoist dietary movements, folk taboos regarding meat, Buddhist scriptures, and the actions of kings. It is possible that the vegetarianism of Manichaean Christianity has exerted a small role here as well.[74]

For at least three thousand years, Chinese culture and religion have revolved around sacrifices and feasting, with this combination constituting the heart of Chinese religion for some scholars.[75] As described in a variety of texts, sacrifices, including meat sacrifices, have to be offered at various points in the calendar, as a response to events, or to honor ancestors, making sacrifice an enduring element of Chinese folk religion. After being offered to spirits, the sacrificed food then becomes a meal for humans. This communal, ritual sacrifice and feasting has a long history in China. To this day, weddings, business deals, political operations, and so on, still typically unfold during a communal meal. It should be noted, though, that because of a widespread Confucian belief that ancestors should receive meat offerings, this has not been, in general, a vegetarian-friendly practice. It was common in the past, for example, to hold biannual communal animal sacrifices and meat feasts to engender the favor of the local gods of the soil (*she*) in order to ensure agricultural success.[76]

Beginning in the early centuries CE, Daoists began to attack the gods of the old sacrifice-and-feast model without attacking the sacrifice-and-feast model itself. To distinguish themselves from Confucians and others, they replaced old spirits with their own pantheon of deities and, in so doing, depicted the old gods as bloodthirsty demons because of their appetite for meat sacrifices. The new gods, bringers of long life rather than death, forbade meat sacrifices, reflecting Daoist ethical mores against harming or killing others.[77] Thus, when in the early centuries CE the Celestial Masters sect developed its ritual feast of the Daoist Kitchen, offerings and feasts excluded meat and included only vegetables.

Celestial Masters vegetarianism, however, was not mandated for every meal, only for the ritual, and Daoists appeared to commonly continue to eat meat in their daily lives.[78] Moreover, some Daoist *fangshi* seekers of immortality abstained from grains and sometimes meat but were not vegetarian as a rule.[79] Beyond the Celestial Masters group, the general Daoist sensibility involved moderation toward, not abstinence from, meat, which perhaps is not surprising, given the Daoist sage Zhuangzi's use of a butcher to demonstrate holiness.[80] In this vein, Daoists commonly referred to the naturalness of animal-eats-animal to support meat eating.[81]

But requiring that the Daoist Kitchen holy feast ritual be vegetarian helped establish the idea that true holiness and vegetarianism go together, with the Daoists further appealing in this regard to an ancient funerary practice of vegetarianism while mourning the loss of a relative.[82] The vegetarian Daoist Kitchen ritual, then, fixed in the minds of many in China that, everyday reality aside, genuine spirituality involves some measure of vegetarianism. Starting in the ninth century CE, Daoists took this line of thinking even further as they campaigned against the "three revolting meats" (*san yan*)—which included the meat of wild geese, dogs, and cattle—as spiritually polluting. Interestingly, according to the sinologist Vincent Goossaert, this latter movement led to a taboo against beef eating since it portrayed bovines as agricultural partner persons to be protected. In this way, and actually against some Buddhist objections, medieval Daoism created its own homegrown version of the holy cattle protection and veneration that is so famous in Indian cultural spheres.[83]

Although holy Indian cattle did not appear to directly figure in the forces that led to indigenous Daoist bovine protection, they influenced Chinese Buddhist vegetarianism indirectly through the medium of Indian Mahāyāna scriptures. As I noted in chapter 2, it is difficult to discern a vegetarian message, or even a vegetarian Buddha, in the Pāli scriptures, which were first composed in the early centuries BCE, resulting in the Theravāda meat eating that appeared in chapters 3 and 4. Yet some Indian Sanskrit Mahāyāna scriptures, especially those that highlight the doctrine of tathāgata-garbha, or Buddha-nature theory, such as the Laṅkāvatāra Sūtra or the Nirvāṇa Sūtra, stress or insist on a vegetarian diet for Buddhists. These texts were among those that traveled to China and were translated early by luminaries such as Kumārajīva (344–413 CE). In this way, Chinese Buddhism included some Indian arguments for vegetarianism nearly from the start. But what caused the shift in dietary message between the Theravāda and Mahāyāna Indian Buddhist scriptures?

The Indologist Ludwig Alsdorf provides a helpful response to this question. In his seminal work, The History of Vegetarianism and Cow-Veneration in India, Alsdorf relates that in the ancient Brahmanic religion of India that was based on the Vedas, animal sacrifice, including the sacrifice of cattle, was common. Vedic rituals, in fact, mandated the same kind of meat sacrifice followed by ritual feasting that marks Chinese cultural forms. Cattle, being sacred and valuable and hence a good gift for the gods, were the most common sacrifice. Precisely because of its holiness and value, a cow had to be killed for an honored guest, a guest thus being known in the Vedas as go ghna, or "cattle killer."[84] Not eating sacrificial meat carried a heavy penalty including being reborn twenty-one times as a sacrificial animal.[85]

Over time, however, such Indian mores began to change, especially in light of the challenges of nonharm that stemmed from the mid-first millennium BCE religion of Jainism, with its thoroughgoing adherence to ahimsa.[86] Dominant Hindu attitudes, affected as well by ideas of ahimsa found in texts such as the Chāndogya Upaniṣad, over time tilted away from accepting the bloody Vedic sacrifices and more toward ahimsa, including ahimsa-inspired vegetarianism. The growing popularity of the vegetarian god Viṣṇu in the epic and Purāṇic literatures aided this rise of vegetarianism.[87]

Therefore, according to Alsdorf, by the fifth century CE Indian views regarding spirituality and meat had completely flipped; now vegetarianism was considered by many to be the sine qua non of the holy life as well as a marker of high-caste status.[88] Just like some Daoists had developed a cultural equation that identified vegetarianism with higher spirituality, so did India in the early centuries CE. This affected Buddhism since it was later in this process in which some essential Mahāyāna scriptures were composed, when "some monks in India eventually came to insist on a vegetarian diet."[89] These later scriptures drank from Indian vegetarian cultural streams that made the apparent meat eating of the Buddha's time unthinkable. Projecting their experiences into the past, Indian writers of these later Mahāyāna scriptures described a Buddhist tradition that had been vegetarian from the start and perhaps thereby unknowingly changed the shape of some forms of East Asian Buddhism.

Despite this Indian change in vegetarian attitudes, though, not all Mahāyāna scriptures support vegetarianism. The *Saṁdhinirmocana Sūtra* memorably recommends meat cooked in clarified butter as "very satisfying," in fact.[90] But some of the sūtras the Chinese have most treasured do emphasize vegetarianism.[91] The *Lotus Sūtra*, for instance, compares selling meat with prostitution.[92] The *Bodhicaryāvatāra* prohibits killing animals for food.[93] The *Nirvāṇa Sūtra*, translated into Chinese in the early fifth century, argues strongly against meat eating, claiming that the Buddha allowed meat while he was alive but forbade meat eating as a deathbed command. According to the *Nirvāṇa Sūtra*, the Buddha issued this prohibition because eating meat is like eating the flesh of one's own children, thus exhibiting an animist personhood orientation.[94] The *Śūraṅgama Sūtra*, translated into Chinese in the eighth century, states that meat eating is acceptable for beginners but must eventually be given up since humans become animals by eating them. Sponsoring veganism, the *Śūraṅgama Sūtra* further encourages Buddhists to avoid all animal-based products.[95] Moreover, based on the doctrine of Buddha-nature as well as regard for the personhood of animals, the *Aṅgulimāla Sūtra* argues against meat eating because another's flesh is not different from one's own.[96]

Among these religious books that enjoin the avoidance of meat, two especially stand out: the semi-scriptural *Śikṣāsamuccaya Sūtra*, compiled by Śāntideva, and the *Laṅkāvatāra Sūtra*. Both of these texts proscribe meat eating and, along with this, the eating of garlic or onions. This latter prohibition indicates that these dietary rules were shaped by culture, not just ahimsa ethics. Garlic and onions were prohibited to proper Hindus of the Brahmin caste for reasons of ritual purity, and the Indian Buddhist scriptures generally follow this line of thinking.[97] In terms of vegetarianism, the *Śikṣāsamuccaya* allows meat eating for medicinal purposes, but otherwise finds that no meat satisfies the conditions for permissibility given in the Pāli scriptures, thus banning all nonmedicinal meats. Therefore, in the *Śikṣāsamuccaya* selling or eating meat leads to a hell rebirth.[98]

The *Laṅkāvatāra Sūtra*, which was translated into Chinese in the first half of the fifth century, provides a much longer list of reasons to avoid meat, including the fact that forbidden meat is often disguised as acceptable; animals will smell and fear you; you will be sleepless and have bad dreams; you will not have magical powers; the sages of the past were vegetarian; you might like meat so much that you become a cannibal; there would be no slaughterhouses without meat eaters; meat eaters will be reborn as demons, noxious animals, or untouchables; and those who buy and sell meat will be reborn in hell.[99] In the *Laṅkāvatāra Sūtra*, "from meat eating arrogance is born" while "innocent victims" are destroyed.[100] Crucially, like the *Nirvāṇa Sūtra*, together the *Śikṣāsamuccaya* and *Laṅkāvatāra Sūtra*s offer one more reason not to eat animals: animals are persons, our peer comrades in samsara.[101] Animals should not be eaten because they are extended kin to humanity, as the *Laṅkāvatāra Sūtra* vividly describes:

> In this long course of transmigration here, there is not one living being that, having assumed the form of a living being, has not been your mother, or father, or brother, or sister, or son, or daughter, or the one or the other, in various degrees of kinship; and when acquiring another form of life, may live as a beast, as a domestic animal, as a bird, or as a womb-born, or as something standing in some relationship to you; this being so, how can the Bodhisattva-Mahāsattva who desires to approach all living beings as if they were himself and to practice the Buddha-truths, eat the flesh of any living being that is of the same nature as himself?[102]

Just as we should shrink from eating human persons, these scriptures highlight, so should we hesitate to eat animals, who likewise represent samsaric persons. Here, personhood animism drives primary arguments of these scriptures that advocate vegetarianism, indicating one of the ways, along with realities like protected Daoist partner bovine persons, that Chinese vegetarianism undergoes sculpting by personhood relational animism.

Additionally, for many East Asian Buddhists, the *Fanwangjing* (Sanskrit: *Brahmajāla Sūtra*) informs this scriptural mix with further personhood-based vegetarian arguments. Composed in China around 420 CE, despite its Sanskrit alternative title, and displaying an array of ideas regarding traditional Confucian filial piety, the *Fanwangjing* supplies a list of ten major and forty-eight secondary precepts for bodhisattvas, and these precepts commonly have been a part of Chinese bodhisattva ordination ceremonies.[103] In the

Fanwangjing, the first major precept forbids bodhisattvas from killing since instead a bodhisattva should have a mind driven by compassion and filial piety. This injunction then is extended in the third and twentieth of the secondary precepts, where the text calls for strict vegetarianism based on kin animist personhood: "Sentient beings in all six destinies have all been our fathers and mothers. If we were to slaughter and eat them, it would be the same as slaughtering and eating our own parents."[104] In the *Fanwangjing*, eating meat "will cut you off from the seed-lineage of great compassion" because it involves cannibalizing your previous parents and therefore should be avoided.[105]

Of course, Chinese Buddhists of the fourth and fifth centuries may not have fully understood the historical and social contexts of Buddhist scriptures. To a number of Chinese Buddhists, the writings all presented the Buddha's actual words. Many took the Chinese-penned *Fanwangjing* to be an authentic scripture from India and, as a result, it was easy for the Chinese of this period to perceive Buddhism simply as a religion of vegetarianism. Lay movements commenced in which Buddhists attempted to convince as many others as possible to adopt a vegetarian diet. The fifth-century Buddhist writers Zhou Yong and Shen Yue, for example, both argued urgently for vegetarianism for the benefit of animals, with Shen Yue adding a plea to discontinue silk making since it inevitably kills large numbers of silkworms.[106] Nonetheless, most monks before the sixth century probably were not strict vegetarians.[107]

The Vegetarian King Wu of Liang

Within this religious context came King Wu of Liang (464–549 CE), a friend of Zhou Yong and Shen Yue as well as a Buddhist who embraced vegetarianism. Wu famously forbade traditional meat sacrifices for his ancestors, giving them vegetarian noodles instead; outlawed animal sacrifice in state rituals; and banned hunting and fishing in areas near the capital. Wu hoped that his hunting ban would last, but it was quickly forgotten after his death. Yet Wu lives on in his more successful efforts to implant monastic vegetarianism.

King Wu inherited a Buddhist interpretive problem regarding vegetarianism, and this provided a platform for his more enduring contribution. As I have described, the Mahāyāna scriptures known in China at that time carried a heavily vegetarian message, whereas the two monastic *Vinayas* or monastic rules in force at the time in China, the Sarvāstivāda *Vinaya* and the Dharmagupta *Vinaya*, allowed meat eating by monks, reflecting the regulations of the Pāli scriptures. Wu therefore asked, "Is Buddhism vegetarian or not?" The vegetarian king called a council of monastic Buddhist leaders with the intent that they would decide in favor of vegetarianism and was frustrated when they stuck to their meat-liberal monastic rules instead. Not to be stopped, the king then issued five edicts, including the institution of a monastic precept forbidding meat eating, much like one finds in the *Fanwangjing*. By imperial decree backed by the perceived scriptural support of the *Fanwangjing*, the Chinese monastic sangha thereby became vegetarian. From this point in time forward, lay expectations across China were that good monks and nuns eschewed meat, an expectation that persists today.[108]

Because of monastic sangha resistance to Wu's mandate, this vegetarian form did not fully take hold immediately, but instead became ingrained slowly as people remembered the vegetarian ideal but forgot the imperial imposition of policy. For instance, as witnessed by monastic biographies that were composed during the next few centuries, over time monastic vegetarianism became less of an issue and more taken for granted.[109] In the end, therefore, King Wu got his way since from his time until today most monks and nuns in China consider vegetarianism to be a Buddhist lifestyle requirement, an expectation that then was exported to Korea, Japan, and Vietnam. However, despite the fact that the *Fanwangjing* requires vegetarianism of lay bodhisattvas, because the king's direct quarrel was with monastics only, King Wu did not mandate lay vegetarianism, although some lay Chinese Buddhists still practice it, especially on holy days. Personhood arguments for vegetarianism thereby continue to reverberate among East Asian Buddhist monastics and laypeople alike.

Nature Mystical Elements

The quest to develop Buddhist vegetarianism betrays a variety of influences from the Chinese religious realm. Multiple influences likewise coalesce to shape a form of nature mysticism at the Shaolin temple, which is perhaps the most famous Buddhist temple in the world because of its martial arts practices. Shaolin lies at the foot of Songshan, which is one of the five Daoist sacred mountains, and an active Daoist temple remains at the peak's summit. Besides its location at a holy mountain, though, Shaolin also retains fame as the place where the Buddhist patriarch Bodhidharma (Chinese: Da Mo) meditated for years in a cave, which still serves as a pilgrimage site. Being a man for whom history has fabricated many talents, Bodhidharma perhaps falsely enjoys credit for being a founder of the Chan Buddhism of Shaolin.

He may have inspired early Chan, but many scholars believe that he lived too early to actually found the Chan school.[110] Shaolin myth also credits Bodhidharma with the establishment of its Buddhist martial arts practices, such as with the *qigong* martial arts manual *Marrow-Cleansing Classic* (*Xisuijing*) that wrongly carries his imprimatur.[111] A closer look at Shaolin martial arts history actually reveals a more complex tale than the authorship of just one man, and this tale is instructive.

The monks of Shaolin monastery trace their martial ways to the transition into the Tang dynasty (618–907 CE), when Shaolin monks fought to enthrone the emperor Li Shimin.[112] Li then rewarded the monks with a land grant and a special dispensation to drink wine and eat meat.[113] This, and the ongoing need to defend against bandits, established a martial ethos at Shaolin, where traditional boundaries separating fighting from monkhood began to crumble. The ascendancy of the martial celestial bodhisattva Vajrapāni as the patron saint of Shaolin accelerated this process, because monks considered fighting for the Dharma to be acceptable since Vajrapāni did it, too. The monks then had the ideological equipment they needed to navigate the paradox of monks who are sworn to nonviolence and yet engage in warfare, even if just for sport. Vajrapāni additionally made it acceptable to eat meat since that is part of his cult, so Shaolin monks have long been notorious for skirting rules regarding vegetarianism, although today the temple serves only vegetarian fare.

Until the sixteenth century, Shaolin monks possessed fame for their fighting with staffs, the same weapon used by Vajrapāni. In the transition from the Ming to the Qing dynasty (1644–1911 CE), however, Shaolin monks turned more to weaponless hand-fighting techniques, like those for which they are now so well known.[114] This switch required a loss of mooring in Buddhist myth regarding Vajrapāni and a greater reliance, borrowed from Daoism, on techniques for manipulating qi energy internally, and the result was a vitalization of the spiritual side of Shaolin martial practice. For instance, Buddhist *mudrās* (sacred hand gestures) combined with notions from acupuncture were united with Shaolin hand-fighting styles during this time.[115] More importantly, Shaolin martial practice additionally integrated Daoist mystical techniques based on animal powers.

Daoists celebrated a long tradition of integrating animal energies into their martial arts practices. Speculation among many scholars holds that the ancient Chinese imitated animals in order to capture their powers. For example, the crane, called "no mere bird" by the ecologist Aldo Leopold, is thought to have a long life, so that if one imitates and in a sense becomes a crane, one assimilates the power of long life into oneself.[116] For many of the same reasons, much of classical dance was based on animal movements.[117] By the third century CE, such thinking had been standardized into formats such as the Five Animals Play, a Daoist exercise in which one manipulates internal qi through the emulation of a tiger, deer, bear, ape, and bird.[118]

In time such lessons became aligned with techniques of qi energy manipulation, so that martial masters emphasized actually being the animal, in a meditative state, in the fight. As the Asian studies scholar Harriette Grissom puts it, "Merely imitating the animals' movements, styles, or attitudes— though it may develop some fighting proficiency—will not bring about the highest level of accomplishment. Ultimately, the practitioner must become a medium for the animal's spirit."[119] This mediumship may spark a nondual nature mystical state, because, as Grissom claims, "When a person imitated a tiger, consciousness moved to a different level. The experience of losing oneself completely in the emulation of another being, especially an animal, creates a sense of freedom from the constraints of self."[120] In this mystical state, translated into Shaolin Buddhist thinking, one experiences the Buddhist "suchness" (*tathātā*), or essence, of the animal, rather than just imitating its movements, and thereby imbibes the animal's power in a deep, instinctual manner.[121] The practice of energy manipulation as directed by animal-inspired martial arts exercises therefore spiritually transformed the theoretical basis of Shaolin Buddhist practice, while its outer forms also evolved, resulting in the birth of many Shaolin techniques as we know them, around the same time that recognizably modern *taiji* practices bloomed within Daoist universes.[122]

In *The Essence of Shaolin White Crane*,[123] Dr. Yang Jingming, an expert on the White Crane style of Shaolin martial arts, shares how these inner mystical states produce effects in martial arts training. "The reason for imitating the fighting techniques of animals," he says, "came from the belief that animals possessed natural talents and skills for fighting in order to survive in the harsh natural environment. The best way to learn effective fighting techniques was by studying and imitating these animals" (5).

In terms of the white crane, it possesses longevity because it "knows how to conserve and protect its essence," so, for Dr. Yang, the Shaolin White Crane fighter must follow suit if he is to have a long and successful fighting career (90). Because the "weak" white crane must "know how to dodge and evade an incoming powerful attack," according to Dr. Yang, such tactics lie at the core of White Crane martial arts techniques, including, for instance, an emphasis on generating power from the torso (101). A crane defends itself by relying on jumping, striking with its wings, and pecking with its beak, so such defenses are built into White Crane movements, including quick strikes with fingers held in beaklike postures (103). It is thought that cranes may fly for long distances because they use their chest muscles, rather than relying on their wings alone, so the White Crane style, in the words of Dr. Yang, "specializes in the training of the torso and the chest" (105). Finally, since a crane is quick but frail, it must calmly and patiently wait in defense until it strikes like lightning in a moment of vulnerability for its opponent. Similarly, Shaolin White Crane fighters train to be good and patient defenders while also smart and agile in the attack (106). Those who manage to externally imitate and internally assimilate the spirit of the white crane in these ways will realize the greatest accomplishment both in terms of fighting and in terms of spiritual development.

Therefore, in this perspective, one may cultivate nature mystical experiences of animals through Buddhist meditative martial arts practices and, ideally, arrive at the ultimate Shaolin goal, the realization of Buddhahood, by embodying an animal.[124] Shaolin practices thereby fascinatingly combine personhood respect for animals as well as Buddhist nature mystical techniques for integrating these animal personhoods into oneself.

Chinese Buddhism and Nature

The monastics at Shaolin draw our attention to an important feature of Chinese Buddhism: tendencies toward nature mysticism, given the immanent spirit and relational animism of much of Chinese religion. In their martial arts forms and mental states, Shaolin fighting monks seek an unusual state that is as nondual with the spiritual essence of the animal as possible, meeting this book's definition of nature mysticism. Some other examples of Chinese Buddhist nature mysticism involve the mandalization of mountains, like Wutaishan, as well as folk possession practices. Of course, many such instances arise only through the addition of non-Buddhist elements that are sometimes uniquely Chinese, so that these cases of nature mysticism with Buddhist actors cannot be described as purely Buddhist, nor can they reasonably be expected to sprout spontaneously in other Buddhist cultural worlds. Nevertheless, the nature mystical features of Chinese Buddhism stand out when compared to some other Buddhist locales.

Along with this nature mysticism, the universe of Chinese Buddhism significantly consists of vivid relational animist relationships. For example, the practice of fengshui demands that respectful attention be paid to realizing harmony with natural entities. Buddhists also revere the spirits of mountains. However, maybe nowhere else in the Buddhist world but China do animist personhood relationships like these also inspire a vegetarian diet. Deriving in part from arguments in favor of the personhood of animals found in Indian Mahāyāna scriptures such as the *Nirvāṇa*, *Śikṣāsamuccaya*, and *Laṅkāvatāra Sūtras*, along with similar arguments in the Chinese *Fanwangjing*, Buddhism has long been understood by many in China as a religion that excludes meat eating. Indeed, early Buddhists such as Zhou Yang and Shen Yue used personhood reasoning to create the ambiance in which King Wu of Liang declared the monastic community to be meat-free. Of course, not all Chinese Buddhists have followed suit, like one sees with the meat eating that has occurred over time at the Shaolin temple. But, notably regarding plants, Chinese Buddhists have often hesitated to accord the same type of personhood to flora that they do to animals, perhaps thereby easing a vegetarian conscience.

Despite this general ethos, the Chinese masters Jizang and Zhanran nonetheless did extend personhood to plants; they were audaciously willing to consider plants as enlightened beings. Therefore, in China we find the unusual Buddhist case in which plants may practice the religion in ways not unlike humans. Animals can practice religion, too. Stories from the life of Xuyun express the idea that land mammals and birds can practice Buddhism, because a tiger, duck, raven, and rooster all practiced Buddhism not unlike humans, inspiring Xuyun to remark specifically on the similarity between his rooster Dharma friend and the Buddha himself.

In this study of Chinese Buddhist realities, mountains have played roles as spirits, tigers have practiced religion like humans, and Buddhists have expressed a variety of forms of intimacy with the natural world. When Chinese Chan Buddhism spread from China to Korea, it helped create Sŏn Buddhism, retaining some of this intimacy with nonhumans and leading to a story about a fox as told by the Korean Sŏn school master Daehaeng Kun Sunim. One day a tiger chased a fox, who, while fleeing, fell into a hole so deep that he could not escape. At first terrified for his lack of food and water, as time passed the fox settled down, eventually accidentally falling into a deep state of meditation in which he experienced his Buddha-nature. Seeing this, the god Indra flew to earth, landed by the fox's hole, and bowed before the fox in spiritual respect. The fox responded by saying, "What good is bowing? Get me out of this hole!" Indra pulled the fox from the hole and then offered fine embroidered silk robes to the awakened fox as a recognition of his spiritual accomplishment. Grateful but frustrated, the fox blurted out "What good are clothes to me?" before bounding away into the forest, thereby eschewing both divine praise and a luxury gift. Concluding the tale, Master Daehaeng urges Buddhists not to be like this fox, "who is still trapped by his own habits and fixed way of thinking."[125]

Foxes, forests, and the latter-day offspring of Chan Buddhism exist as well in today's Japan, like they do in Korea. Some special Buddhist approaches to the natural world exist in Japan, too, so now this investigation turns to the Green Archipelago to explore its unique Buddhist approaches to the natural world.

CHAPTER 6

Japanese Water Buddhas

Ruling parts of Japan in perhaps 100 CE, the great pre-Buddhist monarch Emperor Keikō struggled with a country that was too turbulent. While Keikō governed his own territory with strength, demonic and vengeful kami spirits on his borders sometimes instigated chaos and death, a kami being a traditional Japanese spirit. Kamis in themselves have no shape or tangible features, so they need to inhabit *yorishiros*, or material vessels, if they are to influence the material world. Examples of yorishiros include a body of water, mountain, tree, agricultural field, stone, animal, or human. Kamis may also be encountered in dreams or omens in animal form.[1] While kamis can be quite benevolent, when angered they can be malevolent and dangerous, such as a river kami who kills all who attempt to cross without first making an offering. To bring order to the kamis who were causing problems in his kingdom, Keikō commissioned his son, the crown prince Yamato Takeru no Mikoto, or "Conquering Yamato," on a pacification expedition to bring the kamis to heel.

Having set out for glory, at one point Conquering Yamato's ship was assailed by a storm, and all on board feared for their lives. In response, one poor concubine, Oto Tachibana Hime, was cast overboard as a sacrifice to the kami of the sea, and the storm quickly abated. Arriving safely on land, Conquering Yamato then went to the Shimano mountain pass, where he met the kami of the mountain, known for causing illness to travelers, in the form of a white deer.[2] The ever-ready Conquering Yamato set aside his famous sword and was able to locate a sprig of garlic, which he jabbed into the eye of the wicked deer, thereby killing it. Having eliminated the evil white deer of Shimano as a threat, Conquering Yamato then became confused and lost in the mountains, but luckily he was rescued and led to safety by a magical and kind white wolf.[3]

After this, Conquering Yamato visited Mount Ibuki, where he met the *yama no kami*, the spirit of the mountain, in the form of a giant serpent. Foolishly, Conquering Yamato mistook the snake to be simply a messenger of the mountain god, not the mountain god himself, and ignored the serpent as not worthy of his time. The serpent-shaped kami, now angered by Conquering Yamato's disrespect, sent a hailstorm down upon Conquering Yamato, causing him to contract a nasty illness and die.[4]

Conquering Yamato may have lost his life for disrespecting a mountain deity, but his mythological example, despite deriving from pre-Buddhist Japan, remains important if we are to properly understand the interactions between Japanese Buddhists and the natural world of their archipelago. A tension persists in which, on the one hand, respect is shown to natural beings as abodes of deities who are pleased with gifts, such as with the storm-ending sacrifice of an unfortunate woman on behalf of the sea kami. On the other hand, natural deities who oppose humans must be deposed through the exertion of human mastery, such as with the slaying of the deer kami. The story of Conquering Yamato, at once respecting and warring with non-human nature, provides an insight into Japanese Buddhism, which simultaneously extends unique biospherically sustainable formulations that are not found elsewhere in the Buddhist world while conversely supporting attitudes of human superiority and license to conquer the natural world for human benefit. We must keep this tension in mind to best appreciate those moments when Japanese Buddhists have been at their ecofriendly best as well as when they have been at their worst.

In this chapter we will see that instances of this tension between nature-loving and nature-exploiting help shape multiple Japanese attitudes toward the issue of Buddhist vegetarianism. More decisively, the personhoods of nonhumans within this tension manifest as an ecocentric variety of nonhumans who may practice religion, leaving plants to be regarded by some people as Buddhas and the entire natural world to teach like a Buddhist preacher. Moreover, within these personhood relationships, nature mysticism with mountain persons, like you find with the Shugendō movement, has influenced Japanese culture and history significantly. We can find examples of all these outcomes if we consider, as we do in this chapter, Japanese Buddhist attitudes toward plants, Vajrayāna nature mysticism, and the work of the Buddhist philosopher Dōgen. First, however, we need to better appreciate the tensive context provided by the human and nonhuman environments of the Green Archipelago.

The Japanese World

As the story of Conquering Yamato reveals, the tension between nature loving and nature exploiting already existed in the kami-worshipping forms of religion as presented within the ancient Japanese chronicles *Kojiki* (712 CE) and *Nihonshoki* (720 CE). The Japan specialist Allan G. Grapard helpfully explores the character of this tension.[5] In Japan, there is an intimacy between humans and the natural world, Grapard writes, because both humans and nonhumans are the offspring of deities, yet at the same time clear cultural distinctions arise between the human and nonhuman realms. Grapard states, "Nature has, in Japanese mythology, an ambivalent character: though it looks beautiful, it also is the realm of change, decay, and putrefaction, to which is opposed the purification of culture. . . . It might be said that what has been termed 'the Japanese love of nature' is actually 'Japanese love of cultural transformations and purification of the world which, if left alone, simply decays.' So that the love of culture takes in Japan the form of a love of nature."[6] Grapard tells us that the Japanese seek this cultural purification by reading nonhuman nature since nature speaks a language that needs to be "decoded"; this insight is important for understanding the Japanese Buddhist teachings of Kūkai and Dōgen that we will explore later in this chapter.[7]

Unfortunately, an ocean of literature does not maintain this tension between respect for and conquest of nature since many works fall into one-sided glorification of a supposedly inherent Japanese love for the natural world. Much of this discourse stems from Japanese nationalism, which attempts to establish a Japanese identity in contradistinction to the West in terms of Japanese harmony with, not superiority to, nature, such as in the works of Watsuji Tetsurō and Daisetz T. Suzuki. This oversimplified discourse aside, the tension remains between respect for and domination of nature, and two recent studies by the environmental studies specialist Stephen R. Kellert support Grapard's contention that this tension arises from attempts to enculturate and purify the natural world. Through surveys and interviews, Kellert studied 450 Japanese adults and found no special Japanese love for the natural world. Japanese people tended to respond positively in strong ways to individual animals, especially those like Hello Kitty that are humanlike or considered cute, but showed little awareness of or ethical responsibility toward larger ecosystems. Kellert's respondents, in fact, preferred their nature tamed since they placed the "greatest emphasis on the experience and enjoyment of nature in very controlled, confined, and highly idealized circumstances."[8] In a follow-up study comparing citizens of Japan, Germany, and the United States, Kellert found that people in all three countries reacted powerfully to individual animals, especially if they were among the higher vertebrates. More than in the other two countries, though, Japanese people responded most positively to animals with "unusual aesthetic and cultural appeal," but otherwise also exhibited attitudes that were more "dominionistic and negativistic."[9]

A brief peek at the history of Japanese forests illustrates the forces at play here. During the Jōmon period (14,500–300 BCE), Japanese hunter-gatherers, relatively small in number and perhaps the first in the world to develop pottery, stripped the forest of large mammals such as Naumann's elephants (*Palaeoloxodon naumanni*), giant deer, bison, and woolly mammoths, which all went extinct in Japan earlier than 10,000 BCE because of climate change and the development of better weapons such as the bow and arrow.[10] But Japanese hunter-gatherers appeared to live with trees in a relatively sustainable way, and Jōmon culture beliefs developed into forms in which many trees were thought to be holy abodes for kami spirits, so that sacred trees still exert part of the power of the most holy Shintō shrine of Ise even today.

Nonetheless, Japanese trees began to meet their enemies starting around 600 BCE, when wet field rice agriculture was introduced perhaps from Korea. Rice farming then quickly spread throughout southern Japan, and in many lowland places fields soon replaced forest stands.[11] This felling of trees created wood shortages as early as the construction of the first real capital city, Nara, in 710 CE. The next capital, Kyoto, was never completed as planned in 794 CE because the builders ran out of wood that could reasonably be hauled to the site.[12] In other words, by at least the eighth century CE, the forest shortage that haunts Japan today had already begun.

Along with many nonreligious factors, Buddhism had a hand in this since in Nara the construction of the massive Tōdaiji temple in the eighth century alone required 900 hectares, or 2,200 acres, of timber.[13] Across the islands, because numerous temples were built for the new religion of Buddhism after its reception in 552 CE, temples arose to please kami-worshipping sensibilities as well, and the religious building boom of the Nara period and beyond made countless trees into religious martyrs in the name of spreading Buddhist compassion and kami adoration. As a result, when the Tōdaiji temple burned down in the twelfth century, replacement lumber was difficult to find.[14] While many aspects of Japanese life must have contributed to this outcome, an intense hunger for building many wooden religious buildings added an unsustainable element to the mix.

Buddhism participated in deforestation in other ways, too. In pre-Buddhist Japan, it was considered taboo to climb holy mountains because this was understood as disrespectful of the kamis and spirits of the dead who resided there.[15] As I will describe later, Buddhism erased this taboo, endorsing pilgrimages all the way to the top of sacred peaks, thus removing some disincentives to completely deforesting a mountain.

The warring period from the twelfth to the sixteenth century also took its toll on Japanese forests because the building of castles and military fortifications, as well as the smelting of iron into weapons, demanded huge quantities of wood. A sixteenth-century eyewitness estimated that eight out of every ten mountains faced complete deforestation, the mountains sadly being about the only places where forests could exist.[16] Indeed, at this point, Japan south of the island of Hokkaido came dangerously close to passing the point of no return in deforestation, where the woodland is so damaged that it cannot regenerate, leaving behind a relatively permanent treeless landscape.[17] But Japanese citizens recognized their peril, and the first agricultural tree plantations began to appear along with forest protection initiatives, so that today tree plantations take up more than 25 percent of the total land area of Japan.[18] Wooden buildings also intentionally became smaller in the medieval period.[19] Therefore, through restraint, the implementation of more sustainable solutions, and good luck, many Japanese mountains are greener today.

How are we to assess this history? On the one hand, the Japanese people should be commended for their ecological sensitivity and positive action in pulling themselves back from the brink of environmental disaster. Given the duration and density of human habitation in the islands, the land could have been in worse shape in terms of forest cover, and in fact the islands could have been bare of trees today like so many other overcut places, such as Easter Island. Instead, today Japan sports a beautiful emerald color in many places, somewhat justifying the self-proclaimed description of Japan as *midori no rettō*, the Green Archipelago.

However, it was also Japanese people who drove the forests to the brink in the first place. The human-created artificial forests that now dot the islands, which enjoy only 5 percent of primary forest, do not represent the true historical ecosystem.[20] Red pines, for instance, being economically unproductive, are not planted as often and are thus underrepresented. Also lacking are the Hokkaido wolf (*Canis lupus hattai*), which was exterminated with shocking speed in the late nineteenth-century modernization efforts, as well as the Japanese wolf (*Canis lupus hodophylax*) that prowled Kyushu, Shikoku, and the big island of Honshu. These wolf extinctions occurred despite the fact that for centuries many Japanese people worshipped wolves as helpful deities, as exemplified by the magical white wolf who rescued Conquering Yamato. Wolf shrines remain today in at least twenty places.[21] Japanese trees and wolves provide yet more examples in which a reputation for sacredness does not necessarily protect a natural entity from human harm.

The complex tension between respect for and domination of nature appears as well in Japanese dietary habits. Historically, the Japanese diet has not featured many meats from terrestrial animals. Instead, protein has often been derived from marine animals, nuts, and soy. The ancient Jōmon people hunted and practiced limited animal husbandry with boars, and raising animals for food continued after this. However, this practice may not have been pervasive since in 290 CE the Chinese travelog *Wajinden* described the Japanese diet as consisting simply of vegetables.[22] The introduction of Buddhism, however, led to a diminution of any practice of animal husbandry, anyway, given Buddhism's injunctions against killing animals.[23] Thus, although farmers kept oxen and horses to pull the rice field plow since the eighth century pigs, goats, sheep, fowl, cows, and other animals have not often been raised as food sources. Until the nineteenth century, Japan had no developed tradition of animal husbandry.[24] Because of this, it is fair to say that the traditional Japanese diet has been more vegetarian than in many other locations, especially those that customarily raise land animals for food.[25]

As for hunted animals, rather than domestic ones, Buddhist calls for nonharm seem to have diminished hunting somewhat through the medieval period, but hunting still persisted as a common occupation.[26] Hunting even became Buddhicized through an ideology from the Heian period (794–1185 CE) that hunting compassionately freed animals to move on to better rebirths, and hunters received a Buddhist transmission through Shugendō lineages (to be discussed more fully later) that sanctioned hunting for this reason.[27] Then, with the opening up of Japan in the Meiji era starting in 1868, the Japanese government, followed by the Japanese people, began raising more barnyard animals for food like in the West, so that today chicken, pork, and beef frequently appear in Japanese dinner bowls. Therefore, it may fairly be argued that the Japanese are more spontaneously vegetarian than many Buddhists, while at the same time they are not truly vegetarian since they eat meat in response to its availability and may offer Buddhist reasons in favor of hunting. Nonetheless, the appearance of the vegetarian eating of flora invites our attention to the fascinating role of plants in Japanese Buddhism.

Plants as Buddhas

Given the positive side of the tension between Japanese nature embrace and nature conquest, perhaps there is no better place in the Buddhist world than Japan to be a plant, because Japanese Buddhists have distinctively extended friendliness and respectful personhood to plants in remarkable ways. As mentioned in earlier chapters of this book, in early Theravāda and Mahāyāna Buddhism, at best plants were ambiguous in spiritual regard and were usually regarded as insentient and hence religiously irrelevant, serving instead as part of an inert stage for religious dramas that are only performed by humans or animals. Then, in the Mahāyāna world of China, attitudes began to change since universalizing tendencies within Buddhism led teachers like Jizang to claim the theoretical Buddhahood of plants and others like Zhanran to assert that plants can become Buddhas. But the issue of the sentience of plants was largely a marginal issue in Chinese Buddhism, and when the Chinese Tiantai sect went into decline, so did much of the Chinese concern for the Buddhahood of plants.

Unfortunately, Zhanran in China failed to explain exactly how a plant becomes a Buddha, but Buddhist masters from the Tendai sect, the Japanese outgrowth of Chinese Tiantai Buddhism, caught the fever of universal liberation that was part of Chinese Buddhism and thereby continued and creatively extended the conversation. The Japanese Tendai patriarch Annen (841–895? CE), for instance, taught in his *Bodaishingi* that plants are not only Buddhas because of their participation in nirvana but they are also sentient, thus allowing them to advance on the spiritual path under their own agency. For Annen, in an interconnected and nondual universe, everything gets enlightened together, including existents that are thought to be insentient, and therefore "since plants are mind, they become Buddhas."[28] Thus, like Zhanran in China, Annen collapsed the distinction between sentience and insentience in treating plants as respected holy persons.

Annen's successor, Ryōgen (912–985 CE), not only continued to credit plants with spiritual agency but, interestingly, he also explained how plant spirituality works. Sentient beings, he taught, possess life cycles with four stages: birth, stability, alteration, and extinction. Since humans realize enlightenment within life, for Ryōgen, the life cycle is also an enlightenment cycle, so that the four stages of life correspond to a four-level schema of Buddhist realization: arousing the desire for enlightenment, religious practice, enlightenment, and full nirvana. With homologies between life cycles and the Buddhist path established, Ryōgen spotlighted that plants, like humans, also undergo the same life cycles, which in the case of plants consist of sprouting, growing, changing, and dying. Therefore, plants must be counted among fellow sentient beings who practice on the path to nirvana—as Ryōgen felt the *Lotus Sūtra* assures us—since they "arouse the desire for enlightenment, perform religious practices, and become Buddhas."[29] Although Ryōgen's plant-friendly attitude stands out in the Buddhist world for its clarity and originality, it is in an ecocentric sense more limited than Annen's approach since Ryōgen's understanding of sentience, religious agency, and enlightenment should not be applied to things like stones that may not pass through Ryōgen's four stages of life.

At this point some of my readers, living in cultural universes that consider plants to lack thoughts because they lack brains and central nervous systems, will consider Annen's and Ryōgen's assertions of plant consciousness to be fanciful, metaphorical, or gibberish. But in terms of contemporary botanical science, these thinkers appear to have been centuries ahead of their time. In evolutionary terms, plants are our distant cousins, so we should not be surprised to find some sort of commonality, and in terms of internal communication, plants and humans are remarkably similar. Botanists, for example, constantly provide more information which indicates that consciousness may not be reliant on architecture, like a brain and a central nervous system, but on electrical chemistry. In a human, internal communications and consciousness result from electrical discharges that are modulated by calcium, sodium, and potassium, with the central nervous system and brain merely providing physical pathways for these electrical discharges. Plants, likewise, communicate internally through electrical discharges modulated by calcium, sodium, and potassium, but of course their pathways for expressing these discharges differ greatly from those of humans.[30] Nonetheless, their electrical discharges allow plants to behave as if they had brains. Take, for instance, the familiar example of a plant that turns a leaf to catch more sun, with this movement, called phototropism, taking place through chemical reactions. In turning its leaf, the plant must locate the sun, initiate a process of movement, and then respond appropriately to the situation; in humans, all of this indicates sensory awareness, some form of cognition, and intentional agency. Therefore, although quite differently from humans, plants can, in a sense, think and react, and do so in ways that are not entirely alternative to human mechanisms.

These botanical facts appear to support plant-friendly positions such as those of Annen and Ryōgen. Another intriguing Tendai response to the question of plant Buddhahood appears in the curious document *Kankō ruijū*, which is said to have been composed by the Tendai master Chūjin (1065–1138 CE) but actually first appeared after his death.[31] As described by this text, all living things, including humans, animals, and plants, are dual in composition, possessing both a heart and a mind. Existents differ, however, in how they manifest these features. With humans, mind exists in the foreground and heart remains in the background. But in the *Kankō ruijū*, with plants this situation is reversed because plant hearts occupy the foreground.[32] With plants' minds in the background, they appear to be insentient to humans, but in fact they are sentient. And because they are sentient in the *Kankō ruijū*, plants can become Buddhas. In fact, in the *Kankō ruijū*, plants already express their Buddhahood. In a notably nonanthropocentric turn, the *Kankō ruijū* cautions us not to expect plants to show their Buddhahood as humans do. Instead, plants exhibit their manifest Buddhahood through their "roots, stem or trunk, branches, and leaves."[33] Nevertheless, reflecting the tension between spiritual respect for plants and the need to eat them that arose in the chapter on China as well as the Japanese tension between respect and exploitation of nature, the *Kankō ruijū* does not explicitly oppose killing plants, even if they are manifest Buddhas.[34]

The Japanese Buddhists' teachings on plants I have mentioned are notable in the ways they extend some form of respectful personhood to flora, making Buddhist personhood regard for plants a distinctive feature of Japanese Buddhism which retains the potential to inspire greater biospheric sustainability. Further, as brief as their expositions are, Ryōgen's voice is perhaps the most advanced in terms of describing what a Buddhist path for plants might look like, and the perspective of the *Kankō ruijū* likely supplies the best portrait of how the ends of plants' spiritual paths might appear. However, given that their voices are both a millennium old and undeveloped, Buddhism may be overdue for a substantial reevaluation of its attitudes toward flora.

Such a reevaluation should note that plant-respectful voices like that of the *Kankō ruijū* have never existed in Japan without contention. Just within the Tendai school of Annen, Ryōgen, and the *Kankō ruijū*, a later monk, Shōshin (1136–1220 CE), rolled the conversation regarding plants back somewhat. In a conservatism that was unsympathetic to ideas which made Buddhism too easy, Shōshin politely considered the previous Tendai discussion of plant enlightenment to be nonsense. He argued that no scripture asserted the Buddhahood of plants.[35] Moreover, it was clear to Shōshin that plants phenomenally have no mind and no sentience, and therefore they cannot have religious agency, nor can they become Buddhas by other means. Although Shōshin was criticized by some of his Tendai colleagues for lacking the proper spirit of universalism, Shōshin's rejection of sentience, Buddha-hood, or religious agency for plants has been shared, for various reasons, by many other Japanese Buddhists. Regard for flora as insentient and nonagen-tive remains a common Japanese attitude toward plants.[36]

Kūkai and Plants

Up to this point, I have refrained from mentioning the contribution to the discussion on plant sentience from the Shingon sect and its founder, Kūkai (774–835 CE), who was one of the first Japanese Buddhists to clearly assert the Buddhahood of plants as well as their religious agency through the phrase *mokuseki busshō*, "the Buddha-nature of trees and rocks."[37] Known also as Kōbō Daishi, Kūkai was a monumental figure in Japanese Buddhist history for the way he systematized the Buddhism at his disposal to pro-duce a uniquely new approach to liberation. Important for our purposes, this innovative approach included a healthy dose of nature-friendly elements, and some of these elements continue to thrive in today's world. Indeed, although sustainability in Japanese religions is often attributed solely to the influences of kami-based spirituality, Kūkai, though a sympathizer with kami-based religion, provides a fully Buddhist environment-respecting voice within Japanese culture. Kūkai single-handedly renders simplistic Shintō/Buddhism ecofriendly dualisms obsolete with his teachings not just regard-ing the spirituality of plants but also those regarding celestial bodies, moun-tains, and other nonhuman forms.

Concerning plants, Kūkai begins his exposition by appealing to the Mahāyāna philosophical model of the Three Bodies (*trikāya*). In the Three Body perspective, the universe appears, depending on one's point of view, simultaneously as *nirmāṇakāya*, or a physical form body; as *dharmakāya*, which is ultimate reality, or nirvana; or as *sambhoghakāya*, a view of real-ity that straddles and mediates these other two worlds of material form and formless ultimate reality. Uniquely, Kūkai describes how the void of the dharmakāya manifests the other two bodies from itself and refers to the dharmakāya as Dainichi Nyorai, or "Great Sun Buddha," the major Mahāyāna deity Vairocana. Dainichi's solar nature aids the integration between Buddhism and kami-based religion since his image merges with that of Japan's great sun kami, Amaterasu.[38] In Kūkai's thought, Dainichi is ultimate reality and physical reality is Dainichi's self-expression. To some, this may sound like the creativity of a monotheistic god, but Kūkai describes the universe and its emergence by referring to the Buddhist concept of dependent arising (Sanskrit: *pratītya-samutpāda*) and the interactions of the six great elements: earth, water, fire, air, space, and mind. The first five elements provide tangibility to the universe, while the sixth supplies an ever-present enlightened mind to all things. Thus, for Kūkai, the entire universe arises inseparably from mind and from Dainichi, so that everything participates in enlightenment. Nothing is inanimate and nothing is insentient because all existents live and express the Dharma as extensions of Dainichi.

Following this route, Kūkai collapses the distinctions of animate-inanimate and sentient-insentient; without these distinctions, for Kūkai, nothing bars plants from enlightenment. Therefore, he teaches that each plant, which is inseparable from Dainichi, has its own consciousness and its own spiritual agency. In fact, he averred, "Plants and trees are the *dharmakāya*."[39] In his *Unjigi* he wrote,

Waves do not exist apart from water;
Within the mind are the objects of mind.
If plants and trees were devoid of Buddhahood,
Waves then would be without humidity.[40]

In this way, for Kūkai, plants can navigate their own ways to nirvana, although he does not tell us how. Nevertheless, for him, because Dainichi teaches constantly and universally at the nirmāṇakāya level of form, plants not only are enlightened mind, they preach the Buddhist religion constantly, as do mountains, bodies of water, stones, foxes, and all the other beings found in the nonhuman world. Because of this fascinating doctrine of *hosshin seppō*, the preaching of the natural world, in Kūkai's thought the environment of humans becomes a scripture to be read and studied like a written tome: "Being painted by brushes of mountains, by ink of oceans, / Heaven and earth are the bindings of a *sūtra* [scriptural text] revealing the truth."[41] However, in this perspective the reading of nature requires spiritual intuition, developed through practice, because it is not done in a human language. Later in this chapter, the Zen master Dōgen will make a similar claim about nature's preaching Buddhist teachings, so that Japanese leaders like Kūkai and Dōgen have carved a unique place for Japanese Buddhism through their doctrines that Buddhist scriptures are not found just in monastery libraries, they surround us in the natural world at all times.

Vajrayāna Nature Mysticism

In Kūkai's Shingon thought, all symbols are dual in function since they not only signify something else but they also nondually participate in what they signify. In this way, the Sanskrit syllable A not only symbolizes Dainichi, in a sense it *is* him, so that meditation on the A syllable forms an important aspect of Shingon practice. Most intriguingly, through the influence of the esoteric Buddhist text *Bodaishinron* (*Bodhicitta-śāstra*), Kūkai allied meditation on the A syllable with an earlier Japanese meditation on the disk of the moon, the moon being thought to be at once inseparable from nirvana, the syllable A, and the meditator's mind.[42] Kūkai wrote that defilements obscure our Buddhahood like clouds block out the bright moon, so that the moon in Shingon represents an important symbol for the enlightened mind, thus provoking a meditation practice that is centered on our moon.[43]

In Kūkai's moon meditation practice, which can take from ten minutes to one hour, you visualize a golden Sanskrit A syllable resting on the white disk of the moon, with the moon's disk sitting on a white lotus flower with eight petals.[44] For beginners, it may take some time to stabilize this visualization. Once the image is stable, however, practitioners are encouraged to expand the moon in their visualizations, ideally contemplatively filling the entire universe with the lunar dharmakāya luminescence of both figurative and literal enlightenment. Throughout the meditation, however, the practitioner must be sure not to view the A syllable, the moon, or the practitioner's mind as separate. In this practice, the moon is the mind and vice versa, so that in knowing the moon, you know your mind, eventuating in Buddhahood.[45] Therefore, this meditation that encourages experiential nonduality between the practitioner and the moon appears to offer an example of distinctively Buddhist nature mysticism. It seems to fit the definition of a powerful altered state of consciousness experience of human nonduality specifically with a nonhuman natural entity within a physical human habitat that I mentioned in the introduction to this book.

But this moon meditation is not the only nature mystical aroma to arise from relatively nature-friendly Shingon Buddhism, given that Shingon also contains a fascinating Morning Star meditation on the planet Venus. It can be argued, in fact, that it was the Morning Star meditation that gave rise to Japanese Shingon in the first place. As a young man in college, Kūkai mingled with members of the small Natural Wisdom school (*Jinen chishū*), which was headquartered at the Hisosanji temple in Yoshino. Natural Wisdom Buddhists soured on what they felt was the overly formalized Buddhism of the capital, so they sought to practice in mountain retreats from which they could emphasize experience more than study. One of their primary practices involved meditation on Venus in conjunction with the recitation of mantras for the great bodhisattva Kokūzō (Sanskrit: Ākāśagarbha), who in Kūkai's later Six Element system presided over the element of space.[46] Kūkai tried this Morning Star practice and it changed his life. As he described it, "From that time on, I despised fame and wealth and longed for a life in the midst of nature."[47] Dissatisfied with his training options in Japan, he left to study in China, where eventually the Chenyen Tantric master Huiguo named Kūkai his successor, thereby initiating Kūkai's career as a Buddhist teacher.

As Shingon Buddhists portray it, the Morning Star meditation is much more rigorous and taxing than is the brief moon meditation that I just described. Following principles of Vajrayāna deity yoga, the goal is to realize your sameness with an enlightened being, in this case the bodhisattva Kokūzō, who is not separate from the planet Venus. Unlike many other meditation halls, the hall for Morning Star meditation must be isolated and somewhat open to the sky, so that the meditator can see Venus directly. The practice requires between fifty and one hundred days of repetition. The closing ritual must be done during a lunar or solar eclipse, so the beginning of the schedule is figured by counting backward from the anticipated eclipse event. During the ritual period, the practitioner chants the mantra for Kokūzō one million times as counted on a rosary made of *kaya* or oak tree wood. Once started, the practice should not be stopped even for illness. Again and again, one venerates the morning star and repeats the mantra throughout the day, all the while focusing on the nonduality of oneself, Venus, and the spaciousness of the enlightened bodhisattva Kokūzō. As such, one should not be surprised that this practice generates experiences that appear to be nature mystical in character. Taikō Yamasaki offers us an account of such a nature mystical experience arising from Morning Star meditation:

> Coming out of meditation and leaving the practice hall, the sense of the vastness of the universe would remain, as though I were seeing the world for the first time. The trees were no longer separate from myself, but seemed a part of me, as if we were a single being.
>
> This sense of unity with all things remained in my mind even after the practice ended and I returned to the world. A profound feeling of gratitude and a new appreciation for life came to affect everything I did.[48]

The gratitude and appreciation gained from Yamasaki's contemplation might point to the emotional content of this meditation, meaning that, at least as done by Yamasaki, this Morning Star routine seems to fit this book's definition of nature mysticism. The practitioner seeks an unusual nondual experience specifically with a natural being in the phenomenal human habitat, and this appears to include an uncommon affective component. Thus, this Shingon practice, and perhaps the practice of moon meditation as well, appears to express authentic Buddhist nature mysticism. These practices are not just Buddhist, of course, because, over time, folk Indian, Chinese, and kami-worshipping traditions have had a hand in shaping them. But, in the case of Yamasaki and presumably many others, Buddhists self-consciously pursue the Morning Star meditation by chanting Buddhist words and engaging in Buddhist meditation to meet the Buddhist end of liberation. Detractors of Vajrayāna forms of Buddhism may not approve of this approach, but it is difficult to say that this nature mysticism is not at least partly Buddhist.

While Kūkai undoubtedly taught a form of Buddhism with nature-friendly facets, one learns significantly more about Buddhism if one also attends to the limits of Kūkai's sustainable practices. Although he lived for a long time in Kyoto, the capital city at that time, Kūkai grew up in a rural environment and always preferred rustic settings, even after he became a highly regarded Buddhist leader. He taught, in fact, that "discipline in the woods alone lets us soon enter the eternal realm."[49] Following this philosophy, he built his headquarters monastery on Mt. Kōya, which at the time was in the middle of a remote, densely forested wilderness. In building the isolated monastery, the toll on human workers would have been extreme, but the environment bore an altogether different burden. The mountaintop was largely deforested, ground was leveled, and streams were diverted in order to create the monastery's campus. Stones had to be moved or broken. The building and its furnishings demanded a great deal of wood, thus requiring the felling of many trees, which were also cut down, in part, to make the wood-bead rosaries that were necessary for Vajrayāna practice. Other trees perished to print scriptures.

All of this, of course, is just part of the story of building a Buddhist monastery anywhere. Like many Buddhists before and since, Kūkai felt that to establish the authentic tradition, one needed a monastery, and where there is a monastery, pine trees, badgers, and other natural beings must give way, at least to some extent. Institutional Buddhism may embrace nature in theory but, as with all human endeavors, must utilize nature in some form in practice, especially when it comes to creating monasteries and other religious buildings.

Shugendō Nature Mysticism

The practices of the moon meditation and the Morning Star meditation in Shingon are thought to aid progress toward Buddhahood, which is achieved as well through practice involving Vajrayāna mandalas. Mandalas, in an ordinary sense, are used in meditation as two-dimensional sacred art objects that depict three-dimensional enlightened worlds. In Shingon, practitioners do not simply look at mandalas, they enter them meditationally, so that they may realize their nonduality with nirvana. While there are myriad mandalas in the Buddhist world, Shingon focuses its attention especially on two. The first is the *Taizōkai* or Matrix mandala (Sanskrit: *Garbhakośadhātu maṇḍala*), which represents the five most tangible of the Six Elements, or the enlightened universe understood from the standpoint of compassion.[50] The second mandala, inseparable from the first, is the *Kongōkai* or Diamond mandala (Sanskrit: *Vajradhātu maṇḍala*), which represents the element of mind, or the enlightened universe from the standpoint of wisdom.[51] Practitioners explore each mandala individually in detail, but ultimately Shingon teachings stress meditation on the inseparability of the mandalas, with their union symbolizing many things, such as the marriage of wisdom and compassion, the inseparability of nirvana and samsara, and the nonduality of matter and mind.

As noted, early in life Kūkai was acquainted with members of the Natural Wisdom sect, who blended esoteric Buddhist teachings, pursuit of Daoist immortality and magic, and kami veneration. Its members fled the formality and restrictions of Buddhism in the capital, preferring instead to practice in the rustic mountain wildernesses, at that time, of the Yoshino peaks, which were lionized in the early Japanese poetry collection *Manyōshū*. Influenced by them, Chinese precedents, and the preaching of the Buddha from mountains like Vulture Peak in many sūtras, Kūkai placed the headquarters for his Shingon sect, which specializes in esoteric teachings, on remote Mount Kōya. Also extending respect for mountain settings, the founder of the Tendai sect Saichō, who was a colleague of both Kūkai and Natural Wisdom members, located the headquarters for his school, which also includes esoteric teachings, on Mount Hiei. But enthusiasm for mountain practice meant that soon Shingon and Tendai monks left even these peaks to practice in solitude in their own isolated mountain huts and caves.[52] Their Buddhism led them to reside on mountaintops, rather than avoiding summits as the land of the gods following the taboos of pre-Buddhist religion.[53] This movement then helped give rise to the distinctive Japanese quasi-Buddhist practice of Shugendō, the "way of supernatural power," with its practitioners called *yamabushi*, "those who rest in the mountains," or *shugenja*, "those who obtain supernatural powers."

The example of the legendary hermit En no Gyōja, about whom little hard historical fact can be produced, provided a template for these Shugendō seekers. Apparently exiled from the capital in 699 CE for teaching Buddhism to the masses, which was forbidden at the time, En no Gyōja appeared to combine Daoist teachings on longevity, Japanese shamanic lore, chanting, and ascetic practices called *gyō*, resulting in noteworthy supernatural power. According to his legend, the acquisition of such power begins with the repetitive chanting of spells and spiritually powerful words. The words to be chanted, as taken up by Shugendō practitioners, come from a variety of sources. One may recite the name of a holy mountain, a kami, a Buddha, or a bodhisattva; the Buddhist mantras of various deities; or Buddhist scriptures. Common chants include the entirety of the short *Hannya shingyō*, or *Heart Sūtra*; the mantra of Fudō Myōō, a fierce protector deity who commonly stands guard in statue form at the entrances to Japanese Buddhist temples and is associated with fire and serpents; or perhaps the most powerful of all, the last line of the *Heart Sūtra* in Japanese style: "Gyate haragyate harasogyate bochi sowaka hannya shingyō."[54]

The words on their own are useless, however, unless one generates inner power through asceticism that can infuse one's words with charisma. These ascetic practices include fasting and cold water purifications. The fasting, as taken up by many Shugendō practitioners, includes refraining from meat, which is likely a Buddhist influence, and grains, which appears to reflect the influence of Daoist fangshi immortality seekers. Instead, Shugendō practitioners may be "tree eaters," subsisting merely on nuts, berries, bark, and pine needles.[55]

But it is not just fasting that empowers Shugendō chanting since cold water purifications (*suigyō*) do so as well, and Shugendō perhaps is most famous for these. While a cup of cold water poured over one's head can be purificatory, real Shugendō adepts do not stop there; instead, they seek purification by standing under a waterfall. The water should be as cold as possible, so ideally the purifying is done in the middle of winter and between the hours of two and three in the morning. As they stand in pools of water barely above freezing temperature while frigid fluid pounds their heads and cascades down their bodies, seekers recite the *Heart Sūtra*, or some other formula, at least one hundred times. Some will visualize the waterfall as the Buddha or as Fudō Myōō, rendering the waterfall as a respected holy person.

Kūkai added to such practices by describing the landscape as a realized mandala, so that instead of being a realm of suffering, the environment should be understood as the realm of enlightenment.[56] From this thinking, the two main esoteric Buddhist mandalas became superimposed on sites that were already being used for sacred retreats. Mount Kimpu (also known as Mitake) in Yoshino became so closely identified with the *Kongōkai* mandala that it was thought that the mountain *was* the mandala, and in traversing the mountain, one voyaged through the stages of Buddhist consciousness.[57]

Shugendō practitioners extended a similar understanding to the highlands of Kumano in the southern Kii peninsula as the incarnated *Taizōkai* mandala, with the same comprehension accruing that meditatively to traverse and climb a mountain was the same as entering states of consciousness as portrayed within the respective mandala. By physically climbing both mountains, the yamabushi completed identification with both mandalas in a highly embodied way, just as esoteric Buddhist teachings requested. Later Mount Ōmine, which stands between Kimpu and Kumano, was added as a third element that explicitly united both mandalas, this joining representing an esoteric Buddhist experiential goal.[58] Further, other places throughout Japan became mandalized, such as the Dewa area in northwestern Honshu, the eighty-eight Holy Places of the island of Shikoku, and the mountains of Hiko, Hōman, and Fukuchi along with the Kunisaki peninsula in Kyushu.[59]

Of course, meditational art works did not map neatly to the terrain, so various rocks, trees, waterfalls, and so on were taken to be symbolic of different elements of the mandala. Ascent of the mountains was thought to occur in ten stages, reflecting the ten levels of the enlightened mind: the six realms of rebirth from hell to god, followed by *śrāvaka*, *pratyekabuddha*, bodhisattva, and fully realized Buddha levels, leaving the mountain summit, which must be reached, to symbolize the realization of nirvana. Through this mandalization of the landscape, the earth became Buddhicized, mountaintops lost the ancient taboo against visiting them, and yamabushis thereby undertook otherworldly journeys by using this-worldly mountains as support.

For about a millennium, Shugendō practitioners, "a cornerstone of Japanese culture," roamed holy mountains throughout Japan, becoming a "ubiquitous" element in the religious life of the country.[60] Many laypeople made pilgrimages to the holy mountain mystics to seek their wisdom or simply to absorb their imposing presences. The magical power that developed from Shugendō practices at times was used for rainmaking rituals, for instance, and yamabushis became assimilated in the popular mind with the mountain kamis of old who brought water and fertility.[61]

Whether these yamabushis practiced Buddhism or not, though, remains somewhat debatable. On the one hand, the impetus for the movement, as well as many of its practices and practitioners, come from the Buddhist fold, and some yamabushis would be quite offended to be told that they are not Buddhists. Further, Buddhist temples are typically the empowered overseers of Shugendō peaks. On the other hand, Shugendō has blended a mix of voices from the beginning, and some of its practices and practitioners evidence few Buddhist roots or elements. Moreover, as the name of the movement, the "Way of Supernatural Powers," implies, many of its practitioners have pursued the this-worldly goal of magical power rather than the more sublime Buddhist goal of nirvana.

But whether this is a Buddhist movement or not, it has left its traces on Japanese culture, history, and politics because over time the yamabushis came to view virtually every place in the islands, which consist of 74 percent mountainous territory, as part of a holy mandala. Then they passed on these teachings as they roamed. Eventually, these notions of Japan as a sacred mandala came to fuel concepts of Japan as a special place, and later ripened into sometimes militant nationalism.[62]

In fact, a paradox of the Shugendō story begins with its banning as a superstition by a government modernization drive in 1872. Shugendō consisted of a great deal of oral teachings, and the government ban caused the loss of a number of them.[63] Therefore, when the idea of Japan as a special place perhaps reached a crescendo in the first half of the twentieth century, one of its instigators, Shugendō, had been diminished. Nonetheless, Shugendō retreats continue today as there has been a resurrection of these practices since the 1950s. But the present-day situation does not reflect well the heyday of Shugendō, when Japan was populated with quasi-Buddhist nature mystics who sought spiritual power in nature.

Dōgen

Buddhist practice in the mountains also informed the renowned teacher Dōgen Kigen (1200–1253 CE), the originator of the Sōtō school of Japanese Zen Buddhism, although his perspective on mountain spirits led him to understand human relationships with nonhumans differently than Shugendō adepts do. Dōgen's inventively ecocentric Buddhist teachings regarding Buddhism and the natural world have been significantly influential internationally, especially since the nineteenth century, and he has served as an inspiration for the Deep Ecology of Arne Naess. If we are to understand Japanese religious relationships with nonhumans, we therefore need to probe Dōgen's perspectives along with those of Shugendō.

Like Kūkai, but living four hundred years later, Dōgen was influenced by the Daoist text *Zhuangzi* and its claims that the sacred persists in all things.[64] As part of the Tendai school as a young monk, Dōgen was also exposed to Kūkai's meditations on the moon and Venus, and these themes appear in his writing. Finally, and most centrally, both Kūkai and Dōgen taught that the nonhuman natural world preaches the Buddhist Dharma constantly. But Dōgen was more influenced than Kūkai by the Mahāyāna *Diamond Sūtra*, which may radically be read to collapse not just notions of species but also discriminations between what is animate and what is inanimate.[65] Because of his reading of the *Diamond Sūtra*, for Dōgen, the Buddha, his teachings, his enlightenment, and all natural forms exist nondually, so that ponds and hills can preach because they participate in enlightenment every bit as much as humans. As such, Dōgen's insistent nondualism births some rather startling insights and teachings regarding humans and nature, especially his doctrine of *mujō seppō*, which asserts that everything, including so-called insentient existents, teach religion.

Born in Kyoto, Dōgen lost both of his parents as a child and was adopted within the powerful Minamoto clan. Perhaps having his parents die taught him early lessons in impermanence because at the young age of thirteen he chose be ordained as a Tendai monk. Chan Buddhist teachings from China were just starting to enter Japan as an accessory practice within the Tendai school, leaving Dōgen without a choice of a qualified master if he wanted to enter those teachings. His own teacher, Myōzen, felt the same lack, so in 1223 the two departed to seek a qualified teacher in China, with Dōgen staying there until 1227. During his stay Myōzen died, but at the Tiantong monastery, Dōgen found his true teacher, the strict Chan master Rujing, who taught Dōgen to meditate "as intensely as you would extinguish a fire in your hair."[66] Impressed by Dōgen's fortitude, Rujing made him a Dharma heir, sending him back to Japan to establish Zen (the Japanese counterpart of the Chinese Chan school) there.

Some of Rujing's instructions have stuck with the Sōtō Zen school that Dōgen thereafter created. Following the *Fanwangjing* regulations that we have already examined from China, Rujing taught the strict avoidance of meat.[67] In fact, Rujing forbade Dōgen even to see a slaughterhouse or view herds of pigs or sheep.[68] For Rujing, pets should not be kept by monastics, one should not meditate where the wind blows, and one must live remotely, in a place with "steep mountains and dark valleys."[69] While this last injunction of Rujing's has not always been practical, it remains a Zen ideal for some and, over time, motivated some of the urban rock gardens that appear in Zen temples since the stones in these dry gardens may be explicitly understood as stand-ins for mountains.[70]

Deriving from this training, the originality of Dōgen's insights shines through in his psychologization of the realms of rebirth as states of mind, rather than literal places, somewhat like Buddhadāsa in Thailand did. For Dōgen, there is no objective natural world that is given the same to all beings because all beings experience things according to their natures. Within *Treasury of the True Dharma Eye*,[71] Dōgen wrote, "It seems that there is water for various beings but there is no original water—there is no water common to all types of beings" (159). While humans experience water as flowing, a hungry ghost experiences it as fire, and a fish experiences water as a palace (159). Fish, in fact, would be quite astonished to hear that water flows since for Dōgen this is not their experience (161). Thus, in a remarkably anti-anthropocentric turn, Dōgen warns that the human manner of perceiving the natural world is only one of many ways to perceive nature and certainly not the final and authoritative way. Irreverently in terms of Japanese traditions, he tells us that mountains are not really the abodes of kamis; this belief is just an ordinary human perception (163). Further, he informs us that the distinction between sentience and insentience is another commonplace human delusion, not an objective description of reality. In sermon after sermon, he attacks the division between sentience and insentience proposed by the *Nirvāṇa Sūtra*, using against the scripture its own examples of grass, walls, tiles, and pebbles as supposedly insentient. He says, "Water is seen as dead or alive depending on the seer's causes and conditions," so that "to regard grass and trees as insentient beings is not thoroughgoing" (550). Therefore, for Dōgen, mountains walk, but it is not like human walking, and only those with more enlightened understanding can witness the phenomenon (154–55).

Taking his nondualism one step further, Dōgen teaches that all things interpenetrate, including the worlds of humans, rocks, and rabbits. Stones even may have genders (156). Because of this interpenetration, everything is sacralized by the presence of Buddhas. Dōgen writes, "Even in a drop of water innumerable Buddha lands appear" (160). Therefore, "it is not only that there is water in the world, but there is a world in water. It is not merely in water. There is a world of sentient beings in clouds. There is a world of sentient beings in the air. There is a world of sentient beings in fire. There is a world of sentient beings on earth. . . . There is a world of sentient beings in a blade of grass. . . . Wherever there is a world of sentient beings, there is a world of Buddha ancestors" (164).

Because of this universal interpenetration of Buddhas, in Dōgen's view natural entities already are enlightened, just as they are. In truth, they could not exist otherwise since to consider this to be so invites dualism as far as he is concerned. It is important to note that, for him, this Buddhahood of the natural world does not appear to be a metaphor or simile; it is not the case that Dōgen's nature is merely like a Buddha. Although Dōgen's literary imagery is rich, dense, and sometimes stunning, he does not intend this teaching as the whimsy of a poet, using words about natural beings to make a human point. Instead, Dōgen's natural world literally is enlightened. Mountains are "Buddha ancestors" and have "practice realization" (156–57). Moreover,

"Buddha ancestors always take up water and make it their body and mind, make it their thought" (161). Water models enlightenment itself because water always is what it is and is nothing else: "Because water practices and realizes water, water expresses water. . . . Water is just the true thusness of water" (158, 164). Therefore, like Kūkai taught that nature is a scripture to read, so did Dōgen because the religion is "carved on trees and rocks," but of course not carved by human hands (162). Dōgen asked, "What place in mountains and oceans is not Buddha scripture?" (600).

For Dōgen, by reading the scripture of nature, one becomes enlightened since "mountains and waters of themselves become wise persons and sages" (164). He implores, "Look to trees and rocks, fields and villages, to expound dharma" (73). A revised version of the story of the fox and Indra that ended chapter 5 is proof, for him, that animals teach, as does everything in the universe.[72] Because "the moment of enlightenment emerges through mountains and waters," Dōgen assures us that "when you have true practice, then valley sounds and colors, mountain colors and sounds, all reveal the eighty-four thousand verses," meaning that mountains, valleys, and all others in nature appear as preaching Buddhist persons (94).

Of course, as with Kūkai's thought, for Dōgen, taking teachings from nature defies some expectations since the teaching of nature is not audible. For example, in one of the Japanese Buddhist poet Bashō's most noted haikus, a frog jumps into water and makes a splashing sound—for Dōgen, this sound is not the teaching of nature. Dōgen relates, "Foolish people may think that the sound of trees, or the opening and falling of leaves and flowers, is insentient beings speaking dharma. Such people are not studying the Buddha dharma" (550). Instead, for Dōgen, the preaching of nature is not available to ordinary senses, but only to deep consciousness, which is why common people do not "hear" it but sages do since sages enigmatically know how to hear the teachings "with the eye" (551, 555). In order to hear it, Dōgen advises listening with one's body first and the mind last and listening from the place "before your parents were born" (553). Dōgen tells us that we can take teachings from nature by "dropping body and mind" (shinjin datsuraku), a phrase that, for him, encapsulates the Buddhist teachings and, understood experientially, is synonymous with nirvana. Thus, in order to learn Dharma from nature, Dōgen says, "With the entire body and mind, study the realm where the ear, nose, and eye are neither old nor new. This is how blossoms and rain open up the world" (536).

Obviously, there is an ecocentric horizon to Dōgen's teachings. After all, "The body and mind of the Buddha way is grass, trees, tiles, and pebbles, as well as wind, rain, water, and fire" (650). But there are limits to biospheric sustainability in Dōgen's thought, and recognizing these limits instructs that a multitude of attitudes toward nature may coexist, not just within Buddhism but even in the person of one Buddhist. Despite the way that he is often portrayed, for instance, Dōgen was not sentimentalist or romantic about the natural world, preferring a matter-of-fact approach that views nature as it is, not as one wants it to be or how one wants it to look in a lovely landscape painting. He wrote, "Mountains, rivers, and earth mind are just mountains, rivers, and the earth. There are no extra waves or sprays in this mind. The sun, moon, and stars mind is just the sun, moon, and stars, there is no extra fog or mist" (46).

Moreover, sometimes a conservative despite his extreme psychologizing language, Dōgen clearly presents the classic Buddhist notion of the animal, hungry ghost, and hell realms as lower rebirths (7). Opposed to chanting by itself as a Buddhist practice, Dōgen unflatteringly describes chanters as frogs (8). Further, bad monks are dogs and those with mistaken views are worse than "beasts," a comparison not meant to compliment animals (683, 684). In these ways, along with his more sustainable attitudes, like many humans in history Dōgen demeaned animals by symbolically painting them with a critical brush that was intended for humans.

His thought faces other environmentalist limitations. Sometimes he is championed as the sustainable thinker who will lead us out of our current environmental quagmires, but it is important to recognize that his understanding of nature as a holy Buddha does not resolve some ecological difficulties. If we follow Dōgen by deciding that a mountain chain is a Buddha and so protect it with a large park, this could have a positive ecological effect. But the unbelievable pollution in the Ganges River as it flows through the holy Indian city of Varanasi, plus many other examples that appear in this book, should be enough to show that designating nonhuman things as sacred is not enough to protect them despite a commonly found belief.

Further, if we reverence every last thing in nature as a Buddha like Dōgen does and hence move to protect it, this means that we must protect everything, including problematic things like oil spills or the anthrax bacterium. Humans need a useful environmental ethic that provides the tools to decide which natural phenomena need protecting and which need removal. But because it values everything as a Buddha, Dōgen's theory of the Buddhahood of everything does not help us make these tough and often confusing choices, other than choosing what is best for humans alone, and thus does not take us all the way to a fully sustainable form of Buddhism. Although employing the doctrine of dependent arising like Dōgen does can help level senses of human ascendance over nature, just like we saw with the Thai

Buddhist environmentalists Phrakhru Manas Nathiphitak and Buddhadāsa, it cannot in itself enable value-laden ecological choices.

Japanese Buddhists and Their Environments

Dōgen's ecocentrism brings us to a point from which we can understand long-term trends in Japanese Buddhist relationships with nature. As this chapter has shown, within a Japanese cultural tension between respect for and exploitation of nature, the respectful personhood interactions that mark relational animism appear to bloom in the universe of Japanese Buddhism. In so-called inanimate realms, the moon, sun, and Venus receive regard as holy persons, being inseparable from divine persons within the Buddhist pantheon. Even waterfalls, understood as the embodiment of the Buddha or the deity Fudō Myōō by Shugendō practitioners, garner personhood respect. Moreover, and uncommonly within the Buddhist world, for Annen, Ryōgen, Kūkai, and the *Kankō ruijū*, personhood is extended to plants in such respectful ways that plants manifest as Buddhas, creating animist relationships in which even flora practice religion. The writings of Dōgen vibrantly express this personhood respect since, for him, every existent is a Buddha-person. Additionally, Dōgen's thought, along with Kūkai's, demonstrates a unique outcome of this personhood respect: the doctrines of hosshin seppō or mujō seppō, in which all of nature can be read as a self-reciting Buddhist scripture. Here, all of nature practices religion much like a human Buddhist preacher. As in other parts of the Buddhist world, Japanese natural beings can sometimes practice Buddhism, with these Japanese examples offering some quite interesting ecocentric features. Moreover, the idea that nature teaches important religious truths can lead to more biospherically sustainable attitudes.

In terms of diet, as this chapter demonstrates, vegetarian attitudes are complex in Japan. From one point of view, it may fairly be argued that the Japanese are more spontaneously vegetarian than some other peoples, as the historical lack of a land animal husbandry tradition indicates. Moreover, imported from China, the *Fanwangjing* can enforce vegetarianism in Japanese Buddhist monastic worlds; this effect can be so great that Dōgen was forbidden by his teacher even to look at pigs. At the same time, general Japanese diets do not appear to have ever been completely animal-free, especially when one considers the sea as a human food source, and once Western terrestrial meat-eating practices became available, the Japanese quickly adopted them. One therefore could also argue that the Japanese have never really been vegetarian. Perhaps this vegetarian tension emerges most clearly in Shugendō, which has counseled fasting from meat as a spiritual regimen yet has also condoned hunting as a Buddhist practice, leaving us with an unclear sense of its biospheric sustainability.

Regarding contemplative experiences in nature, reflecting the Japanese cultural purification of natural processes that Grapard described, the nature mysticism that appears in Japanese Buddhist worlds may represent the most robust examples of nature mysticism in this book. Shingon counsels nondual meditation on the moon, the meditator, and nirvana as inseparable, sparking a broad Japanese spiritual appreciation for the moon. Likewise, Shingon sponsors the Morning Star meditation, in which the practitioner seeks a nondual state where Venus, the practitioner, and liberation are experienced as not plural. Additionally, the nature mysticism in Shugendō seems especially rich, because Shugendō may involve these meditations on the moon or Venus while it also encourages deep contemplative states, gained from an immersion in uninhabited places, in which enlightened mandalas from the Mahāyāna scriptures, mountains, and Buddhists themselves experientially arise as inseparable and nondual. While the roots of this nature mysticism reflect diverse sources, these practices have often been understood as Buddhist and pursued to reach the Buddhist goal of enlightenment and, thus, in at least some measure, may be considered to be Buddhist.

This chapter has revealed intimate sacred relationships with animals like wolves but perhaps without the same valence as the funeral request of the pious Buddhist monarch of nineteenth-century Cambodia, Ang Duang. While on his deathbed, out of compassion Ang Duang ordered that his body be fed to animals immediately after his demise. With attendants using swords that had been blessed with water consecrated by Buddhist monks, Ang Duang's chopped-up body, served on golden platters, thereby provided food for birds of prey.[73] But it is not just in Cambodia that one finds such funeral practices; offerings of one's corpse to animals is attested to from across the Buddhist world. However, no place is more famous for this practice than Tibet, as we will see in the next chapter.

CHAPTER 7

Releasing Animals in Tibet

In his memoir *Tibet Is My Country*, Taktser Rinpoché, a revered Tibetan Buddhist teacher in his own right as well as the eldest brother of the Fourteenth Dalai Lama, offers a unique window into rural life in the northeastern Tibetan region of Amdo in the 1930s and 1940s.[1] In narrating stories from his childhood, Taktser Rinpoché relates that his family farm rested in the sight of Kyiri, the snow-covered Happiness Mountain, where the deity of happiness Kyi maintained residence.[2] As the *yül lha* or local god of the territory, Kyi controlled everything that happened within his reach, engendering prosperity or adversity as he saw fit. The deity Kyi's alpine throne, Happiness Mountain, consisted of a magnificently soaring snow peak under which Taktser Rinpoché's childhood unfolded. Because of the felt intimacy with the mountain engendered by this childhood relationship, Taktser Rinpoché describes Kyi, who iconographically appears as a horseman with a pointed black beard, as a beloved holy person to whom he directed his youthful prayers, and Kyi's "majestic glacier" mountain seat as "the symbol of a full life" (51–52).

In order to show their devotion to the montane spirit, residents of Taktser Rinpoché's village would frequently burn juniper sticks, the smoke from which is adored by Tibetan mountain gods, in a fire at Kyi's temple in the hamlet, thus creating an incense offering. At other times, they would place more stones on Kyi's *la tsé*, or rock cairn, for which Buddhist monks led annual rituals (53).[3] Each summer, the denizens of the thirty cottages in the village would make a weeklong pilgrimage to Happiness Mountain, where adults would offer more incense at the peak's snow line while the young stayed at the base and played, as Taktser Rinpoché describes it, in the ecologically marred remains of gold mining (53).

Figure 8.   A Tibetan woman offers juniper sticks in a large communal incense burner. Jokhang Temple, Lhasa, Tibet.

Farmers in Taktser Rinpoché's village typically grew oats, wheat, or the Tibetan staple of barley. Taktser Rinpoché's family kept a pet cat named Zhimi, a temporary pet musk deer, and a dog, Khyimo, who, being "powerful and rather savage," stayed tethered to a chain throughout the day (48). For food and wool, Taktser Rinpoché's family raised pigs, chickens, and sheep (47). Sheep were sheared for their wool in early summer and slaughtered in the autumn, although fresh mutton was eaten at other times due to "emergency slaughtering," a seeming reference to euthanasia (27, 47). Matter-of-fact about sheep carcasses' hanging in the family barn, Taktser Rinpoché shares that he relished the mutton dishes cooked by his mother Dékyi Tséring since eating meat is standard in the Tibetan Buddhist world, the focus of this chapter (27).

One can save one's own livestock and still eat meat if one hunts, so Taktser Rinpoché tells us that "hunting played quite a role in our lives" (55). His father enjoyed such proficiency in hunting with a sling, in fact, that he refused to use a gun. Members of his village would hunt for wild sheep, deer, lynxes, foxes, and wolves. Unlike the perceived good wolves of the traditional Japanese, Tibetans, more enthusiastic about pastoralism, have long regarded wolves as their enemies, given wolves' depredations of livestock.[4] Because of negative attitudes toward wolves, killing them was often celebrated, and Taktser Rinpoché writes, "Whoever managed to kill a wolf not only had the satisfaction of having destroyed a dangerous beast, but also the much-desired skin," all part of a publicly admired heroic action (56). Interestingly, similar to the old Japanese binary perception of the wolf as friend and the deer as foe, but with a different valence, Taktser Rinpoché portrays bears as friends to be protected. "A Tibetan would never dream of hunting a bear," he tells us, since "awe-inspiring" bears in Tibet are both "feared and respected" like human persons (160).

Besides the taboo against killing bears, animals who were not slaughtered or hunted sometimes prospered due to local Buddhist practices. For instance, the first monastery in which Taktser Rinpoché stayed as a young monk banned the hunting of animals in its environs, so that musk deer, with nothing to fear from humans, ambled tamely around the hermitage (73). Further, Taktser Rinpoché shares a touching story from his childhood in which he discovered that a number of small fish had been trapped by a drying stream and faced losing their fluid habitat altogether. Motivated by the Buddhist ideals of compassion that surrounded him, he took a piece of pottery and scooped up the fish, walking them home afterward to be placed in the giant urn that held the family's drinking water. Unfortunately, he lost his balance while checking on the fish, pulling over the urn and watching it smash on the floor. His parents refrained from punishing him for breaking the family water urn because he had moved to benefit the fish, a deed that in Buddhist sentiments represents a virtuous activity (42–43).

As we will see in this chapter, the complex attitudes toward the natural world exhibited by Taktser Rinpoché include diverse approaches to the natural world that reflect the broader Tibetan cultural milieu. Fish are protected from harm but sheep are eaten, complicating the issue of Buddhist vegetarianism. Additionally, the highest mountains in the world, like Taktser Rinpoché's Happiness Mountain, receive personhood treatment, enabling a unique breed of Buddhist alpine nature mysticism. The personhood of natural beings also become expressed in the sharing of their souls with humans, who then care for animals with Buddhist compassion by liberating them from harm, like the fish that Taktser Rinpoché released. Yet these personhood attitudes sometimes do not inhibit animal sacrifices, despite the visible ecological teachings of Taktser Rinpoché's brother, the Fourteenth Dalai Lama. The way to make sense of these sometimes conflicting attitudes is to grasp the Tibetan cultural ideal of sustainable taming.

The Ideal of Sustainable Taming

The elements of hunting and mining in the story of Taktser Rinpoché's childhood call attention to a central motif in Tibetan religion, one with strong ramifications for relationships with the natural world, the theme of *dülwa*, or taming.[5] According to Tibetan legends, fierce powers of nature prevented the implantation of Buddhism in Tibet until those nature gods were defeated by a Vajrayāna Buddhist magician and saint from eighth-century India, Padmasambhava, also known as Guru Rinpoché. Padmasambhava roamed Tibet while subduing many different nature spirits, including the mountain deity Nyenchen Tanglha, the central montane divinity of one of the most imposing of mountain ranges in Tibet, whom Padmasambhava transformed into a protector of Buddhism.[6] This taming by Padmasambhava was part of a long historical process through which Nyenchen Tanglha changed from a local montane warrior god to a beloved divine ancestor of Tibetan emperors and then to a Buddhist protector of the lineage of Dalai Lamas. Some other Tibetan mountain gods have received relatively similar treatments.

Notable in this episode is the fact that Padmasambhava did not kill but rather transformed Nyenchen Tanglha, who in this way was tamed, and sustainably so, enabling his powers to continue into the future. This idea of sustainable taming is quite useful in explaining Tibetan religious experiences with the natural world because Tibetans through history have tried to tame nature and in the ideal have done so sustainably, like Padmasambhava did with Nyenchen Tanglha. Humans being humans, though, sometimes the ideal of sustainability is not reached in the course of taming, just like humans fail to reach many of their ideals.[7] Nonetheless, that Tibetans seek sustainable taming of nonhuman nature, which is not entirely unlike some contemporary concepts of sustainable development, helps illuminate Tibetan religious relationships with nature much better than do the simplistic presentations of old Tibet as a paradisiacal sustainable biosphere where animals simply meandered without fear or that of the opposite view, that of old Tibet as an ecological nightmare. Recognizing the ideal of sustainable taming as well as its limitations better explains Tibetan religious relationships with nature than do the many polarized arguments that one often finds regarding Tibet.

The Tibetan World

Before we enter the world of sustainable taming further, I should better delineate the object of our focus. The area of cultural Tibet is enormous, far exceeding the boundaries of the present-day political Tibet Autonomous Region since, in longitude, cultural Tibet stretches from western Sichuan province in China in the east to Ladakh in the west and, in latitude, from southern Bhutan northward to Mongolia. At an average altitude of 3,660 meters (12,000 feet), the Tibetan plateau is the earth's highest feature, having risen over 45 million years due to the subduction of the Indian geological plate under the Asian plate. Most of the major rivers of Asia begin on the Tibetan plateau, leaving 40 percent of humanity dependent on Tibet for its water supply and making the health of the mountains and their snowy fresh water reserves a crucial issue.

When humans arrived in these highlands no later than the Neolithic era, it seems they entered a world which, despite its altitude and cold, teemed with wildlife. William Rockhill, the late nineteenth-century traveler, wrote that "the country was everywhere literally alive with game," being replete with deer of various subspecies, snow leopards, bears, wolves, rabbits, ducks, geese, grouse, and partridges.[8] In fact, numerous reports of large numbers of animals occupy Tibetan history into the 1950s. Some of the animals that Rockhill met were distinctively Tibetan, such as *chirus* or Tibetan antelopes (*Pantholops hodgsoni*, Tibetan: *tsö*), Tibetan gazelles (*Procapra picticaudata*), white-lipped deer (*Cervus albirostris*), *kyang* wild asses (*Equus kiang*), yaks and *dris* (yak being the male, *dri* being the female of *Bos grunniens* or *Bos mutus*), and argali (*Ovis ammon hodgsoni*) as well as blue (*Pseudois nayaur*) wild sheep. Numerous species of birds, including black-necked cranes, vultures of different types, kites, and sparrows inhabit the high altitudes, with ravens and crows possessing the powers of oracles.[9] Snakes may dwell near hot springs. Foxes, wolves, and bears feast on *pikas* (various species in the genus *Ochotona*), which are Himalayan rodents that look like hares yet are the size of mice. Animals subsist on each other and on a variety of vegetation, from dense forests on the eastern edge of the plateau in Kham to the almost treeless but not grassless vast spaces of the cold and dry Changtang region in the northwest.

Tibetans in Nature

Like the tale of natural history that I just recounted, the eleventh-century Tibetan historical chronicle *Mani Kabum* claims that animals filled Tibet when humans arrived.[10] According to the *Mani Kabum*, the great *mahāsattva* of compassion, Chenrézik (Sanskrit: Avalokiteśvara) needed humans to enter Tibet since he wished to spread Buddhism, which animals in this *Mani Kabum* passage cannot practice. Therefore, Chenrézik incarnated as a monkey on a mountain near the Yarlung valley in southeastern Tibet, where he mated with the Tibetan Buddhist mahāsattva great spirit of mercy, Drölma (Sanskrit: Tārā), who appeared as a rock ogress. Their offspring, who represent the seeds of the legendary first six Tibetan clans, in the beginning were monkeys who took after their simian father and had tails. Over several generations, the divine progeny lost their tails and transformed into modern humans, although some did not evolve as much and now remain as supposed yetis.[11]

In this mythological origin story, Tibetan humans descended from animals and rocks, so that one cannot draw a sharp line between humans and nonhumans. This allows a blurring of the boundaries between the human and the nonhuman that, as we will see, is a common feature of Tibetan relationships with nature. At the same time, the whole point of Chenrézik's creating humans involved enabling the practice of religion, which in this view animals cannot practice, thus legitimizing the sustainable taming of animals by religiously superior human beings.

Beyond animal ancestry, boundaries between humans and nonhumans further lose definition in light of soul sharing within the Tibetan *la né* soul residence complex.[12] In varying formulations of what must be old Tibetan folk beliefs combined with a sprinkling of Buddhist theory, traditional Tibetans broadly embrace the idea that humans share souls with a variety of entities in the natural world, binding humans and nonhumans together. While there exist many different systems, if one follows the Tibetologist R. A. Stein, one can appreciate that at birth each individual human commences spiritual ties through which the person shares souls with a specific horse, ox, bird, tree, or lake, with this bond lasting for life.[13] Sometimes the partners are even born on the same day.

This tie between humans and nonhumans is actualized through the activities of wandering souls. Although Buddhism itself is phobic regarding soul concepts, many Tibetan Buddhists have conflated an indigenous concept of a *la*, or soul, with the Buddhist notion of the consciousness component of a human, known in Sanskrit as *vijñāna* or in Tibetan as *namshé*, just as we saw Thai Buddhists conflate vijñāna with their local soul concepts.[14] It is this namshé consciousness component, appearing as the la soul, that separates from the body and wanders, during sneezes, moments of fright, or just ordinary sleep, when our dreams represent records of the travels of our souls. A disembodied wandering soul is prey to demons and black magicians, however, so it needs safe havens.[15]

The natural beings with whom one shares a birth bond provide these havens, as they represent la né soul residences in which one's soul may safely rest. In this way, each Tibetan shares a traveling soul with a specific horse, ox, bird, tree, or lake, problematizing boundaries between humans and nonhumans and turning soul residences into persons, too, because they share human souls.[16] Partners in these ties share fates, so that if my soul horse dies, I may get sick or die, but if I prosper, my soul bird should flourish as well. In a contemporary story regarding this nexus, it seems that not long ago a man named Chimé Namgyel suffered from chronic back pain that would not leave. Examining his case, the Buddhist leader Lama Achuk Rinpoché said that his family's soul-shared cypress tree had a broken branch that needed healing. Chimé put medication on the broken branch, covered it with a respectful *khata* ceremonial scarf, and created a support to hold up the branch. The tree healed and, as it did so, Chimé's back pains disappeared.[17]

Like one sees in an element of Chimé Namgyel's story, continued Tibetan blurring of personal boundaries occurs when one considers that some soul residences, especially trees, lakes, and mountains, may not pertain to just one individual, but instead are shared by families, clans, or populations of entire valley systems. In a common traditional belief, for example, everyone in a locality shares her or his soul with the resident yül lha, or local god, usually thought to be the same as, or resident on, an important large mountain, like Taktser Rinpoché's childhood peak Happiness Mountain.[18] Typically, one cannot hunt or gather plants on the high slopes of a divine yül lha mountain because animals and plants may be thought to belong to the yül lha him- or herself. As a result, yül lha mountains may serve as sustainable nature sanctuaries, much like the Dai-regarded mountains that we saw in the chapter on Thailand.

Further, the yül lha deity, often considered to be an ancestor to local people as well as a practitioner of Buddhism, retains the power to control all events in his or her orbit, so both prosperity and disaster may be attributed to the personality of the yül lha.[19] For this reason, new building constructions or wedding engagements may be announced to the yül lha both as good etiquette and to avoid divine wrath. Yül lhas may also serve as Masters of Animals, or hunting gods.[20] The powers of some of these yül lha mountains can be quite literal because their extreme physical height both alters storm patterns and creates sunny and shadowed alpine patches, with sometimes severe temperature differentials obtaining between bright areas that enjoy a summerlike climate and shady spots a stone's throw away that at the same moment are below freezing.

Typically, but not always, these yül lhas manifest as male, but the male mountain spirits often have their female counterparts in nearby sacred lakes that also serve as soul residences for entire communities. For instance, many Tibetans claim that they share their souls with the gorgeous high-altitude lake Namtso, a local counterpart of the mountain deity Nyenchen Tanglha, in central Tibet.[21] Both mountain and lake deities, because of their soul-sharing spiritual ties with their communities, frequently enjoy consideration as community member persons in their own right, like Taktser Rinpoché expressed in his memories of the alpine spirit Kyi. In this vein, at times Tibetans may perceive the deities of special lakes and mountains to be the ultimate parents of members of the human community.[22] The names of many soul residence lakes and mountains, in fact, often bear respectful familial names, expressing their perceived personhood. The "Anyé" in the name of the notable northeastern Tibetan yül lha Anyé Machen stands for "Grandfather," for instance, and other yül lhas carry names including *achi*, or grandmother; *apa*, or father; or *jobo* or *jomo*, meaning respected elder brother or sister.[23] Further personhood elements arise in terms of Anyé Machen's anthropomorphic iconography since the yül lha is "a golden figure wearing a helmet and a cuirass of gold, a white cloak, and numerous jewels." He rides a white horse, so the major pilgrimages to his peak happen in the year of the horse. Additionally, Anyé Machen holds a lance with a flag attached to it, thus appearing much like the person of a human king.[24]

These Tibetan soul-sharing beliefs appear to inhibit any sharp delineation of a human realm as completely distinct from either the nonhuman or the sacred. Humans blend into their individual soul horses and shared-soul mountains, these latter also representing manifest divinities, so that no

FIGURE 9. The holy lake goddess Namtso rests in the foreground. Her companion mountain deity, Nyenchen Tanglha, is partially surrounded by clouds in the background. Namtso, Tibet.

decisive demarcation between individual human, corporate human, deity, and nonhuman nature obtains. Of course, it is not that Tibetans cannot understand themselves as individuals, but the lack of some of the rigid boundaries between humans and nonhumans that may be found in other religious cultures helps facilitate the relational animist personhood relationships with nonhumans that appear so brilliantly in the Tibetan Buddhist world. Given that soul-sharing partners share fates, so that caring for one partner means caring for the other as well, these beliefs also retain strong implications for an environmental ethic that is sustainable for humans and nonhumans alike. With these beliefs Tibetans culturally tame a landscape but do so in a way that perhaps allows greater opportunities for nonhumans to thrive.

Typically, local protective yül lha mountains with which communities share souls receive pilgrimages in order to enable sustainable relationships of mutual ecological prosperity, like the one we saw with Taktser Rinpoché's childhood. Indeed, pilgrimage, or *nékor*, perhaps marks the most important and distinctive of all Tibetan spiritual practices.[25] Holy lakes receive pilgrimages as well. Of interest, according to research by the anthropologists Åshild Kolås and Monika Thowsen, pilgrimages and festivals in honor of yül lha persons are today experiencing a renaissance in eastern Tibet after their prohibition during the Cultural Revolution from 1966 to 1976.[26] It is unclear whether a growing contemporary sustainability movement in eastern Tibet aids political realities in stimulating this situation.

Vajrayāna Power Mountains

Despite the importance of pilgrimages to yül lha mountains and lakes, the biggest mountain pilgrimages typically do not pertain to local protector mountain or lake spirits but to a conceptually different category of Tibetan sacred mountain, this time Buddhist in a more straightforward way: the *néri*, or Tantric power mountain.[27] Tantric power mountains are experienced as persons but not like regional protector yül lha persons. Instead, Tantric power mountains incarnate Vajrayāna Buddhist deities. Depending on whom one asks, the Tantric power mountain is the abode of the Vajrayāna deity, the body of the deity, the mandala or enlightened realm of the deity, or all these perspectives simultaneously. Perhaps the peak known widely as Mt. Kailash, called Kang Rinpoché or Tisé by Tibetans, best exemplifies a Tantric power mountain since Kailash provides an often-visited location for encountering the Vajrayāna deity Déchok (Sanskrit: Cakrasaṃvara). While the noninitiated may see just piles of stones, those with spiritual insight encounter a holy paradise in mountain form instead.[28]

Because of the mandalization of Tantric power mountains, advanced practitioners may regard néri mountains as charismatic nature mystical places for deepening their Buddhist experiences. These practitioners understand traversing the mountain as synonymous with spiritual travel through a mandala, not entirely unlike some Chinese pilgrims to Wutaishan or the Shugendō practitioners who appeared in the chapter on Japan. Differences accrue, however, since Tibetans typically do not climb to the top of Tantric power mountains as symbolic of conquering nirvana, like Shugendō practitioners do. For many Tibetans, climbing to summits remains disrespectful of the various gods and spirits who live there, and, further, the extreme altitude of many Tantric power mountains may make climbing to the top impractical anyway. Thus, Tibetans move through mandalas in the process of the circumambulation of the mountain, called *korra*, on relatively horizontal, rather than vertical, paths, with a common arrangement being a path around the base, a path around the midsection of the mountain, and a path around the upper reaches, but not the summit, of the peak, with many landmarks on alternate paths representing various elements of the mandalas. This mandalization separates Tantric power mountains from yül lha protector mountains, which are not Buddhicized as mandalas, although some peaks, such as Anyé Machen or Mudo, provide both Tantric power and yül lha protector functions.[29]

By the way, this mandalization process as an example of the spiritual taming of mountains does not lack critics; the Tibetologist Charles Ramble, for one, laments the violence done to the landscape by imposing human religious concepts on nonhumans, such as by insisting that mountains are not just mountains, they are mandalas.[30] Following Padmasambhava's example, in Tibetan religious logic the wildness of mountains must be Tantrically tamed for human use through mandalization, asserting human control by taming nonhuman things for human religious uses. But, from Ramble's sustainability-friendly point of view, mountains may be better off if they are perceived as just mountains, rather than as emanations of Vajrayāna gods, the latter representing human religious projections that mountains themselves of course did not request.

Animals for Ordinary and Sacrificial Foods

Historically speaking, many rituals in honor of yül lhas have concluded with the sacrifice of an animal to provide a meat offering since protector deities are often carnivorous, and in some places today these sacrifices continue. Therefore, again in this book instances emerge in which Buddhist actors participate in animal sacrifice but not without controversy. On the one hand, in many places Tibetan Buddhist leaders have successfully urged the replacement of actual animals in the sacrifice with effigies, such as seminaturalistic dough sculptures that serve as more pacific offerings. As a result, today few animal sacrifices happen in central Tibet and many Tibetans remain horrified by the very notion of animal sacrifice. However, in other locations, local Buddhist leaders may lack the power to stop sacrifices and so pretend to ignore the proceedings, or at uncommon moments village clergy participate.

Animal sacrifices are difficult to stop in some areas in part because Bön, a form of pre-Buddhist Tibetan religiosity that became codified with the arrival of Buddhism, prescribes some animal sacrifices despite its manifestations, which often speak against such practices.[31] From the beginning of their shared history, Bön and Buddhism intermingled, so that many centuries later they resemble each other so greatly that some people speak of Bön as the fifth school of Tibetan Buddhism, along with the Nyingma, Kagyü, Sakya, and Géluk schools.[32] In the minds of some Tibetans, there is little that separates Bön from Buddhism other than the direction of circumambulation (Bön practitioners circumambulate counterclockwise), so that the sacrifices prescribed by Bön may be perceived as a manifestation of

Buddhism, regardless of what scholars or Buddhist leaders may think. But even Tibetan Buddhism itself may provide an impetus for animal sacrifices since the pre-Communist Tibetan state run by the Dalai Lamas knowingly sponsored the ostensibly non-Buddhist animal sacrifice that marked part of the large pilgrimage to the Tantric power mountain of Tsari in southeastern Tibet.[33]

Another reason why animal sacrifices continue is because of the perception that the prosperity and welfare of the people depend on the good will of the yül lha even if the deity is carnivorous. This motivates some Tibetans to participate in animal sacrifices despite a reluctance to do so, like one finds in the fieldwork of the anthropologist Stan Royal Mumford. In the 1980s, Mumford lived in the Gyasumdo valley of northern Nepal, where on one side of the Marsyandi River members of a Gurung Hindu settlement named Tapje practiced animal sacrifice to the yül lha Akyenedong. In the Tibetan Buddhist community of Tshap on the other side of the river, these sacrifices were mostly scorned during the time of Mumford's fieldwork; instead, Buddhists engaged in merit-making activities to counteract the martyrdom of animals during the Tapje animal sacrifice festival. However, earlier in history, Tibetans had participated in the yül lha animal sacrifices. Only in the early 1960s did Tibetans give up participating since to escape Chinese rule in 1962 the Buddhist leader Lama Chog Lingpa arrived in Tshap from Tibet and thereafter commandingly forbade the continuance of "red offerings" among Tibetans. But in 1968 a landslide buried much of the Buddhist village of Tshap, destroying numerous homes and killing many people, although it spared the animal-sacrificing Hindu village of Tapje. In the wake of this disaster, Hindus and some Buddhists blamed the landslide on the lack of Tibetan Buddhist animal sacrifices for the yül lha Akyenedong, who had withdrawn his favor from the Buddhists. Although in Mumford's ethnography Tibetans seemed divided in opinion, even decades after the 1968 landslide there were some Tibetans who expressed the need to offer an animal to the yül lha to prevent a repeat landslide occurrence.[34]

In Tibetan religiosity, it is not just many folk protector spirits like yül lhas who request meat because the deities of the Vajrayāna Buddhism of Tibet do as well, and a number of Vajrayāna Buddhist *tsok* rituals specify that meat must be offered.[35] Participants often consume the meat from both folk and Vajrayāna rituals after it has been offered first to the divinities. Perhaps this religious taste for meat helps support the widespread habit among Tibetan Buddhists of eating animal flesh since "for many, a meal without meat is not a full meal," but other reasons have been given as well.[36] Ecologically, it is difficult to grow vegetables on the Tibetan plateau due to the altitude, unpredictable weather, and a short growing season. However, yaks and other animals have evolved special tongues that allow them to consume the short Tibetan *stipa* alpine grasses, and then humans can eat these animals, creating an environmental reason for Tibetan carnivory.[37]

It should further be noted that the Chinese *Fanwangjing*, so influential in stimulating East Asian Buddhist vegetarianism among monastics, as we have seen, did not take hold in Tibet. Instead, Tibetan monastics follow the Mūlasarvāstivādin *Vinaya*, which like the Theravāda *Vinaya* allows monastic meat eating as long as meat is not specifically requested and as long as the animal has not been seen, heard, or suspected of being killed for the sake of the monastic involved. The Mūlasarvāstivādin *Vinaya* even states that "meat, fish, and dried flesh" are "excellent."[38] Thus, there exist both religious and environmental reasons why Tibetan monasteries in Tibet itself usually do not share the vegetarianism of many East Asian Buddhist outposts. Meat eating is so integrated into Tibetan culture, in fact, that in pre-Communist Tibet the Dalai Lama's office used to give away meat as part of the Losar, or New Year, festivities.[39]

For Tibetan settled agriculturalists, meat is a standard dietary adjunct to the high-altitude crops they grow, like one sees in stories from the childhood of the Dalai Lama's brother. Moreover, for the mobile pastoralists who have traditionally made up around a third of the Tibetan population, meat eating has at times been a virtual survival requirement, so their animals represent their *nor*, or wealth, as walking food stores.[40]

Unfortunately, a common method for the slaughter of these domestic animals creates a troublesome Buddhist situation. Tibetan pastoralists frequently eschew using a knife in the slaughtering process since cutting the throat of the animal is considered a direct form of killing and thus a contravention of the Buddhist nonharm precept. However, if the animal is strangled by tying its mouth shut and plugging its nostrils, then one can say that the animal simply died, rather than was killed.[41] Strangulation may also be thought to result in more delicious meat. Because suffocation in this way may be perceived as a lesser violation of the ahimsa precept than using a knife and/or may be perceived as producing better meat, it is the preferred method of slaughter for many Tibetans.[42] With this practice, however, the animal dies slowly and painfully rather than quickly, with as many as thirty agonizing minutes elapsing before the animal expires, which from the animal's point of view appears to be a greater violation of the ahimsa precept than is quickly cutting the throat.[43] Hence, despite the many claims by outsiders that Tibetans treat animals gently and kindly in life, this suffocation practice can mitigate this reputation somewhat in death.[44]

In order to avoid such realities, rich Tibetans may be able to pay others to do their slaughtering. But poorer people may not have this option, so slaughtering may be viewed as a necessary evil component of relative poverty, with piety on this issue being a luxury of the affluent.[45] Alternatively, sometimes to avoid slaughtering, Tibetans drive animals to markets and sell them live, leaving the butchering to others. One can further try to counteract the negative karma from animal slaughter by temporarily practicing vegetarianism, especially during the holy Buddhist month of Saga Dawa in late spring, and many Tibetans choose this option.[46]

As I have indicated, among both settled agriculturalists and mobile pastoralists, Tibetans often augment the meat from domesticated animals with food gained from hunting since this helps preserve the domestic herd while it also provides animal skins that can be sold for cash and supplies for making medicines. From the time of the advent of firearms in Tibet around the eighteenth century, hunters have most often used muskets or rifles for hunting, although the slingshot used by the Dalai Lama's father appears to have been more common in the past, as were a leghold snare, the bow and arrow, and the use of dog teams.[47]

Like slaughtering, hunting has always been a double-edged sword for Tibetan Buddhists because, on the one hand, it makes economic sense in a land where vegetables are relatively scarce due to the climate, a mobile lifestyle, or both. In an old Tibet full of wildlife, the animals appeared to be there for the taking. On the other hand, as my reader has learned throughout this book, the Buddha discouraged hunting and traditionally hunting has been viewed by some Buddhists as a more heinous violation of the ahimsa precept than the slaughter of domestic animals is. Tibetan literature therefore remains full of stories in which humans relish wild meat and thereafter receive reprimands for hunting by Tibetan Buddhist leaders because, as the Tibetologist Toni Huber has stated, hunting in Tibet has long occurred "in an atmosphere of stark contradiction between ideals and practices."[48] You get a sense of how deep these contradictions run when you consider that some monastic estates in pre-Communist Tibet privately encouraged individual lay people to hunt for them to provide the monasteries with trade goods at the same time that the resident monastics dissuaded hunting in their public teachings.[49]

Limits to Compassion

Tibetan Buddhist leaders offer many teachings to discourage hunting, yet Tibetan hunting has not ended.[50] Numerous monasteries forbid hunting in their environs, but a hunter can always move to another spot. Further, and quite instructive, for many Tibetans who live close to subsistence level, hunting is either necessary for survival or seen as a sensible economic activity, blunting calls of the clergy to stop hunting. Some contemporary Tibetans have said, for example, that they have given up hunting perhaps not so much for religious scruples, but because Chinese government officials confiscated their guns.[51] These limitations highlight an important weakness of Buddhist compassion when applied to the natural world, especially regarding realizing Rolston's ideal of a sustainable biosphere: its individual-oriented limited biocentrism, which in this case may not account for the needs of many beings, including those of impoverished humans.

Certainly, Buddhist compassion toward animals like in the story of Taktser Rinpoché's saving of fish adds an animal-friendly component to Buddhism, and, because of that, Buddhist compassion can be a powerful tool in furthering animal rights causes. But Buddhist compassion as traditionally conceived is directed only toward individual animals. Compassion for things that are more complex than individuals, like ecosystems, is difficult to conceive and practice, because one may have to encourage a wolf to kill a deer and a tiger then to kill the wolf, if that is what creates healthy ecosystem sustainability.

Related to this, the extension of compassion primarily to animals alone, rather than also to plant, water, or mineral entities, almost always places intrinsic value only on humans and animals, creating a limited biocentric vision that generally neither accounts nor cares for nonanimal elements of the ecosystem. This lack of an ecocentric vision or an ability to account for ecocentric complexities, which include human needs, places a great limit on Buddhism when it comes to establishing a viable environmental ethic. The foundational environmentalist Aldo Leopold asserted in his *Sand County Almanac* that the total land must be treated as a complex system, with individuals valued primarily for their places in that system, and the individual-oriented limited biocentrism of Buddhist compassion hampers such an approach.[52] Because of this limit, Buddhist compassion for nature, as inspiring and animal-friendly as it can be, does not support "modern conservation principles," as one study stated, because it does not retain solidly ecocentric perspectives.[53]

It is not difficult to find examples of this shortcoming anywhere in the Buddhist world, but I will restrict myself to just one from Tibet, in which an eagle caused commotion in the life of the Tibetan saint Shabkar (1781–1851 CE). While staying at Tsonying, Shabkar noticed that an eagle came each day to the many nests along the shore of Blue Lake and ate a baby bird that had not yet learned to fly. He watched as the eagle "tore out and devoured their hearts while they were still alive," inciting compassion within him for the baby birds but also anger toward the eagle. One day the eagle returned and Shabkar intentionally hit the eagle with a stone from his slingshot, nearly killing the bird. Afterward, Shabkar encouraged other humans nearby to similarly protect the fledglings from eagles.[54]

While the compassion for fledglings that one finds in this story is admirable and provides a nice window into Buddhist animal-welfare sentiments, it lacks a systematic understanding of the natural world. Eagles play important roles in ecosystem health, and from this point of view if one looks only at individual eagle catches, and not at the complicated system in which eagles and their catches participate, one is not fully able to care even for fledglings who live within the system, much less for eagles. Whether one likes predatory eagles or not, the eagles in this story act as they should. Human vegetarians, when faced with the fact that eating vegetables may destroy small creatures that live in plants, occasionally respond, "You have to eat something!," this being a statement with which these innately carnivorous eagles could agree.

Putting this insight into ecological terms, the environmentalist Arne Naess stated, "The ecological viewpoint presupposes acceptance of the fact that big fish eat small."[55] Indeed, in order to promote ecosystem health in some situations, we may even wish to encourage eagle predation rather than pelting eagles with stones like Shabkar did. In other words, this story involves sentimental compassion for baby animals but limited compassion for eagles, whom in fact Shabkar actively attacks. There is little compassion for the entities that died for the sake of the fledglings' diet, either, or for the water or minerals that fed those entities. Although Shabkar later expressed regret for his aggression toward the eagle, still this tale exhibits the common themes of myriad Buddhist compassion stories in which some ecological individuals matter (usually animals who are most like humans or whom humans most like), while others, such as eagles or animals used for human food, do not.

In this way, the Buddhist ethic of compassion, as traditionally taught, understood, and applied by people like Shabkar, does not make for a complete, viable environmental ethic. Despite the notion of broad dependent arising within the religion, its limited biocentric concept of compassion for individual animals is constrained in application to ecosystems. We will see the American Buddhist environmentalist Gary Snyder further this line of criticism in the next chapter.

Spurning Meat

Despite his assaulting of eagles with stones, Shabkar is a well-known figure in Tibetan circles as an animal lover and represents perhaps the most notable of a long list of Buddhist vegetarian dissenters against the Tibetan meat-eating norm. Traveling widely through a variety of Tibetan lands, Shabkar developed compassion for many animals he encountered, and based on this compassion he declared that Buddhists should without fail avoid eating animal flesh, resulting in several texts of his that promote vegetarianism. Shabkar based his vegetarian arguments on several authoritative Mahāyāna and Vajrayāna sources, including the *Śikṣāsamuccaya Sūtra*, *Nirvāṇa Sūtra*, *Aṅgulimāla Sūtra*, *Kālacakra Tantra*, and perhaps most of all, the *Laṅkāvatāra Sūtra*, in the end providing numerous counsels against meat eating. These vegetarian teachings of Shabkar coalesce with other forces in our current twenty-first-century world to incite a greater meat-shunning sensibility among Tibetans, especially in the eastern Tibetan region of Kham, according to the researchers Geoffrey Barstow and Holly Gayley.[56]

In his memoir, Shabkar states that, for him, both butchery and meat eating result in hell rebirths, and selling meat leads to a rebirth as a hungry ghost (66–69). In Shabkar's view, meat eating causes a loss of energy, diminishes compassion, inhibits mental functioning, and results in a lack of access to both nirvana and omniscience (70, 81, 83, 100). He claims that meat carries toxins, causes animals to flee your smell, makes Buddhism look bad, and may even lead you to become a cannibal for love of meat (80, 89, 113). Thinking more economically, Shabkar, like the *Laṅkāvatāra Sūtra*, further indicates that meat eating creates an avoidable market for killing, saying, "If there is no meat eater, there is no animal killer" (101). Finally, and most importantly, Shabkar also frames his call for vegetarianism with personhood principles. He informs us that animals, despite being "stupid creatures," represent the reincarnations of our previous family and friends. By eating them, one eats persons, both kin and otherwise, and Shabkar finds this intolerable. Begging Buddhists to reflect on the realities of reincarnation, Shabkar asks, "Who would be able to eat the flesh of their own parents and children?" (84).

Notably, in order to dissuade people from eating meat, Shabkar refuses to support the common practice of pronouncing mantras, such as the mantra of compassion *Om mani padme huṃ*, over the animal during or after the slaughter. Mantras are phrases that are infused with spiritual power, so that, for example, by reciting the mantra of compassion, compassionate energies are thought to arise in the universe. The intention behind chanting such mantras over slaughtered animals involves the creation of the merit necessary to send the animal to a better rebirth as well as to prevent poor karma for the slaughterer. For Shabkar, this practice may soften some human guilt, but from the animal's point of view it is a charade. He, in fact, compared the chanting of mantras over slaughtered animals to the taunting of a mouse by a cat (108). Shabkar said, "Showing compassion for animals after they have been killed and the meat is being eaten—reciting mantras for the animal's sake—is nothing but a silly game" (109).

Releasing Animals

Besides vegetarianism, in order to pursue sustainable taming Shabkar also fondly promoted the Buddhist ritual of animal release. Known from all over the Buddhist world, including in germinal form in ancient Indian scriptures such as the *Vessantara Jātaka*, the practice of animal release involves freeing animals who would otherwise be facing death. The freed animals ideally enjoy release into safe and healthy habitats, thus being compassionately protected from harm. In some instances, this practice can additionally dovetail with vegetarianism, such as the myriad releases performed in eastern Tibet by Khenpo Tsültrim Lodrö, who intentionally liberates animals that are marked for human consumption.[57] For many Buddhists, this distinctive practice of animal release adds a very animal-friendly dimension to the tradition.

Understanding these animal release practices requires context, although this contextualization remains a bit difficult. First, consider that in their study of Buddhist animal release practices, the scholars Henry Shiu and Leah Stokes flatly claimed, as others have done, that the ritual of Buddhist animal release began in China.[58] However, despite the otherwise fine research done by Shiu and Stokes, the origins of the ritual actually may be less settled than this. It is true that in China the third-century CE Daoist text *Liezi* briefly discusses freeing animals out of kindness to them, perhaps indicating a Chinese cultural preparedness for such rituals.[59] Further, the Chinese Buddhist *Fan-wangjing* enjoins fangsheng, or animal release, commanding, "You should compassionately engage in the practice of releasing captive animals into the wild."[60] Moreover, one of the greatest proponents of Buddhist animal release rituals was the Chinese Buddhist monk Zhuhong (1535–1615 CE).[61]

These elements notwithstanding, animal releases have historically occurred across the Buddhist world, among all three great sects, not just in the sphere of Chinese influence.[62] For instance, elements of animal release practices exist in many ancient Indian Buddhist texts, albeit without any sense of an organized ritual, and numerous Indian scriptural jātaka stories in the Theravāda scriptures portray freeing animals from perilous situations to be a virtuous activity. In one Theravāda jātaka story, for instance, a man buys a fish intended for human consumption and thereby compassionately frees it, much as we find in animal release rituals in China.[63] Further, as a justification for their practice of animal release, Mahāyāna Buddhists, including within

Tibet, often cite the story of Jalavāhana from the Indian *Suvarṇabhāsottama Sūtra* in which grateful fish are saved from harm.[64] Moreover, although Siming Zhili's medieval liturgy provides a long-valued template for Chinese animal release rituals, there is no standard traditional Chinese Buddhist scripture or liturgy that describes the ritual that we know today.[65] Therefore, the claim that the ritual began in China remains uncertain, although animal releases undoubtedly have taken on some specifically Chinese hues in the Middle Kingdom.

In Tibet itself, animal releases, or *tsé tar*, may have occurred before the arrival of Buddhism as part of the worship of yül lha mountains, like one finds in the Mani Rimdu ritual discussed below.[66] However, Buddhist animal release liturgies do not appear in the ancient Dunhuang texts. One can be more certain that, in Tibetan Buddhism, animal releases have occurred at least since their appearance in the biography of Ra Lotsawa (1000–1080 CE) and their mention in the fifteenth-century historical chronicle *Blue Annals* (*deb ther sngon po*).[67] Whenever these practices started in Tibet, Tibetan animal release ritual texts that we have now arise from Vajrayāna principles of meditational generation and completion stages, typical of Tibetan Vajrayāna works but atypical of Chinese Mahāyāna texts. Thus, there appears to be no direct transmission from China to Tibet of the Tibetan ritual as it exists today.

In historical Tibetan cultures, animal release has been practiced both as a formal ritual and as a more informal, personal practice, such as when mobile pastoralists free an animal from their own herds as a way to atone for the malfeasance of animal slaughter.[68] Often, animals that receive their freedom through this latter, more informal method are white or piebald, ideally also being healthy and strong since they represent gifts to deities.[69] Although they may be released into the wild, frequently the animals that are informally freed by pastoralists remain with the herd and may still be used as transport or as a source of wool, but the liberated animals will not have to worry about being slaughtered for food, no matter how old or lacking in human uses they become.[70] Freed animals receive decorations of tassels, colored ribbons, or other markers of their inviolate nature since the killing of a liberated animal can be considered worse than killing a hundred humans.[71] These freed animals therefore avoid being used for human food, but they remain social markers within the human world because having many freed animals in one's herd is a conspicuous sign of wealth.

During the karmically powerful holy month of Saga Dawa in late spring that celebrates the Buddha's birth, enlightenment, and death, in Tibet people may release animals as a mass merit-making phenomenon.[72] Alternatively, and more formally, in an autumn ritual at Thyangboche monastery among the ethnically and culturally Tibetan Sherpas of northern Nepal, instead of being sacrificed for a yül lha, a yak enjoys ceremonial release in honor of a mountain goddess during the Mani Rimdu holiday festivities. As described by the scholar and alpinist Luther Jerstad, part of Mani Rimdu involves prayers and offerings to the local yül lha goddess Miyo Langzang, who is one of the group of Five Sisters of Long Life goddesses who rule the mountains in the environs of Mount Everest.[73] During the chant to the goddess of Everest that forms part of the Mani Rimdu liturgy, a yak is tied in the monastery's courtyard and respectfully smeared with butter and libated with milk before silk banners are affixed to the four-legged guest of honor. The yak's head, ears, shoulders, and tail are especially consecrated to the goddess. Then the yak, which no longer does work in any outcome, is turned loose theoretically to roam the wild mountainsides as a living offering to the yül lha goddess.[74]

Outside of calendric occasions such as Mani Rimdu, formal animal release rituals may be performed at any time, like one finds with one of the foremost practitioners of formal animal release rituals today, Lama Zopa Rinpoché. A monk from the Géluk sect, Lama Zopa, with Lama Yeshe, founded the Kopan monastery in Kathmandu, Nepal, as well as the Foundation for the Preservation of the Mahāyāna Tradition (FPMT). Besides being an accomplished institution builder, for decades Lama Zopa has ardently promoted animal release practices and on his internet site he claims to have freed or inspired the freeing of over 200 million animals.[75]

In his animal release manual, *Liberating Animals from the Danger of Death*,[76] Lama Zopa asserts that several benefits derive from the practice. First, the animals themselves ideally are benefitted since one practices worship on behalf of the animals while one physically frees them (45). But human gains further accrue to Lama Zopa's animal liberation practice, and in fact these human benefits remain more salient in Lama Zopa's text than do boons for animals. Liberating animals, for example, can protect a human from an untimely death. The practice of animal release, according to Lama Zopa, can also heal one from life-threatening diseases, including AIDS and cancer (7). Liberating animals further builds health and nourishes humans like a wholesome diet, so that it forms a proactive part of wellness, too (7). For Lama Zopa, animal liberations can additionally serve as nice social events (43).

Moreover, in a Buddhist sense, Lama Zopa emphasizes that the practice of animal release helps in the development of *bodhicitta*, the compassionate mind of enlightenment, thus aiding human spiritual progress as well. Lama Zopa asks us to look upon animals with compassion since, he says, their suffering is intense. Yet, as is frequently stressed in Buddhist scriptures, animals have been our mothers in previous lifetimes, so humans owe them gratitude and care. Even when we ourselves were born as animals, Lama Zopa says, our animal mothers nurtured us. Thus, in Lama Zopa's personhood-laden teachings, we should feel as close to and as compassionate toward animals "as we do our present family" (10).

It is easy to appreciate the potentially compassionate, sustainable, and ecofriendly goals of animal release practices like Lama Zopa's, but they have problems, some of which may countervail the kinder aspects of the ritual. First, in their study of animal release practices, Shiu and Stokes indicate that animal releases often create a market for animal catches. Market cycles in Taiwan have been traced from orders placed for birds by Buddhists to pet shops, with hunters then filling the orders on behalf of the Buddhists, pet shops selling the birds, and then hunters waiting to recapture the birds upon their release.[77] Lama Zopa himself tells a story of buying all the worms in a store, which inconvenienced fishers until the store raised the number of worms that it stocked. Of course, this overstocking diminished the sense of freeing worms since economics dictated that liberated worms be replaced by nonliberated ones.[78]

Another problem with animal releases concerns a high mortality rate. Preparatory capture and captivity sometimes kills animals before the release ceremony starts, or animals may die soon after the ceremony due to habitat mismatch, waiting predators, or another reason. In this light, John K. Nelson reports that, at the animal release ceremony at today's Honkōji temple in Kyoto, Japan, numbers of birds of prey, well-positioned downstream, eagerly feast on fish that have just been supposedly liberated.[79]

A further trouble with animal releases concerns the introduction of invasive species. For instance, animal release ceremonies have been shown to significantly impact the number of invasive species in Taiwan, and in Guangzhou, China, a native turtle has nearly gone extinct as an effect of many released Brazilian turtles.[80] Even when true invasions do not occur, local species may become hybridized by newcomers, and the results can be unpredictably troublesome.

Finally, animal release advocates from China's Zhuhong to Tibet's Lama Zopa Rinpoché may stress the benefits of the practice for humans more than the benefits for the animals themselves, leaving questions about the possible motivations for animal release rituals. Der-Ruey Yang, for instance, describes a quest for "positive changes to the temperament, mental capability, or personality of the practitioners" as motivating the current movement in China for animal releases, not simply a focus on animal welfare.[81] For reasons such as these, Shiu and Stokes conclude their study of Buddhist animal release practices by surmising that formal, large-scale animal release rituals are generally selfish, intended more for the karmic benefit of humans than they are for the real benefit of animals.[82] Whether or not Shui and Stokes are correct on this last point, it is true that Buddhists who perform animal release practices sometimes claim to seek a more sustainable biosphere yet fail to fully realize this goal.

The Fourteenth Dalai Lama

Many Tibetans seek the opportunity through animal release and other practices to act environmentally, but perhaps there is no more famous environmentalist in the Tibetan world than Taktser Rinpoché's brother, Tenzin Gyatso, the current and Fourteenth Dalai Lama. Granted, so that he may better serve as a political and social leader, the Dalai Lama sometimes overstates his visions of a past ecofriendly Tibet, and "the image of Green Tibetans was largely created in Dharamsala" by his office.[83] But the Dalai Lama's analyses of environmental destruction in Tibet and beyond, as well as his prescriptive cures, provide a distinctive ecological perspective that receives respect from many international environmentalists, Buddhist or not.[84]

The Dalai Lama began issuing statements regarding environmental issues in 1986 as part of his political and social resistance to Chinese rule in Tibet. These statements were later collected and published in the volume *On Environment*.[85] In the midst of decrying numerous human rights abuses that he attributed to the Chinese, he began mentioning the Chinese record with Tibet's natural world, focusing at first on Chinese plans to dump nuclear wastes in Tibet. The Chinese brought to Tibet not just a threat to Tibet's culture, the Dalai Lama taught, but also to what he claimed as being a previously "unspoiled" natural world (9).

Tibet was unblemished, the Dalai Lama states, because in following their overall cultural forms, pre-Communist Tibetans lived in harmony with their natural world, which they protected from distress out of respect for nonhumans. The construction of la tsé stone cairns for mountain deities, for example, teaches one Tibetan-style respect for the natural world, according to the Dalai Lama (53, 77). He wrote, "For more than 1,000 years we Tibetans have adhered to spiritual and environmental values in order to maintain the delicate balance of life across the high plateau on which we live. Inspired by the Buddha's message of nonviolence and compassion and protected by our mountains, we have sought to respect every form of life" (54). Exhibiting this ecofriendliness for the current Dalai Lama, in 1642 CE the then–Dalai Lama's government banned hunting, thereby attempting to turn central Tibet into a large wildlife sanctuary, although rats and wolves did not appear as part of the ban (87).

While some elements of the Dalai Lama's story of an old, ecofriendly Tibet appear to be true, one also already knows from the childhood tales of his brother, Taktser Rinpoché, that hunting remained alive and well in their village, despite the Buddhist ban described by the Dalai Lama. Because the political control of the Dalai Lamas extended tenuously outside of central Tibet, the hunting ban that the Dalai Lama mentioned never enjoyed a pervasive reach and may not have been particularly enforced even in central Tibet, a difficulty noted by the Dalai Lama (51).[86]

Nonetheless, at least before the seventeenth-century introduction of firearms, pre-Communist Tibetans appeared to be sustainable enough in their practices that Tibetan and foreign travelers alike marveled at the large numbers of wild animals inhabiting the plateau. Yet this abundance has disappeared dramatically over the last few decades.[87] Therefore, with some justification the Dalai Lama says, "Sadly, this profusion of wildlife is no longer to be found. Partly due to hunting but primarily due to loss of habitat, what remains half a century after Tibet was occupied is only a small fraction of what there was. . . . Whereas before wild animals would often come close to the house, today they are hardly anywhere to be seen" (76).

Along with this massive loss of wildlife, the Dalai Lama also laments the vast deforestation that creates not just habitat loss but also landslides, erosion, and floods in a country with so many vertical slopes. He tells us, "In the past, the hills were all thickly wooded; today those who have been back [from exile to Tibet] report that they are clean shaven like a monk's head. The government in Beijing has admitted that the tragic flooding of western China, and further afield, is in part due to this" (76). While recognizing that Tibetans have participated in this quagmire, the Dalai Lama holds the Beijing government to be especially accountable, given what he calls its "iniquitous and wanton destruction of the Tibetan environment" (21). Of course, the Dalai Lama further realizes that what is happening in Tibet is in some ways just part of a larger crisis of global proportions since "we hear about hot temperatures and rising sea levels, increasing cancer rates, vast population growth, depletion of resources, and extinction of species. Human activity everywhere is hastening to destroy key elements of the natural ecosystems all living beings depend on" (29).

Buddhism teaches that human suffering comes from indulgence in the three poisons of attachment, aversion, and ignorance, and the Dalai Lama transposes this formula into an environmental view when he claims that all ecological destruction—whether it be deforestation in Tibet, loss of water resources in Mexico, or human-caused climate change—results from indulg-ing in "ignorance, greed, and lack of respect for the earth's living things."[88] As Buddhist teachings seek to reverse such mental qualities, environmental action, for the Dalai Lama, runs on a parallel track because "in order to change the external situation we must first change within ourselves" (32). In this vein, the Dalai Lama teaches that technological repairs alone will not suffice because it is not the environment that needs fixing, it is us (78).[89]

Based on Buddhist values and indirectly reflecting some principles found in the Deep Ecology movement, the Dalai Lama states that we can heal the world by embodying a sense of "universal responsibility" for our planetary home, with this sense of universal responsibility, for him incumbent on all human beings, being founded on "love and compassion and clear awareness" (14). Following an understanding of dependent arising, Buddhism teaches a close interdependence between sentient beings and their environments, the Dalai Lama says, providing a starting point for developing this ecological "clear awareness." By firmly realizing our rich connections within the web of the universe, we can more positively respond to these connections with lovingkindness and ahimsa.

Interestingly, for the Dalai Lama himself, a sense of personhood relation-ship with the environment motivates his ecological actions. For instance, he describes Anyé Machen, the great yül lha and Tantric power mountain of northeastern Tibet, as a "special friend" (53). Further, because all sentient beings have in the past been our mothers, "we must show respect to all forms of life in the same way we do to our own mother" (87). This last advice, for him, applies to his own understanding of the planet as "Mother Earth." He says, "Until now Mother Earth has somehow tolerated sloppy house habits. But now human use, population, and technology have reached that certain stage where Mother Earth no longer accepts our presence with silence. In many ways she is now telling us, 'My children are behaving badly'" (16). The Dalai Lama, the most visible of Tibetan Buddhist environmentalists, there-fore fits a familiar Buddhist pattern in which relational animist personhood sentiments ground greater efforts toward realizing a greener, more sustain-able biosphere.

Buddhism and Nature in Tibet

As we have seen, Tibetan Buddhist attitudes toward nature revolve around the notion of sustainable taming, in which nonhuman resources are put to human use but, ideally, in a manner that is sustainable. Yet environmental problems occur when Tibetan Buddhists, unlike the Dalai Lama with Mother

Earth, do not consider nonhumans to be fully Buddhist persons, such as with eagles and wolves who are disliked despite their ecological contributions or with animal sacrifices. The uneven extension of personhood sentiments is felt in the limitations of Buddhist compassion, as shown by Shabkar's baby birds who received compassion but also the eagles, plants, and others who did not. Therefore, the ideal of sustainable taming appears difficult to realize when Tibetans do not fully extend relational animist personhood sentiments and because of the boundaries imposed by limited biocentric attitudes.

That said, the extension of personhood to a wide variety of beings helps enable Tibetan efforts toward sustainable Buddhist living while also creating vivid relational animist relationships. Taktser Rinpoché reverences fish, bears, and holy mountains as persons, and many other Tibetans similarly extend respectful personhood to the mountain and lake protectors in their neighborhoods. Natural beings share souls with humans and thus participate in social personhood relationships, and Tantric power mountains manifest the potent persons of the Vajrayāna Buddhist pantheon. Personhood sentiments further drive strong arguments for vegetarianism and animal releases for Lama Zopa and others, and the released animals receive Buddhist teachings and blessings, much like human persons. Finally, the current Dalai Lama, noted for his ecological teachings, is influenced by his own personhood relationships with sacred mountains and the planet itself, which he describes as a maternal person.

Despite these vibrant relational animist outcomes, though, Tibetans generally follow the Buddhist mainstream in denying animals the ability to practice religion. Indeed, the *Mani Kabum* makes it clear that humans were specifically created because only humans can practice religion, thus legitimating the taming of animals. Animals still practice religion indirectly, though, since the sharing of souls with animals leads to spiritual development among all the interconnected beings, so that even if only humans practice religion, nonhumans may still advance spiritually. Similarly, while animals may not practice religion in this life, they can in future lives, so animal release rituals make a point of preaching to animals for their religious welfare in times to come. Alternatively, in this life, apocryphal instances of the practice of religion by animals appear in Tibetan tales, perhaps most famously with the saint Milarepa's taming of a deer and a hunting dog, each of whom realize Buddhist liberation by practicing advanced meditations that they received from the saint.[90]

Additionally, Tibet evidences some Buddhist nature mysticism as part of its network of natural persons. Tantric power mountains represent persons, the manifest deities in the Vajrayāna Buddhist world, and Vajrayāna practitioners explicitly attempt to realize their nonduality with these deities. This creates a situation in which direct numinous nondual experience of a nonhuman in the human habitat results, this being nature mysticism. From this point of view, in fact, nature mysticism becomes an important part of Tibetan Buddhist practice for some people, who may retreat to and meditate on Tantric power mountains for long periods of time. This practice is not required of the vast majority of Tibetan Buddhists, though, so it is not a central feature, but it does inject a potent nature mystical dimension into Tibetan Buddhist spirituality.

Not far from Tibet's capital of Lhasa, one of the places for holy Vajrayāna retreats, Drak Yerpa, is an ancient sacred hill that is dotted with caves. For generations meditators have utilized caves there as isolated and quiet meditation spots, thus blending age-old Tibetan alpine veneration with the practice of Buddhism. Across Central Asia in Mongolia, which shares many cultural traits with Tibet, one encounters a similar situation at the Yalkhoi caves near Khamaryn Khiid. On a mountainside, caves "for the 108 meditation students" remain guarded by the yül lha–like deity of the mountain Yalkhoi, who in art appears riding a red goat. The summit of the promontory is called "Offering Hill" since it is here that a vulture, seeking the protection of the mountain god Yalkhoi, leaves offerings of dead rodents.[91] In sacrificing to a deity what is valuable in species-specific terms like this bird does, it practices religion very much like a human being. No matter how remarkable this vulture may be, though, to some Western Buddhists, trees go beyond this because trees may not simply practice devotional religion, they may meditate. Given this perceived capacity of flora, now it is time to explore the Buddhism of the West.

CHAPTER 8

Natural Persons in the West

Achan Sumano Bhikkhu, a contemporary Theravāda Buddhist monk originally from Chicago in the United States, relates an interesting encounter abroad that he had with a mosquito.[1] Living and meditating in a cave in a remote area of Thailand where mosquitoes thrive, Achan Sumano once became so bothered by a flying antagonist that he trapped it in a jar. While he held it captive, Achan Sumano attempted to "reprogram it through telepathic suggestion" by mentally encouraging it to believe that it was a butterfly, not a mosquito, and should act accordingly. After some time, Achan Sumano set the mosquito loose, and the mosquito immediately went for Achan Sumano's blood. As Achan Sumano humorously describes it, this mosquito taught Achan Sumano that he lacks telepathic powers. But, more seriously, the mosquito also instructed Achan Sumano to respect her or his personhood as a mosquito. Achan Sumano teaches, "The mosquitoes are acting the way they should. It is we humans who see a problem where there is none. . . . Learning to coexist with everything is part of becoming a mature person."[2] In this story, Achan Sumano interacts with a being from the nonhuman natural world who is experienced as a person, or a subject who maintains its own sense of agency. As such, Achan Sumano's interesting interaction highlights some of the roles that respectful personhood attitudes toward nonhuman nature can play in developing sustainable approaches regarding the nonhuman environment, such as acting to benefit mosquitoes, who may perform important ecosystem roles despite their fraught relationships with humans.

Throughout this book, we have seen similar instances in which attending to personhood relationships with the nonhuman natural world can shed new light on Buddhism, and this is true for Achan Sumano's Buddhism of the West, which reveals some intriguing and novel features to add to the characteristics of Western Buddhism that have previously been identified. Already some scholars have probed what, if anything, makes Western Buddhism distinctive, and from this questioning they have arrived at a variety of answers, including the ecumenical character of Western Buddhism; forms of Buddhism that were historically isolated now mingle freely in the West, as they interact with Judaism, Christianity, and other religions.[3] As another feature of the West, the late scholar of Buddhist philosophy C. W. Huntington helpfully portrayed the common, if sometimes troublesome, blending of Buddhism and Western psychologies, such as with some forms of mindfulness-based psychotherapies.[4] Separate congregations of birthright and "convert" Buddhists, or Western-born people who are Buddhist by personal choice rather than family heritage, typify Western Buddhism in Paul Numrich's much-discussed study.[5] Alternatively, Richard Hughes Seager mentions unintentional Christianization, family-centered lay practices, an emphasis on gender equity, and, important to this chapter, an environmentalist sensibility.[6] Extending Seager's insights, James William Coleman discusses feminization processes and laicization in Western Buddhism in his book *The New Buddhism*.[7] Coleman isolates features such as the leveling of hierarchies, including between monastic and lay, and a stressing of meditation practices and correlated retreats.[8]

If there truly is a "New Buddhism" in the West, as Coleman asserts, what we find in this chapter instructs us to add relatively prominent relational animism and nature mysticism to these features as we probe the Western Buddhisms of Bhikkhu Nyanasobhano, Philip Kapleau Roshi, Stephanie Kaza, and Gary Snyder. Each of these Buddhists, including the relatively staid Bhikkhu Nyanasobhano, evidences some form of relational animism, and some of these appearances arise quite vividly. In addition, as I will discuss, while nature mysticism emerges in a less powerful way than relational animism, the experiences of nonduality of Stephanie Kaza and Gary Snyder awaken us to the personhood-laden nature mysticism that is a vital thread of Western Buddhist discourse.

Because of their historical places, Western Buddhists in this chapter can appreciate ecological economics or climate change dynamics in ways that old masters like Buddhaghoṣa or Dōgen never could, thereby supplying some fresh environmentalist perspectives. At the same time, though, we find that contemporary Western Buddhists, like their forebears, still struggle ecologically with limits arising from anthropocentric, biocentric, and ecocentric approaches alike. As I will describe more fully, the vivid ecocentrism of some of these ecological positions may strike some Buddhists as incoherent or too untraditional. Likewise, the focused biocentrism of other Western Buddhist perspectives may limit their broad ecosystem applicability, like one finds, perhaps, with the teachings of Bhikkhu Nyanasobhano, the first Buddhist to be discussed in this chapter.

Bhikkhu Nyanasobhano

Called the "Thoreau of American Buddhism" by Bhikkhu Bodhi, Bhikkhu Nyanasobhano, a Theravāda monk, was born in Louisville, Kentucky, with the name Leonard Price.[9] He attended Dartmouth College, where he majored in English before he became an actor and writer.[10] Drawn to the Dhamma, he lived in Sri Lanka and Thailand and was ordained as a monk at Wat Mahādhātu in Bangkok in 1987.[11] As a monk he has authored numerous works through the Buddhist Publication Society, including *Nothing Higher to Live For*, *To the Cemetery and Back*, and *Radical Buddhism*.[12] Especially notable among his works are *Landscapes of Wonder*, *Longing for Certainty*, and *Available Truth*, in which Nyanasobhano encourages Buddhists to learn teachings from everything in the nonhuman natural world.[13]

Nyanasobhano's prose is often both elegant and moving as he describes hikes through woodlands and meadows in terms of nature's meanings for a Buddhist life. Communing with wild animals, trees, stones, and other elements of the nonhuman natural world helps us attune our minds to the deep processes of the universe, Nyanasobhano says, and in this way nature does not just reflect the teachings of the Buddha, nature *is* the Dhamma (*LW*, 10). Nyanasobhano states, "All this thinking, this habitual noise we take as a self, seems lost in the greater speech of nature around us—or would be lost, perhaps, if we could let go of it now, so immense and strange is the change of the tumbling river" (*LW*, 43). While such communion with nature cannot replace more traditional practices like meditation, for him peering deeply into the natural world can offer profound enhancement of those traditional methods. Moreover, Nyanasobhano says, experiences with nature are common and readily available: "Perhaps we rounded a corner at sunset and saw the landscape charged with rare light, or whirled away from company into a dark street where snow swooped down in a hush, or crossed a bridge, a field, a clearing in solemn pines, and experienced a mood half of pain and half of exultation" (*LW*, 1). Nyanasobhano encourages Buddhists to pursue such moments intentionally and consciously so that they may learn Buddhist lessons from the natural world.

Since "the river speaks Dhamma to those who approach with their hearts prepared," encounters with nature offer Nyanasobhano bountiful lessons for the Buddhist spiritual life, with the fur, leaves, and pebbles of nonhuman nature incarnating the teachings of the Buddha for him (*LW*, 163). Nyanasobhano teaches that we come to see the purpose in life in nature, perhaps foremost because the natural world powerfully instructs us about the keystone Buddhist philosophical notion of impermanence. Nyanasobhano says, "The theme of impermanence revisits us in the immediacy of nature, as our feet swing through cool grass, where still an unseen thorn will scratch us. Remembered words come back to us under the chatter of insects, telling of change and ripening in change as we walk and breathe. What, indeed, can we trust in among all the sparkling of sensation more than this underlying, elemental fact of change?" (*AT*, 173).

In order to understand impermanence, Nyanasobhano invites Buddhists to contemplate a fallen, decaying log that is "crumbling to the dark soil it came from" (*LW*, 26). The log was once a tree, now it is a disintegrating mass, and in the future its molecules will recombine to produce other beings, providing a model for understanding our own human lifeworlds. In addition, according to him, we can learn about our own deaths from observing chrysanthemums in Buddhist temples since they were flowers that once grew free, then beautified a sacred space, and later were disposed of once they wilted and became discolored. In this way, temple chrysanthemums teach humility (*LW*, 154–55; *LC*, 150). Even the most apparently banal experiences with nature can instruct in this way, as long as one attends closely to natural beings and processes, so that learning from nature aids in the development of meditative mindfulness (*LC*, 149). As a plus, this attention includes learning the Buddhist idea of no-self from the natural world because when we look closely, he claims, we appreciate that we have no more self than the decomposing log does (*LW*, 28).

For Nyanasobhano, nature can teach us lessons like these because the natural world is "revealed Dhamma" (*LC*, 45). He says, "The negligent see their days and seasons as the tricky dice of fate, to be sweated over and implored. The attentive do not rely on uncontrollable twists of events but make their quiet progress by the lamps of nature—for Dhamma is nature rightly examined and rightly known. A resolute attention to the course of things, to the laws that shape the course, strikes off the sparks of insight that light our darkness" (*LW*, 10).

In Nyanasobhano's view, we learn lessons from nature perhaps best from animals, our compatriots on the wheel of reincarnation. Closely observing animals "not only reinforces appreciation of the fragility of life but draws us into a deeper contemplation of our own predicament in the immense revolving cosmos," he states (LW, 58). To him, this observation includes regarding animals as persons, as "morally significant beings in their own rights" because human and animal lives are quite similar (LW, 54). Indeed, Nyanasobhano states that we can see our own suffering in animals (LW, 59). He says, "Crows hopping in the cornfields and dogs romping on suburban lawns are surely living, intending, and acting with as dear a regard for their own welfare as we have for ours. Have we ever before paid much mind to the fact?" (AT, 30). Due to rebirth, Nyanasobhano's humans are temporarily superior to animals, but not in an absolute sense, so humans must be charitable to animals (LW, 54). Buddhists should avoid killing animals, even household pests, and animal vivisection in scientific research violates Buddhist ethics (LW, 55, 57). Thus, lively personhood relational animism with animals enriches the teachings of this American Theravāda monk.

Nyanasobhano's nonharm and animal animism nevertheless have limits. He relates that harming nonhumans in the course of agriculture is acceptable as long as one is mindful of one's interactions (LW, 58). Further, perhaps reflecting the Theravāda Buddhist milieu that we observed in chapters 2, 3, and 4, Nyanasobhano is tolerant of meat eating since, in his view, so was the Buddha. To be sure, he states that in a perfect world, animals would not die for our food, but we do not live in a perfect world. The act of eating is morally neutral in itself, he claims, and "what one eats affects one's internal organs, not one's spiritual standing" (LW, 56). Diet choice poses complex questions, among which there are no "moral absolutes," so while he has some sympathy for vegetarian lifestyles, Nyanasobhano leaves dietary choices up to individual Buddhists without condemning a meat diet (LW, 57).

Revealing another animist limit, while he enjoys personhood animist relations with animals, the same cannot be said for his interactions with plants. He certainly admires plants as teachers of impermanence and selflessness and, like Ryōgen in Japan from chapter 6, describes human maturation on the Buddhist path with the analogy of the growth of a plant (LC, 165). But, although he often discusses the need for nonharm toward the natural world, he does not extend this nonharm specifically to plants. In his discussion of dietary choices, he evidences no sense of limit on plant use and implicitly condones any human consumption of flora. Nyanasobhano's approach to the plant world thus is purely instrumental, being focused on what humans can derive from nature.

These instrumental orientations perhaps led Nyanasobhano to clearly explain that one should not take refuge in the natural world (*LC*, 57–58). Unlike what we saw with Dōgen in Japan, Nyanasobhano's natural world is not liberated. Instead, nature is dukkha, being fraught with instability, suffering, and death. Besides the low place of plants in Nyanasobhano's thought, he states that animals are driven purely by instinct and utterly lack the capacity for wisdom required to advance on the Buddhist path. The best that nature can do is to show us ourselves (*LW*, 147). Therefore, we should not look to the nonhuman world for enlightenment, he teaches, because the path to nirvana is not to be found there. Instead, nirvana arises from overcoming nature by escaping the cycle of samsara that makes up the human and nonhuman universe. In other words, it is not enough to savor nature since one must go beyond it. Hence, to him, an excellent symbol for the Buddha's teaching is a dead fish (*LW*, 167).

The image of the dead fish highlights that Nyanasobhano does not promote Buddhist approaches to nature that consist of unbridled ecstasy. For him, mindfulness of nature's beauty, which he definitely admires in some lovely prose, also includes mindfulness of less-pretty degeneration, decomposition, and mortality. In his perspective, marvelous experiences with nature can be spiritual obstacles because they may cement a sense of subjectivity rather than a sense of nature as not-self (*AT*, 46, 111). Further, not only is natural splendor subjective, unlike the way that he describes the experience of nirvana; negativity and disgust at less-pleasant elements of the natural world are also simply human projections that need to be overcome (*AT*, 113; *LC*, 59). Instead, Nyanasobhano teaches, Buddhists must use reason to penetrate both magnificent and horrific encounters with the nonhuman world. Practitioners should attend to the decaying and repulsive as they attend to the beautiful if they are to maximally learn the truth of impermanence, so that dispassion leads to insight (*LC*, 37–39). He writes, "What we observe are repeated facts and signs of the working of nature that we should use for mature reflection, not merely sensual enjoyment, so that we may regard them without delusion and passion and thereby free ourselves from the misery of clinging" (*LC*, 38).

On this note, Nyanasobhano states that "the beauties of the world abound, undeniably, and they arouse a kind of wistfulness and spiritual longing, but when clung to they disguise the landscape of reality," thus leading him to speak against the kind of nature mysticism that is found later in this chapter. Nyanasobhano stresses that the Buddha left home for the forest seeking quiet solitude for meditation, not nature mystical experiences, since "he did not regard the beauties of nature as sufficient in themselves to precipitate liberation" (*LC*, 60). Further, Nyanasobhano states that, although the environment in which one practices may help or hinder you, no environment on its own can lead you to liberation. Nature should not be appreciated for the sensory experience alone nor should one seek self-gratification through experiences with nature, so that nature mysticism, in his view, involves attachments to be avoided, not nirvanic states to be embraced (*LC*, 62). Therefore, in his thought, nature mysticism is not just lacking, it is significantly rejected. Nonetheless, Nyanasobhano's teachings still contain colorful relational animist experiences with animals, as do the pronouncements of another important American Buddhist teacher, Philip Kapleau Roshi.

Philip Kapleau Roshi

As we have seen, Nyanasobhano's spirited personhood relationships with animals do not lead him to call unequivocally for vegetarianism. The same cannot be said for Philip Kapleau Roshi, the American Zen master and founder of the Rochester Zen Center, who presents a dynamic and influential example of vegetarian personhood regard for animals. Born in New Haven, Connecticut, in 1912, Kapleau served as chief court reporter for the Allies at the Nuremburg trials and was later called to Japan for more trials there. While in Japan, Kapleau became deeply interested in Zen Buddhism. A return trip to Japan resulted in a thirteen-year stay, during which time he studied with three different teachers. In 1965 Hakun Yasutani Roshi ordained him and gave him permission to teach within the Sanbōkyōdan lineage, which combines elements of both Sōtō and Rinzai Zen practice. In that same year, Kapleau returned to the United States and published *The Three Pillars of Zen*, an enduring classic in American Buddhist literature. Over the next few decades, he led the Rochester Zen Center to prominence within the American Buddhist world while also writing many books on the practice of Zen. Kapleau died on May 6, 2004, from complications of Parkinson's disease.[14]

Kapleau's influence continues to reverberate throughout Western Buddhism, not just in Zen worlds, in part because of his much-beloved book, *To Cherish All Life: A Buddhist Case for Becoming Vegetarian*.[15] In this text, Kapleau's relational animism with animals, whom he says possess "innate dignity and wholeness (holiness)," is every bit as rich as other forms of animism that appear in this chapter. Animals clearly are persons for him since humans and animals share a "basic kinship," given their interchangeable places within the wheel of reincarnation in which animals are reborn as humans and vice versa (6). Human incarnations are temporarily "karmically superior" but are not supreme creations, leaving "no demarcation between humans and animals" in terms of hierarchy (6, 21). In fact, following an argument from the *Laṅkāvatāra Sūtra*, to him animals and humans are kin, peers to each other, so that we must respect the subjectivities of animals just as we respect those of our human kin.[16] We need nonhuman animals and animals need us, and further we share the problematic outcomes of environmental degradation with animals, so that human and animal worlds are interrelated networks of peers (6–7).

Interestingly, given our personhood connections, Kapleau even encourages the development of "interspecies communication" with animal persons since there is much that we can learn from them: "Animals, we know, are gifted with senses and psychic powers far keener than our own, and they can teach us much about our own animal nature . . . provided we respect their uniqueness and do not patronize or exploit them" (6–7). On the other hand, to him, a lack of communication with animals inevitably results from not treating them with an ethic of kin personhood respect and care (23).

In Kapleau's view, a poignant example of such a lack of personhood respect for animals appears with the human habit of eating meat, given that we cannot enhance our relationships with nonhuman persons while we are eating them (55). In fact, Kapleau's animal animism motivates him to a rather strident advocacy for Buddhist vegetarianism since, for him, eating animals violates the precept of ahimsa, or nonharm, with the eating of animals in reality representing a "war of aggression" against animals (1). Eating meat by itself, even if one does not kill the animal oneself, violates Kapleau's sense of ahimsa since it makes one an accessory after the fact to animal killing as well as to animal cruelty, given that neither traditional pastoralism nor modern factory farms are cruelty-free (9, 15, 19). The basic moral goodness of our Buddha-nature, Kapleau teaches, fosters engaging in nonharm, so that meat eating entails estrangement not just from our animal personhood relationships but also from our own Buddha-natures. To him, this estrangement is not just unethical, it is also pointless because, he claims, unlike other animals, humans can choose to be herbivores.

Intriguingly, the idea that relational animist personhood shapes ethical dietary values appears even in the negative for him. Attempting to be culturally tolerant, Kapleau states that it is acceptable for members of groups like the Inuit people to eat meat since they ritualize the hunt and regard their quarry respectfully as persons (54). Thus, Kapleau essentially argues that we should not eat animals because of their personhood, but he excuses Inuit people from this moral understanding precisely because they openly regard animals as persons. Either way, to Kapleau, personhood relationships determine Buddhist dietary norms.

While he teaches that animals suffer from human meat eating, Kapleau relates that humans suffer from the practice, too; this point is educational in terms of understanding his relational animism. Representing the second human fall after Adam and Eve, meat eating leads to "terror, violence, bloodshed, the slaughter of humans, and ultimately war" (1).[17] Kapleau teaches—as did Augustine, Aquinas, and Kant in the Christian tradition—that an attitude of cruelty toward animals leads to a similar attitude toward humans, so, to him, meat eaters enable an inexorable cycle of human violence (16–17).[18] Further, in an influential passage, Kapleau argues that eating meat means ingesting the "fear and terror" of the animals, and these negative energies become a part of you, preventing the growth of peaceful mental states (30). Instructively, however, he warns against adopting vegetarianism for one's own benefit since this can become an attachment, like Thailand's Achan Cha argued in chapter 4. Instead, to Kapleau, the proper reason to adopt vegetarianism is for the sake of our animal kin, thus exhibiting the relational animism that forms the core of Kapleau's vegetarian Buddhist ideals (56).

Kapleau knows that his portrayal of the Buddhist religion as a vegetarian one attracts challenges from other places in the Buddhist world. He bemoans Buddhist teachers and monastics in Japan for their consumption of animal flesh, decries what he calls the "waffling permissiveness" of meat eating in the Theravāda world, and recognizes climactic difficulties regarding the practice of vegetarianism in Tibet (35, 39). To him, in most of these instances Buddhists have lost sight of the Buddha's essential message regarding our proper relationships with animals. Kapleau portrays the Buddha as, without a doubt, an uncompromising vegetarian. To him, translations of the Buddha's last meal, sūkara-maddava or "pig's delight," as a pork dish simply could not be correct, so that, for Kapleau, the Buddha certainly died from eating "a bad mushroom" (3). Because meat eating creates a market for killing, there is no chance that the Buddha would have approved of the custom, he says (30–31). Eating meat is worse to him than eating after noon, like Theravāda monks avoid doing, because eating at the wrong time is victimless (33). Kapleau further states that the acceptance of meat eating found in numerous passages of the Pāli canon was contrived by the scriptures' authors, who were monks with an attachment to meat, so that when it comes to meat, "The Buddha could not have uttered the words attributed to him in the Pāli scriptures" (3, 40).

Taking a cue from Kapleau in terms of the recognition of different approaches to nature, it is important to note again that his vegetarianism-motivating animism includes animals, but only animals, as respected persons within the nonhuman realm. The plant persons on whom Japanese masters like Annen and Ryōgen focused are invisible in Kapleau's text outside of their presence on our dinner plates. Kapleau grants plants a "rudimentary" consciousness, but implicitly denies them the ability to suffer (54). Humans are anatomically designed to eat plants, he avers, and require plants, but not meat, in order to survive. Moreover, he says, one can pick a fruit from a plant without harming the plant itself, despite the somewhat erroneous nature of this assertion (55).[19] Nowhere does Kapleau apply the notion of nonharm to plants or otherwise consider their value apart from human food. Therefore, to Kapleau, plants are not persons, nor are water and mineral entities. In his limited biocentric view, we should not eat animals because they are respected persons, but we are free to eat plants because they are not.

The dismissal of plant personhood by Kapleau and Nyanasobhano is a common attitude in the Western Buddhist world. But another Buddhist, Stephanie Kaza, clearly disagrees with these leaders when it comes to treating flora as persons, and this disagreement bears implications for establishing a sustainable biosphere.

Stephanie Kaza and Green Gulch

Both Nyanasobhano and Kapleau have a sense of limited biocentrism, in which plants are valued merely instrumentally while only animals are significantly valued in themselves. However, across the universes of Western Buddhism, one finds many points of view that are less animal-centered and much more ecocentric than those of Nyanasobhano and Kapleau, like that of Stephanie Kaza. Kaza is a professor of environmental studies at the University of Vermont who has distinguished herself as a scholar and an academic leader. She also intentionally cultivates a public identity as a Buddhist student of Sōtō Zen's Kōbun Chino Roshi; she has published several works foremost as a Buddhist and only secondarily as an environmental scientist, and I will focus on these more Buddhist works of hers. A leader within the Buddhist Peace Fellowship, she has authored or edited books such as *Mindfully Green: A Personal and Spiritual Guide to Whole Earth Thinking, Dharma Rain: Essays in Buddhist Environmentalism*, and *Hooked!: Buddhist Writings on Greed, Desire, and the Urge to Consume*.

Kaza's book, *The Attentive Heart: Conversations with Trees*,[20] may contain the most luminous example of relational animism in the Western Buddhist universe since in it Kaza exquisitely expresses the importance of enjoying sacred, intimate experiences with trees. In this book, Kaza's writing resembles that of the American naturalist John Muir in that nonhuman beings appear as persons, a broadly ecocentric perspective arises, and ecstatic experiences with nature enliven the narrative. Also like Muir, Kaza deeply regrets excess human destruction of the nonhuman environment, with this concern having caused her to enter into the field of conservation biology in the first place. She states that current Western economic philosophies are unsustainable because their goal of never-ending growth cannot be realized, given the expansion of human population on a finite planet. They are also alienating, according to Kaza, since by design they regard nonhumans instrumentally, or only for what resources they offer to humans. While Kaza recognizes that some human use of nonhumans is inevitable, she contends that Western economic philosophies prevent our experiencing them in noninstrumental ways, and such a one-sided approach to nature leads, she feels, inevitably to ever-greater environmental devastation. In other words, she argues that the social ethics of contemporary Western economies do "not include any thoughtful basis for mutually respectful relationships with trees" (AH, 4).

Because we have a "moral obligation to forests and woodlands," Kaza stresses that we must embrace a sense of natural beings as subjects, as entities with value in their own right, if we are to act both morally and sustainably (AH, 5). Like the mid-twentieth-century American ecologist Aldo Leopold, Kaza insists on our renewing our communion with the land and its inhabitants. Kaza says, "The environmental movement is, as much as anything, a struggle to reclaim the land and relationship with the land for the common people" (AH, 8). She stresses this renewal because of what she describes as the moral challenge of the natural world to humanity as "a place of truth, generating ethical power by its very existence" (AH, 8). Reclaiming the land further aids with fighting environmental destruction since "acknowledgement of and participation in relationships with trees, coyotes, mountains, and rivers is central to the philosophy of Deep Ecology" (AH, 10).

In order to renew her own sense of relation to the land, for a period Kaza studied at Starr King School for the Ministry. For one of her projects, she chose to go to the forest specifically to explore the spiritual dimensions of her interactions with trees. Inspiration for this journey came from Dōgen's *Mountains and Waters Sūtra*, in which Dōgen spoke of a mountain contemplatively being a mountain, then no longer being a mountain, and then being a mountain again. For her part, Kaza wished to experience trees as trees; trees as no longer trees, but beings who "carry painful stories of fear, killing unconsciousness, and objectification"; and then trees as trees again (AH, 13). Her method for this experiment was Zen *shikantaza*, or sitting meditation. She would sit with a tree and then, in Zen fashion, try to drop all her projections, preconceptions, and so on, so that she could commune with the bare tree as it was. In the process, Kaza emphasized that the practice should not be anthropomorphic, or humanize a tree as one might find in a children's story. Instead, she sought to experience trees in themselves, with as much human subjectivity stripped away from the process as possible. Calling this method "the attentive heart," Kaza says that one tries to interact as openly, respectfully, and substantially as possible with another being, human or non-human, since "the attentive heart" is "the heart that feels the presence of others and the call to respond, the heart that lives in relationship with other beings" (*AH*, 158).

The scholar of religion Evan Berry showed that, in the early twentieth-century United States, the establishment of national parks combined with the advent of the automobile to get to the parks sponsored a back-to-nature movement that was not purely secular, but instead took on a tone of pilgrimage.[21] Similarly, Kaza describes her journey to the forest as a pilgrimage (*AH*, 32–33). A grove of redwoods, for instance, provided her with a kind of temple, and once there she cavorted with her sequoia sangha community (*AH*, 154). But Kaza, ecocentrically recognizing that "all beings are Buddhas with teachings to offer," also interacted with a broad array of entities as persons; at one point a glacier, the sun, wind, snow, and ice were her friends.[22] She says, "Each introduction to salamander and shrew is a step toward seeing the pattern of lives and movement that define the forest. To say hello to trillium and redwood sorrel is to meet the friends of the tall trees" (*AH*, 42).

But despite her many friends, in this experiment Kaza has come to converse specifically with trees, although of course not conversing with ordinary human speech. The scientist Kaza retains a sense of sobriety as she seeks to avoid human sentimentalism and anthropomorphism in her interactions. She admits that she does not understand "the language of these alders," whom she describes as "water people" (*AH*, 26, 46). But she can still sense some wordless communication since plants, as biology teaches, are beings who communicate through the use of chemicals. For Kaza, conversations with trees thereby begin with the recognition of personhood, not human verbal aptitude. For instance, she hears, but not with ordinary human speech, redwood trees calling her to friendship (*AH*, 39). Redwoods also serve as models for a straight back during meditation since they are the "yogis of the forest," and, as the "people of time," they teach impermanence (*AH*, 128, 131). She insists on knowing trees by species name, just as one must be "properly introduced" before interacting with human persons (*AH*, 81). She also startlingly describes her perception of a madrone tree using semi-erotic language usually reserved for humans, including, "I feel the sweetness of reaching out to touch the muscular limbs, the leaning branches, the solid trunk" (*AH*, 74).

Further, she found that communication with a tree may occur through touch. If we remember that plants are complex systems of electrical interactions, we can appreciate that repeatedly she lovingly laid her hands on trees, telling us, "It is difficult to imagine the scale and complexity of activity that goes on inside a tree. I sense in my hands some charge, some energetic force at work here. Joining palms to trunk, I form a circle of energy with this tree. Listening through my hands, I meet this tree from my own experience of sunlight and stillness" (*AH*, 28).

Kaza enjoys these communicative encounters not as a dominant human with a mindless object but as a peer within "a co-created field of experience, generated as much by tree as by [human] person" (*AH*, 10). As peer friends, "trees tell stories of fire, agriculture, and commercial cultivation" (*AH*, 12). However, in order to work, Kaza's "attentive heart" method requires a time investment since "it takes time to see the deeply encoded patterns of destruction and transgression against trees and other nonhuman beings. It takes time to cultivate a relational sensitivity that is compassionate and not pathological" (*AH*, 164).

Kaza feels that the practice of "the attentive heart" may lead to something like Rolston's concept of a sustainable biosphere since it helps one peer more deeply into the lives of nonhumans while it also inspires one energetically to seek solutions to problems. One thereby finds these movements in Kaza's prose. At times, she describes ecstasy in the forest, lucidly portraying her appreciative experiences of nonhumans in intimate and holy terms. These passages represent fine examples of American nature writing at its most exuberant, such as when she exclaims regarding the natural persons who surround her, "Such a lovely gathering of children and friends on a sweet, sunny afternoon" (*AH*, 43). These ecstatic experiences motivate her to act on behalf of nonhumans.

At the same time, just as with human friendships, when her tree friends suffer and die, she experiences genuine grief. When an elm tree was felled because its roots were encroaching on the foundation of her mother's home, Kaza created an impromptu funeral ritual for the elm as she mourned its "murder" (*AH*, 96). She also movingly shared her experiences with an oak tree she had befriended. Being distracted by human concerns, she left the oak for a long time; upon her return, she discovered that it had been cut down. In response, she said, "The tree soul in me screamed with the shock of sudden loss" (*AH*, 124). She moaned, "My friend, taken apart by a chainsaw. AAaaayyy! The instrument of torture cut through my own limbs" (*AH*, 124). She felt complicit in the death of her oak friend, and not just because she had left it unguarded for so long. While dealing primarily with human issues, she had also lost her empathic connection with her oak friend and cut herself off from "learning the wisdom of time in a wild context" (*AH*, 124). With these attitudes regarding attention and empathy, Kaza modeled how, in her teachings, the practice of "the attentive heart" may lead to deeper perceptions of environmental problems as well as positive enthusiasm to create change for the better.

Her experiences led Kaza to comprehend her similarities with trees, despite obvious differences in outward form. For instance, as she describes it, both trees and Kaza follow the same life rhythms of day and night through the four seasons (*AH*, 19). Thus, having for some time caringly practiced meditation and "the attentive heart" at the foot of a manzanita tree, she says, "If I stayed here long enough, it seems like I would grow into a manzanita. Put down roots and join back to back with you, Old One [manzanita tree]. That would be fine; some part of me is tree" (*AH*, 67). In this feeling of sameness with trees, Kaza encounters trees as peers, as respected subjects in their own right and as partners in the job of living, rather than as meaningless objects. In other words, Kaza's approach to the nonhuman world evidences clear and vivid personhood relational animism with flora.

I mentioned previously that, besides brilliant animism, Western Buddhism sometimes embodies dynamic nature mysticism as well, and Kaza's writings further demonstrate this. Of the landscape of her childhood she said, "I didn't realize how much it supported my entire life and worldview. Like roots growing up through my toes, the land had entered my body. The creek water flowed in my veins, the night stars shone in my eyes" (*AH*, 122). Her nature mysticism even blends with her animism, as she says of a powerful experience in Yosemite, "The shock of this expansiveness awakens the truth of interpenetrating realities. I am the sky, I am the rock, I am the pine. The wind is in me, in my breath; the stone is in me, in my body; the tree is in me, in my mind. The truth of this is real; I recognize the depth of it. . . . The sense of unity with this rock, with these trees, speaks to me. They are my relations" (*AH*, 235–36).

Kaza developed her nature mystical and relational animist attitudes in part during long periods spent at Green Gulch, the rural northern California retreat center that is affiliated with the prominent San Francisco Zen Center. As Kaza describes it in a book chapter titled "American Buddhist Response to the Land,"[23] due to ecofriendly impulses that adopt Buddhist modes of expression, the twenty-five or so residents of Green Gulch approach their setting with an attitude of Buddhist gratitude. Previously, the land had been a cattle ranch on which herbicides were used to suppress native brush so, beginning with the acquisition of the property in 1975, Green Gulch residents started renewing the plot. Over time, they planted numerous trees such as Monterey cypress, Monterey pine, redwood, Douglas fir, and live oak, while culling non-native trees and shrubs like eucalyptus, acacia, broom sedge, and ivy, with residents seeking to restore the presumed primary forest (*AB*, 221, 229). Today, the second Sunday of each month occasions a "watershed work party day," in which self-described "ecosattvas" remove invasive species, plant local species, and initiate ecosystem cleanups.[24] Due to these activities, the Green Gulch precincts now encourage sustainable biodiversity despite still resting in a larger region that has been significantly denuded by logging.

Reflecting impulses toward the development of a sustainable biosphere, ritualized expressions of gratitude at Green Gulch are sometimes offered not just to the Buddha, the Dharma, and the sangha, but to the local landscape as well (*AB*, 227). Such expressions of gratitude appear in multiple ways at mealtimes. Before the meal, practitioners chant this supplication, whose lines include references to the land:

Innumerable labors brought us this food
We should know how it comes to us
Receiving this offering let us consider whether our virtue or practice deserve it
Desiring the natural order of mind, let us be free from greed, hate, and delusion
We eat to support life and to practice the way of the Buddha. (*AB*, 228)

Meat is never served at the center, which is thoroughgoing vegetarian due both to its Zen lineage—which includes employment of the *Fanwangjing* injunctions that we studied in the chapter on China—and its efforts to live compassionately with the environment. By following a vegetarian diet, residents feel that they are avoiding participation in the cruelty of the industrial factory farm system while also reducing the desire among others to fell forests in favor of animal ranches (*AB*, 231). In order to support vegetable over meat consumption, Green Gulch maintains a resident-run farm that is a member of the California Organic Farming Association and provides many of its own plant-based edibles at mealtimes. Using no artificial pesticides or fertilizers, Green Gulch farmers condition the soil with their own compost, manure, and green manure provided by a wintertime fava bean crop. Farmers keep the use of machines to a minimum and weed and harvest as much as possible by hand as down-to-earth Zen practices (*AB*, 229).

Gratitude for the nonhuman world also appears in a number of holiday rituals at the center, such as at the four cardinal points of the solar year, during which times gratitude is extended to the rising sun, the garden, its produce, and other natural entities (*AB*, 228). Arbor Day witnesses the planting of trees as a cherished center tradition. Earth Day celebrations have included memorial services for animals as well as tree ordinations of live oaks, these last receiving inspiration from the Thai tree ordination practices explored in chapter 4. The Buddha's birthday may be celebrated with praise for local wildflowers and the American holiday of Thanksgiving includes expressions of gratitude for the vegetable produce of the Green Gulch gardens.[25]

The community also seeks to be simultaneously ecofriendly and compassionate through other means, such as its treatment of waste. Residents compost or recycle all eligible materials, with the compost then enriching the organic gardens. Paper towels, napkins, and office supplies come from recycled resources. Water conservation is practiced year-round but is especially focused on the driest period of August and September. Night lights provide nocturnal safety but are otherwise kept to a minimum, so as to diminish light pollution. Finally, residents often offer classes on green living to the many visitors of the center, as well as a farm and garden apprenticeship program, thus expanding the reach of Green Gulch's twenty-first-century Buddhist activities.[26]

However, despite the noteworthy environmental activities of the center, limits constrain the Zen center's ability to help establish something like Rolston's sustainable biosphere because all forms of religion, sooner or later, face limits to their nature-friendliness.[27] Kaza tells us, for example, that the primary goal of Green Gulch, like other Buddhist institutions, is to maintain and transmit the teachings, not simply to be a positive environmental example, so compromises in green living must sometimes be made. Green Gulch's very success, in fact, occasions many of the compromises since wild land must be taken to provide parking for the greater number automobiles of visitors who through their numbers also exert pressure on the available water, sewage, and energy resources (*AB*, 239–41). Additionally, for residents of Green Gulch raising food in the gardens means trapping gophers and removing snails.[28] Such limits on Buddhist sustainable biospheric living inform the work of another important American Zen Buddhist, the poet Gary Snyder.

Gary Snyder

Kaza has spent considerable time in the forests of northern California, as has the American writer and environmental activist Gary Snyder, whom Max Oelschlaeger called "the poet laureate of Deep Ecology."[29] Like Kapleau, Snyder trained in Zen in Japan in the 1960s, and Snyder's thought echoes that of Kapleau in its potent relational animism. However, like Kaza, Snyder is much more ecocentric than Kapleau in his concern.

Born in 1930, Snyder spent his childhood on a farm in remote Oregon, where chopping wood and tending chickens were daily activities. Always a lover of the outdoors, in his teens Snyder mountaineered with the Mazamas club before working as both a logger and a forest ranger. During this time, he became enamored of many aspects of the Native American cultures of the Pacific Northwest, later integrating these influences into his thought. Snyder then went to San Francisco in the early 1950s, changing his life forever. In the city, he explored Chinese landscape painting, Chinese poetry, and Japanese Zen while he undertook Chinese and Japanese language study at the University of California. Around this time, he also began publishing his poetry as a member of both the San Francisco Renaissance and Beat Generation movements.

Seeking the real Zen coin, Snyder then moved for a number of years to the Japanese city of Kyoto, where he was a de facto Rinzai Zen monk as well as an English teacher. Returning to the United States, he established a home in the Sierra Nevada foothills and his writing career blossomed spectacularly thereafter, with his book *Turtle Island* winning the Pulitzer Prize for Poetry in 1975 and his *Axe Handles* garnering an American Book Award in 1984.[30] In part because of their powerful evocations of nonhuman nature, Snyder's writings are influential not just in Western Buddhist circles but also within non-Buddhist American literary and environmentalist communities.

For all of his life an amateur naturalist, it seems no surprise that Snyder laments the environmental devastation currently ravaging our globe. In *A Place in Space* and *The Practice of the Wild*,[31] sometimes using incendiary words, he attributes ecological problems to a variety of causes, including overpopulation, otherworldly religions, the unequal distribution of wealth, and a lack of intrinsic valuation of nature in Western cultures (*PS*, 33, 60, 209; *PW*, 98). Agriculture was a mistake from the start, he says, relying as it does on the monoculture of annual plants. Like Kaza, he indicts contemporary capitalist economic philosophies, whose ultimate goal of eternal growth cannot be met on a planet that does not expand in carrying capacity (*PS*, 60; *PW*, 97). Snyder also blames the widespread anthropocentric attitude of human superiority to the natural world, including within Buddhism. On this note, he insightfully avoids the common error of overly valorizing approaches to nature in East Asia, given that he trenchantly criticizes the environmental records of both China and Japan, "who have long given lip service to nature" (*PW*, 6), in his poem "Mother Earth: Her Whales."[32]

In response to our environmental crises, Snyder insists that Buddhist eco-friendly attitudes must develop through an intentional, unique, and deeply personal process including with the help of Buddhist practices such as Zen sitting meditation. Snyder calls this process "the practice of the wild." By "practice," Snyder intends "a deliberate, sustained, and conscious effort to be more finely tuned to ourselves and to the way the actual existing world is" (PW, x). This practice involves not just sitting meditation, though, but a whole-being, critical self-evaluation to uncover genuinely nature-friendly, deceptively nature-friendly, and not nature-friendly attitudes within oneself. One should overcome one's attachments, aversions, and delusions regarding one's interactions with nonhumans so that one may be open to profoundly interacting with a multitude of natural beings as respected persons with whom one relates. He asks us to "engage in more than environmentalist virtue, political keenness, or useful and necessary activism. We must ground ourselves in the dark of our deepest selves . . . within the 'natural nations' shaped by mountain ranges, river courses, flatlands, and wetlands" (PW, xi). The practice manifests differently across individuals since there "is a 'going' but no goer, no destination," but, for Snyder personally, it entails events such as conversing with wood and having a cedar tree as an adviser, much like Kaza did (PW, 114, 127, 162).

Snyder's own "practice of the wild" intriguingly also includes bear persons. From his perspective, bears, "the closest of all animals to humans," are fond of humans, having "decided long ago to let the humans join them at the salmon-running rivers and the berryfields" (PW, 175). In honor of bears, Snyder devotes a large section of his book The Practice of the Wild to a lively retelling of the old Native American myth, "The Woman Who Married a Bear," in which bears clearly exist as respected persons (PW, 166–86). But perhaps no bear means more to Snyder than Smokey the Bear, the fictional mascot of the United States Forest Service whose famous motto is "Only you can prevent wildfires." To Snyder, in creating the figure of Smokey the Bear, the Forest Service unwittingly uncovered a sacred Buddhist incarnation, perhaps not unlike the discovery of ter ma hidden spiritual treasures by Tibetans.[33] This is because, for Snyder, Smokey the Bear is a contemporary emanation of the "Ancient One" Buddha, identified by Snyder in his Smokey the Bear Sutra as Vairocana, the Great Sun Buddha of the Mahāvairocana Sūtra.[34]

Teaching long ago, this "Ancient One" Buddha only gave her teachings to "mountain and river spirits, wild creatures, storm gods, whale ascetics, bison philosophers, and a few lost human stragglers."[35] Now incarnated as the "Sacred Cub" or the "Great Bear," this Buddha, through the figure of Smokey the Bear, brings "a rich and complex teaching of Non-Dualism."[36] Although some may doubt the power of the holy Smokey the Bear, Snyder relates that "it might take this sort of Buddha to quell the fires of greed and war and to help us head off the biological holocaust that the twenty-first

century may well prove to be" (*PS*, 30). Therefore, Smokey the Bear wages
battle against rampant human desire and its destructiveness on behalf of a
variety of beings, both human and nonhuman:

> Bearing in his right paw the Shovel that digs to the
> truth beneath appearances; cuts the root of useless attachments,
> and flings damp sand on the fires of greed and war;

> His left paw in the Mudra of Comradely Display—
> indicating that all creatures have the full right to live to their limits
> and that deer, rabbits, chipmunks, snakes, dandelions,
> and lizards all grow in the realm of the Dharma.[37]

Smokey the Bear Buddha alerts us to Snyder's implementation of the
word *wild* in "practice of the wild," which stands several common uses on
their heads. For Snyder, "the wild" is not a thing or place, such as a happy
meadow in which foxes and grasshoppers play. Instead, it is a process, a universal flux that runs through, shapes, and informs all things, "constantly
going on without human intervention," as the mutability that the Buddha
described as impermanence.[38] Snyder says, "'Wild' is a name for the way that
phenomena continually actualize themselves" as "interconnected, interdependent, and incredibly complex" (*PS*, 168). The "wild" is both inner and
outer since it forms the reality through which we experience our true, unde-
luded selves in relationship with everything, including the natural beings that
people our universe.

Because of this use of the word *wild*, Snyder says that both New York City
and Tokyo are "natural" but not "wild," since their human-oriented habitats
inhibit realization of relationships with nonhuman beings, thus limiting felt
wholeness, and "to speak of wilderness is to speak of wholeness" (*PW*, 12).
Cities, in Snyder's view, remain chaotic and disorganized since, to him, all
human activities are disorganized, while true order resides in the transhu-
man (*PW*, 100). Nonhuman nature is always organized, and, not unlike what
we find in the work of the anthropologist Claude Lévi-Strauss, to Snyder our
notions of social order derive from the order of nature (*PW*, 19).

To be fair, a critic might say that Snyder, otherwise so allergic to dualisms, here falls prey to a troublesome dualism of his own making by dividing
the "natural" from the "wild" in order to "speak of wilderness." Snyder's
implied concept of "wilderness" as a place devoid of human influence, as
the environmental historian William Cronon has taught us, presupposes a
nonexistent reality since humans participate in physically uninhabited locations even if only culturally. Cronon states, "Wilderness embodies a dualistic

vision in which the human is entirely outside the natural."[39] For example, today's space age cultures prompt some humans to ponder the planet Neptune, meaning that even far away Neptune, which is physically uninhabited, is culturally inhabited by the human mind and therefore is not a human-free wilderness area. Thus, Snyder's usual thoroughgoing ecocentrism may stumble a bit with his bifurcating distinction between what is "natural" and what is "wild" in the "wilderness."

This difficulty notwithstanding, Snyder's "wild" also supplies the locus of the sacred since the Buddhist individual self may arise as an artifact of culture but the "wild" manifests as nirvanic realization. In Snyder's view, the classic Buddhist struggle with the individual self appears both as the path to nirvana as well as the path to healing our relationships with the natural world. Snyder claims, "Self-realization, even enlightenment, is another aspect of our wildness—a bonding of the wild in ourselves to the (wild) process of the universe," so that the "wild" is "not far from the Buddhist term *Dharma* with its original senses of forming and firming" (PW, xi, 11).

Instead of relying on Buddhism as it is to be a sustainable biosphere panacea like so many others have done, Snyder, like Bhikkhu Nyanasobhano and Stephanie Kaza, encourages augmenting traditional Buddhist practices with direct, aware, and respectful encounters with the nonhuman world understood, as the environmental ethicist Thomas Berry put it, as a community of subjects rather than a collection of objects.[40] In this effort, Snyder emphasizes the bioregional need for a deep sense of place. He criticizes Westerners, whom he says are always on the move and distracted from the nonhuman world, thus never getting a substantial sense of where they are in terms of the many animals, insects, plants, bodies of water, and rocks that provide their immediate surroundings. For Snyder, without a clear and locally grounded sense of place, we are alienated not just from the nonhuman world but also from the sacred "wild" within ourselves.

We must reverse this process of alienation and acquire a grounded sense of place, says Snyder the bioregionalist, if we are to cultivate greater eco-friendliness. Doing this means realizing one's interconnections in wise and compassionate ways that begin in one's backyard and, without this local support, cannot continue. With this local support, though, one can be truly oneself. Thus, Snyder asserts, "The wild requires that we learn the terrain, nod to all the plants and animals and birds, ford the streams and cross the ridges" (PW, 26). Only with such a sense of place can we be truly in touch with long-term natural rhythms, so that we can see more clearly what is truly problematic and what represents an organic process of healing with which we should not interfere. For Snyder, considering nature to be sacred is not required, but listening to nature like we do to human persons is, because "mind is fluid, nature is porous, and both biologically and culturally we are always fully part of the whole" (*PW*, 103; *PS*, 81). For this listening, one must be fully present in the moment with natural beings since "to see a wren in a bush, call it 'wren,' and go on walking is to have (self-importantly) seen nothing. To see a bird and stop, watch, feel, forget yourself for a moment, be in the bushy shadows, maybe then feel 'wren'—that is to have joined in a larger moment with the world" (*PS*, 179).

Therefore, "the practice of the wild" differs across individuals, not just because of divergent mental worldviews but also because the place-based practice occurs among the varying flora, fauna, water bodies, mineral formations, and climates between locations. But "the practice of the wild" need not occur only in bucolic settings; it should stay with us in urban environs because, Snyder says, "Great Brown Bear is walking with us, Salmon is swimming upstream with us, as we stroll a city street" (*PW*, 101). With natural beings as our leaders, perhaps "the spirits of douglas fir, redwood, cedar, live oak, manzanita, and especially salmon will guide us past gridlock and smog to a new culture."[41]

Snyder's environmentalism fascinatingly does not lead to a plea for vegetarianism like it does for so many other ecologically minded Western Buddhists. Snyder ecocentrically perceives human and nonhuman worlds meshed as a process involving a variety of respected persons, so that he feels no compulsion to favor animal existences over plant or any other existences. Rather than create a moral boundary between animals and plants like Kapleau does, Snyder instead values "the total ecological health of the region" (*PW*, 34). Therefore, for Snyder, "the very distinction 'vegetarian/nonvegetarian' is too simple" because "the First Precept goes beyond a concern just for organic life" (*PW*, 67, 70). He does not oppose vegetarianism and deeply criticizes the techniques of modern factory farms yet, for him, the crucial factor is respectful recognition of the relational animist personhood of the nonhuman Other, not which category of person one will eat and not valuing animal persons more than plant persons. He says, "Every boulder on a talus slope is different, no two needles on a fir tree are identical. How could one part be more central, more important, than any other?" (*PW*, 164). The influence of Native American religions on him shines through with this issue since he considers everything we eat to be a natural person, and as long as we collect food and eat with respect, the question of whether that person is an animal or a plant is not overly relevant (*PW*, 22). Indeed, Snyder invites us to enter the "wild" reality that we are both eater and eaten within a much larger universe, and in fact the constant dining of the natural world shows us its essence as a holy, sacramental reality (*PW*, 20). Therefore, establishing a sustainable biosphere does not demand Buddhist vegetarianism for Snyder as it does for Kapleau. This clash of perspectives invites us to take stock of Western Buddhist interactions with nonhuman nature.

The Environment of Western Buddhism

Each thinker in this chapter embodies a multitude of divergent influences, reflecting the cosmopolitan ethos of the Buddhist West. Each of these Buddhists further exhibits energetic relational animism of some kind, from the animal animism of Nyanasobhano and Kapleau to the ecocentric personhood relationships of Kaza and Snyder. Of anthropological and social interest, with these Buddhists one finds relational animism arising comfortably in the midst of Euro-American culture, contrary to the expectations of those like the anthropologist Edward Tylor, who described animism as appearing primarily within non-Western cultures. But even the most closely related among these Buddhists exhibit differences in animist manifestations. For Nyanasobhano and Kapleau, animals are persons, but the two disagree about whether this fact prevents their consumption by humans. Kaza and Snyder maintain visions deriving from Chan-family Buddhist schools, but Snyder sometimes advocates meat eating while Kaza, although sympathetic to vegetarianism, feels that the choice of diet must be navigated by each Buddhist in her or his own way.[42]

Perhaps even more interestingly, animism blends into nature mysticism in the thought of Kaza as well as Snyder. This nature mysticism of Western Buddhism, which also manifests in the Western Buddhist works of Thich Nhat Hanh, Joanna Macy, and Charles S. Fisher, is more apparent and outspoken than it has been in some other chapters of this book and therefore appears to mark a distinctive characteristic of Western Buddhism when compared to other Buddhist forms.[43] Perhaps the influences of ecocentric Deep Ecology, Leopold's land ethic, and East Asian Buddhist nature mysticism contribute to this orientation which, along with vibrant relational animism, appears to mark the Buddhist world of the West. Given the diversity of Western Buddhist attitudes toward the environment, however, this nature mystical orientation is not shared by all Western Buddhists, as Bhikkhu Nyanasobhano's teachings against nature mysticism reveal.

Every Western Buddhist in this chapter encourages respect for natural entities in some form or another, and, in so doing, they reflect sentiments expressed in the ancient Pāli jātaka tales. For instance, a story from the *Macchuddāna*

Jātaka tells us that, in a lifetime before he was our Buddha, the Buddha-to-be was once born into a wealthy family. The father of the family died, leaving the Buddha-to-be and his younger brother to collect debts owed to their deceased father. Having received a great deal of money, the brothers were returning home when they stopped on the banks of the Ganges River for a quick meal. The Buddha-to-be threw the remains of his food into the river as an offering to Ganga, the water spirit who lived there, and the spirit of the river received the Buddha's gift gratefully. The Buddha-to-be's younger brother, however, did not possess the same integrity, and sought to defraud the Buddha-to-be of all the money. The younger brother's plan backfired, however, when he mistakenly threw all the funds into the river. The spirit of the river Ganga, appearing as a fish, swallowed the bundle of money before the spirit-as-fish was caught by fishers. Eventually, the fishers brought the fish full of money to the Buddha-to-be's house, and the Buddha-to-be bought the fish and retrieved the money. Just then, the spirit of the Ganges River appeared floating in midair and asserted that the Buddha's funds had been returned to him because of the respect that he showed to the river spirit.[44]

Similar personhood respect for natural beings arises in every chapter of this book. In the concluding chapter, we will explore what these varying expressions of personhood respect mean.

Conclusion

A meditator named Kukkuripa, who lived in the region where the Buddha spent his childhood but more than a thousand years later, was a follower of late Indian Vajrayāna Buddhism, according to Abhayadatta's Sanskrit hagiography, *Caturaśītisiddhapravṛtti*. As part of his saintly practice, Kukkuripa would roam free like a deer through northern India, just like many other Buddhist adepts. On one occasion, Kukkuripa came across a sad and hungry puppy in the road and decided to care for her. Gathering provisions, Kukkuripa found a cave and established it as a new domicile for the two. The pair then spent the next twelve years developing a close friendship, during which time Kukkuripa's meditation practice deepened.

In response to Kukkuripa's advancement in practice, one day a group of gods appeared at the cave and invited Kukkuripa to join them in the joyful Heaven of the Thirty-Three (Sanskrit: Trāyastriṃśa). Kukkuripa accepted the invitation, thereafter rising into the sky to cavort with gods in their blissful realm. In the meantime, the dog, back on Earth, somehow found food and water by digging in the cave and so stayed there, alone.

In heaven Kukkuripa fondly remembered his dog friend and, missing her, began to return to Earth. The gods implored him stay, repeatedly telling him that worries about a dog were beneath his new position among the deities, so he decided to remain in heaven. Eventually, however, Kukkuripa longed for his canine pal so much that he decided not to listen to his divine comrades, thereafter returning to his cave. When he patted the dog in greeting upon his homecoming, she shape-shifted to reveal that she was a *ḍākinī*, a Vajrayāna Buddhist feminine celestial spirit of goodness and wisdom. She praised Kukkuripa for refusing the sidetrack to spiritual progress that heaven represented, telling him "You have purified your wrong views," and then gave him advanced Buddhist teachings.[1] Following these teachings, Kukkuripa reached the highest stages of the practice.

The heartwarming tale of Kukkuripa and the dog arises from different streams of attitudes toward the nonhuman world, thus expressing some trends found throughout the Buddhist tradition as a whole. Seen positively, the overall tenor of the story is that kindness to animals is more spiritually rewarding than a place among the gods. This reflects a strength of the Buddhist tradition in terms of its general concern for animal welfare, especially for animals that are not used for human food. As an outcome of this strength, Kukkuripa finds that attending to empirical natural phenomena, rather than heavenly concerns, pays spiritually.

At the same time, though, the story embodies nature-friendly limits in terms of realizing Rolston's sustainable biosphere. The dog in the tale is not an ordinary canine, the type that does not abruptly shape-shift into goddess form, so that the holy and wise dog in the story does not really elevate the position of nonmagical dogs. Moreover, the component in which Kukkuripa reaps benefit for himself, while not overtly a problem in this story, can be troublesome in other Buddhist venues, such as with those who carelessly release animals more for themselves than for the sake of animals, as we have seen.

Environmental tensions like these that are found in the tale of Kukkuripa encapsulate some of the ecological dilemmas that we have found throughout the Buddhist tradition. As I will describe more fully in this final chapter, multivalent Buddhist interactions with the nonhuman natural world especially influence Buddhist relationships with natural beings, environmental limitations in the climate change era, dietary propensities, spiritual experiences, and speculations about the possible religious talents of nonhuman beings.

Natural Persons in Buddhism

A common feature of these diverse streams of attitudes toward nature, both in the story of Kukkuripa as well as in the larger Buddhist tradition, involves the extension of respectful personhood to nonhumans. Attending to these personhood moments reveals how nature religious elements, while sometimes arising from local religions, also percolate from within Buddhism itself, thus scuttling the old model of animism that held Buddhism and nature religion separate from each other.

Reflecting this, personhood elements proliferate throughout the Buddha's previous and final lives in terms of his friendly relationships with many beings such as elephants, lions, swans, nāgas, and trees. Attempting to emulate this example of the Buddha in various ways, in Sri Lanka Buddhists extend personhood reverence to trees, mountains, and a rice goddess as expressions of devotion, while forest monastics send lovingkindness to the snake and bear persons whom they feel need it. In Thailand, trees become symbolic monks, and Buddhist leaders compassionately traffic and beautify buffaloes, while dangerous undomesticated animals are tamed specifically through the extension of respectful personhood. Natural persons in China emerge as holy mountains, enlightened plants, or in the animal forms of Shaolin martial arts practice. Japanese Buddhists like Kūkai and Dōgen extend personhood respect so broadly that, for them, the entire natural world acts as a Buddhist preacher. Tibetans do not respect just their local mountain protector god, a practicing Buddhist, but also Tantric power mountain deities, while they share consciousness elements with a variety of nonhuman persons. Personhood relationships also drive concern for animals for Western Buddhists such as Bhikkhu Nyanasobhano and Philip Kapleau Roshi while they propel more ecocentric attitudes for Buddhists such as Stephanie Kaza and Gary Snyder.

This book's examination of the world of Buddhism and nonhuman nature reveals that personhood elements within the Buddha's biography later helped incite personhood nature religious impulses in the tradition as a whole, with these malleable impulses expressing themselves in a variety of canonical and noncanonical ways. Given the numerous respectful friendships the Buddha shared with nonhuman persons, such manifestations of relational animism, although not always directly prescribed by the scriptures, make sense in a Buddhist universe when looked at from a personhood point of view. Examples of nonhuman people in the Buddha's life reveal the dynamic effectiveness of using a personhood-based relational animist model for investigating Buddhist relationships with nonhuman nature.

Buddhist Environmentalism

Of course, sometimes Buddhists do not extend personhood respect to nonhumans and in these moments Buddhists may be at their least sustainable. While animal releases gone bad, disappearing elephants in China, or clear-cut forests in Japan could provide examples of this point, perhaps most surprising along these lines to many readers of this book may be the practice of animal sacrifice, which appears in many places in the Buddhist world albeit on the margins of everyday practice. Animals to be sacrificed may be treated quite well while living since one wants to offer the sacred the happiest and healthiest gift possible. But at the moment of sacrifice itself, Buddhist sacrificers do not extend personhood respect to animals, or, if they do, the sense of personhood is not compelling in a way that admonishes adherence to the ahimsa precept.

In the case of animal sacrifices, an argument could be made that sacrificers commonly eat the meat, rendering animal sacrifice functionally no more animal-unfriendly than the routine slaughter for human food that occurs daily throughout much of the Buddhist universe. But this slaughter for the sake of humans still provides a sharp limit to claims that can be made regarding Buddhism's concern for animal welfare. Special trouble arises in those moments when the merging of slaughter and ahimsa go terribly wrong, such as with the distressingly slow killing of animals by suffocation enacted by some Thai fishers, Tibetan pastoralists, and other Buddhists.

However, leaving the realities of sacrifices and human food sources aside, the tradition otherwise significantly provides a rather strong platform for animal welfare efforts. Sri Lankan Buddhism possesses a movement seeking the positive treatment of protected cattle, Thai Buddhists protect and beautify buffaloes, and by precept Chinese Buddhists may abjure eating animals. In Japan, Buddhists release animals with accompanying wishes for their happiness, while some Tibetans save animals from slaughter and a number of Western Buddhists attempt to follow suit. This Buddhist concern for animals, which is stronger than in some other religious traditions, arises from the ethic of ahimsa. But it arises as well from calls to extend compassion and lovingkindness to animals, with these calls often being driven by personhood, even kin personhood, sentiments. After all, numerous Buddhists from across sects insist that we must treat animals, our loving family members from previous lifetimes, with kindness.

The compassionate concern for animals that sponsors Buddhist actions for animal welfare, however, also imposes a limit on the tradition in terms of supporting a sustainable biosphere, given that this attitude cannot, as it is, result in a viable environmental ethic that attends to the complexities of ecosystems with many preying individuals. For most Buddhists, notions of reincarnation result in the targeting of compassion toward animals but not toward plants, minerals, or water, resulting in a limited biocentric orientation as a complementary addition to Buddhism's erstwhile anthropocentrism.

This limited biocentric attitude substantially lacks the ecocentric elements required by a full environmental ethic, which must recognize that plant, mineral, and water resources, too, need to be valued in order to create ecosystem health, as the environmentalist Arne Naess has written.[2]

Moreover, despite the religion's depiction of a broadly interconnected universe, Buddhist compassion is directed at individuals, creating difficulties when it comes to addressing compassionate nonharm to the complexities of ecosystems that persist through constant predation of some type. In this light, the environmental philosopher J. Baird Callicott states that, within genuine environmental ethics, it is foolish to conceive of organisms "apart from the field, the matrix of which they are modes," so that Buddhism's almost exclusive attention to individual animals within an ecosystem, rather than the ecosystem itself, fails to muster the resources of a viable environmental ethic.[3] Due to its focus on individual animals, the same animal-friendly components that may draw attention to Buddhism as an ecofriendly way of life also provide obstacles to the development of full environmental thinking from within Buddhism itself despite the doctrine of dependent arising. Perhaps this is why deforestation woes appear in every chapter of this book: it is not due to an encouragement of animosity toward trees, but because Buddhism contains an implicit, if restrained, admiration for agriculture and at the same time offers trees little defense against the economic desires of humans given its limited biocentric approach, which focuses more on individual animals than it does on the habitats in which they reside.

Therefore, while Buddhism maintains many beautiful thoughts and practices that may lead to a sustainable biosphere, in order to produce an environmental ethic that is capable of responding to twenty-first-century difficulties of ecosystems Buddhism needs help or must change. Buddhist notions of compassion will need to be refashioned to work beyond their individual-only focus, which means setting aside some customary precedents in thought and practice. Further, from the standpoint of many Buddhist systems but contrary to some realities of the climate change age, there is no point in extending compassion to or even giving much consideration to the realities of plants, minerals, and water. In response, to become more ecologically potent in itself, Buddhism requires a more ecocentric, less limited biocentric, focus.

Of course, as we have seen, ecocentric voices such as those of Dōgen or more recently the Vietnamese master in the West Thich Nhat Hanh do occur in the tradition. Nonetheless, a problem arises from the fact that ecocentric Buddhist formulations like Dōgen's, based on the concept of dependent arising, often do not aid the navigation of dilemmatic ecological choices since they lead one to value everything equally. If everything must be valued because everything is connected to everything else, then we must treasure not just dogs and dolphins but also toxic waste and oil spills. That is, keeping a clean environment requires difficult choices, and a worldview that values all existents equally provides an unsteady platform for making these value-laden choices. Or, put differently, explicit and implicit claims that Buddhism represents an essentially ecological religion solely because of its stress on dependent arising have been belied throughout this book. Instead, we find more evidence supporting a current environmental studies contention that, when it comes to ecology, "knowledge and values alone do not prompt action," and many Buddhist environmentalists, being overreliant on the doctrine of dependent arising, may fail to recognize this.[4]

When accomplished in a way that facilitates choices, though, ecocentric Buddhism could maintain its relatively animal-friendly voices while it broadens the environmental reach of Buddhist thought and practice. With the inspiration of the current generation of ecologically minded Buddhists, perhaps the religion can adapt to overcome some of its environmental shortcomings. For instance, traditional notions of rebirth result in an ontological split between humans and animals on one side and the rest of the natural world on the other, thus leading to a worldview that is tilted more toward limited biocentrism than it is toward ecocentrism. But if Buddhism lessened its grip on traditional rebirth worldviews and instead adopted a more naturalistic approach, Buddhism could become more ecocentric and hence more capable when dealing with ecosystems.

Consider, for instance, that in traditional Buddhist rebirth beliefs, I cannot be reborn as a mineral. Looked at naturalistically, though, things appear differently. No matter the method of disposal of my corpse, the molecules in my bones and flesh eventually will recombine into other forms, including mineral formations, meaning that, naturalistically, I will in fact physically reincarnate, in a way, as minerals. Perspectives like this naturalism could inspire changes that result in the extension of positive Buddhist personhood sentiments much more broadly across the nonhuman world than to just humans and animals, perhaps leading in the direction of a more universal sense of compassionate kinship, even with supposedly inanimate elements, expressed not just in theory but also in practice.

The essential Buddhist concept of dependent arising, for instance, can be enhanced with alternate mindfulness, intention, and flexibility so that it embraces human interactions with abiotic elements as robustly as it does human interactions with humans and other animals. Given that battling global warming means directing some ethical value to abiotic entities like gases and stones, Buddhism would be more environmentally potent in the climate change era if it could help us value and navigate difficult decisions regarding abiotic ecologies. Hence, as with other religious environmental ethics, the future of Buddhist ethics involves the development of more wholesome ethical outlooks regarding beings considered to be nonliving. For instance, some American Buddhists extend attitudes of nonharm specifically to abiotic landscapes on Mars, thereby opening the door for the tradition to innovate in terms of the greater valuation of abiotic ecologies within a dependent arising outlook.[5]

Another part of the problem with the development of a sustainable Buddhist biosphere arises with the tradition's myriad, and sometimes conflicting, conceptual approaches to the nonhuman world. For one example, animal sacrifice is forbidden as evil but is not always beyond the pale if one must express one's disaffections or keep a mountain god contented. Further, some Buddhist monastics stand practically side by side with others, with one group arguing for felling trees in the name of Buddhist development while the others petition against chopping trees, also for Buddhist reasons.

In order to slice through the theoretical conundrums residing within examples such as these, the scholar Seth Devere Clippard asserts that perhaps Buddhists would be more ecofriendly if they relatively de-emphasized theory in developing ecoBuddhism and instead returned to the ground and focused on the practical. In exploring the world of Thai tree ordinations, Clippard states that tree ordination practitioners who begin with specific problems in designated communities build a kind of ecofriendly Buddhist speech through empirical action and in so doing enjoy greater environmental success than do humans who follow more purely textual or doctrinal approaches.[6] Stressing hands-on activities in concert with the nonhuman world, Clippard says, "The mixture of symbolism, rhetoric, and activism coming together in the ritual of ordination [of trees] makes the emergent discourse more effective in establishing a meaningful Buddhist environmental ethic."[7]

Of course, a danger of Clippard's practice-first approach involves the loss of an anchor within Buddhism itself, in that non-Buddhist ideals and practices in Buddhist wrapping may eventually become fobbed off as the real coin. This is a serious obstacle since a few of the best-known figures in today's Buddhist environmentalism, both in Asia and in the West, have been deemed by some Buddhists as not sufficiently authentic, their Buddhism being considered diminished through admixture with other, non-Buddhist environmentalist elements. As a result, their voices sometimes sing beautifully to a small environmentalist choir but not to a wider Buddhist audience, perhaps with a concomitant loss of helpful lessons. Clippard recognizes this danger, saying that within practice-first approaches the scriptures still have a function in terms of theoretical guidance, thereby supplying a reliable anchorage in the teachings.[8]

Naturally, Clippard's practice-first approach represents just one option, and one would think that Buddhists moving forward might develop other potentially positive strategies, too. Like all religions, Buddhism struggles to support consistent, wholesome human relationships with the natural world, but the tradition retains some useful tools and has the potential to develop new ones. Thus, even if it is not a full-scale ecofriendly religion today in terms of establishing a sustainable biosphere, Buddhism provides some possible resources for environmentalists everywhere. As the Buddhist environmental ethics scholar John J. Holder said, Buddhism "has some important ideas to contribute to the current conversations on environmental ethics—especially among the scientific community where naturalism (not theism) is a common conceptual framework."[9]

Vegetarianism, Religious Practice, and Nature Mysticism

Along with exploring some of Buddhism's sustainability credentials, throughout this book I have probed three touchpoints for comparison: Buddhist vegetarianism, the practice of religion by animals and other natural beings, and nature mysticism. As for the vegetarian comparative touchpoint, the Buddhist personhood approaches that aid the creation of some sustainable practices, especially toward animals, also help determine vegetarianism, or a lack of it, in the Buddhist world. In the Theravāda Buddhist universe, for example, it is easy to argue on the basis of personhood that one should not eat animals since they were our kin in previous lives, and some Theravāda Buddhists make this argument. However, Theravāda scriptures do not deliver this plea as substantially as some Mahāyāna texts do. Instead, the Pāli scriptural Buddha and his disciples took meat eating for granted, leaving meat a standard ingredient in many Theravāda Buddhist diets. Due to historical changes in Indian culture, however, some authoritative Mahāyāna sources that appeared later than the Theravāda texts, such as the Nirvāṇa, Śūraṅgama, and Śikṣāsamuccaya Sūtras, do make strong pleas for Buddhist vegetarianism based on a variety of factors, especially including personhood arguments. Perhaps the most influential among these is the Laṅkāvatāra Sūtra, which, in personhood fashion, implores Buddhists to avoid eating animals in part because they embody our parents from previous lives.

Indian Mahāyāna scriptural personhood arguments such as those of the Laṅkāvatāra Sūtra seem to have proven themselves insufficient in establishing much vegetarianism. For instance, they exist in Tibetan literature, yet to date they have affected only a minority of Tibetan vegetarians. Instead, in creating the greater vegetarian atmosphere that marks the world of Chinese Mahāyāna Buddhism and its offshoots, the role of the Chinese text *Fanwangjing*, with its own kin personhood arguments for vegetarianism, is crucial. Armed with this document, the sixth-century Chinese king Wu of Liang mandated vegetarianism among Buddhist monastics by government decree rather than decision by the religious community, and this ethic continues to reverberate throughout the East Asian Buddhism that stems from China. Wu of Liang's vegetarian mandate therefore makes Wu one of the more influential Buddhists in history, even if his decree did not necessarily affect nonmonastics and perhaps has become a bit forgotten in China-influenced Japan, Korea, and Vietnam.

The personhood of natural entities that fuels some vegetarian pleas also leads in a different direction in which animals or other natural beings, in their own species-specific ways, are said to practice Buddhism. Of course, the mainstream of the tradition denies the ability of any being other than a human to practice Buddhism, as we saw clearly in Tibet's *Mani Kabum*. However, numerous stories from across the Buddhist world including Tibet nonetheless indicate the spurious practice of religion by a broad array of natural entities. Animals frequently practice religion in jātaka tales and even winds, the moon, trees, and the earth expressed devotional grief at the Buddha's passing. Buddhism was not established in Sri Lanka without the help of a sambar deer, a couple of holy elephants, and some rather remarkable pious trees. A variety of nonhuman spirits are Buddhist practitioners themselves in Thailand, where insightful elephants may found monasteries and personally serve Buddhist monastics. Even plants practice religion, according to the Chinese masters Jizang and Zhanran, as they do for the Japanese masters who think that all of nature constantly preaches like a monastic. Tibetan natural entities share souls with enlightened beings, and liberated animals receive teachings for the sake of their future lives. Moreover, to ecocentric Western Buddhists like Kaza and Snyder, all beings in nature, even fictional natural beings like Smokey the Bear, practice religion like a Buddha. These instances in themselves, of course, do not rigorously establish that nonhuman beings practice Buddhism, coming as they do from folk stories, scriptural proclamations, and philosophic speculations that sometimes complicate things by including anthropomorphic impulses. Nonetheless, with interest in the possible practice of religion by animals growing within the academic community, these examples could provoke further research.

As for the third comparative touchpoint of nature mysticism, those who describe Buddhism as essentially a form of nature mysticism may be disappointed by the conclusions of this book since nature mysticism may exist in many places in the Buddhist world but it does so at best on the margins. Buddhist nature mysticism seems to thrive particularly in China, where religious forms blend so much that it would be surprising if Buddhism did not team up with some homegrown Chinese nature mysticism. Not only in China but also beyond China, nature mysticism further appears in the imposition on the landscape of Vajrayāna scriptures and their associated mandalas, which represent the spiritual utopias and truths of deities. Although frequently found in two dimensions, mandalas inherently embody three-dimensional spiritual paradises, which Buddhists in China, Korea, Japan, Tibet, Mongolia, and other places affected by Vajrayāna Buddhism project onto revered mountains. In this way, mountains become incarnate divine persons of sorts, and in communing with and traversing mountains, Buddhist practitioners attempt to directly experience Buddhist realities through nonhuman forms. Thus, Buddhist nature mysticism appears to shine especially brightly in the light of Vajrayāna practices that mandalize a landscape. Moon and Morning Star meditations add to this nature mystical mix in Japan's Shingon Buddhism and Shugendō, with these practices having arisen in combination with some non-Buddhist Daoist and indigenous Japanese elements.

Interestingly, like we see with Kaza's mystical experiences with trees, the contemporary West provides another location for active Buddhist nature mysticism, one that does not necessarily rely on Vajrayāna mandalization of the landscape. Perhaps this element of sometimes vibrant nature mysticism, which helps distinguish Western Buddhism from other forms of the tradition, results from fewer traditional boundaries to thought and practice in the West, where Buddhists have enjoyed some freedom to refashion the cultural clothing that Buddhism wears. For example, the Transcendentalist writers of the nineteenth century such as Thoreau and Emerson helped integrate Buddhism culturally, and in their works Buddhism and nature mysticism are not always held conceptually separate.

The notable presence of nature mysticism in Western Buddhism allows us to close the circle on our exploration of Buddhism and nature. Nature mysticism involves a powerful, extraordinary experience of nonduality with a nonhuman, and Shalipa, a later Indian Buddhist saint, may have sought such an experience in a quite unusual way. Being of low caste, Shalipa lived near a cemetery, and the howling of wolves in the home of the dead caused him tremendous fear and anxiety. One day he met a Buddhist monk and Shalipa requested a practice to generate fearlessness. The monk asked if Shalipa feared the sorrows of samsara, and Shalipa replied that everyone fears samsara, but his own personal problem concerned his terror of howling wolves. The monk then urged Shalipa to move to the center of the cemetery and to "meditate unceasingly on the fact that all the various sounds of the world are identical to the howl of a wolf." Shalipa followed the monk's advice and practiced for some time. Eventually, he became free of his fear of wolf howls when "he realized that all sounds were inseparable from emptiness," thereby producing "an unbroken state of great joy." Continuing to meditate until he realized full enlightenment, the eccentric Buddhist thereafter carried a wolf on his shoulders, earning him the name Shalipa, or Wolf-man.[10]

Luckily, the Buddha did not prescribe the wearing of wolves like Shalipa donned, so that Buddhists can overlook that part of Shalipa's example in favor of his greater lesson. Shalipa, deeply mired in what Buddhism considers to be false views regarding the natural world, at first embodies a profoundly negative attitude toward wolves. Then, with the help of Buddhist practices, he enriches his consciousness regarding the character of the universe and especially of wolves. In this way, his negative attitude toward natural beings disappears, thus dramatically shifting the consciousness that he inhabits and sponsoring for him a sense of intimacy with wolves. Although Abhayadatta's version of the story does not give the reason why Shalipa wore a wolf, one may imagine that he did so to cement his newfound sense of spiritual identity with wolves, not unlike some Native American usages of spirit animal talismans. But whether this last speculation is true or not, Shalipa shows Buddhists that even quite strong-rooted and problematic approaches to non-human nature can be overcome, perhaps inspiring Buddhists to look both within and outside of themselves in order to help create worlds that are more sustainable and friendly toward humans and nonhumans alike.

GLOSSARY OF TERMS AND CONCEPTS

ahimsa Ahimsa represents the ethic of nonharm that appears in one form or another in all religions born in India. In Buddhism ahimsa marks the first of the Five Precepts. The ethic of ahimsa counsels the avoidance of physical, verbal, or emotional harm to or killing of other beings, including humans, animals, and, in the eyes of some Buddhists, perhaps other entities.

anthropocentrism Among the approaches to nature including biocentrism and ecocentrism, anthropocentrism provides a human-centered approach to nonhuman nature. With strong anthropocentrism, only humanity retains intrinsic value, and the rest of the natural world retains value only instrumentally, or in terms of its use for humans. Weak anthropocentrism intrinsically values humans and only instrumentally values other entities, with some exceptions, such as family pets.

biocentrism Among the approaches to nature including anthropocentrism and ecocentrism, biocentrism provides an approach to nonhuman nature that focuses on supposed living beings, such as animals and/or plants along with humans. With biocentrism, living beings retain intrinsic value, while entities perceived as nonliving are valued only instrumentally. A great deal of animal rights discourse, which typically extends intrinsic value to animals, reflects biocentric perspectives. Plants often mark the border between limited biocentrism and full biocentrism since sometimes plants are valued intrinsically as living beings (full biocentrism), while at other times they are not (limited biocentrism).

bodhisattva The bodhisattva ideal exists in all forms of Buddhism, although it is most emphasized in Mahāyāna and Vajrayāna worlds. Bodhisattvas seek spiritual attainments not just for themselves but also so that they may lead all others to nirvana first. In postponing their own nirvanic departure from samsara, bodhisattvas sacrifice themselves for the good of others, so their hallmark is compassion. Although ordinary humans may take the vow to become a bodhisattva, especially powerful bodhisattvas appear as *mahāsattva* celestial deities, such as the well-known Mahāyāna Pure Land deity Amitābha.

Buddha-nature Found in Mahāyāna and Vajrayāna Buddhism, the doctrine of Buddha-nature asserts that existents such as humans, and perhaps animals, plants, or stones, already enjoy the qualities and capacities of a Buddha, with this everpresent spark of Buddhahood being known as *tathāgata-garbha* or Buddha-nature. Following this way of thinking, Buddhists conceptualize the religious path less as adding something to the practitioner and more as uncovering innate positive spiritual realities that currently remain hidden.

dependent arising (Pāli: *paṭicca-samuppāda*, Sanskrit: *pratītya-samutpāda*) A fundamental doctrine of the Buddhist tradition, dependent arising describes a universe in which every existent is interconnected with every other existent across time and space. Since all things arise as effects from one or more causes, and in turn become causes, nothing exists independently in either time or space, and all things thereby form a vast web of interrelations.

Dhamma (Pāli) or Dharma (Sanskrit)   This multifaceted term is used in this book to refer to Buddhist teachings and practices, or to the Buddhist religion as a whole, much as Buddhists themselves may employ it at times. Following scriptural preferences, the Pāli form "Dhamma" arises more commonly in Theravāda universes, while the Sanskrit form "Dharma" finds employment in Mahāyāna and Vajrayāna realms.

dukkha   The Buddha taught that *dukkha* represents one of the fundamental characteristics of the physical universe, along with *anicca* (impermanence) and *anatta* (no-self). Although it is often translated into English simply as "suffering," *dukkha* actually possesses a much broader meaning since *dukkha* encompasses ideas of imperfection, meaningless, instability, and suboptimality in all their manifestations.

ecocentrism   Among the approaches to nature including anthropocentrism and biocentrism, ecocentrism provides an approach to nonhuman nature that focuses value on an entire ecosystem, including existents that remain perceived both as animate and inanimate. With ecocentrism the entire natural world, including minerals and water, enjoys intrinsic value, and in its fullest version, nothing is valued only in terms of its instrumental use by humans. A great deal of environmentalist discourse reflects ecocentric perspectives.

Five Precepts   These are fundamental injunctions against harming living beings (the ahimsa precept), taking what is not given, engaging in uncompassionate sexual behavior, uttering false speech, and consuming intoxicants. In theory, all Buddhists, both lay and monastic, should adhere to the Five Precepts.

jātakas   The *jātakas* represent a genre of Buddhist canonical literature that relates stories of the previous lives of the Buddha before his enlightenment, during which time he took birth in a variety of human and other animal bodies. *Jātaka* tales are often used in the Buddhist world to educate people about the religion, especially in terms of ethical ideals. Although they appear in a number of scriptures, most *jātaka* stories are collected together into 547 tales in the *Khuddaka Nikāya* section of the Pāli canon or 34 stories in Āryaśūra's Sanskrit work *Jātakamālā*, which is influential in the Mahāyāna world.

Mādhyamaka   Along with the Yogācāra school, the Mādhyamaka school represents one of the fundamental divisions of Mahāyāna Buddhist philosophy. Emerging from the work of the second-century Indian writer Nāgārjuna, the principles of this school include an emphasis on overcoming all forms of dualism. This results in a worldview in which all existents are considered to be *śūnya*, or "empty," meaning that all things, no matter how tangible or intangible, lack an abiding or individual essence.

mahāsattva   A *mahāsattva* is an advanced bodhisattva who has accrued significant spiritual power despite remaining in samsara. The prominent deities of Mahāyāna Buddhism, such as the spirit of compassion Avalokiteśvara, are *mahāsattvas*.

Mahāyāna Along with Theravāda and Vajrayāna, Mahāyāna represents one of the Three Vehicles, or major divisions, of Buddhism. The roots of Mahāyāna Buddhism may be traced to the last few centuries BCE in India, while Mahāyāna itself became a self-conscious movement, based principally on Sanskrit-language scriptures, in the early centuries CE. Mahāyāna approaches generally include greater emphasis on the bodhisattva ideal, the practice of Buddhism by laypeople, and a more cosmic and less purely human understanding of the Buddha. Although global in reach today, Mahāyāna Buddhism can most easily be found in China, Taiwan, Japan, Korea, and Vietnam.

mandala Used especially in Vajrayāna Buddhist worlds but also in Mahāyāna Buddhism, mandalas are two- or three-dimensional artistic representations of three-dimensional spiritual utopias, such as the abodes of various divine beings. Mandalas typically appear ornate, intricate, and colorful so that they may most effectively be employed by meditators, who intentionally contemplate their own presence in the sacred places that are depicted.

mantra A mantra is a holy phrase, usually derived from scriptures, that encapsulates holy power. By repeating the phrase over and over, you train your mind in the quality, such as compassion, represented by the sacred phrase. Further, there exists some belief that chanting mantras can karmically alter happenings in the phenomenal world, so that, for instance, chanting mantras for compassion can increase compassionate outcomes.

metta One of the four *brahmavihāras*, or Four Immeasurables, of Buddhist teachings, *mettā*, or lovingkindness, represents the sincere wish to bring happiness to others and should be radiated to all humans and other animals, all living beings including plants, or all existents, depending on who is preaching. *Mettā* is said to be able to dispel anger and hate both within oneself and within others.

nāga A *nāga* is being who is at once a serpent, a shape-shifter with serpentine default form, and a spiritual charismatic. *Nāgas* appear in the Indian scriptures of all three great sects of Buddhism while their rough counterparts show up in the pre-Buddhist folk traditions of many Buddhist locations, like one finds with the dragons of China. Frequently understood to be humanlike in many ways and often artistically represented as such, *nāgas* in Indian Buddhism often were renowned for their spiritual accomplishments, genuine devotion to the Buddha and his teachings, associations with hidden treasures, and their ability to bring rain.

nature mysticism Nature mysticism is a powerful altered state of consciousness experience of human nonduality specifically with a nonhuman natural entity within a physical human habitat, with this experience significantly lacking in dimensions of time and space and possessing a sensory or emotive quality, although perhaps unlike ordinary senses and emotions.

nirvana (**Pāli:** *nibbāna*, **Sanskrit:** *nirvāṇa*) This is the goal experience of Buddhism as described by the Third Noble Truth. Meaning something like "extinction," nirvana denotes the eradication of the three poisons of attachment, aversion, and ignorance, and thus, the end of *dukkha* unsatisfactoriness. Nirvana may also be understood as the direct experience of no-self or the deepest experience of dependent arising.

no-self (Pāli: *anatta*, Sanskrit: *anātman*) One of the three fundamental characteristics of the universe along with impermanence and *dukkha*, the notion of no-self denies that humans (and perhaps other existents) possess selves that are continuous in time or separate in space. Ordinary forms of experienced selfhood deceive since they imply an abiding essence that in Buddhism does not exist. Because of the essenceless nature of things, Buddhism generally rejects soul concepts, although due to various conditions such concepts nonetheless sometimes still manifest in universes in which Buddhism appears.

Pāli scriptural canon Also known as the *Tipiṭaka* or *Three Baskets*, the Pāli canon represents the essential scriptural resource that is shared more or less the same across the Theravāda Buddhist realm. Three sections divide the canon into the *Vinaya-piṭaka*, or rules for monastics; the *Sutta-piṭaka*, or sermons of the Buddha; and the *Abhidhamma-piṭaka*, or philosophical discourses. The *Tipiṭaka* was composed in Pāli in the last few centuries BCE.

refuge in the Three Jewels The ritual of refuge is often taken to indicate formal acceptance of Buddhism and entry into the tradition. In this ritual, one expresses taking refuge in the person of the Buddha; in the collection of his teachings, or Dharma; and in the community of Buddhists, or *sangha*. Hence, the Buddha, Dharma, and *sangha* remain known collectively as the *Triratna*, which may be translated as something like Three Jewels or Triple Gem.

relational animism Relational animism consists of a form of belief and/or practice in which nonhuman entities are relationally experienced as persons in their own right, with respect accorded to their specific agencies through linguistic, ritual, or other interactions.

samsara Samsara represents the Buddhist universe in which rebirth takes place. Realms of rebirth appear on a spectrum from the highest realm, the god or *deva* realm, manifesting the least suffering, to the lowest realm, hell or *niraya*, which presents the most suffering. Above hell in ascending order exist rebirths as a ghost or *peta* (Sanskrit: *preta*), an animal, a human, and, in some common six-tier systems, a fighting demigod (*asura*) world just above the human realm and below the highest realm, that of the pleasure-enjoying *deva* gods.

sangha One of the Three Refuges along with the Buddha and his teachings, the *sangha* consists of the community of monastics or the community of all Buddhists, depending on the context.

Sanskrit scriptural canon Also known as the *Tripiṭaka* or *Three Baskets*, the Sanskrit canon represents the essential scriptural resource for the Mahāyāna Buddhist realm as well as a scriptural resource for Vajrayāna Buddhism, which grew out of Mahāyāna circles. Although the Sanskrit scriptures contain much of the material that is found in the Pāli scriptures of Theravāda Buddhism, for various reasons the Sanskrit scriptures further offer some alternative doctrines from the Pāli scriptures, such as *tathāgata-garbha* Buddha-nature theory. Different Mahāyāna Buddhist locations possess alternate collections of texts, or, in the cases of ubiquitous scriptures like the *Lotus* and *Laṅkāvatāra Sūtras*, emphasize textual alternatives in diverse fashions. The *Tripiṭaka* was composed in Sanskrit starting perhaps in the last century BCE.

tantra Please see the glossary entry for Vajrayāna.

Theravāda Along with Mahāyāna and Vajrayāna, Theravāda represents one of the Buddhist Three Vehicles or major divisions. Theravāda stresses adherence to the Pāli canon and relatively emphasizes a humanlike Buddha and the high place of monastics compared to some other Buddhist systems. Although Theravāda may be discovered globally, concentrations of Theravāda Buddhists can be found in Sri Lanka, Burma, Thailand, and Cambodia.

trikāya The *trikāya* or Three Body theory of Mahāyāna Buddhism asserts that the phenomenal universe, or alternatively the Buddha, may be regarded from three points of view that are simultaneously true. A *nirmāṇakāya* appearance emerges as a physical form body, like the material body of the Buddha who lived in India 2,500 years ago. From another point of view, the *dharmakāya*, the universe manifests as ultimate reality, nirvana, or empty of inherent existence. The *sambhoghakāya* body mediates the two other perspectives in blurring form and ultimate truth while it provides the point of view from which humans regard powerful *mahāsattva* beings like the bodhisattva of wisdom Mañjuśrī.

Vajrayāna One of the Buddhist Three Vehicles or major divisions, Vajrayāna, also known as Tantra, exhibits Mahāyāna influences while supplying a path to nirvana that is said to be quicker. Based on scriptures called *tantras* as well as the Mahāyāna Sanskrit scriptural canon, Vajrayāna was the last of the three great sects to develop in India and today can be found most centrally in Tibet and Mongolia, although Vajrayāna outposts exist in many places worldwide, including within Kūkai's Japanese Shingon Buddhism of chapter 6.

Vinaya Existing in many versions that differ according to time and place, the *Vinaya* provides the essential ethical, practical, and living codes for Buddhist monastics.

Yogācāra One of the most important schools of Mahāyāna philosophy, Yogācāra systematizes meditative experiences into a view in which phenomenal reality arises as a perception of the mind. Empirical existents lack solidity in this view since they are created by the mind on the basis of various predispositions.

Notes

Introduction

1. Joanna F. Handlin Smith, "Liberating Animals in Ming-Qing China: Buddhist Inspiration and Elite Imagination," *Journal of Asian Studies* 58, no. 1 (1999): 58, https://doi.org/10.2307/2658389.

2. Kerry S. Walters and Lisa Portmess, eds., *Religious Vegetarianism: From Hesiod to the Dalai Lama* (Albany: State University of New York Press, 2001), 82, 83.

3. Smith, "Liberating Animals in Ming-Qing China," 59.

4. Henry Shiu and Leah Stokes, "Buddhist Animal Release Practices: Historic, Environmental, Public Health and Economic Concerns," *Contemporary Buddhism* 9, no. 2 (2008): 190–192, https://doi.org/10.1080/14639940802556529.

5. John K. Nelson, *Experimental Buddhism: Innovation and Activism in Contemporary Japan* (Honolulu: University of Hawai'i Press, 2013), 161.

6. Shiu and Stokes, "Buddhist Animal Release Practices," 189.

7. David Ross Komito, "Eco-Bodhicitta and Artful Conduct," *Tibet Journal* 17, no. 2 (1992): 45–46, http://www.jstor.org.lynx.lib.usm.edu/stable/43300433.

8. Grace G. Burford, "Hope, Desire, and Right Livelihood: A Buddhist View on the Earth Charter," in *Buddhist Perspectives on the Earth Charter*, ed. Boston Research Center for the 21st Century (Boston, MA: Boston Research Center for the 21st Century, 1997), 32–33.

9. David E. Cooper and Simon P. James, *Buddhism, Virtue, and Environment* (Aldershot: Ashgate, 2005), 106.

10. Peter Harvey, "Buddhist Attitudes to and Treatment of Non-Human Nature," *Ecotheology* 4 (1998): 39, https://doi.org/10.1558/ecotheology.v3i1.35; Francis H. Cook, "The Jewel Net of Indra," in Callicott and Ames, *Nature in Asian Traditions of Thought*, 218.

11. Alan Drengson and Bill Devall, ed., *Ecology of Wisdom: Writings by Arne Naess* (Berkeley, CA: Counterpoint, 2008), 195; Deane Curtin, "A State of Mind Like Water: Ecosophy T and the Buddhist Traditions," in *Beneath the Surface: Critical Essays in the Philosophy of Deep Ecology*, ed. Eric Katz, Andrew Light, and David Rothenberg (Cambridge, MA: MIT Press, 2000), 254.

12. Leslie E. Sponsel and Poranee Natadecha-Sponsel, "A Theoretical Analysis of the Potential Contribution of the Monastic Community in Promoting a Green Society in Thailand," in Tucker and Williams, *Buddhism and Ecology*, 47.

13. Duncan Ryūken Williams, "Animal Liberation, Death, and the State: Rites to Release Animals in Medieval Japan," in Tucker and Williams, *Buddhism and Ecology*, 156.

14. Deanna G. Donovan, "Cultural Underpinnings of the Wildlife Trade in Southeast Asia," in Knight, *Wildlife in Asia*, 88.

15. William Edelglass, "Moral Pluralism, Skillful Means, and Environmental Ethics," *Environmental Philosophy* 3 (2006): 12.

16. Yale University Center for Environmental Law and Policy, "2020 Environmental Performance Index," accessed June 4, 2020, http://epi.yale.edu.

17. Galen Rowell, "The Agony of Tibet," in Kaza and Kraft, *Dharma Rain*, 222–230; Liu Jianqiang, *Tibetan Environmentalists in China: The King of Dzi*, trans. Ian Rowen, Cyrus K. Hui, and Emily T. Yeh (Lanham, MD: Lexington Books, 2015).

18. Pragati Sahni, *Environmental Ethics in Buddhism: A Virtues Approach* (Abingdon: Routledge, 2008), 9.

19. Thich Nhat Hanh, "The Sun My Heart," in Kaza and Kraft, *Dharma Rain*, 83–91.

20. Fourteenth Dalai Lama, "Make Tibet a Zone of Peace," in Kaza and Kraft, *Dharma Rain*, 231–235.

21. Sivaraksa Sulak, "The Religion of Consumerism," in Kaza and Kraft, *Dharma Rain*, 178–182.

22. Seth Devere Clippard, "The Lorax Wears Saffron: Toward a Buddhist Environmentalism," *Journal of Buddhist Ethics* 18 (2011): 238, http://blogs.dickinson.edu/buddhistethics/2011/06/06/3120.

23. Roger S. Gottlieb, *A Greener Faith: Religious Environmentalism and Our Planet's Future* (New York: Oxford University Press, 2006), 144.

24. Daniel Capper, "The Search for Microbial Martian Life and American Buddhist Ethics," *International Journal of Astrobiology* online (2019): 6, https://doi.org/10.1017/S1473550419000296.

25. Marc Bekoff, *Rewilding Our Hearts: Building Pathways of Compassion and Coexistence* (Novato, CA: New World Library, 2014), 4.

26. Environmental ethicists debate what roles anthropocentrism, biocentrism, and ecocentrism should play in a viable environmental ethic, so here I speak in terms of relative orientations. At least some measure of ecocentrism appears to be required.

27. Aldo Leopold, *A Sand County Almanac* (London: Oxford University Press, 1949), 204.

28. Arne Naess, *Ecology, Community and Lifestyle* (Cambridge: Cambridge University Press, 1990), 57.

29. Ian Harris, "Attitudes to Nature," in *Buddhism*, ed. Peter Harvey (London: Continuum, 2001), 245, 253.

30. Johan Elverskog, *The Buddha's Footprint: An Environmental History of Asia* (Philadelphia: University of Pennsylvania Press, 2020), xiii.

31. Holmes Rolston III, *A New Environmental Ethics: The Next Millennium for Life on Earth* (New York: Routledge, 2012), 37–38.

32. Rolston, *New Environmental Ethics*, 218, 220.

33. Rolston, *New Environmental Ethics*, 37–38.

34. E. F. Schumacher, *Small Is Beautiful: Economics as If People Mattered* (New York: Harper Perennial, 1973), 31.

35. Rolston, *New Environmental Ethics*, 38.

36. Andrew Balmford, *Wild Hope: On the Front Lines of Conservation Success* (Chicago: University of Chicago Press, 2012), 75.

37. Murray Gray, *Geodiversity: Valuing and Conserving Abiotic Nature* (Chichester: John Wiley and Sons, 2004), 166–167.

38. Katie McShane, "Individualist Biocentrism vs. Holism Revisited," *Les ateliers de l'éthique* 9, no. 2 (2014): 132, https://doi.org/10.7202/1026682ar.

39. Along with Mahāyāna and Vajrayāna, Theravāda represents one of the Buddhist Three Vehicles or major divisions. Theravāda stresses adherence to the Pāli canon and relatively emphasizes a humanlike Buddha and the high place of monastics compared to some other Buddhist systems. Although Theravāda may be discovered globally, concentrations of Theravāda Buddhists can be found in Sri Lanka, Burma, Thailand, and Cambodia.

40. J. J. Jones, trans., *The Mahavastu*, vol. 3 (London: Luzac, 1956), 422.

41. I. B. Horner, trans., *The Book of the Discipline* (Oxford: SuttaCentral, 2014), 656–657.

42. A. Irving Hallowell, "Ojibwa Ontology, Behavior, and World View," in *Contributions to Anthropology*, ed. A. Irving Hallowell (Chicago: University of Chicago Press, 1976), 357–390.

43. In his studies of Buddhist bioethics, Damien Keown asserts that the notion of ethical personhood "would be rejected by Buddhism in that it involves a narrowing of the moral universe, whereas the Buddhist inclination is to expand it." But Keown's statement applies only given his philosophical premise that the paradigm for the concept of personhood be a "rational human adult." This premise fails to recognize the numerous times when Buddhists precisely treat nonhuman beings as persons, if not necessarily rational human adult persons, as well as recent ecocentric trends in environmental thinking. See Damien Keown, *Buddhism and Bioethics* (New York: Palgrave, 2001), 27–37.

44. Horner, *Book of the Discipline*, 1706–1707.

45. Daniel Capper, "Animism among Western Buddhists," *Contemporary Buddhism* 17, no. 1 (2016): 30–48, https://doi.org/10.1080/14639947.2016.1189130.

46. Geoffrey Samuel, *Civilized Shamans* (Washington, DC: Smithsonian Institution Press, 1995).

47. Eric Katz, *Nature as Subject: Human Obligation and Natural Community* (Lanham, MD: Rowman and Littlefield, 1997), 22.

48. Bruno Latour, *Down to Earth: Politics in the New Climatic Regime* (Cambridge: Polity Press, 2018), 40–41.

49. "New Zealand River Granted Same Legal Rights as Human Being," *Guardian*, March 16, 2017, accessed September 26, 2017, https://www.theguardian.com/world/2017/mar/16/new-zealand-river-granted-same-legal-rights-as-human-being. Exhibiting the potent if limited role of personhood approaches in ecology, environmental law has begun to embrace personhood arguments as a way of protecting ecosystems. This movement began perhaps with a 1972 article in which Christopher D. Stone, attempting to influence the United States Supreme Court, ecocentrically proposed that "we give legal rights to forests, oceans, rivers, and other so-called 'natural objects' in the environment—indeed, to the natural environment as a whole." See Christopher D. Stone, "Should Trees Have Standing? Towards Legal Rights for Natural Objects," *Southern California Law Review* 45 (1972): 456, http://heinonline.org/HOL/LandingPage?handle=hein.journals/scal45&div=17&id=&page.

50. David R. Loy, *Ecodharma: Buddhist Teachings for the Ecological Crisis* (Somerville, MA: Wisdom Publications, 2018), 96–97.

51. Capper, "Animism among Western Buddhists," 30–48.

52. Donovan O. Schaefer, *Religious Affects: Animality, Evolution, and Power* (Durham, NC: Duke University Press, 2015); Stewart Elliott Guthrie, *Faces in the Clouds: A New Theory of Religion* (New York: Oxford University Press, 1993), 202; Jane Goodall, "The Dance of Awe," in Waldau and Patton, *Communion of Subjects*, 653–654.

53. Hjalmar S. Kühl et al., "Chimpanzee Accumulative Stone Throwing," *Scientific Reports* 6 (2016): 1–8, https://doi.org/10.1038/srep22219.

54. Barbara Smuts, "Encounters with Animal Minds," *Journal of Consciousness Studies* 8, nos. 5–7 (2001): 300–301, http://www.ingentaconnect.com/content/imp/jcs/2001/00000008/f0030005/1213.

55. R. C. Zaehner, *Mysticism Sacred and Profane* (New York: Oxford University Press, 1961), 41.

56. Zaehner, *Mysticism Sacred and Profane*, 34; italics in the original.

57. W. T. Stace, *Mysticism and Philosophy* (Los Angeles: Jeremy P. Tarcher, 1960), 79.

58. Stace, *Mysticism and Philosophy*, 110.

59. Laurie Cozad, *Sacred Snakes: Orthodox Images of Indian Snake Worship* (Aurora, CO: Davies Group, 2004), 96.

1. Some Methods in Buddhist Environmental Ethics

1. Susan M. Darlington, "The 'Spirits' of Conservation in Buddhist Thailand," in *Nature across Cultures: Views of Nature and the Environment in Non-Western Cultures*, ed. Helaine Selin (Dordrecht: Kluwer Academic, 2003), 129.

2. King Bhumibol Adulyadej, *The Story of Tongdaeng: Biography of a Pet Dog* (Bangkok: Amarin, 2002).

3. King Bhumibol Adulyadej, *Story of Tongdaeng*, 10.

4. King Bhumibol Adulyadej, *Story of Tongdaeng*, 10, 68.

5. It should be noted that human emulation of Tongdaeng is limited by the fact that comparing a human to an animal, particularly a dog or a monkey, is deeply insulting to many Thais. See Leslie E. Sponsel, Poranee Natadecha Sponsel, and Nukul Ruttanadakul, "Coconut-Picking Macaques in Southern Thailand: Economic, Cultural, and Ecological Aspects," in Knight, *Wildlife in Asia*, 117.

6. King Bhumibol Adulyadej, *Story of Tongdaeng*, 68.

7. Edward B. Tylor, *Primitive Culture*, vol. 1 (London: John Murray, 1871), 383.

8. James George Frazer, *The Golden Bough* (New York: Macmillan, 1922), 128.

9. Maurice Walshe, trans., *The Long Discourses of the Buddha* (Boston, MA: Wisdom Publications, 1995), 83.

10. Frazer, *Golden Bough*, 128, 129.

11. Melford E. Spiro, *Burmese Supernaturalism* (Englewood Cliffs, NJ: Prentice-Hall, 1967), 253–257.

12. Jacob von Uexküll, "A Stroll through the Worlds of Animals and Men," in *Instinctive Behavior: The Development of a Modern Concept*, ed. Claire H. Schiller (New York: International Universities Press, 1957), 6.

13. See Carl Safina, *Beyond Words: What Animals Think and Feel* (New York: Henry Holt, 2015), 26–30.

14. Thomas Nagel, "What Is It Like To Be a Bat?," *Philosophical Review* 83, no. 4 (1974): 435–450, https://www.jstor.org/stable/i338273.

15. Jacques Derrida, *The Animal That Therefore I Am* (New York: Fordham University Press, 2008), 4–6.

16. Katz, *Nature as Subject*, 22.

17. Marc Bekoff, *The Emotional Lives of Animals* (Novato, CA: New World Library, 2007).

18. David Abram, *Becoming Animal: An Earthly Cosmology* (New York: Pantheon Books, 2010), 43, 49.

19. David L. Haberman, *People Trees: Worship of Trees in Northern India* (New York: Oxford University Press, 2013).

20. Matthew Hall, *Plants as Persons: A Philosophical Botany* (Albany: State University of New York Press, 2011), 12.

21. Graham Harvey, *Animism: Respecting the Living World* (New York: Columbia University Press, 2006), 28.

22. G. Harvey, *Animism*, xi.

23. E. B. Cowell, ed., *The Jātaka*, vol. 4 (Cambridge: Cambridge University Press, 1901), 221.

24. Daniel Capper, *Guru Devotion and the American Buddhist Experience* (Lewiston, NY: Edwin Mellen Press, 2002).

25. See Barbara Noske, *Beyond Boundaries: Humans and Animals* (Montreal: Black Rose Books, 1997); and Mary Midgley, *Beast and Man: The Roots of Human Nature* (Ithaca, NY: Cornell University Press, 1978).

26. Val Plumwood, *Environmental Culture: The Ecological Crisis of Reason* (London: Routledge, 2002), 6.

27. Paul Waldau, *Animal Studies: An Introduction* (New York: Oxford University Press, 2013), 44–65.

28. Tim Ingold, "Hunting and Gathering as Ways of Perceiving the Environment," in *Redefining Nature: Ecology, Culture, and Domestication*, ed. Roy Ellen and Katsuyoshi Fukui (Oxford: Berg, 1996), 117.

29. Ingold, "Hunting and Gathering as Ways of Perceiving the Environment," 120.

30. Ingold, "Hunting and Gathering as Ways of Perceiving the Environment," 121.

31. Bhikkhu Bodhi, trans., *The Connected Discourses of the Buddha*, vol. 1 (Boston, MA: Wisdom Publications, 2000), 952.

32. According to the evolutionary biologist David P. Barash, modern Western biological science shares with Buddhism the idea of a dependent arising universe. See David P. Barash, *Buddhist Biology: Ancient Eastern Wisdom Meets Modern Western Science* (Oxford: Oxford University Press, 2014).

33. For a Pāli scripture model of a five gati universe, see Bhikkhu Ñāṇamoli and Bhikkhu Bodhi, trans., *The Middle Length Discourses of the Buddha* (Boston, MA: Wisdom Publications, 1995), 168–169; for a Mahāyāna universe of six gatis, see Daisetz Teitaro Suzuki, trans., *The Lankavatara Sutra: A Mahayana Text* (London: Routledge and Kegan Paul, 1973), 274.

34. At the center of the Wheel of Life, one finds three animals that represent the Three Poisons (*triviṣa*), or three states of mind that create suffering and therefore should be avoided: a pigeon or other bird symbolizes greed (*rāga*), a snake represents hatred (*dveṣa*), and a pig personifies delusion (*moha*). Stephen F. Teiser, *Reinventing the*

Wheel: Paintings of Rebirth in Medieval Buddhist Temples (Seattle: University of Washington Press, 2006), 55.

35. K. R. Norman, trans., *The Group of Discourses (Sutta-Nipāta)* (Oxford: Pali Text Society, 2001), 80.

36. Norman, *Group of Discourses*, 81.

37. Lambert Schmithausen claims that in some commentaries killing an animal is worse than killing a human because animals do not have wrong views. See Schmithausen, "The Early Buddhist Tradition and Ecological Ethics," *Journal of Buddhist Ethics* 4 (1997): 46, http://dharmaflower.net/_collection/earlybuddhist.pdf.

38. Horner, *Book of the Discipline*, 1742.

39. Horner, *Book of the Discipline*, 1518.

40. Ian Harris, "'A Vast Unsupervised Recycling Plant': Animals and the Buddhist Cosmos," in Waldau and Patton, *Communion of Subjects*, 208.

41. Sometimes I drop the qualifier *nonhuman* before the word *nature* for the sake of literary elegance but eventually return to a reminder that humans are not intrinsically separate from nature in my definitions.

42. Thomas Pradeu and Edgardo D. Carosella, "The Self Model and the Conception of Biological Identity in Immunology," *Biology and Philosophy* 21 (2006): 235–252, https://doi.org/10.1007/s10539-005-8621-6.

43. Florin Deleanu, "Buddhist 'Ethology' in the Pāli Canon: Between Symbol and Observation," *Eastern Buddhist* 32, no. 2 (2000): 85.

44. Walshe, *Long Discourses of the Buddha*, 241.

45. For an example of trees in hells, see Bhikkhu Ñāṇamoli and Bhikkhu Bodhi, *Middle Length Discourses of the Buddha*, 1034.

46. Ellison Banks Findly employs the descriptor "inconsistent" rather than "ambiguous." See Ellison Banks Findly, *Plant Lives: Borderline Beings in Indian Traditions* (Delhi: Motilal Banarsidass, 2008), xxix.

47. Christopher Key Chapple, *Nonviolence to Animals, Earth, and Self in Asian Traditions* (Albany: State University of New York Press, 1993), 9–12.

48. Lambert Schmithausen, *Plants in Early Buddhism and the Far Eastern Idea of the Buddha-Nature of Grasses and Trees* (Lumbini, Nepal: Lumbini International Research Institute, 2009), 29.

49. Bhikkhu Bodhi, trans., *The Connected Discourses of the Buddha*, vol. 2 (Boston, MA: Wisdom Publications, 2000), 1813.

50. Bhikkhu Bodhi, trans., *The Numerical Discourses of the Buddha* (Boston, MA: Wisdom Publications, 2012), 570.

51. Norman, *Group of Discourses*, 48.

52. Schmithausen, *Plants in Early Buddhism*, 51.

53. Schmithausen, *Plants in Early Buddhism*, 51.

54. Lambert Schmithausen, *The Problem of the Sentience of Plants in Earliest Buddhism* (Tokyo: International Institute for Buddhist Studies, 1991), 81.

55. T. W. Rhys Davids, trans., *The Questions of King Milinda*, vol. 1 (Delhi: Motilal Banarsidass, 1988), 241.

56. Burton Watson, trans., *The Lotus Sutra* (New York: Columbia University Press, 1993), 99–100; Burton Watson, trans., *The Vimalakirti Sutra* (New York: Columbia University Press, 1997), 35; Garma C. C. Chang, trans., *A Treasury of Mahāyāna*

Sūtras: Selections from the Mahāratnakūta Sūtra (University Park: Pennsylvania State University Press, 1983), 273.

57. Mark L. Blum, trans., *The Nirvana Sutra*, vol. 1 (Berkeley, CA: BDK America, 2013), 281.

58. Jan Nattier, trans., *A Few Good Men: The Bodhisattva Path according to "The Inquiry of Ugra" (Ugraparipṛcchā)* (Honolulu: University of Hawai'i Press, 2003), 229–230.

59. T. W. Rhys Davids, trans., *The Questions of King Milinda*, vol. 2 (Delhi: Motilal Banarsidass, 1993), 85–86; Cecil Bendall and W. H. D. Rouse, trans., *Śikṣā Samuccaya: A Compendium of Buddhist Doctrine* (Delhi: Motilal Banarsidass, 2006), 210.

60. Findly, *Plant Lives*, 6.

61. C. A. F. Rhys Davids and K. R. Norman, trans., *Poems of Early Buddhist Nuns (Therīgāthā)* (Oxford: Pali Text Society, 2009), 32–33.

2. The Buddha's Nature

1. Cozad, *Sacred Snakes*, 32. In the Pāli canon, *nāga* is less commonly used to refer to a type of elephant or an accomplished meditator.

2. Horner, *Book of the Discipline*, 1505.

3. Horner, *Minor Anthologies*, 3:37.

4. Cozad, *Sacred Snakes*, 43.

5. Robert Decaroli, "'The Abode of the *Nāga* King': Questions of Art, Audience, and Local Deities at the Ajaṇṭā Caves," *Ars Orientalis* 40 (2011): 142–161, http://www.jstor.org.lynx.lib.usm.edu/stable/23075934.

6. Horner, *Minor Anthologies*, 3:5. *Supaṇṇas* are spirit-birds that early Buddhists transformed from a single Garuda into an entire species.

7. Irfan Habib, *Man and Environment: The Ecological History of India* (New Delhi: Tulika Books, 2010).

8. Bhikkhu Bodhi, *Connected Discourses of the Buddha*, 1:1020–1021. Perhaps the reputation for holy fasting among nāgas results from snakes' lack of generation of their own body heat, unlike mammals who warm themselves but therefore must eat more often than snakes are required to do.

9. Watson, *Lotus Sutra*, 188.

10. Cowell, *Jātaka*, 4:284.

11. Cowell, *Jātaka*, 4:116–121.

12. Andy Rotman, trans., *Divine Stories (Divyāvadāna, Part 1)* (Boston, MA: Wisdom Publications, 2008), 119.

13. Cozad, *Sacred Snakes*, 110.

14. Edward O. Wilson, *Biophilia* (Cambridge, MA: Harvard University Press, 1984), 86, 93.

15. Rotman, *Divine Stories*, 119.

16. T. Rhys Davids, *Questions of King Milinda*, 1:28.

17. See, for example, Horner, *Book of the Discipline*, 2126.

18. Cozad, *Sacred Snakes*, 96.

19. Reginald A. Ray, *Buddhist Saints in India* (New York: Oxford University Press, 1994), 75.

20. Cozad, *Sacred Snakes*, 111, 115.

21. Horner, *Minor Anthologies*, 3:29, 43–44, 47.

22. Sarah Shaw, *The Jātakas: Birth Stories of the Bodhisatta* (Gurgaon, India: Penguin Books, 2006), xx, liv.

23. Simon P. James, "How 'Green' is Buddhism?," *SHAP: World Religions in Education* (2008/2009), accessed July 19, 2015, http://www.shapworkingparty.org.uk/journals/articles_0809/james.pdf.

24. Reiko Ohnuma, *Unfortunate Destiny: Animals in the Indian Buddhist Imagination* (New York: Oxford University Press, 2017), 52.

25. Deleanu, "Buddhist 'Ethology' in the Pāli Canon," 81, 86, 114.

26. Ohnuma, *Unfortunate Destiny*, 44.

27. Ohnuma, *Unfortunate Destiny*, 45.

28. Midgley, *Beast and Man*, 25–40.

29. There are some passages in the Pāli canon, namely the *Koṭisimbali*, *Kāliṅgabodhi*, *Hatthipāla*, and especially the *Bhaddasāla Jātaka*s, that may lead to the interpretation that the tree spirit is the tree itself, rather than being a detachable spirit. In the *Bhaddasāla Jātaka*, for example, a tree spirit reproaches a king who wishes to cut down the tree for tearing apart its body, as if the tree spirit and the tree were the same. But this passage is exceptional since in other cases tree spirits are not as afraid of death for having their bodies destroyed by having a tree felled as they are of dying because they have no home. Because of the unique character of the passage, the scholar Lambert Schmithausen considers it to be just a "tolerated" holdover of Indian folk belief. Whether he is correct about this or not, the overwhelming spirit of the Pāli canon holds tree spirits to be separable from trees, so that passages like that found in the *Bhaddasāla Jātaka* represent exceptions rather than the rule. For example, the Pāli Pāṭimokkha code of monastic conduct discourages harming trees specifically for the spirits that will be displaced. See Schmithausen, *Plants in Early Buddhism*, 68–81.

30. E. B. Cowell, ed., *The Jātaka*, vol. 2 (Cambridge: Cambridge University Press, 1895), 157–158. I thank Geoffrey Barstow for pointing out that this story also indicates an early Indian appreciation for ecosystems and the potential dangers of human interference in them.

31. Bhikkhu Ñāṇamoli and Bhikkhu Bodhi, *Middle Length Discourses of the Buddha*, 174.

32. Harris, "Attitudes to Nature," 244; Chapple, *Nonviolence to Animals, Earth, and Self*, 10; E. B. Cowell, ed., *The Jātaka*, vol. 3 (Cambridge: Cambridge University Press, 1897), 177.

33. Walshe, *Long Discourses of the Buddha*, 397.

34. Lambert Schmithausen, "Buddhism and the Ethics of Nature—Some Remarks," *Eastern Buddhist* 32, no. 2 (2000): 56.

35. Bendall and Rouse, *Śikṣā Samuccaya*, 207.

36. Lambert Schmithausen, *Buddhism and Nature* (Tokyo: International Institute for Buddhist Studies, 1991), 30.

37. Schmithausen, "Buddhism and the Ethics of Nature," 47.

38. Sakka is the Buddhist version of the Vedic deity Indra.

39. Cowell, *Jātaka*, 3:35–37.

40. Several other traditions give fig tree rather than *sāl* tree. The Chinese pilgrim Xuanzang identified it as an *aśoka* tree. See Li Rongxi, trans., *The Great Tang Dynasty Record of the Western Regions* (Berkeley, CA: Numata Center for Buddhist Translation and Research, 1996), 179.

41. E. H. Johnston, *Asvaghoṣa's Buddhacarita or Acts of the Buddha* (Delhi: Munshiram Manoharlal, 1995), 4.

42. Bhikkhu Ñāṇamoli, *The Life of the Buddha* (Seattle, WA: Buddhist Publication Society, 1992), 5.

43. Johnston, *Asvaghoṣa's Buddhacarita*, 7.

44. Dharmachakra Translation Committee, *The Play in Full: Lalitavistara* (New York: 84000, 2013), 95.

45. The purport of this story, in which the Buddha meditates while others concern themselves with agricultural rituals, is one of many stories in the Pāli canon in which the Buddha's religious practice appears as a superior vocation to agriculture.

46. Walter Henry Nelson, *Buddha* (New York: Jeremy P. Tarcher, 1996), 30–32.

47. Despite claims to the contrary, the Four Immeasurables on their own do not provide for a viable environmental ethic. Lovingkindness and compassion are directed toward individuals, rather than the complexities of ecosystems, so that the Four Immeasurables do not always help in making tough ecological choices. Yet, through their focus on specific individuals, the Four Immeasurables do establish a strong and vital approach to the welfare of individual animals.

48. Tenzin Chögyel, *The Life of the Buddha*, trans. Kurtis R. Schaeffer (New York: Penguin Books, 2015), 41.

49. Reiko Ohnuma highlights that in some stories, such as in the *Nidānakathā*, Kaṇṭaka neighs in joyful approval of the Buddha's leaving home, rather than in attempted subversion of the Buddha's plans. Nonetheless, even in stories like those in the *Nidānakathā*, in the end Kaṇṭaka dies of grief over the absence of the Buddha. See Ohnuma, *Unfortunate Destiny*, 105–106.

50. Trāyastriṃśa heaven in Sanskrit. J. J. Jones, trans, *The Mahavastu*, vol. 2 (London: Luzac, 1952), 156, 182–183.

51. Patrick Olivelle, trans., *Life of the Buddha* (New York: New York University Press, 2009), 163.

52. The scriptural Buddha recommended that monastics "roam about free as deer." See Bhikkhu Ñāṇamoli and Bhikkhu Bodhi, *Middle Length Discourses of the Buddha*, 246; J. J. Jones, trans., *The Mahavastu*, vol. 3 (London: Luzac, 1956), 422.

53. Walshe, *Long Discourses of the Buddha*, 200.

54. Cowell, *Jātaka*, 4:142–148.

55. Chögyel, *Life of the Buddha*, 55.

56. It is important to note that the Pāli canon informs us that the Jetavana monastery, while in a forest setting, was designed specifically to shield monastics from heat, cold, and dangerous animals. See Bhikkhu Ñāṇamoli, *Life of the Buddha*, 95.

57. Haberman, *People Trees*, 97.

58. Herbert A. Giles, trans., *Record of the Buddhistic Kingdoms* (London: Trübner, 2004), 76–77.

59. Dharmachakra Translation Committee, *Play in Full*, 210, 213–214.

60. Olivelle, *Life of the Buddha*, 371.

61. Dharmachakra Translation Committee, *Play in Full*, 243, 257, 297.

62. T. W. Rhys Davids, trans., *Buddhist Birth-Stories* (London: George Routledge and Sons, 1878), 197–198.

63. Horner, *Book of the Discipline*, 1386–1393.

64. Chögyel, *Life of the Buddha*, 71.

65. Norman, *Group of Discourses*, 46; E. B. Cowell, ed., *The Jātaka*, vol. 5 (Cambridge: Cambridge University Press, 1905), 514.

66. K. R. Norman, trans., *Poems of Early Buddhist Monks (Theragāthā)* (Oxford: Pali Text Society, 1997), 73.

67. Walshe, *Long Discourses of the Buddha*, 254.

68. Bhikkhu Ñāṇamoli and Bhikkhu Bodhi, *Middle Length Discourses of the Buddha*, 993.

69. Ṭhānissaro Bhikkhu, trans., *Udāna: Exclamations* (Ṭhānissaro Bhikkhu, 2012), 67–68.

70. Horner, *Book of the Discipline*, 2261–2263. Xuanzang presents an alternate story in which the elephant was named Dhanapāla and the Buddha tamed him by producing five lions from the tips of his five fingers. See Rongxi, *Great Tang Dynasty Record*, 268–269.

71. Johnston, *Asvaghoṣa's Buddhacarita*, 59; Rotman, *Divine Stories*, 333.

72. Rotman, *Divine Stories*, 334.

73. Rotman, *Divine Stories*, 243–245.

74. E. B. Cowell, ed., *The Jātaka*, vol. 1 (Cambridge: Cambridge University Press, 1895), 86.

75. Norman, *Group of Discourses*, 90; T. Rhys Davids, *Questions of King Milinda*, 1:12.

76. Bhikkhu Ñāṇamoli and Bhikkhu Bodhi, *Middle Length Discourses of the Buddha*, 165.

77. Giles, *Record of the Buddhistic Kingdoms*, 40.

78. Giles, *Record of the Buddhistic Kingdoms*, 44.

79. Giles, *Record of the Buddhistic Kingdoms*, 69–70.

80. Walshe, *Long Discourses of the Buddha*, 318.

81. Giles, *Record of the Buddhistic Kingdoms*, 25.

82. Ian Harris, "Landscape Aesthetics and Environmentalism: Some Observations on the Representations of Nature in Buddhist and Western Art," *Contemporary Buddhism* 8, no. 2 (2007): 156, https://doi.org/10.1080/14639940701636125.

83. Bhikkhu Ñāṇamoli and Bhikkhu Bodhi, *Middle Length Discourses of the Buddha*, 600. For stories about non-Buddhist saints who possess power over natural beings, see Daniel Capper, *Learning Love from a Tiger: Religious Experiences with Nature* (Oakland: University of California Press, 2016).

84. Rotman, *Divine Stories*, 97.

85. Ray, *Buddhist Saints in India*, 192.

86. Horner, *Book of the Discipline*.

87. Deryck O. Lodrick, "Symbol and Sustenance: Cattle in South Asian Culture," *Dialectical Anthropology* 29, no. 1 (2005): 66–67, 71, https://doi.org/10.1007/s10624-005-5809-8; Chapple, *Nonviolence to Animals, Earth, and Self*, 15. See also chapter 3 of this book for a discussion of changes in ancient Indian attitudes toward meat eating.

88. Horner, *Book of the Discipline*, 1694. For one example of disciples eating meat, see Horner, *Book of the Discipline*, 1715.

89. Horner, *Book of the Discipline*, 478; Bhikkhu Bodhi, *Numerical Discourses of the Buddha*, 669.

90. Bhikkhu Ñāṇamoli and Bhikkhu Bodhi, *Middle Length Discourses of the Buddha*, 476.

91. Norman, *Group of Discourses*, 30–31.

92. Walshe, *Long Discourses of the Buddha*, 572.

93. Suzuki, *Lankavatara Sutra*, 217–220.

94. Blum, *Nirvana Sutra*, 1:111.

95. Charles Luk, trans., *The Śūraṅgama Sūtra* (London: Rider, 1966), 154.

96. Bendall and Rouse, *Śikṣā Samuccaya*, 130.

97. Chögyel, *Life of the Buddha*, 82.

98. Rotman, *Divine Stories*, 346.

99. Walshe, *Long Discourses of the Buddha*, 270.

100. Walshe, *Long Discourses of the Buddha*, 271.

101. Johnston, *Asvaghoṣa's Buddhacarita*, 103.

102. John J. Holder, "A Suffering (But Not Irreparable) Nature: Environmental Ethics from the Perspective of Early Buddhism," *Contemporary Buddhism* 8, no. 2 (2007): 123, https://doi.org/10.1080/14639940701636091.

103. Rongxi, *Great Tang Dynasty Record*, 198.

3. The Clever Bee of Sri Lanka

1. Dick de Ruiter, trans., *Buddhist Folk Tales from Ancient Ceylon* (Havelte, Netherlands: Binkey Kok Publications, 2005), 84–85.

2. Manuel Komroff, trans., *The Travels of Marco Polo* (New York: Modern Library, 2001), 234.

3. James L. A. Webb Jr., *Tropical Pioneers: Human Agency and Ecological Change in the Highlands of Sri Lanka, 1800–1900* (Athens: Ohio University Press, 2002), 4, 10.

4. T. Somasekaram et al., eds., *Arjuna's Atlas of Sri Lanka* (Dehiwala, Sri Lanka: Arjuna Consulting, 1997), 36.

5. Somasekaram et al., *Arjuna's Atlas of Sri Lanka*, 40.

6. Webb, *Tropical Pioneers*, 21.

7. Webb, *Tropical Pioneers*, 13–14.

8. Webb, *Tropical Pioneers*, 15.

9. Webb, *Tropical Pioneers*, 23.

10. Somasekaram et al., *Arjuna's Atlas of Sri Lanka*, 74.

11. Somasekaram et al., *Arjuna's Atlas of Sri Lanka*, 37.

12. Somasekaram et al., *Arjuna's Atlas of Sri Lanka*, 27.

13. Nur Yalman, *Under the Bo Tree: Studies in Caste, Kinship, and Marriage in the Interior of Ceylon* (Berkeley: University of California Press, 1971), 23.

14. Found throughout the Buddhist world at least as temple decorations, the Indian Buddhist gods of the four directions are Dhṛtarāṣṭra (east), Virūḍha (south), Virūpākṣa (west), and Vaiśravaṇa.

15. Richard Gombrich and Gananath Obeyesekere, *Buddhism Transformed: Religious Change in Sri Lanka* (Princeton, NJ: Princeton University Press, 1988), 99.

16. Douglas Bullis, trans., *The Mahavamsa: The Great Chronicle of Sri Lanka* (Fremont, CA: Asian Humanities Press, 1999), 50.

17. Hermann Oldenburg, trans., *The Dīpavamsa: An Ancient Buddhist Historical Record* (New Delhi: Asian Educational Services, 2001), 121–127.

18. Bullis, *Mahavamsa*, 109–111, 119.

19. James John Stewart, *Vegetarianism and Animal Ethics in Contemporary Buddhism* (London: Routledge, 2016), 12.

20. Stewart, *Vegetarianism and Animal Ethics*, 113, 128.

21. Some authorities give Mahinda and Saṅghamittā as Aśoka's brother and sister.

22. Bullis, *Mahavamsa*, 199–207; Stephen C. Berkwitz, trans., *The History of the Buddha's Relic Shrine: A Translation of the Sinhala* Thūpavaṃsa (Oxford: Oxford University Press, 2007), 152.

23. S. Paranavitana, "Pre-Buddhist Religious Beliefs in Ceylon," *Journal of the Ceylon Branch of the Royal Asiatic Society of Great Britain and Ireland* 31, no. 82 (1929): 318, http://www.jstor.org.lynx.lib.usm.edu/stable/43483299; C. G. Seligmann and Brenda Z. Seligmann, *The Veddas* (Cambridge: Cambridge University Press, 1911), 170; Richard F. Gombrich, *Precept and Practice: Traditional Buddhism in the Rural Highlands of Ceylon* (Oxford: Clarendon Press, 1971), 108.

24. Gombrich, *Precept and Practice*, 162.

25. Antonella Serena Comba, "The Bodhi Tree and Other Plants in the Pāli Tipiṭaka," in *Roots of Wisdom, Branches of Devotion: Plant Life in South Asian Traditions*, ed. Fabrizio M. Ferrari and Thomas Dähnhardt (Sheffield: Equinox, 2016), 98–117, 110.

26. Bryan Geoffrey Levman, "Cultural Remnants of the Indigenous Peoples in the Buddhist Scriptures," *Buddhist Studies Review* 30, no. 2 (2013): 166, https://doi.org/10.1558/bsrv.v30i2.145.

27. Gombrich and Obeyesekere, *Buddhism Transformed*, 70.

28. Steven Kemper, *Rescued from the Nation: Anagarika Dharmapala and the Buddhist World* (Chicago: University of Chicago Press, 2015), 435.

29. Swarna Wickremeratne, *Buddha in Sri Lanka: Remembered Yesterdays* (Albany: State University of New York Press, 2006), 160.

30. Wickremeratne, *Buddha in Sri Lanka*, 160.

31. Mahinda Deegalle, *Popularizing Buddhism: Preaching as Performance in Sri Lanka* (Albany: State University of New York Press, 2006), 153–156.

32. H. L. Seneviratne and Swarna Wickremeratne, "*Bodhipuja*: Collective Representations of Sri Lanka Youth," *American Ethnologist* 7, no. 4 (1980): 734–743, https://doi.org/ae.1980.7.4.02a00080.

33. Wickremeratne, *Buddha in Sri Lanka*, 161–165.

34. Gombrich and Obeyesekere, *Buddhism Transformed*, 388–389.

35. For just a couple of examples of mountain gods who control the hunt, see Capper, *Learning Love from a Tiger*, 93, 152, 196–198, 238.

36. Seligmann and Seligmann, *Veddhas*, 132–188.

37. Gombrich and Obeyesekere, *Buddhism Transformed*, 174–175; Wickremeratne, *Buddha in Sri Lanka*, 260.

38. Wickremeratne, *Buddha in Sri Lanka*, 260; Gombrich and Obeyesekere, *Buddhism Transformed*, 175.

39. Bullis, *Mahavamsa*, 51.

40. Gananath Obeyesekere, *The Cult of the Goddess Pattini* (Chicago: University of Chicago Press, 1984), 94.

41. Wickremeratne, *Buddha in Sri Lanka*, 104; S. Paranavitana, "The God of Adam's Peak," *Artibus Asiae Supplementum* 18 (1958): 11.

42. Paranavitana, "God of Adam's Peak," 12.

43. Paranavitana, "God of Adam's Peak," 17.

44. Paranavitana, "God of Adam's Peak," 54.

45. Wickremeratne, *Buddha in Sri Lanka*, 105.

46. Wickremeratne, *Buddha in Sri Lanka*, 106.

47. Wickremeratne, *Buddha in Sri Lanka*, 105.

48. Stewart, *Vegetarianism and Animal Ethics*, 74, 84.

49. Bullis, *Mahavamsa*, 389–390.

50. Bullis, *Mahavamsa*, 385.

51. Rohan Bastin, *The Domain of Constant Excess: Plural Worship at the Munnesvaram Temples in Sri Lanka* (New York: Berghahn Books, 2002), 156.

52. Kate Crosby, *Theravada Buddhism: Continuity, Diversity, and Identity* (Chichester: John Wiley and Sons, 2014), 86.

53. Wilhelm Geiger, trans., *Cūḷavaṃsa: Being the More Recent Part of the Mahāvaṃsa*, vol. 1 (New Delhi: Asian Educational Services, 2003), 22–26.

54. Bhikkhu Ñāṇamoli, trans., *The Path of Purification (Visudhimagga)* (Onalaska, WI: Buddhist Publication Society, 1991).

55. Crosby, *Theravada Buddhism*, 148.

56. Paul Waldau, *The Specter of Speciesism: Buddhist and Christian Views of Animals* (Oxford: Oxford University Press, 2002), 131.

57. Horner, *Book of the Discipline*, 2786–2787.

58. N. R. M. Ehara, Soma Thera, and Kheminda Thera, trans., *The Path of Freedom* (Kandy, Sri Lanka: Buddhist Publication Society, 1961), 27–28.

59. R. A. L. H. Gunawardana, *Robe and Plough: Monasticism and Economic Interest in Early Medieval Sri Lanka* (Tucson: University of Arizona Press, 1979), 40.

60. Michael Carrithers, *The Forest Monks of Sri Lanka* (Delhi: Oxford University Press, 1983).

61. Bhikkhu Bodhi, *Numerical Discourses of the Buddha*, 456.

62. Cowell, *Jātaka*, 1:51–53.

63. Bruce Kapferer, *Feast of the Sorcerer: Practices of Consciousness and Power* (Chicago: University of Chicago Press, 1997), 45.

64. Bastin, *Domain of Constant Excess*, 53.

65. Bastin, *Domain of Constant Excess*, 103; Gombrich and Obeyesekere, *Buddhism Transformed*, 77.

66. For removing spells, limes are used at the temple to ritually absorb sorcery, and when these limes are halved, the spell is presumed to be cut, thus providing a countersorcery resource. Other exorcists cut pumpkins or use a snake effigy to dispel sorcery. See Kapferer, *Feast of the Sorcerer*, 140, 175.

67. Bastin, *Domain of Constant Excess*, 67, 197.

68. Gombrich and Obeyesekere, *Buddhism Transformed*, 34.

69. Colombo Telegraph, "SC Says Need License for Animal Sacrifice," *Colombo Telegraph*, September 3, 2014, accessed July 24, 2016, https://www.colombotele graph.com/index.php/sc-says-need-licence-for-animal-sacrifice/.

70. Stewart, *Vegetarianism and Animal Ethics*, 23.

71. Pe Maung Tin and G. H. Luce, trans., *The Glass Palace Chronicle of the Kings of Burma* (London: Oxford University Press, 1921), 108.

4. Beautiful Thai Buffaloes

1. "Achan," as a title for recognized Thai Buddhist masters, approximates the Indian *ācārya*.

2. J. L. Taylor, *Forest Monks and the Nation-State: An Anthropological and Historical Study in Northeastern Thailand* (Singapore: Institute of Southeast Asian Studies, 1993), 237.

3. Taylor, *Forest Monks*, 30.

4. Taylor, *Forest Monks*, 12.

5. Taylor, *Forest Monks*, 30.

6. Frank E. Reynolds and Mani B. Reynolds, trans., *Three Worlds according to King Ruang: A Thai Buddhist Cosmology* (Berkeley, CA: Asian Humanities Press, 1982), 5.

7. Justin Thomas McDaniel, *The Lovelorn Ghost and the Magical Monk: Practicing Buddhism in Modern Thailand* (New York: Columbia University Press, 2011), 126; Reynolds and Reynolds, *Three Worlds*, 73.

8. Reynolds and Reynolds, *Three Worlds*.

9. Taylor, *Forest Monks*, 23.

10. Barend Jan Terwiel, *Monks and Magic: Revisiting a Classic Study of Religious Ceremonies in Thailand* (Copenhagen: Nordic Institute of Asian Studies, 2012), 157.

11. Pei Sheng-ji, "Some Effects of the Dai People's Cultural Beliefs and Practices upon the Plant Environment of Xishuangbanna, Yunnan Province, Southwest China," in *Cultural Values and Human Ecology in Southeast Asia*, ed. Karl L. Hutterer, A. Terry Rambo, and George Lovelace (Ann Arbor: Center for South and Southeast Asian Studies, University of Michigan, 1985), 332.

12. Kabilsingh Chatsumarn, *Thai Women in Buddhism* (Berkeley, CA: Parallax Press, 1991), 1; Terwiel, *Monks and Magic*, 11.

13. Donald K. Swearer, Sommai Premchit, and Phaithoon Dokbuakaew, *Sacred Mountains of Northern Thailand and Their Legends* (Chiang Mai, Thailand: Silkworm Books, 2004).

14. Robert L. Winzeler, *The Peoples of Southeast Asia Today* (Lanham, MD: Altamira Press, 2011), 151–152.

15. The scholar of Buddhism Ian Harris relates that this earth goddess is indigenous to Thailand and Cambodia and does not derive from India. He states that her image, in which she wrings water from her hair, adorns the entrance to virtually every monastery. See Ian Harris, "Magician as Environmentalist: Fertility Elements in South and Southeast Asian Buddhism," *Eastern Buddhist* 32, no. 2 (2000): 133.

16. Terwiel, *Monks and Magic*, 174.

17. Rice farming, introduced from China, began in what is now Thailand around 2,500 BCE. Although humans first appeared in Thailand in perhaps 17,000 BCE, because of the difficulties that rainforests pose to hunter-gatherer lifestyles, the human population in Thailand appears to have been small before the introduction of rice agriculture. See Steven Mithen, *After the Ice: A Global Human History, 20,000–5,000 BC* (Cambridge, MA: Harvard University Press, 2003), 353–354.

18. John E. deYoung, *Village Life in Modern Thailand* (Berkeley: University of California Press, 1966), 142–143.

19. deYoung, *Village Life*, 141–142.

20. Stanley J. Tambiah, *Buddhism and the Spirit Cults in Northeast Thailand* (Cambridge: Cambridge University Press, 1970), 243.

21. Tambiah, *Buddhism and the Spirit Cults in Northeast Thailand*, 257.

22. Tambiah, *Buddhism and the Spirit Cults in Northeast Thailand*, 254.

23. On calling the souls of buffaloes, see Michael R. Rhum, *The Ancestral Lords: Gender, Descent, and Spirits in a Northern Thai Village* (DeKalb: Northern Illinois University Press, 1994), 126.

24. Georges Condominas, "Phībān Cults in Rural Laos," in *Change and Persistence in Thai Society*, ed. G. Thomas Skinner and A. Thomas Kirsch (Ithaca, NY: Cornell University Press, 1975), 255.

25. Kitiarsa Pattana, *Mediums, Monks, and Amulets: Thai Popular Buddhism Today* (Chiang Mai, Thailand: Silkworm Books, 2012), 43.

26. Tambiah, *Buddhism and the Spirit Cults in Northeast Thailand*, 264–286.

27. Rhum, *Ancestral Lords*, 76.

28. Stanley J. Tambiah, *The Buddhist Saints of the Forest and the Cult of the Amulets* (Cambridge: Cambridge University Press, 1984), 83–84.

29. Tambiah, *Buddhist Saints of the Forest*, 106; Tiyavanich Kamala, *Forest Recollections: Wandering Monks in Twentieth-Century Thailand* (Honolulu: University of Hawai'i Press, 1997), 87.

30. Ajahn Tate, *The Autobiography of a Forest Monk* (Nongkhai, Thailand: Amarin, 1993), 170.

31. Tambiah, *Buddhist Saints of the Forest*, 89.

32. Tambiah, *Buddhist Saints of the Forest*, 94.

33. Tambiah, *Buddhist Saints of the Forest*, 87–88.

34. Tiyavanich Kamala, *The Buddha in the Jungle* (Chiang Mai, Thailand: Silkworm Books, 2003), 191.

35. Kamala, *Forest Recollections*, 88–89.

36. Kamala, *Buddha in the Jungle*, 171–173.

37. Kamala, *Buddha in the Jungle*, 141.

38. Kamala, *Buddha in the Jungle*, 152–153.

39. Kamala, *Buddha in the Jungle*, 154.

40. Kamala, *Forest Recollections*, 89–90.

41. Kamala, *Buddha in the Jungle*, 165.

42. Tambiah, *Buddhist Saints of the Forest*, 107.

43. Kamala, *Forest Recollections*, 150.

44. Kamala, *Forest Recollections*, 165.

45. Ajahn Chah, *Food for the Heart* (Boston, MA: Wisdom Publications, 2002), 84.

46. Ajahn Chah, *Food for the Heart*, 266–267.

47. Jack Kornfield and Paul Breiter, eds., *A Still Forest Pool: The Insight Meditation of Achaan Chah* (Wheaton, IL: Quest Books, 1985), 112.

48. Ajahn Tate, *Autobiography of a Forest Monk*, 75.

49. Ajahn Tate, *Autobiography of a Forest Monk*, 173.

50. Taylor, *Forest Monks*, 205.

51. Kamala, *Forest Recollections*, 198.

52. Kamala, *Forest Recollections*, 198–199; Tate, *Autobiography of a Forest Monk*, 166.

53. Peter A. Jackson, *Buddhadāsa: Theravada Buddhism and Modernist Reform in Thailand* (Chiang Mai, Thailand: Silkworm Books, 2003), 35.

54. For a discussion of Buddhist modernism as a trend that blends religious pluralism, secularization, globalization, and other forces, see David L. McMahan, *The Making of Buddhist Modernism* (Oxford: Oxford University Press, 2008).

55. Jackson, *Buddhadāsa*, 77.

56. Donald K. Swearer, ed., *Me and Mine: Selected Essays of Bhikkhu Buddhadāsa* (Delhi: Sri Satguru Publications, 1991), 134.

57. Swearer, *Me and Mine*, 143.

58. Swearer, *Me and Mine*, 143.

59. Swearer, *Me and Mine*, 170.

60. Jackson, *Buddhadāsa*, 210.

61. Swearer, *Me and Mine*, 186–187, 196.

62. Swearer, Premchit, and Dokbuakaew, *Sacred Mountains*, 9.

63. Swearer, Premchit, and Dokbuakaew, *Sacred Mountains*, 8–9.

64. Susan M. Darlington, *The Ordination of a Tree: The Thai Buddhist Environmental Movement* (Albany: SUNY State University of New York Press, 2012).

65. Lotte Isager and Søren Ivarsson, "Contesting Landscapes in Thailand: Tree Ordination as Counter-Territorialization," *Critical Asian Studies* 34, no. 3 (2002): 396, https://doi.org/10.1080/1467271022000008947.

66. Just as the tree ordination rituals I mentioned aim to be ecofriendly but remain limited in this regard, so diverse forces also conflict within the reality of the famous "tiger temple," with unfortunate results. Featured in the heartwarming movie documentary, *The Tiger and the Monk*, Wat Pa Luangta Bua Yannasampano in 1999 received an injured tiger cub and nursed it until it died soon thereafter. Based on this experience, other tigers were given to the monastery, which then began, ad hoc at first, self-consciously to serve as a tiger sanctuary. Over time, the temple then marketed itself as a kind of sacred petting zoo, where Thais and foreigners alike could have their photos taken while cuddling tiger cubs or holding the heads of adult tigers in their laps. Sadly, though, nearly from the start the tiger temple was surrounded by accusations of mistreating the animals, engaging in the illegal trade of endangered species, and operating in an unlicensed, unregulated manner. In May and June of 2016, the Thai government investigated, and while removing 137 tigers from the property, investigators found more than 60 dead tiger cubs, as well as other animal parts, preserved in freezers and in formaldehyde in jars, apparent evidence of participation in the illegal black market for tiger parts. Also troubling, a vehicle was stopped while leaving the compound, and in this vehicle two tiger skins, numerous tiger teeth, and between 800 and 900 blessed Buddhist amulets that contained bits of tiger skin were found. Five staff members of the temple were arrested, including three monks. The holy petting zoo then closed. See Azadeh Ansari and Kocha Olarn, "Thai 'Tiger Temple': Five Charged with Possessing Endangered Animal Parts," *CNN*, June 3, 2016, accessed June 26, 2016, http://www.cnn.com/2016/06/03/asia/thailand-tiger-temple-charges/.

67. Kitiarsa Pattana, "Beyond Syncretism: Hybridization of Popular Religion in Contemporary Thailand," *Journal of Southeast Asian Studies* 36, no. 3 (2005): 461, https://doi.org/10.1017/S0022463405000251.

68. Darlington, *Ordination of a Tree*, 12.

69. Philip Hirsch, "Introduction: Seeing Forests for Trees," in *Seeing Forests for Trees: Environment and Environmentalism in Thailand*, ed. Philip Hirsch (Chiang Mai, Thailand: Silkworm Books, 1996), 6.

70. For Mayan agricultural nature mysticism, see Capper, *Learning Love from a Tiger*, 171–173.

71. Ian Harris, *Cambodian Buddhism: History and Practice* (Honolulu: University of Hawai'i Press, 2005), 30–31.

5. Eating the Enlightened Plants of China

1. Xu Yun, *Empty Cloud*, trans. Charles Luk (Worcestor: Element Books, 1988), x.

2. Xu Yun, *Empty Cloud*, 115–116.

3. Xu Yun, *Empty Cloud*, 113.

4. Xu Yun, *Empty Cloud*, 53–54.

5. Xu Yun, *Empty Cloud*, 39.

6. Roel Sterckx, "Transforming the Beasts: Animals and Music in Early China," *T'oung Pao* 86 (2000): 2, https://doi.org/10.1163/15685320051072672.

7. For some Confucian instances, see Keith N. Knapp, "Noble Creatures: Filial and Righteous Animals in Early Medieval Confucian Thought," in *Animals through Chinese History: Earliest Times to 1911*, ed. Roel Sterckx, Martina Seibert, and Dagmar Schäfer (Cambridge: Cambridge University Press, 2019), 82.

8. Martin Palmer, trans., *The Book of Chuang Tzu* (London: Penguin Books, 2006), 20, 147.

9. Xu Yun, *Empty Cloud*, 91.

10. Xu Yun, *Empty Cloud*, 91.

11. D. C. Lau, trans., *Mencius* (London: Penguin Books, 2003), 156.

12. Roel Sterckx, "Attitudes towards Wildlife and the Hunt in Pre-Buddhist China," in Knight, *Wildlife in Asia*, 16.

13. Mithen, *After the Ice*, 364–365.

14. Mithen, *After the Ice*, 361–363.

15. Michael J. Hathaway, *Environmental Winds: Making the Global in Southwest China* (Berkeley: University of California Press, 2013), 152.

16. Mark Elvin, *The Retreat of the Elephants: An Environmental History of China* (New Haven, CT: Yale University Press, 2004), 9, 11.

17. Elvin, *Retreat of the Elephants*, 33–34.

18. Elvin, *Retreat of the Elephants*, 20.

19. David Hawkes, trans., *The Songs of the South* (London: Penguin Books, 1985), 178–179; Elvin, *Retreat of the Elephants*, 48.

20. Elvin, *Retreat of the Elephants*, xvii, 46.

21. Elvin, *Retreat of the Elephants*, 62.

22. Henrik H. Sørensen, "Of Eco-Buddhas and Dharma-Roots: Views from the East Asian Buddhist Tradition," in Meinert, *Nature, Environment and Culture in East Asia*, 91.

23. Heiner Roetz, "Chinese 'Unity of Man and Nature': Reality or Myth?," in Meinert, *Nature, Environment and Culture in East Asia*, 23.

24. Livia Kohn, *Taoist Mystical Philosophy: The Scripture of the Western Ascension* (Albany: State University of New York Press, 1991), 237.

25. Sterckx, "Attitudes towards Wildlife and the Hunt in Pre-Buddhist China," 17.

26. Anthony C. Yu, trans., *The Monkey and the Monk* (Chicago: University of Chicago Press, 2006), 48.

27. Ole Bruun, *Fengshui in China: Geomantic Divination between State Orthodoxy and Popular Religion* (Honolulu: University of Hawai'i Press, 2003), 2; Graham Parkes, "Winds, Waters, and Earth Energies: *Fengshui* and Sense of Place," in *Nature across Cultures: Views of Nature and the Environment in Non-Western Cultures*, ed. Helaine Selin (Dordrecht: Kluwer Academic, 2003), 201.

28. Bruun, *Fengshui*, 2, 6, 82.

29. Chris Coggins, "When the Land Is Excellent: Village Feng Shui Forests and the Nature of Lineage, Polity, and Vitality in Southern China," in Miller, Yu, and van der Veer, *Religion and Ecological Sustainability in China*, 116–117.

30. Bruun, *Fengshui*, 4, 148.

31. Bruun, *Fengshui*, 194–195.

32. Bruun, *Fengshui*, 236.

33. Chris Coggins, "Sacred Watersheds and the Fate of the Village Body Politic in Tibetan and Han Communities under China's Ecological Civilization," *Religions* 10 (2019): 22, https://doi.org/10.3390/rel10110600.

34. Ole Bruun, "Is Chinese Popular Religion At All Compatible with Ecology? A Discussion of Feng Shui," in Miller, Yu, and van der Veer, *Religion and Ecological Sustainability in China*, 177.

35. James Robson, *Power of Place: The Religious Landscape of the Southern Sacred Peak (Nanyue) in Medieval China* (Cambridge, MA: Harvard University Press, 2009), 32.

36. Hawkes, *Songs of the South*, 115–116.

37. Richard E. Strassberg, trans., *A Chinese Bestiary: Strange Creatures from the Guideways through Mountains and Seas* (Berkeley: University of California Press, 2002), 107–108, 192.

38. Strassberg, *Chinese Bestiary*, 146, 147, 149, 153, 159.

39. Christoph Baumer, *China's Holy Mountain: An Illustrated Journey into the Heart of Buddhism* (London: I. B. Tauris, 2011), 129–130.

40. Isabelle Charleux, *Nomads on Pilgrimage: Mongols on Wutaishan (China), 1800–1940* (Leiden: Brill, 2015), 63.

41. Baumer, *China's Holy Mountain*, 4.

42. Baumer, *China's Holy Mountain*, 141; Charleux, *Nomads on Pilgrimage*, 90.

43. Charleux, *Nomads on Pilgrimage*, 90.

44. Baumer, *China's Holy Mountain*, 141.

45. Baumer, *China's Holy Mountain*, 3; Gray Tuttle, "Tibetan Buddhism at Ri bo rtse lnga/Wutai shan in Modern Times," *Journal of the International Association of Tibetan Studies* 2 (2006): 4, http://www.thlib.org/static/reprints/jiats/02/pdfs/tuttleJIATS_02_2006.pdf.

46. Baumer, *China's Holy Mountain*, 127; Charleux, *Nomads on Pilgrimage*, 91.

47. Charleux, *Nomads on Pilgrimage*, 65.

48. Baumer, *China's Holy Mountain*, 143.

49. Charleux, *Nomads on Pilgrimage*, 195.

50. Xu Yun, *Empty Cloud*, 14–16; Charleux, *Nomads on Pilgrimage*, 86.

51. Charleux, *Nomads on Pilgrimage*, 85; Xu Yun, *Empty Cloud*, 52.

52. Charleux, *Nomads on Pilgrimage*, 178.

53. Charleux, *Nomads on Pilgrimage*, 87.

54. Charleux, *Nomads on Pilgrimage*, 67–68.

55. T. Rhys Davids, *Questions of King*, 1:241.

56. Watson, *Lotus Sutra*, 99–100; Watson, *Vimalakirti Sutra*, 35; Chang, *Treasury of Mahāyāna Sūtras*, 273.

57. Blum, *Nirvana Sutra*, 1:281; Schmithausen, *Plants in Early Buddhism*, 113.

58. Nattier, *Few Good Men*, 229–230.

59. Schmithausen, *Plants in Early Buddhism*, 121.

60. Inagaki Hisao, trans., *The Three Pure Land Sutras* (Berkeley, CA: BDK America, 2003), 86.

61. As an alternative to the mainstream view denying a place for animals in Pure Lands, the Pure Land priest Ryūen (1759–1834 CE) said that a dog was reborn in a Pure Land because he had barked in time to the *nembutsu* chant that leads to a Pure Land rebirth. See J. Nelson, *Experimental Buddhism*, 162.

62. Livia Kohn, *Laughing at the Tao: Debates among Buddhists and Taoists in Medieval China* (Princeton, NJ: Princeton University Press, 1995), 115.

63. Paul Williams, *Mahāyāna Buddhism: The Doctrinal Foundations* (London: Routledge, 1989), 96–115.

64. Watson, *Lotus Sutra*, 101–103.

65. Watson, *Lotus Sutra*, 99.

66. William R. LaFleur, "Saigyō and the Buddhist Value of Nature, Part I," *History of Religions* 13, no. 2 (1973): 95, http://www.jstor.org.lynx.lib.usm.edu/stable/1061933.

67. Schmithausen, *Plants in Early Buddhism*, 163; Watson, *Vimalakirti Sutra*, 35.

68. Fabio Rambelli, *Vegetal Buddhas: Ideological Effects of Japanese Buddhist Doctrines on the Salvation of Inanimate Beings* (Kyoto: Scuola Italiana di Studi sull' Asia Orientale, 2001), 8.

69. LaFleur, "Saigyō and the Buddhist Value of Nature, Part I," 95.

70. In much of the literature regarding Buddhism and plants, *Zhanran* is transliterated using the older Wade-Giles system as *Chan-jan*.

71. LaFleur, "Saigyō and the Buddhist Value of Nature, Part I," 96.

72. LaFleur, "Saigyō and the Buddhist Value of Nature, Part I," 96.

73. Daniel Capper, "Learning Love from a Tiger: Approaches to Nature in an American Buddhist Monastery," *Journal of Contemporary Religion* 30, no. 1 (2015): 56, https://doi.org/10.1080/13537903.2015.986976.

74. Daniel L. Overmyer, *Folk Buddhist Religion: Dissenting Sects in Late Traditional China* (Cambridge, MA: Harvard University Press, 1976), 77; John Kieschnick, "Buddhist Vegetarianism in China," in Sterckx, *Of Tripod and Palate*, 207.

75. Jordan Paper, *The Spirits Are Drunk: Comparative Approaches to Chinese Religion* (Albany: State University of New York Press, 1995), 24.

76. Terry F. Kleeman, "Feasting with the Victuals: The Evolution of the Daoist Communal Kitchen," in Sterckx, *Of Tripod and Palate*, 145.

77. Livia Kohn, *Cosmos and Community: The Ethical Dimension of Daoism* (Cambridge, MA: Three Pines Press, 2004), 22.

78. Kleeman, "Feasting with the Victuals," 53–154.

79. Shawn Arthur, *Early Daoist Dietary Practices* (Lanham, MA: Lexington Books, 2013), 49.

80. Kohn, *Cosmos and Community*, 47; Palmer, *Book of Chuang Tzu*, 22–23.

81. E. N. Anderson and Lisa Raphals, "Daoism and Animals," in Waldau and Patton, *Communion of Subjects*, 277.

82. Kieschnick, "Buddhist Vegetarianism in China," 193.

83. Vincent Goossaert, "The Beef Taboo and the Sacrificial Structure of Late Imperial Chinese Society," in Sterckx, *Of Tripod and Palate*, 239, 241–243.

84. Ludwig Alsdorf, *The History of Vegetarianism and Cow-Veneration in India*, trans. Bal Patil (London: Routledge, 2010), 19.

85. Alsdorf, *History of Vegetarianism and Cow-Veneration in India*, 20.

86. W. Norman Brown, "The Sanctity of the Cow in Hinduism," *Economic Weekly* 16, nos. 5–7 (February 1964): 247.

87. Alsdorf, *History of Vegetarianism and Cow-Veneration in India*, 41.

88. Chapple, *Nonviolence to Animals, Earth, and Self*, 15.

89. Kieschnick, "Buddhist Vegetarianism in China," 189.

90. John Powers, trans., *Wisdom of Buddha: The Saṃdhinirmocana Sūtra* (Berkeley, CA: Dharma, 1995), 137.

91. Lambert Schmithausen, *Fleischverzehr und Vegetarismus im indischen Buddhismus*, Teil 1 (Bochum: Projekt Verlag, 2020), 212.

92. Watson, *Lotus Sutra*, 199.

93. Śāntideva, *The Bodhicaryāvatāra*, trans. Kate Crosby and Andrew Skilton (Oxford: Oxford University Press, 1995), 99.

94. Blum, *Nirvana Sutra*, 1:111.

95. Luk, *Śūraṅgama Sūtra*, 90, 153–154.

96. D. Seyfort Ruegg, "Ahiṃsā and Vegetarianism in the History of Buddhism," in *Buddhist Studies in Honor of Walpola Rahula*, ed. Somaratna Balasooriya, Andre Bareau, Richard Gombrich, Siri Gunasingha, Udaya Mallawarachchi, and Edmund Perry (London: Gordon Fraser, 1980), 236.

97. This regulation was not a problem for some in China since tradition had already counseled the avoidance of the "five pungent herbs" (*wuxin*): garlic, onions, leeks, chives, and ginger. The Celestial Masters sect of Daoism especially discouraged their use. See L. Kohn, *Cosmos and Community*, 44.

98. Bendall and Rouse, *Śikṣā Samuccaya*, 130–132.

99. Suzuki, *Lankavatara Sutra*, 213–221.

100. Suzuki, *Lankavatara Sutra*, 217, 220.

101. Bendall and Rouse, *Śikṣā Samuccaya*, 130.

102. Suzuki, *Lankavatara Sutra*, 212.

103. The *Fanwangjing* proposes a winter rather than summer retreat for monastics, a suggestion that some East Asian Buddhists have embraced. A. Charles Muller and Kenneth K. Tanaka, trans., *The Brahmā's Net Sutra* (Moraga, CA: BDK America, 2017), xix, 65.

104. Muller and Tanaka, *Brahmā's Net Sutra*, 55.

105. Muller and Tanaka, *Brahmā's Net Sutra*, 49.

106. Roel Sterckx, "'Of a Tawny Bull We Make Offering': Animals in Early Chinese Religion," in Waldau and Patton, *Communion of Subjects*, 262; Kieschnick, "Buddhist Vegetarianism in China," 196–198.

107. Kieschnick, "Buddhist Vegetarianism in China," 194.

108. Kieschnick, "Buddhist Vegetarianism in China," 201.

109. Kieschnick, "Buddhist Vegetarianism in China," 201.

110. Meir Shahar, *The Shaolin Monastery: History, Religion, and the Chinese Martial Arts* (Honolulu: University of Hawai'i Press, 2008), 13.

111. Shahar, *Shaolin Monastery*, 14.

112. Shahar, *Shaolin Monastery*, 22.

113. Matthew Polly, *American Shaolin* (New York: Gotham Books, 2007), 37.

114. Shahar, *Shaolin Monastery*, 3.

115. Shahar, *Shaolin Monastery*, 120.

116. Leopold, *Sand County Almanac*, 96.

117. Sterckx, "Transforming the Beasts," 19–21.

118. Harriette D. Grissom, "Animal Forms and Formlessness: The Protean Quality of Buddha Nature in Chinese Martial Arts," in *Buddha Nature and Animality*, ed. David Jones (Fremont, CA: Jain, 2007), 63.

119. Grissom, "Animal Forms and Formlessness," 68.

120. Grissom, "Animal Forms and Formlessness," 65.

121. Grissom, "Animal Forms and Formlessness," 73.

122. Shahar, *Shaolin Monastery*, 142.

123. Jwing-ming Yang, *The Essence of Shaolin White Crane: Martial Power and Qigong* (Wolfeboro, NH: YMAA Publication Center, 1996).

124. Jwing-ming Yang, *Qigong: The Secret of Youth* (Boston, MA: YMAA Publication Center, 2000), 9.

125. Daehaeng Kun Sunim, *My Heart Is a Golden Buddha* (Anyang, China: Hanmaum Publications, 2006), 65–67.

6. Japanese Water Buddhas

1. Carmen Blacker, *The Catalpa Bow: A Study of Shamanistic Practices in Japan* (London: George Allen and Unwin, 1986), 38.

2. In the *Kojiki*, Conquering Yamato meets a boar, a traditional antagonist of Japanese farmers, rather than the *Nihonshoki*'s deer, which represents another historical agricultural antagonist.

3. With intensive animal husbandry largely absent from traditional Japan, leading to fewer fears of wolves' eating livestock, the Japanese reverse images of some forest animals vis-à-vis European folk cultures. Over time, Japanese farmers have generally perceived deer as somewhat negative despite their sacredness, because deer eat the rice crop, and wolves as somewhat positive, because they limit the numbers of destructive deer and boar in rice fields. As a matter of form meeting function, deer even have been employed as sacrifices to ensure a good rice harvest. See Hoyt Long, "Grateful Animal or Spiritual Being? Buddhist Gratitude Tales and Changing Conceptions of Deer in Early Japan," in *JAPANimals: History and Culture in Japan's Animal Life*, ed. Gregory M. Pflugfelder and Brett L. Walker (Ann Arbor: Center for Japanese Studies, University of Michigan, 2005), 38.

4. W. G. Aston, trans., *Nihongi*, vol. 1 (New York: Cosimo Classics, 2008), 200–211.

5. Despite widespread misunderstandings, Japanese kami-worshipping and the religion known as Shintō are not necessarily the same. Beginning in 1868, the Meiji

government insisted on separating Buddhism and indigenous religiosity, creating Shintō as a state-directed form of spirituality. Many effects of this attempted separation remain today. But Japanese people sometimes venerate kami spirits in modes not covered by the state Shintō system. Therefore, I follow a manner that is common in the world of Japanese religious studies by using *Shintō* to reference the state-molded form of religiosity and *kami-worshipping* to denote broader kami-based activities that may or may not be subsumed under Shintō.

6. Allan G. Grapard, "Nature and Culture in Japan," in *Deep Ecology*, ed. Michael Tobias (San Marcos, CA: Avant Books, 1988), 243.

7. Grapard, "Nature and Culture in Japan," 244.

8. Stephen R. Kellert, "Japanese Perceptions of Wildlife," *Conservation Biology* 5, no. 3 (1991): 302, https://doi.org/10.1111/j.1523-1739.1991.tb00141.x.

9. Stephen R. Kellert, "Attitudes, Knowledge, and Behaviour toward Wildlife among the Industrial Superpowers: United States, Japan, and Germany," *Journal of Social Issues* 49, no. 1 (1993): 58–59, https://doi.org/10.1111/j.1540-4560.1993.tb00908.x.

10. Conrad Totman, *Japan: An Environmental History* (London: I. B. Tauris, 2016), 32, 35.

11. Totman, *Japan*, 55.

12. Totman, *Japan*, 86.

13. Totman, *Japan*, 86.

14. Totman, *Japan*, 104.

15. Blacker, *Catalpa Bow*, 84.

16. Brett L. Walker, *A Concise History of Japan* (Cambridge: Cambridge University Press, 2015), 122.

17. Totman, *Japan*, 176.

18. John Knight, *Waiting for Wolves in Japan: An Anthropological Study of People-Wildlife Relations* (Honolulu: University of Hawai'i Press, 2006), 31.

19. Totman, *Japan*, 127.

20. Knight, *Waiting for Wolves*, 30.

21. John Knight, "Wolf Reintroduction in Japan?," in Knight, *Wildlife in Asia*, 235; Brett L. Walker, *The Lost Wolves of Japan* (Seattle: University of Washington Press, 2005), 70.

22. Totman, *Japan*, 62.

23. Barbara R. Ambros, *Bones of Contention: Animals and Religion in Contemporary Japan* (Honolulu: University of Hawai'i Press, 2012), 40.

24. Totman, *Japan*, 48.

25. Walker, *Concise History of Japan*, 90.

26. Totman, *Japan*, 138; Ambros, *Bones of Contention*, 40–41.

27. Ambros, *Bones of Contention*, 56.

28. Rambelli, *Vegetal Buddhas*, 15.

29. Rambelli, *Vegetal Buddhas*, 17.

30. Daniel Chamovitz, *What a Plant Knows* (New York: Scientific American, 2012), 137–138.

31. Paul Groner, "A Medieval Japanese Reading of the *Mo-ho chih-kuan*: Placing the *Kankō ruijū* in Historical Context," *Japanese Journal of Religious Studies* 22, no. 1/2 (1995): 53, http://www.jstor.org.lynx.lib.usm.edu/stable/30233537.

32. Rambelli, *Vegetal Buddhas*, 25.

33. Rambelli, *Vegetal Buddhas*, 23.

34. Rambelli, *Vegetal Buddhas*, 27.

35. Yukio Sakamoto, "On the 'Attainment of Buddhahood by Trees and Plants,'" *Proceedings of the IXth International Congress for the History of Religions, Tokyo and Kyoto, 1958* (Tokyo: Maruzen, 1960), 418.

36. Notably, even the celebrated nature poet Matsuo Bashō (1644–1694 CE), self-named for a banana tree, dismissed plant sentience in his encounter with a massive pine tree: "I felt a strange sense of awe and respect, for, though the tree itself was a cold, senseless object, it had survived the punishment of an axe for so many years under the divine protection of the Buddha." Matsuo Bashō, *The Narrow Road to the Deep North and Other Travel Sketches*, trans. Nobuyuki Yuasa (Harmondsworth: Penguin Books, 1966), 56.

37. Rambelli, *Vegetal Buddhas*, 30.

38. Taikō Yamasaki, *Shingon: Japanese Esoteric Buddhism* (Boston, MA: Shambhala, 1988), 53.

39. LaFleur, "Saigyō and the Buddhist Value of Nature, Part I," 98.

40. Yoshito S. Hakeda, *Kukai: Major Works* (New York: Columbia University Press, 1972), 254–255.

41. Hakeda, *Kukai*, 91.

42. Yamasaki, *Shingon*, 198.

43. Yamasaki, *Shingon*, 198.

44. Yamasaki, *Shingon*, 195.

45. Manabu Watanabe, "Religious Symbolism in Saigyō's Verses: A Contribution to Discussions of His Views on Nature and Religion," *History of Religions* 26, no. 4 (1987): 393, https://doi.org/10.1086/463088.

46. Hakeda, *Kukai*, 22.

47. Hakeda, *Kukai*, 102.

48. Yamasaki, *Shingon*, 188–189.

49. Hakeda, *Kukai*, 52.

50. Minoru Kiyota, *Shingon Buddhism: Theory and Practice* (Los Angeles: Buddhist Books International, 1978), 81; Yamasaki, *Shingon*, 128.

51. Yamasaki, *Shingon*, 138.

52. For centuries, Shugendō practitioners have visited Inari Mountain in Fushimi, near Kyoto, as one of their power places. But Inari Mountain does more religiously than attract *yamabushis* since it also provides an inviting site for less strenuous popular mountain pilgrimages, given that the mountain serves as the foremost home of the immensely influential Buddhist and Shintō deity Inari. Lacking a specific gender, Inari typically appears as a fox with a jewel in its mouth, under a paw, or resting at the tip of its upraised tail, with the deity's identity as a fox symbolically connecting Inari with notions of prosperity. Today, Inari is the main deity in one-third of all kami-worshipping shrines, while the holy fox appears as well in numerous Buddhist temples by the name Dakiniten, making this spirit one of the most visible manifestations of contemporary Japanese popular religion. Perhaps Inari's presence as a deity of prosperity explains some of the god's celebrity, for there is a saying, "For sickness pray to Kūkai, for desires to Inari." In granting wishes, Inari is the leader of all fox spirits, with beliefs in fox spirits rife throughout East Asia, not just in Japan; they

have occurred in China at least since the Han dynasty and likely earlier. Fox spirits maintain a reputation for capriciousness because they may bestow wealth or power for little to no reason, yet also create disease, material damage, and even death without apparent cause. In Japan, as in much of East Asia, fox spirits engage in activities and enact their personhood by entering the world of humans through either fox apparitions, in which a numinous fox shape-shifts into human form, or through fox possession (*kitsune tsuki*), in which a fox spirit maintains agency from within a human being. Symptoms of fox possession include unusual eating habits, inappropriate use of language, inability to follow social norms, wanting to always be outside, being profligate with money, being destructive or violent, spitting, crawling on all fours, and, more positively, new literacy skills, such as sudden proficiency in the classical Chinese language. A fox spirit may possess someone to avenge a perceived slight or the spirit may just wish to have a physical body to pursue desires for food or to have a shrine built in its honor. See Karen A. Smyers, *The Fox and the Jewel: Shared and Private Meanings in Contemporary Japanese Inari Worship* (Honolulu: University of Hawai'i Press, 1999), 22, 178; Blacker, *Catalpa Bow*, 52; and Xiaofei Kang, *The Cult of the Fox: Power, Gender, and Popular Religion in Late Imperial and Modern China* (New York: Columbia University Press, 2005), 14.

53. Blacker, *Catalpa Bow*, 84.

54. Blacker, *Catalpa Bow*, 96.

55. Blacker, *Catalpa Bow*, 87.

56. Allan G. Grapard, "Flying Mountains and Walkers of Emptiness: Toward a Definition of Sacred Space in Japanese Religions," *History of Religions* 21, no. 3 (1982): 207–208, https://doi.org/10.1086/462897.

57. Allan G. Grapard, *Mountain Mandalas: Shugendō in Kyushu* (London: Bloomsbury, 2016), 112.

58. Grapard, "Flying Mountains and Walkers of Emptiness," 210.

59. Grapard, *Mountain Mandalas*, 191–194.

60. Grapard, *Mountain Mandalas*, 1–2.

61. Grapard, *Mountain Mandalas*, 62, 116.

62. Grapard, "Flying Mountains and Walkers of Emptiness," 210–218.

63. Shigeru Gorai, "Shugendo Lore," *Japanese Journal of Religious Studies* 16, no. 2/3 (1989): 128, http://www.jstor.org.lynx.lib.usm.edu/stable/30234004.

64. Palmer, *Book of Chuang Tzu*, 205.

65. Mu Soeng, trans., *The Diamond Sutra: Transforming the Way We Perceive the World* (Boston, MA: Wisdom Publications, 2000), 80.

66. Takashi James Kodera, *Dogen's Formative Years in China: An Historical Study and Annotated Translation of the "Hōkyō-ki"* (Boulder, CO: Prajñā Press, 1980), 137.

67. Kodera, *Dogen's Formative Years in China*, 119.

68. Kodera, *Dogen's Formative Years in China*, 120.

69. Kodera, *Dogen's Formative Years in China*, 121, 122, 128.

70. Joseph D. Parker, *Zen Buddhist Landscape Arts of Early Muromachi Japan (1336–1573)* (Albany: State University of New York Press, 1999), 162.

71. Kazuaki Tanahashi, ed., *Treasury of the True Dharma Eye: Zen Master Dogen's Shobo Genzo* (Boulder, CO: Shambhala, 2012).

72. Dōgen tells the story differently than did Master Daehaeng Kun Sunim in chapter 5. In Dōgen's tale, the fox in the hole does not meditate, but takes refuge in

myriad Buddhas. Indra does not offer robes, so none are rejected. And instead of running away to the forest, the fox stays to teach Indra and other deities. See Tanahashi, *Treasury of the True Dharma Eye*, 74, 848–849.

73. Harris, *Cambodian Buddhism*, 48.

7. Releasing Animals in Tibet

1. Thubten Jigme Norbu, *Tibet Is My Country* (New York: E. P. Dutton, 1961). I should mention that "Rinpoché," meaning "Precious," is a title that demarks a Tibetan Buddhist saint and so appears in several names in this chapter. Further, I remind my reader that I rely on the Tibetan and Himalayan Library Simplified Phonetic system for my primary transliterations of the Tibetan language while additionally supplying the more literarily precise but also more difficult to pronounce Wylie transliteration form when it seems appropriate for specialists.

2. Wylie Tibetan: *skyid ri.*

3. Wylie Tibetan: *la btsas.*

4. For a discussion of a recent Tibetan dislike of wolves, see George B. Schaller, *Wildlife of the Tibetan Steppe* (Chicago: University of Chicago Press, 1998), 301.

5. Wylie Tibetan: *'dul ba.*

6. Erik Pema Kunsang, trans., *The Lotus Born: The Life Story of Padmasambhava* (Boston, MA: Shambhala, 1993), 63. Wylie Tibetan: *gnyan chen thang lha.*

7. Providing an example of sustainable taming gone awry, the scholar Elizabeth Allison offers an intriguing instance from Bhutan in which Tibetan Buddhism inadvertently sponsors irresponsibility toward nonhumans. Bhutan embraces a culture heavily imbued with Tibetan influences, including widespread adherence to Tibetan Buddhism. Because of this, Bhutan takes pride in cultivating an ecofriendly Buddhist public identity, having initiated a number of works to make the nation's biosphere healthier and embraced a constitution that requires at least 60 percent forest cover. But, as Allison portrays it, Bhutanese government action based on Western ecological principles for responsibly managing local waste, such as the phrase "reduce-reuse-recycle" to eliminate "pollution," has significantly failed. According to Allison, this is because the word *drip* (*sgrib*), or "pollution," takes on Buddhist purity, not environmentalist, overtones for much of the Bhutanese populace. *Drip* pollution, which is spiritual and thus normally invisible, occurs in a variety of ways, such as eating religiously wrong foods or mistreating the deities. This Buddhist usage of the concept of inner pollution, in many Bhutanese minds, is disconnected from the idea of pollution as a dirty outer environment. Thus, Bhutanese people may see nonbiodegradable waste, a fairly new thing in Bhutan, as positive, even pretty. Allison tells us, "Plastic packaging and consumer goods, small electric appliances, and fluorescent tube lights did not engender the sense of disgust necessary to subject them to self-initiated regimes of local control." Households thereby sometimes indiscriminately dump their wastes and littering remains rampant, leading to a Bhutanese countryside that in many places is covered in rubbish, despite efforts to live sustainably otherwise. Allison relates, "Items that are no longer needed are discarded in nearly any place that is convenient. Villagers reported that they did not find plastic wrappers to be particularly 'dirty' or disturbing because of their shiny, manufactured appearance. More importantly, plastic wrappings are not considered to be dirty or polluting because

they lack the qualities that cause *drip.*" According to Allison, at the intersection of Buddhist notions of purity, government initiatives, globalization, and twenty-first-century ecological realities, Tibetan Buddhism tries but fails to sustainably tame the contemporary environment. See Elizabeth Allison, "At the Boundary of Modernity: Religion, Technocracy, and Waste Management in Bhutan," in *Religion and Modernity in the Himalayas,* ed. Megan Adamson Sijapati and Jessica Vantine Birkenholtz (London: Routledge, 2016), 164–172. For a similar situation among Sherpas, see Lionel Obadia, "The Conflicting Relationships of Sherpa to Nature: Indigenous or Western Ecology," *Journal for the Study of Religion, Nature, and Culture* 2, no. 1 (2008): 120, https://doi.org/10.1558/jsrnc.v2i1.116.

8. William Woodville Rockhill, *The Land of the Lamas* (Varanasi: Pilgrims, 2000), 157.

9. Berthold Laufer, "Bird Divination among the Tibetans," *T'oung Pao* 15, no. 1 (1914): 1–110, https://doi.org/10.1163/156853214X00014.

10. Wylie Tibetan: *ma ni bka' 'bum.*

11. Daniel Capper, "The Friendly Yeti," *Journal for the Study of Religion, Nature, and Culture* 6, no. 1 (2012): 77–78, https://doi.org/10.1558/jsrnc.v6i1.71.

12. Wylie Tibetan: *bla gnas.*

13. R. A. Stein, *Tibetan Civilization* (Stanford, CA: Stanford University Press, 1972), 227.

14. Ferdinand D. Lessing, "Calling the Soul: A Lamaist Ritual," in *Semitic and Oriental Studies,* ed. Walter J. Fischel (Berkeley: University of California Press, 1951), 265. Wylie Tibetan: *bla, rnam shes.*

15. Samten G. Karmay, *The Arrow and the Spindle,* vol. 1 (Kathmandu: Mandala Books, 1998), 314–315.

16. Interestingly, despite the general Tibetan derision of wolves, according to some Tibetans one may share one's soul with a wolf. Matthew T. Kapstein, *The Tibetans* (Malden, MA: Blackwell, 2006), 38.

17. Jianqiang, *Tibetan Environmentalists in China,* 284–285.

18. These local protective mountains do not retain uniformity in terminology or concept. Some Tibetans call them *zhidak* (*gzhi bdag*) rather than *yül lha,* while for others a *zhidak* is the higher level chieftain mountain deity among a community of lesser *yül lhas.*

19. Karmay, *Arrow and the Spindle,* 1:426.

20. Toni Huber, *The Cult of Pure Crystal Mountain: Popular Pilgrimage and Visionary Landscape in Southeast Tibet* (New York: Oxford University Press, 1999), 219.

21. René de Nebesky-Wojkowitz, *Oracles and Demons of Tibet* (Graz, Austria: Akademische Druck-u Verlagsamstalt, 1975), 482.

22. Karine Gagné, "The Materiality of Ethics: Perspectives on Water and Reciprocity in a Himalayan Anthropocene," *Wiley Interdisciplinary Reviews: Water* 7:e1444 (2020), https://doi.org/10.1002/wat2.1444.

23. Samten G. Karmay, "The Tibetan Cult of Mountain Deities and Its Political Significance," in *Reflections of the Mountain: Essays on the History and Social Meaning of the Mountain Cult in Tibet and the Himalaya,* ed. Anne-Marie Blondeau and Ernst Steinkellner (Vienna: Verlag der Österreichischen Akademie der Wissenschaften, 1996), 61. Wylie Tibetan: *a myes rma chen.*

24. Nebesky-Wojkowitz, *Oracles and Demons,* 211.

25. Kapstein, *Tibetans*, 237, 243.

26. Åshild Kolås and Monika P. Thowsen, *On the Margins of Tibet: Cultural Survival on the Sino-Tibetan Frontier* (Seattle: University of Washington Press, 2005), 61.

27. Wylie Tibetan: *gnas ri*.

28. Katia Buffetrille, "The Great Pilgrimage of A-myes rma-chen," in *Maṇḍala and Landscape*, ed. A. W. Macdonald (New Delhi: D. K. Printworld, 1997), 96.

29. Karmay, *Arrow and the Spindle*, 1:433. Wylie Tibetan: *dmu rdo*.

30. Charles Ramble, "The Politics of Sacred Space in Bon and Tibetan Popular Tradition," in *Sacred Spaces and Powerful Places in Tibetan Culture*, ed. Toni Huber (Dharamsala: Library of Tibetan Works and Archives, 1999), 27.

31. David L. Snellgrove, ed., *The Nine Ways of Bon: Excerpts from gZi-brjid* (Boulder, CO: Prajna Press, 1980), 107.

32. Kapstein, *Tibetans*, 205.

33. Huber, *Cult of Pure Crystal Mountain*, 173–174.

34. Stan Royal Mumford, *Himalayan Dialogue: Tibetan Lamas and Gurung Shamans in Nepal* (Madison: University of Wisconsin Press, 1989), 33, 135.

35. Robert B. Ekvall, *Religious Observances in Tibet* (Chicago: University of Chicago Press, 1964), 169; Geoffrey Barstow, *Food of Sinful Demons: Meat, Vegetarianism, and the Limits of Buddhism in Tibet* (New York: Columbia University Press, 2017), 98.

36. Barstow, *Food of Sinful Demons*, 1.

37. Barstow, *Food of Sinful Demons*, 115.

38. Charles S. Prebish, *Buddhist Monastic Discipline: The Sanskrit Prātimokṣa Sūtras of the Mahāsāṃghikas and Mūlasarvāstivādins*. Delhi: Motilal Banarsidass, 1996), 81.

39. Kapstein, *Tibetans*, 49.

40. Schuyler Jones, *Tibetan Nomads: Environment, Pastoral Economy, and Material Culture* (Copenhagen: Carlsberg Foundation, 1996), 56.

41. Ekvall, *Religious Observances*, 75.

42. Robert B. Ekvall, *Fields on the Hoof: Nexus of Tibetan Nomadic Pastoralism* (Prospect Heights, IL: Waveland Press, 1983), 48.

43. Rinzin Thargyal, *Nomads of Eastern Tibet: Social Organization and Economy of a Pastoral Estate in the Kingdom of Dege*, ed. Toni Huber (Leiden: Brill, 2007), 87.

44. For two examples of praises of animal treatments by Tibetans, see Ekvall, *Religious Observances*, 76–77; and Marco Pallis, *Peaks and Lamas* (Washington, DC: Shoemaker and Hoard, 1949), 72, 104.

45. Thargyal, *Nomads of Eastern Tibet*, 28.

46. Barstow, *Food of Sinful Demons*, 171.

47. Schaller, *Wildlife of the Tibetan Steppe*, 295.

48. Toni Huber, "The Chase and the Dharma: The Legal Protection of Wild Animals in Premodern Tibet," in Knight, *Wildlife in Asia*, 37.

49. Huber, "Chase and the Dharma," 49.

50. Tsangnyön Heruka, *The Hundred Thousand Songs of Milarepa*, trans. Christopher Stagg (Boulder, CO: Shambhala, 2016), 285–297. Relevant to the title of this book, Milarepa's intense asceticism, simple lifestyle, and constant wanderings worried his sister Peta so much that, in her own way, she implored Milarepa not to roam free like a deer: "Brother, rather than fleeing from one place to another like a deer chased by dogs and hiding in rocky caves, stay in one place. That way your meditation will improve and it will be easier for me to find you." See Tsangnyön

Heruka, *The Life of Milarepa*, trans. Andrew Quintman (New York: Penguin Books, 2010), 159–160.

51. Emily Woodhouse et al., "Religious Relationship to the Environment in a Tibetan Rural Community: Interactions and Contrasts with Popular Notions of Indigenous Environmentalism," *Human Ecology* 43 (2015): 303, https://doi.org/10.1007/s10745-015-9742-4.

52. Leopold, *Sand County Almanac*, 194–198.

53. Woodhouse et al., "Religious Relationship to the Environment in a Tibetan Rural Community," 304.

54. Shabkar Tsogdruk Rangdrol, *The Life of Shabkar*, trans. Matthieu Ricard (Albany: State University of New York Press, 1994), 139.

55. Naess, *Ecology, Community and Lifestyle*, 195.

56. Barstow, *Food of Sinful Demons*, 193; Holly Gayley, "The Compassionate Treatment of Animals: A Contemporary Buddhist Approach in Eastern Tibet," *Journal of Religious Ethics* 45, no. 1 (2017): 29–57, https://doi.org/10.1111/jore.12167.

57. Matthieu Ricard, *A Plea for the Animals: The Moral, Philosophical, and Evolutionary Imperative To Treat All Beings with Compassion* (Boulder, CO: Shambhala, 2016), 281n93.

58. Shiu and Stokes, "Buddhist Animal Release Practices, 183. See also Pu Chengzhong, *Ethical Treatment of Animals in Early Chinese Buddhism: Beliefs and Practices* (Cambridge: Cambridge Scholars, 2014), 1, 3.

59. Shiu and Stokes, "Buddhist Animal Release Practices," 183.

60. Muller and Tanaka, *Brahmā's Net Sutra*, 55.

61. On Zhuhong, see Smith, "Liberating Animals in Ming-Qing China, 58.

62. David Holler, "The Ritual of Freeing Lives," in *Religion and Secular Culture in Tibet*, ed. Henk Blezer (Leiden: Brill, 2002), 207.

63. Cowell, *Jātaka*, 1:87–88.

64. For Jalavāhana's story, see R. E. Emmerick, *The Sūtra of Golden Light: A Translation of the "Suvarṇabhāsottama Sūtra"* (Delhi: Motilal Banarsidass, 2016), 80–87.

65. Alan Gerard Wagner, for example, highlights a little-known alternative text by Layman Ruru in which animals remain fully equipped for enlightenment. In this liturgy humans still perform the ritual simply because animals cannot speak the words themselves. See Alan Gerard Wagner, "Dumb Animals? Comparing Chan and Tiantai Views of Animals' Abilities in Two Song Liturgies for Releasing Living Creatures," paper presented at the annual meeting of the American Academy of Religion, San Diego, CA, November 23, 2019. Moreover, Der-Ruey Yang stresses the informal, ad hoc nature of many contemporary animal release liturgies in China. See Der-Ruey Yang, "Animal Release: The Dharma Being Staged between Marketplace and Park," *Cultural Diversity in China* 1 (2015): 152, https://doi.org/10.1515/cdc-2015-0008.

66. Wylie Tibetan: *tshe thar*.

67. Holler, "Ritual of Freeing Lives," 210–211.

68. Holler, "Ritual of Freeing Lives," 210.

69. Thargyal, *Nomads of Eastern Tibet*, 75; Holler, "Ritual of Freeing Lives," 215.

70. Ekvall, *Religious Observances*, 178.

71. Holler, "Ritual of Freeing Lives," 213.

72. Holler, "Ritual of Freeing Lives," 208.

73. Luther G. Jerstad, *Mani-Rimdu: Sherpa Dance Drama* (Seattle: University of Washington Press, 1969), 110. Wylie Tibetan: *mi g.yo glang bzang, tshe ring mched lnga*.

74. Jerstad, *Mani-Rimdu*, 110.

75. Foundation for the Preservation of the Mahayana Tradition, "The Official Homepage for Lama Zopa Rinpoche," accessed June 28, 2017, http://fpmt.org/teachers/zopa.

76. Lama Zopa Rinpoche, *Liberating Animals from the Danger of Death* (Portland, OR: Foundation for the Preservation of the Mahayana Tradition, 2007).

77. Shiu and Stokes, "Buddhist Animal Release Practices," 189.

78. Lama Zopa Rinpoche, *Liberating Animals from the Danger of Death*, 44.

79. J. Nelson, *Experimental Buddhism*, 161.

80. Shiu and Stokes, "Buddhist Animal Release Practices," 190–192.

81. Der-Ruey Yang, "Animal Release, 152.

82. Shiu and Stokes, "Buddhist Animal Release Practices," 194.

83. Toni Huber, "Green Tibetans: A Brief Social History," in *Tibetan Culture in the Diaspora*, ed. Frank J. Korom (Vienna: Verlag der Österreichischen Akademie der Wissenschaften, 1997), 104.

84. Woodhouse et al., "Religious Relationship to the Environment in a Tibetan Rural Community," 295.

85. Fourteenth Dalai Lama, *On Environment: Collected Statements* (Dharamsala: Central Tibetan Administration, 2007).

86. As one moved away from Lhasa through old Tibet, the Dalai Lama's powers generally weakened, but the powers of yül lha mountain gods became stronger. Karmay, *Arrow and the Spindle*, 1:387.

87. Schaller, *Wildlife of the Tibetan Steppe*, 313; Dawa Tsering and John D. Farrington, "Human-Wildlife Conflict, Conservation, and Nomadic Livelihoods in the Chang Tang," in *Tibetan Pastoralists and Development: Negotiating the Future of Grassland Livelihoods*, ed. Andreas Gruschke and Ingo Breuer (Wiesbaden: Dr. Ludwig Reichert Verlag, 2017), 142.

88. Fourteenth Dalai Lama, "An Ethical Approach to Environmental Protection," in *Tree of Life: Buddhism and Protection of Nature*, ed. Buddhist Perception of Nature (Buddhist Perception of Nature, 1987), 5.

89. John Stanley, David R. Loy, and Gyurme Dorje, eds., *A Buddhist Response to the Climate Emergency* (Boston, MA: Wisdom Publications, 2009), 23.

90. Tsangnyön Heruka, *Hundred Thousand Songs of Milarepa*, 285–297.

91. Michael Kohn, *Lama of the Gobi: How Mongolia's Mystic Monk Spread Tibetan Buddhism in the World's Harshest Desert* (Hong Kong: Blacksmith Books, 2010), 72.

8. Natural Persons in the West

1. Along with Mahāyāna and Vajrayāna, Theravāda represents one of the Buddhist Three Vehicles or major divisions. Theravāda stresses adherence to the Pāli canon and relatively emphasizes the high place of monastics compared to some other Buddhist systems. Although Theravāda may be discovered globally, concentrations of Theravāda Buddhists can be found in Sri Lanka, Burma, Thailand, and Cambodia.

2. Ajahn Sumano Bhikkhu, *Questions from the City, Answers from the Forest* (Wheaton, IL: Quest Books, 1999), 122.

3. Charles S. Prebish, *Luminous Passage: The Practice and Study of Buddhism in America* (Berkeley: University of California Press, 1999), 268–269.

4. C. W. Huntington, Jr., "The Triumph of Narcissism: Theravāda Buddhist Meditation in the Marketplace," *Journal of the American Academy of Religion* 83, no. 3 (2015): 624–648, https://doi.org/10.1093/jaarel/lfv008.

5. Paul David Numrich, *Old Wisdom in the New World: Americanization in Two Immigrant Theravada Buddhist Temples* (Knoxville: University of Tennessee Press, 1999). Following Peter Gregory, with the term *convert* I refer to "Americans (regardless of ethnicity) who are not Buddhist by birth but who take up various forms of Buddhist practice without necessarily undergoing a dramatic experience that could be characterized as a religious conversion." Peter N. Gregory, "Describing the Elephant: Buddhism in America," *Religion and American Culture* 11 (2001): 233–63, https://doi.org/10.1525/rac.2001.11.2.233.

6. Richard Hughes Seager, "American Buddhism in the Making," in *Westward Dharma: Buddhism beyond Asia*, ed. Charles S. Prebish and Martin Baumann (Berkeley: University of California Press, 2002), 108; Richard Hughes Seager, *Buddhism in America* (New York: Columbia University Press, 1999), 215, 242.

7. James William Coleman, *The New Buddhism: The Western Transformation of an Ancient Tradition* (Oxford: Oxford University Press, 2001), 218–219.

8. Coleman, *New Buddhism*, 13–14.

9. Bhikkhu Nyanasobhano, *Landscapes of Wonder: Discovering Buddhist Dhamma in the World around Us* (Boston, MA: Wisdom Publications, 1998).

10. Bhikkhu Nyanasobhano, "Bhikkhu Tissa Dispels Some Doubts," accessed March 20, 2016, http://www.accesstoinsight.org/lib/authors/price/bl102.html.

11. Bhikkhu Nyanasobhano, "Nothing Higher to Live For," accessed March 20, 2016, http://www.accesstoinsight.org/lib/authors/price/bl124.html.

12. Bhikkhu Nyanasobhano, "Buddhist Publication Society," accessed March 20, 2016, http://www.bps.lk/library-search.php?t=01&c=00&s=0&a=Nyanasobhano&first=0.

13. Nyanasobhano, *Landscapes of Wonder*; Bhikkhu Nyanasobhano, *Longing for Certainty: Reflections on the Buddhist Life* (Boston, MA: Wisdom Publications, 2003); Bhikkhu Nyanasobhano, *Available Truth: Excursions into Buddhist Wisdom and the Natural World* (Boston, MA: Wisdom Publications, 2007). Page numbers are given in the text, preceded by an abbreviation: *LW*, *LC*, or *AT*.

14. Buddhanet, "Philip Kapleau Roshi," accessed February 27, 2016, http://www.buddhanet.net/masters/kapleau.htm.

15. Philip Kapleau, *To Cherish All Life: A Buddhist Case for Becoming Vegetarian* (Rochester, NY: Zen Center, 1986), 6.

16. Suzuki, *Lankavatara Sutra*, 212.

17. I have rendered this passage more gender neutral by substituting "humans" for the original "men."

18. The French Buddhist writer Matthieu Ricard agrees with Kapleau, saying, "We maintain a kind of moral schizophrenia that has us lavishly pampering our pets and at the same time planting our forks in the pigs that have been sent to slaughter in the millions, even though they are in no way less conscious, less sensitive to pain, or less intelligent than our cats and dogs." Ricard, *Plea for the Animals*, 4.

19. Plants typically possess greater sensitivities to being touched than humans do, so the loss of a picked fruit does not go unnoticed. Through chemicals, plants reconfigure themselves in response to a loss of fruit, showing that the autonomous striving of the plant has been harmed. Further, plants produce fruits to reproduce themselves, not to feed humans, so picking a fruit harms the autonomous striving of plants in another way since the plant's prospective children are taken away. Additionally, many raw vegetables, such as tomatoes, still ripen after being picked, showing that they are still alive while being eaten. For these reasons, out of a sense of nonharm, some Jains refuse to pick fruits from plants, instead waiting until the fruits fall naturally, but this sensibility has historically been absent from Buddhism. Of course, when it comes to root vegetables such as potatoes, the claim that picking the fruit causes no harm is almost always fallacious since harvesting potatoes commonly kills the entire plant. Carrot tops may be replanted so that they regrow, but this agricultural strategy is uncommon. Moreover, part of agriculture involves removing unwanted plant visitors that are arbitrarily labeled as "weeds," and these plants are killed as a common plan. Hence, Kapleau's claim that harvesting a vegetable does not harm plants remains problematic. On plants' sense of touch, see Brian J. Ford, *The Secret Language of Life* (New York: Fromm International, 2000), 185–189; and Chamovitz, *What a Plant Knows*, 137–138.

20. Stephanie Kaza, *The Attentive Heart: Conversations with Trees* (New York: Fawcett Columbine, 1993). Page numbers are given within the text, preceeded by the abbreviation *AH*.

21. Evan Berry, *Devoted to Nature: The Religious Roots of American Environmentalism* (Oakland: University of California Press, 2015), 133.

22. Stephanie Kaza, "A Community of Attention," *Context* 29 (1991): 35, http://www.context.org/iclib/ic29/kaza; Kaza, *Attentive Heart*, 237.

23. Stephanie Kaza, "American Buddhist Response to the Land: Ecological Practice at Two West Coast Retreat Centers," in Tucker and Williams, *Buddhism and Ecology*, 219–248. Page numbers are given in the text, preceeded by the abbreviation *AB*.

24. San Francisco Zen Center, "Green Gulch," accessed February 27, 2017, http://sfzc.org/green-gulch/green-gulch-watershed/watershed-work-party-days.

25. Kaza, "Community of Attention," 33–34.

26. Kaza, "American Buddhist Response to the Land," 231–234; San Francisco Zen Center, "Apprenticeship," accessed February 27, 2017, http://sfzc.org/green-gulch/farm-garden/farm-and-garden-apprenticeship-program.

27. Capper, *Learning Love from a Tiger*, 237–240.

28. Wendy Johnson, "Garden Practice," in Kaza and Kraft, *Dharma Rain*, 337.

29. Max Oelschlaeger, *The Idea of Wilderness: From Prehistory to the Age of Ecology* (New Haven, CT: Yale University Press, 1991), 437.

30. Oelschlaeger, *Idea of Wilderness*, 437.

31. Gary Snyder, *A Place in Space: Ethics, Aesthetics, and Watersheds* (Berkeley, CA: Counterpoint, 1995); Gary Snyder, *The Practice of the Wild* (Berkeley, CA: Counterpoint, 1990). Page numbers are given in the text, preceded by an abbreviation: *PS* or *PW*.

32. Gary Snyder, *Turtle Island* (New York: New Directions Books, 1974), 47–49.

33. *Ter ma* (*gter ma*) in the Tibetan world represent texts or other artifacts that were hidden by ancient masters for later discovery. Finding these *ter ma* thus provides Tibetan religion with an ongoing renewal of spiritual resources.

34. Gary Snyder, *Back on the Fire: Essays* (Emeryville, CA: Shoemaker and Hoard, 2007), 124.

35. Snyder, *Back on the Fire*, 123–124.

36. Snyder, *Back on the Fire*, 123.

37. Snyder, *Back on the Fire*, 125.

38. Gary Snyder, *Nobody Home: Writing, Buddhism, and Living in Places* (San Antonio, TX: Trinity University Press, 2014), 84.

39. William Cronon, "The Trouble with Wilderness; Or, Getting Back to the Wrong Nature," in *Uncommon Ground: Toward Reinventing Nature*, ed. William Cronon (New York: Norton, 1995), 69–90.

40. Thomas Berry, *The Sacred Universe* (New York: Columbia University Press, 2009), 86.

41. Snyder, *Back on the Fire*, 96.

42. Stephanie Kaza, "Penetrating the Tangle," in *Hooked!: Buddhist Writings on Greed, Desire, and the Urge to Consume*, ed. Stephanie Kaza (Boston, MA: Shambhala, 2005), 139.

43. See, for instance, Thich Nhat Hanh, *Love Letter to the Earth* (Berkeley, CA: Parallax Press, 2013), 69; Joanna Macy and Molly Young Brown, *Coming Back to Life: Practices to Reconnect Our Lives, Our World* (Gabriola Island, BC: New Society, 1998), 161–164; Charles S. Fisher, *Meditation in the Wild: Buddhism's Origin in the Heart of Nature* (Winchester: Changemakers Books, 2013), 124–125.

44. Cowell, *Jātaka*, 2:288–289.

Conclusion

1. James B. Robinson, trans., *Buddha's Lions* (Berkeley, CA: Dharma, 1979), 128–130.

2. Naess, *Ecology, Community and Lifestyle*, 29.

3. J. Baird Callicott, "The Metaphysical Implications of Ecology," in Callicott and Ames, *Nature in Asian Traditions of Thought*, 59.

4. Charles R. Strain, "Reinventing Buddhist Practices to Meet the Challenge of Climate Change," *Contemporary Buddhism* 17, no. 1 (2016): 139, https://doi.org/10.1080/14639947.2016.1162976.

5. Daniel Capper, "American Buddhist Protection of Stones in Terms of Climate Change on Mars and Earth," *Contemporary Buddhism* (2020), online, https://doi.org/10.1080/14639947.2020.1734733.

6. Clippard, "Lorax Wears Saffron," 233–234.

7. Clippard, "Lorax Wears Saffron," 217.

8. Clippard, "Lorax Wears Saffron," 233–234.

9. Holder, "Suffering (But Not Irreparable) Nature," 125.

10. Robinson, *Buddha's Lions*, 96–97.

BIBLIOGRAPHY

Abram, David. *Becoming Animal: An Earthly Cosmology*. New York: Pantheon Books, 2010.

Ajahn Chah. *Food for the Heart*. Boston, MA: Wisdom Publications, 2002.

Ajahn Sumano Bhikkhu. *Questions from the City, Answers from the Forest*. Wheaton, IL: Quest Books, 1999.

Ajahn Tate. *The Autobiography of a Forest Monk*. Nongkhai, Thailand: Amarin, 1993.

Allison, Elizabeth. "At the Boundary of Modernity: Religion, Technocracy, and Waste Management in Bhutan." In *Religion and Modernity in the Himalayas*, edited by Megan Adamson Sijapati and Jessica Vantine Birkenholtz, 164–181. London: Routledge, 2016.

Alsdorf, Ludwig. *The History of Vegetarianism and Cow-Veneration in India*. Translated by Bal Patil. London: Routledge, 2010.

Ambros, Barbara R. *Bones of Contention: Animals and Religion in Contemporary Japan*. Honolulu: University of Hawai'i Press, 2012.

Anderson, E. N., and Lisa Raphals. "Daoism and Animals." In Waldau and Patton, *Communion of Subjects*, 275–290.

Ansari, Azadeh, and Kocha Olarn. "Thai 'Tiger Temple': Five Charged with Possessing Endangered Animal Parts." *CNN*, June 3, 2016. Accessed June 26, 2016. http://www.cnn.com/2016/06/03/asia/thailand-tiger-temple-charges/.

Arthur, Shawn. *Early Daoist Dietary Practices*. Lanham, MD: Lexington Books, 2013.

Aston, W. G., trans. *Nihongi*. Vol. 1. New York: Cosimo Classics, 2008.

Balmford, Andrew. *Wild Hope: On the Front Lines of Conservation Success*. Chicago: University of Chicago Press, 2012.

Barash, David P. *Buddhist Biology: Ancient Eastern Wisdom Meets Modern Western Science*. Oxford: Oxford University Press, 2014.

Barstow, Geoffrey. *Food of Sinful Demons: Meat, Vegetarianism, and the Limits of Buddhism in Tibet*. New York: Columbia University Press, 2017.

Bashō, Matsuo. *The Narrow Road to the Deep North and Other Travel Sketches*. Translated by Nobuyuki Yuasa. Harmondsworth: Penguin Books, 1966.

Bastin, Rohan. *The Domain of Constant Excess: Plural Worship at the Munnesvaram Temples in Sri Lanka*. New York: Berghahn Books, 2002.

Baumer, Christoph. *China's Holy Mountain: An Illustrated Journey into the Heart of Buddhism*. London: I. B. Tauris, 2011.

Bekoff, Marc. *The Emotional Lives of Animals*. Novato, CA: New World Library, 2007.

——. *Rewilding Our Hearts: Building Pathways of Compassion and Coexistence*. Novato, CA: New World Library, 2014.

Bendall, Cecil, and W. H. D. Rouse, trans. *Śikṣā Samuccaya: A Compendium of Buddhist Doctrine*. Delhi: Motilal Banarsidass, 2006.

Berkwitz, Stephen C., trans. *The History of the Buddha's Relic Shrine: A Translation of the Sinhala* Thūpavaṃsa. Oxford: Oxford University Press, 2007.

Berry, Evan. *Devoted to Nature: The Religious Roots of American Environmentalism.* Oakland: University of California Press, 2015.

Berry, Thomas. *The Sacred Universe.* New York: Columbia University Press, 2009.

Bhikkhu Bodhi, trans. *The Connected Discourses of the Buddha.* Vol. 1. Boston, MA: Wisdom Publications, 2000.

———, trans. *The Connected Discourses of the Buddha.* Vol. 2. Boston, MA: Wisdom Publications, 2000.

———, trans. *The Numerical Discourses of the Buddha.* Boston, MA: Wisdom Publications, 2012.

Bhikkhu Ñāṇamoli, trans. *The Life of the Buddha.* Seattle, WA: Buddhist Publication Society, 1992.

———, trans. *The Path of Purification (Visudhimagga).* Onalaska, WI: Buddhist Publication Society, 1991.

Bhikkhu Ñāṇamoli and Bhikkhu Bodhi, trans. *The Middle Length Discourses of the Buddha.* Boston, MA: Wisdom Publications, 1995.

Bhikkhu Nyanasobhano. *Available Truth: Excursions into Buddhist Wisdom and the Natural World.* Boston, MA: Wisdom Publications, 2007.

———. "Bhikkhu Tissa Dispels Some Doubts." Accessed March 20, 2016. http://www.accesstoinsight.org/lib/authors/price/bl102.html.

———. "Buddhist Publication Society." Accessed March 20, 2016. http://www.bps.lk/library-search.php?t=01&c=00&s=0&a=Nyanasobhano&first=0.

———. *Landscapes of Wonder: Discovering Buddhist Dhamma in the World around Us.* Boston, MA: Wisdom Publications, 1998.

———. *Longing for Certainty: Reflections on the Buddhist Life.* Boston, MA: Wisdom Publications, 2003.

———. "Nothing Higher to Live For." Accessed March 20, 2016. http://www.accessto insight.org/lib/authors/price/bl124.html.

Blacker, Carmen. *The Catalpa Bow: A Study of Shamanistic Practices in Japan.* London: George Allen and Unwin, 1986.

Blum, Mark L., trans. *The Nirvana Sutra.* Vol. 1. Berkeley, CA: BDK America, 2013.

Brown, W. Norman. "The Sanctity of the Cow in Hinduism." *Economic Weekly* 16, nos. 5–7 (February 1964): 245–256.

Bruun, Ole. *Fengshui in China: Geomantic Divination between State Orthodoxy and Popular Religion.* Honolulu: University of Hawai'i Press, 2003.

———. "Is Chinese Popular Religion At All Compatible with Ecology? A Discussion of Feng Shui." In Miller, Yu, and van der Veer, *Religion and Ecological Sustainability in China*, 164–180.

Buddhanet. "Philip Kapleau Roshi." Accessed February 27, 2016. http://www.budhanet.net/masters/kapleau.htm.

Buffetrille, Katia. "The Great Pilgrimage of A-myes rma-chen." In *Maṇḍala and Landscape*, edited by A. W. Macdonald, 75–132. New Delhi: D. K. Printworld, 1997.

Bullis, Douglas, trans. *The Mahavamsa: The Great Chronicle of Sri Lanka.* Fremont, CA: Asian Humanities Press, 1999.

Burford, Grace G. "Hope, Desire, and Right Livelihood: A Buddhist View on the Earth Charter." In *Buddhist Perspectives on the Earth Charter*, edited by Boston Research Center for the 21st Century, 27–35. Boston, MA: Boston Research Center for the 21st Century, 1997.

Callicott, J. Baird. "The Metaphysical Implications of Ecology." In Callicott and Ames, *Nature in Asian Traditions of Thought*, 51–64.

Callicott, J. Baird, and Roger T. Ames, eds. *Nature in Asian Traditions of Thought*. Albany: State University of New York Press, 1989.

Capper, Daniel. "American Buddhist Protection of Stones in Terms of Climate Change on Mars and Earth." *Contemporary Buddhism* (2020). Online. https://doi.org/10.1080/14639947.2020.1734733.

——. "Animism among Western Buddhists." *Contemporary Buddhism* 17, no. 1 (2016): 30–48. https://doi.org/10.1080/14639947.2016.1189130.

——. "The Friendly Yeti." *Journal for the Study of Religion, Nature, and Culture* 6, no. 1 (2012): 71–87. https://doi.org/10.1558/jsrnc.v6i1.71.

——. *Guru Devotion and the American Buddhist Experience*. Lewiston, NY: Edwin Mellen Press, 2002.

——. "Learning Love from a Tiger: Approaches to Nature in an American Buddhist Monastery." *Journal of Contemporary Religion* 30, no. 1 (2015): 53–69. https://doi.org/10.1080/13537903.2015.986976.

——. *Learning Love from a Tiger: Religious Experiences with Nature*. Oakland: University of California Press, 2016.

——. "The Search for Microbial Martian Life and American Buddhist Ethics." *International Journal of Astrobiology* (2019): 1–9. Online. https://doi.org/10.1017/S1473550419000296.

Carrithers, Michael. *The Forest Monks of Sri Lanka*. Delhi: Oxford University Press, 1983.

Chamovitz, Daniel. *What a Plant Knows*. New York: Scientific American, 2012.

Chang, Garma C. C., trans. *A Treasury of Mahāyāna Sūtras: Selections from the Mahāratnakūta Sūtra*. University Park: Pennsylvania State University Press, 1983.

Chapple, Christopher Key. *Nonviolence to Animals, Earth, and Self in Asian Traditions*. Albany: State University of New York Press, 1993.

Charleux, Isabelle. *Nomads on Pilgrimage: Mongols on Wutaishan (China), 1800–1940*. Leiden: Brill, 2015.

Chatsumarn, Kabilsingh. *Thai Women in Buddhism*. Berkeley, CA: Parallax Press, 1991.

Chengzhong, Pu. *Ethical Treatment of Animals in Early Chinese Buddhism: Beliefs and Practices*. Cambridge: Cambridge Scholars, 2014.

Chögyel, Tenzin. *The Life of the Buddha*. Translated by Kurtis R. Schaeffer. New York: Penguin Books, 2015.

Clippard, Seth Devere. "The Lorax Wears Saffron: Toward a Buddhist Environmentalism." *Journal of Buddhist Ethics* 18 (2011): 210–248. http://blogs.dickinson.edu/buddhistethics/2011/06/06/3120.

Coggins, Chris. "Sacred Watersheds and the Fate of the Village Body Politic in Tibetan and Han Communities under China's Ecological Civilization." *Religions* 10 (2019): 1–31. https://doi.org/10.3390/rel10110600.

——. "When the Land Is Excellent: Village Feng Shui Forests and the Nature of Lineage, Polity, and Vitality in Southern China." In Miller, Yu, and van der Veer, *Religion and Ecological Sustainability in China*, 97–126. London: Routledge, 2014.

Coleman, James William. *The New Buddhism: The Western Transformation of an Ancient Tradition*. Oxford: Oxford University Press, 2001.

Comba, Antonella Serena. "The Bodhi Tree and Other Plants in the Pāli Tipiṭaka." In *Roots of Wisdom, Branches of Devotion: Plant Life in South Asian Traditions*, edited by Fabrizio M. Ferrari and Thomas Dähnhardt, 98–117. Sheffield: Equinox, 2016.

Condominas, Georges. "Phĭbăn Cults in Rural Laos." In *Change and Persistence in Thai Society*, edited by G. Thomas Skinner and A. Thomas Kirsch, 252–277. Ithaca, NY: Cornell University Press, 1975.

Cook, Francis H. "The Jewel Net of Indra." In Callicott and Ames, *Nature in Asian Traditions of Thought*, 213–229.

Cooper, David E., and Simon P. James. *Buddhism, Virtue, and Environment*. Aldershot: Ashgate, 2005.

Cowell, E. B., ed. *The Jātaka*. Vol. 1. Cambridge: Cambridge University Press, 1895.

——, ed. *The Jātaka*. Vol. 2. Cambridge: Cambridge University Press, 1895.

——, ed. *The Jātaka*. Vol. 3. Cambridge: Cambridge University Press, 1897.

——, ed. *The Jātaka*. Vol. 4. Cambridge: Cambridge University Press, 1901.

——, ed. *The Jātaka*. Vol. 5. Cambridge: Cambridge University Press, 1905.

Cozad, Laurie. *Sacred Snakes: Orthodox Images of Indian Snake Worship*. Aurora, CO: Davies Group, 2004.

Cronon, William. "The Trouble with Wilderness; Or, Getting Back to the Wrong Nature." In *Uncommon Ground: Toward Reinventing Nature*, edited by William Cronon, 69–90. New York: Norton, 1995.

Crosby, Kate. *Theravada Buddhism: Continuity, Diversity, and Identity*. Chichester: John Wiley and Sons, 2014.

Curtin, Deane. "A State of Mind Like Water: Ecosophy T and the Buddhist Traditions." In *Beneath the Surface: Critical Essays in the Philosophy of Deep Ecology*, edited by Eric Katz, Andrew Light, and David Rothenberg, 253–267. Cambridge, MA: MIT Press, 2000.

Daehaeng Kun Sunim. *My Heart Is a Golden Buddha*. Anyang, China: Hanmaum Publications, 2006.

Darlington, Susan M. *The Ordination of a Tree: The Thai Buddhist Environmental Movement*. Albany: State University of New York Press, 2012.

——. "The 'Spirits' of Conservation in Buddhist Thailand." In *Nature across Cultures: Views of Nature and the Environment in Non-Western Cultures*, edited by Helaine Selin, 129–146. Dordrecht: Kluwer Academic, 2003.

DeCaroli, Robert. "'The Abode of the *Nāga* King': Questions of Art, Audience, and Local Deities at the Ajaṇṭā Caves." *Ars Orientalis* 40 (2011): 142–161. http://www.jstor.org.lynx.lib.usm.edu/stable/23075934.

Deegalle, Mahinda. *Popularizing Buddhism: Preaching as Performance in Sri Lanka*. Albany: State University of New York Press, 2006.

Deleanu, Florin. "Buddhist 'Ethology' in the Pāli Canon: Between Symbol and Observation." *Eastern Buddhist* 32, no. 2 (2000): 79–127.

Derrida, Jacques. *The Animal That Therefore I Am*. New York: Fordham University Press, 2008.

deYoung, John E. *Village Life in Modern Thailand*. Berkeley: University of California Press, 1966.

Dharmachakra Translation Committee. *The Play in Full: Lalitavistara*. New York: 84000, 2013.

Donovan, Deanna G. "Cultural Underpinnings of the Wildlife Trade in Southeast Asia." In Knight, *Wildlife in Asia*, 88–111.

Drengson, Alan, and Bill Devall, eds. *Ecology of Wisdom: Writings by Arne Naess*. Berkeley, CA: Counterpoint, 2008.

Edelglass, William. "Moral Pluralism, Skillful Means, and Environmental Ethics." *Environmental Philosophy* 3 (2006): 8–16.

Ehara, N. R. M., Soma Thera, and Kheminda Thera, trans. *The Path of Freedom*. Kandy, Sri Lanka: Buddhist Publication Society, 1961.

Ekvall, Robert B. *Fields on the Hoof: Nexus of Tibetan Nomadic Pastoralism*. Prospect Heights, IL: Waveland Press, 1983.

——. *Religious Observances in Tibet*. Chicago: University of Chicago Press, 1964.

Elverskog, Johan. *The Buddha's Footprint: An Environmental History of Asia*. Philadelphia: University of Pennsylvania Press, 2020.

Elvin, Mark. *The Retreat of the Elephants: An Environmental History of China*. New Haven, CT: Yale University Press, 2004.

Emmerick, R. E. *The Sūtra of Golden Light: A Translation of the "Suvarṇabhāsottama Sūtra."* Delhi: Motilal Banarsidass, 2016.

Findly, Ellison Banks. *Plant Lives: Borderline Beings in Indian Traditions*. Delhi: Motilal Banarsidass, 2008.

Fisher, Charles S. *Meditation in the Wild: Buddhism's Origin in the Heart of Nature*. Winchester: Changemakers Books, 2013.

Ford, Brian J. *The Secret Language of Life*. New York: Fromm International, 2000.

Foundation for the Preservation of the Mahayana Tradition. "The Official Homepage for Lama Zopa Rinpoche." Accessed June 28, 2017. http://fpmt.org/teachers/zopa.

Fourteenth Dalai Lama. "An Ethical Approach to Environmental Protection." In *Tree of Life: Buddhism and Protection of Nature*, edited by Buddhist Perception of Nature, 5. Buddhist Perception of Nature, 1987.

——. "Make Tibet a Zone of Peace." In Kaza and Kraft, *Dharma Rain*, 231–235.

——. *On Environment: Collected Statements*. Dharamsala: Central Tibetan Administration, 2007.

Frazer, James George. *The Golden Bough*. New York: Macmillan, 1922.

Gagné, Karine. "The Materiality of Ethics: Perspectives on Water and Reciprocity in a Himalayan Anthropocene." *Wiley Interdisciplinary Reviews: Water* 7:e1444 (2020). https://doi.org/10.1002/wat2.1444.

Gayley, Holly. "The Compassionate Treatment of Animals: A Contemporary Buddhist Approach in Eastern Tibet." *Journal of Religious Ethics* 45, no. 1 (2017): 29–57. https://doi.org/10.1111/jore.12167.

Geiger, Wilhelm, trans. *Cūḷavaṃsa: Being the More Recent Part of the Mahāvaṃsa.* Vol. 1. New Delhi: Asian Educational Services, 2003.

Giles, Herbert A., trans. *Record of the Buddhistic Kingdoms.* London: Trübner, 2004.

Gombrich, Richard F. *Precept and Practice: Traditional Buddhism in the Rural Highlands of Ceylon.* Oxford: Clarendon Press, 1971.

Gombrich, Richard, and Gananath Obeyesekere. *Buddhism Transformed: Religious Change in Sri Lanka.* Princeton, NJ: Princeton University Press, 1988.

Goodall, Jane. "The Dance of Awe." In Waldau and Patton, *Communion of Subjects,* 651–656.

Goossaert, Vincent. "The Beef Taboo and the Sacrificial Structure of Late Imperial Chinese Society." In Sterckx, *Of Tripod and Palate,* 237–248.

Gorai, Shigeru. "Shugendo Lore." *Japanese Journal of Religious Studies* 16, no. 2/3 (1989): 117–142. http://www.jstor.org.lynx.lib.usm.edu/stable/30234004.

Gottlieb, Roger S. *A Greener Faith: Religious Environmentalism and Our Planet's Future.* New York: Oxford University Press, 2006.

Grapard, Allan G. "Flying Mountains and Walkers of Emptiness: Toward a Definition of Sacred Space in Japanese Religions." *History of Religions* 21, no. 3 (1982): 195–221. https://doi.org/10.1086/462897.

———. *Mountain Mandalas: Shugendō in Kyushu.* London: Bloomsbury, 2016.

———. "Nature and Culture in Japan." In *Deep Ecology,* edited by Michael Tobias, 240–253. San Marcos, CA: Avant Books, 1988.

Gray, Murray. *Geodiversity: Valuing and Conserving Abiotic Nature.* Chichester: John Wiley and Sons, 2004.

Gregory, Peter N. "Describing the Elephant: Buddhism in America." *Religion and American Culture* 11 (2001): 233–63. https://doi.org/10.1525/rac.2001.11.2.233.

Grissom, Harriette D. "Animal Forms and Formlessness: The Protean Quality of Buddha Nature in Chinese Martial Arts." In *Buddha Nature and Animality,* edited by David Jones, 59–82. Fremont, CA: Jain, 2007.

Groner, Paul. "A Medieval Japanese Reading of the *Mo-ho chih-kuan*: Placing the *Kankō ruijū* in Historical Context." *Japanese Journal of Religious Studies* 22, no. 1/2 (1995): 49–81. http://www.jstor.org.lynx.lib.usm.edu/stable/30233537.

Gunawardana, R. A. L. H. *Robe and Plough: Monasticism and Economic Interest in Early Medieval Sri Lanka.* Tucson: University of Arizona Press, 1979.

Guthrie, Stewart Elliott. *Faces in the Clouds: A New Theory of Religion.* New York: Oxford University Press, 1993.

Haberman, David L. *People Trees: Worship of Trees in Northern India.* New York: Oxford University Press, 2013.

Habib, Irfan. *Man and Environment: The Ecological History of India.* New Delhi: Tulika Books, 2010.

Hakeda, Yoshito S. *Kukai: Major Works.* New York: Columbia University Press, 1972.

Hall, Matthew. *Plants as Persons: A Philosophical Botany.* Albany: State University of New York Press, 2011.

Hallowell, A. Irving. "Ojibwa Ontology, Behavior, and World View." In *Contributions to Anthropology,* edited by A. Irving Hallowell, 357–390. Chicago: University of Chicago Press, 1976.

Harris, Ian. "Attitudes to Nature." In *Buddhism*, edited by Peter Harvey, 235–256. London: Continuum, 2001.

———. *Cambodian Buddhism: History and Practice*. Honolulu: University of Hawai'i Press, 2005.

———. "Landscape Aesthetics and Environmentalism: Some Observations on the Representations of Nature in Buddhist and Western Art." *Contemporary Buddhism* 8, no. 2 (2007): 149–168. https://doi.org/10.1080/14639940701636125.

———. "Magician as Environmentalist: Fertility Elements in South and Southeast Asian Buddhism." *Eastern Buddhist* 32, no. 2 (2000): 128–156.

———. "'A Vast Unsupervised Recycling Plant': Animals and the Buddhist Cosmos." In Waldau and Patton, *Communion of Subjects*, 207–217.

Harvey, Graham. *Animism: Respecting the Living World*. New York: Columbia University Press, 2006.

Harvey, Peter. "Buddhist Attitudes to and Treatment of Non-Human Nature." *Ecotheology* 4 (1998): 35–50. https://doi.org/10.1558/ecotheology.v3i1.35.

Hathaway, Michael J. *Environmental Winds: Making the Global in Southwest China*. Berkeley: University of California Press, 2013.

Hawkes, David, trans. *The Songs of the South*. London: Penguin Books, 1985.

Hirsch, Philip. "Introduction: Seeing Forests for Trees." In *Seeing Forests for Trees: Environment and Environmentalism in Thailand*, edited by Philip Hirsch, 1–14. Chiang Mai, Thailand: Silkworm Books, 1996.

Hisao, Inagaki, trans. *The Three Pure Land Sutras*. Berkeley, CA: BDK America, 2003.

Holder, John J. "A Suffering (But Not Irreparable) Nature: Environmental Ethics from the Perspective of Early Buddhism." *Contemporary Buddhism* 8, no. 2 (2007): 113–130. https://doi.org/10.1080/14639940701636091.

Holler, David. "The Ritual of Freeing Lives." In *Religion and Secular Culture in Tibet*, edited by Henk Blezer, 207–226. Leiden: Brill, 2002.

Horner, I. B., trans. *The Book of the Discipline*. Oxford: SuttaCentral, 2014.

———, trans. *The Minor Anthologies of the Pāli Canon*. Vol. 3. Oxford: Pali Text Society, 2000.

Huber, Toni. "The Chase and the Dharma: The Legal Protection of Wild Animals in Premodern Tibet." In Knight, *Wildlife in Asia*, 36–55.

———. *The Cult of Pure Crystal Mountain: Popular Pilgrimage and Visionary Landscape in Southeast Tibet*. New York: Oxford University Press, 1999.

———. "Green Tibetans: A Brief Social History." In *Tibetan Culture in the Diaspora*, edited by Frank J. Korom, 103–119. Vienna: Verlag der Österreichischen Akademie der Wissenschaften, 1997.

Huntington, C. W., Jr. "The Triumph of Narcissism: Theravāda Buddhist Meditation in the Marketplace." *Journal of the American Academy of Religion* 83, no. 3 (2015): 624–648. https://doi.org/10.1093/jaarel/lfv008.

Ingold, Tim. "Hunting and Gathering as Ways of Perceiving the Environment." In *Redefining Nature: Ecology, Culture, and Domestication*, edited by Roy Ellen and Katsuyoshi Fukui, 117–175. Oxford: Berg, 1996.

Isager, Lotte, and Søren Ivarsson. "Contesting Landscapes in Thailand: Tree Ordination as Counter-Territorialization." *Critical Asian Studies* 34, no. 3 (2002): 395–417. https://doi.org/10.1080/1467271022000008947.

Jackson, Peter A. *Buddhadāsa: Theravada Buddhism and Modernist Reform in Thailand.* Chiang Mai, Thailand: Silkworm Books, 2003.

James, Simon P. "How 'Green' is Buddhism?" *SHAP: World Religions in Education* (2008/2009). Accessed July 19, 2015. http://www.shapworkingparty.org.uk/journals/articles_0809/james.pdf.

Jerstad, Luther G. *Mani-Rimdu: Sherpa Dance Drama.* Seattle: University of Washington Press, 1969.

Jianqiang, Liu. *Tibetan Environmentalists in China: The King of Dzi.* Translated by Ian Rowen, Cyrus K. Hui, and Emily T. Yeh. Lanham, MD: Lexington Books, 2015.

Johnson, Wendy. "Garden Practice." In Kaza and Kraft, *Dharma Rain,* 335–339.

Johnston, E. H. *Asvaghoṣa's Buddhacarita or Acts of the Buddha.* Delhi: Munshiram Manoharlal, 2016.

Jones, J. J., trans. *The Mahavastu.* Vol. 2. London: Luzac, 1952.

Jones, J. J., trans. *The Mahavastu.* Vol. 3. London: Luzac, 1956.

Jones, Schuyler. *Tibetan Nomads: Environment, Pastoral Economy, and Material Culture.* Copenhagen: Carlsberg Foundation, 1996.

Kamala, Tiyavanich. *The Buddha in the Jungle.* Chiang Mai, Thailand: Silkworm Books, 2003.

——. *Forest Recollections: Wandering Monks in Twentieth-Century Thailand.* Honolulu: University of Hawai'i Press, 1997.

Kang, Xiaofei. *The Cult of the Fox: Power, Gender, and Popular Religion in Late Imperial and Modern China.* New York: Columbia University Press, 2005.

Kapferer, Bruce. *Feast of the Sorcerer: Practices of Consciousness and Power.* Chicago: University of Chicago Press, 1997.

Kapleau, Philip. *To Cherish All Life: A Buddhist Case for Becoming Vegetarian.* Rochester, NY: Zen Center, 1986.

Kapstein, Matthew T. *The Tibetans.* Malden, MA: Blackwell, 2006.

Karmay, Samten G. *The Arrow and the Spindle.* Vol. 1. Kathmandu: Mandala Books, 1998.

——. "The Tibetan Cult of Mountain Deities and Its Political Significance." In *Reflections of the Mountain: Essays on the History and Social Meaning of the Mountain Cult in Tibet and the Himalaya,* edited by Anne-Marie Blondeau and Ernst Steinkellner, 59–75. Vienna: Verlag der Österreichischen Akademie der Wissenschaften, 1996.

Katz, Eric. *Nature as Subject: Human Obligation and Natural Community.* Lanham, MD: Rowman and Littlefield, 1997.

Kaza, Stephanie. "American Buddhist Response to the Land: Ecological Practice at Two West Coast Retreat Centers." In Tucker and Williams, *Buddhism and Ecology,* 219–248.

——. *The Attentive Heart: Conversations with Trees.* New York: Fawcett Columbine, 1993.

——. "A Community of Attention." *Context* 29 (1991): 32–36. http://www.context.org/iclib/ic29/kaza.

——. "Penetrating the Tangle." In *Hooked!: Buddhist Writings on Greed, Desire, and the Urge to Consume,* edited by Stephanie Kaza, 139–151. Boston, MA: Shambhala, 2005.

Kaza, Stephanie, and Kenneth Kraft, eds. *Dharma Rain: Sources of Buddhist Environmentalism*. Boston, MA: Shambhala, 2000.

Kellert, Stephen R. "Attitudes, Knowledge, and Behaviour toward Wildlife among the Industrial Superpowers: United States, Japan, and Germany." *Journal of Social Issues* 49, no. 1 (1993): 53–69. https://doi.org/10.1111/j.1540-4560.1993.tb00908.x.

——. "Japanese Perceptions of Wildlife." *Conservation Biology* 5, no. 3 (1991): 297–308. https://doi.org/10.1111/j.1523-1739.1991.tb00141.x.

Kemper, Steven. *Rescued from the Nation: Anagarika Dharmapala and the Buddhist World*. Chicago: University of Chicago Press, 2015.

Keown, Damien. *Buddhism and Bioethics*. New York: Palgrave, 2001.

Kieschnick, John. "Buddhist Vegetarianism in China." In Sterckx, *Of Tripod and Palate*, 186–212.

King Bhumibol Adulyadej. *The Story of Tongdaeng: Biography of a Pet Dog*. Bangkok: Amarin, 2002.

Kiyota, Minoru. *Shingon Buddhism: Theory and Practice*. Los Angeles: Buddhist Books International, 1978.

Kleeman, Terry F. "Feasting with the Victuals: The Evolution of the Daoist Communal Kitchen." In Sterckx, *Of Tripod and Palate*, 140–162.

Knapp, Keith N. "Noble Creatures: Filial and Righteous Animals in Early Medieval Confucian Thought." In *Animals through Chinese History: Earliest Times to 1911*, edited by Roel Sterckx, Martina Seibert, and Dagmar Schäfer, 64–83. Cambridge: Cambridge University Press, 2019.

Knight, John. *Waiting for Wolves in Japan: An Anthropological Study of People-Wildlife Relations*. Honolulu: University of Hawai'i Press, 2006.

——. "Wolf Reintroduction in Japan?" In Knight, *Wildlife in Asia*, 223–254.

——, ed. *Wildlife in Asia*. London: RoutledgeCurzon, 2004.

Kodera, Takashi James. *Dogen's Formative Years in China: An Historical Study and Annotated Translation of the "Hōkyō-ki."* Boulder, CO: Prajñā Press, 1980.

Kohn, Livia. *Cosmos and Community: The Ethical Dimension of Daoism*. Cambridge, MA: Three Pines Press, 2004.

——. *Laughing at the Tao: Debates among Buddhists and Taoists in Medieval China*. Princeton, NJ: Princeton University Press, 1995.

——. *Taoist Mystical Philosophy: The Scripture of the Western Ascension*. Albany: State University of New York Press, 1991.

Kohn, Michael. *Lama of the Gobi: How Mongolia's Mystic Monk Spread Tibetan Buddhism in the World's Harshest Desert*. Hong Kong: Blacksmith Books, 2010.

Kolås, Åshild, and Monika P. Thowsen. *On the Margins of Tibet: Cultural Survival on the Sino-Tibetan Frontier*. Seattle: University of Washington Press, 2005.

Komito, David Ross. "Eco-Bodhicitta and Artful Conduct." *Tibet Journal* 17, no. 2 (1992): 45–51. http://www.jstor.org.lynx.lib.usm.edu/stable/43300433.

Komroff, Manuel, trans. *The Travels of Marco Polo*. New York: Modern Library, 2001.

Kornfield, Jack, and Paul Breiter, eds. *A Still Forest Pool: The Insight Meditation of Achaan Chah*. Wheaton, IL: Quest Books, 1985.

Kühl, Hjalmar S., Ammie K. Kalan, Mimi Arandjelovic, Floris Aubert, Lucy D'Auvergne, Annemarie Goedmakers, Sorrel Jones, Laura Kehoe, Sebastien

Regnaut, Alexander Tickle, Els Ton, Joost van Schijndel, Ekwoge E. Abwe, Samuel Angedakin, Anthony Agbor, Emmanuel Ayuk Ayimisin, Emma Bailey, Mattia Bessone, Matthieu Bonnet, Gregory Brazolla, Valentine Ebua Buh, Rebecca Chancellor, Chloe Cipoletta, Heather Cohen, Katherine Corogenes, Charlotte Coupland, Bryan Curran, Tobias Deschner, Karsten Dierks, Paula Dieguez, Emmanuel Dilambaka, Orume Diotoh, Dervla Dowd, Andrew Dunn, Henk Eshuis, Rumen Fernandez, Yisa Ginath, John Hart, Daniela Hedwig, Martijn Ter Heegde, Thurston Cleveland Hicks, Inaoyom Imong, Kathryn J. Jeffery, Jessica Junker, Parag Kadam, Mohamed Kambi, Ivonne Kienast, Deo Kujirakwinja, Kevin Langergraber, Vincent Lapeyre, Juan Lapuente, Kevin Lee, Vera Leinert, Amelia Meier, Giovanna Maretti, Sergio Marrocoli, Tanyi Julius Mbi, Vianet Mihindou, Yasmin Moebius, David Morgan, Bethan Morgan, Felix Mulindahabi, Mizuki Murai, Protais Niyigabae, Emma Normand, Nicolas Ntare, Lucy Jayne Ormsby, Alex Piel, Jill Pruetz, Aaron Rundus, Crickette Sanz, Volker Sommer, Fiona Stewart, Nikki Tagg, Hilde Vanleeuwe, Virginie Vergnes, Jacob Willie, Roman M. Wittig, Klaus Zuberbuehler, and Christophe Boesch. "Chimpanzee Accumulative Stone Throwing." *Scientific Reports* 6 (2016): 1–8. https://doi.org/10.1038/srep22219.

Kunsang, Erik Pema, trans. *The Lotus Born: The Life Story of Padmasambhava.* Boston, MA: Shambhala, 1993.

LaFleur, William R. "Saigyō and the Buddhist Value of Nature, Part I." *History of Religions* 13, no. 2 (1973): 93–128. http://www.jstor.org.lynx.lib.usm.edu/stable/1061933.

Lama Zopa Rinpoche. *Liberating Animals from the Danger of Death.* Portland, OR: Foundation for the Preservation of the Mahayana Tradition, 2007.

Latour, Bruno. *Down to Earth: Politics in the New Climatic Regime.* Cambridge: Polity Press, 2018.

Lau, D. C., trans. *Mencius.* London: Penguin Books, 2003.

Laufer, Berthold. "Bird Divination among the Tibetans." *T'oung Pao* 15, no. 1 (1914): 1–110. https://doi.org/10.1163/156853214X00014.

Leopold, Aldo. *A Sand County Almanac.* London: Oxford University Press, 1949.

Lessing, Ferdinand D. "Calling the Soul: A Lamaist Ritual." In *Semitic and Oriental Studies*, edited by Walter J. Fischel, 263–284. Berkeley: University of California Press, 1951.

Levman, Bryan Geoffrey. "Cultural Remnants of the Indigenous Peoples in the Buddhist Scriptures." *Buddhist Studies Review* 30, no. 2 (2013): 145–180. https://doi.org/10.1558/bsrv.v30i2.145.

Lodrick, Deryck O. "Symbol and Sustenance: Cattle in South Asian Culture." *Dialectical Anthropology* 29, no. 1 (2005): 61–84. https://doi.org/10.1007/s10624-005-5809-8.

Long, Hoyt. "Grateful Animal or Spiritual Being? Buddhist Gratitude Tales and Changing Conceptions of Deer in Early Japan." In *JAPANimals: History and Culture in Japan's Animal Life*, edited by Gregory M. Pflugfelder and Brett L. Walker, 21–58. Ann Arbor: Center for Japanese Studies, University of Michigan, 2005.

Loy, David R. *Ecodharma: Buddhist Teachings for the Ecological Crisis.* Somerville, MA: Wisdom Publications, 2018.

Luk, Charles, trans. The *Śūraṅgama Sūtra*. London: Rider, 1966.

Macy, Joanna, and Molly Young Brown. *Coming Back to Life: Practices to Reconnect Our Lives, Our World*. Gabriola Island, BC: New Society, 1998.

McDaniel, Justin Thomas. *The Lovelorn Ghost and the Magical Monk: Practicing Buddhism in Modern Thailand*. New York: Columbia University Press, 2011.

McMahan, David L. *The Making of Buddhist Modernism*. Oxford: Oxford University Press, 2008.

McShane, Katie. "Individualist Biocentrism vs. Holism Revisited." *Les ateliers de l'éthique* 9, no. 2 (2014): 132. https://doi.org/10.7202/1026682ar.

Meinert, Carmen, ed. *Nature, Environment and Culture in East Asia*. Leiden: Brill, 2013.

Midgley, Mary. *Beast and Man: The Roots of Human Nature*. Ithaca, NY: Cornell University Press, 1978.

Miller, James, Dan Smyer Yu, and Peter van der Veer. *Religion and Ecological Sustainability in China*. London: Routledge, 2014.

Mithen, Steven. *After the Ice: A Global Human History, 20,000–5,000 BC*. Cambridge, MA: Harvard University Press, 2003.

Muller, A. Charles, and Kenneth K. Tanaka, trans. *The Brahmā's Net Sutra*. Moraga, CA: BDK America, 2017.

Mumford, Stan Royal. *Himalayan Dialogue: Tibetan Lamas and Gurung Shamans in Nepal*. Madison: University of Wisconsin Press, 1989.

Naess, Arne. *Ecology, Community and Lifestyle*. Cambridge: Cambridge University Press, 1990.

Nagel, Thomas. "What Is It Like To Be a Bat?" *Philosophical Review* 83, no. 4 (1974): 435–450. https://www.jstor.org/stable/i338273.

Nattier, Jan, trans. *A Few Good Men: The Bodhisattva Path according to "The Inquiry of Ugra" (Ugraparipṛcchā)*. Honolulu: University of Hawai'i Press, 2003.

Nebesky-Wojkowitz, René de. *Oracles and Demons of Tibet*. Graz, Austria: Akademische Druck-u Verlagsamstalt, 1975.

Nelson, John K. *Experimental Buddhism: Innovation and Activism in Contemporary Japan*. Honolulu: University of Hawai'i Press, 2013.

Nelson, Walter Henry. *Buddha*. New York: Jeremy P. Tarcher, 1996.

Norman, K. R., trans. *The Group of Discourses (Sutta-Nipāta)*. Oxford: Pali Text Society, 2001.

——, trans. *Poems of Early Buddhist Monks (Theragāthā)*. Oxford: Pali Text Society, 1997.

Noske, Barbara. *Beyond Boundaries: Humans and Animals*. Montreal: Black Rose Books, 1997.

Numrich, Paul David. *Old Wisdom in the New World: Americanization in Two Immigrant Theravada Buddhist Temples*. Knoxville: University of Tennessee Press, 1999.

Obadia, Lionel. "The Conflicting Relationships of Sherpa to Nature: Indigenous or Western Ecology." *Journal for the Study of Religion, Nature, and Culture* 2, no. 1 (2008): 116–134. https://doi.org/10.1558/jsrnc.v2i1.116.

Obeyesekere, Gananath. *The Cult of the Goddess Pattini*. Chicago: University of Chicago Press, 1984.

Oelschlaeger, Max. *The Idea of Wilderness: From Prehistory to the Age of Ecology*. New Haven, CT: Yale University Press, 1991.

Ohnuma, Reiko. *Unfortunate Destiny: Animals in the Indian Buddhist Imagination*. New York: Oxford University Press, 2017.

Oldenburg, Hermann, trans. *The Dīpavamsa: An Ancient Buddhist Historical Record*. New Delhi: Asian Educational Services, 2001.

Olivelle, Patrick, trans. *Life of the Buddha*. New York: New York University Press, 2009.

Overmyer, Daniel L. *Folk Buddhist Religion: Dissenting Sects in Late Traditional China*. Cambridge, MA: Harvard University Press, 1976.

Pallis, Marco. *Peaks and Lamas*. Washington, DC: Shoemaker and Hoard, 1949.

Palmer, Martin, trans. *The Book of Chuang Tzu*. London: Penguin Books, 2006.

Paper, Jordan. *The Spirits Are Drunk: Comparative Approaches to Chinese Religion*. Albany: State University of New York Press, 1995.

Paranavitana, S. "The God of Adam's Peak." *Artibus Asiae Supplementum* 18 (1958): 4–78.

——. "Pre-Buddhist Religious Beliefs in Ceylon." *Journal of the Ceylon Branch of the Royal Asiatic Society of Great Britain and Ireland* 31, no. 82 (1929): 302–328. http://www.jstor.org.lynx.lib.usm.edu/stable/43483299.

Parker, Joseph D. *Zen Buddhist Landscape Arts of Early Muromachi Japan (1336–1573)*. Albany: State University of New York Press, 1999.

Parkes, Graham. "Winds, Waters, and Earth Energies: *Fengshui* and Sense of Place." In *Nature across Cultures: Views of Nature and the Environment in Non-Western Cultures*, edited by Helaine Selin, 185–209. Dordrecht: Kluwer Academic, 2003.

Pattana, Kitiarsa. "Beyond Syncretism: Hybridization of Popular Religion in Contemporary Thailand." *Journal of Southeast Asian Studies* 36, no. 3 (2005): 461–487. https://doi.org/10.1017/S0022463405000251.

——. *Mediums, Monks, and Amulets: Thai Popular Buddhism Today*. Chiang Mai, Thailand: Silkworm Books, 2012.

Plumwood, Val. *Environmental Culture: The Ecological Crisis of Reason*. London: Routledge, 2002.

Polly, Matthew. *American Shaolin*. New York: Gotham Books, 2007.

Powers, John, trans. *Wisdom of Buddha: The Saṁdhinirmocana Sūtra*. Berkeley, CA: Dharma, 1995.

Pradeu, Thomas, and Edgardo D. Carosella. "The Self Model and the Conception of Biological Identity in Immunology." *Biology and Philosophy* 21 (2006): 235–252. https://doi.org/10.1007/s10539-005-8621-6.

Prebish, Charles S. *Buddhist Monastic Discipline: The Sanskrit Prātimokṣa Sūtras of the Mahāsāṃghikas and Mūlasarvāstivādins*. Delhi: Motilal Banarsidass, 1996.

——. *Luminous Passage: The Practice and Study of Buddhism in America*. Berkeley: University of California Press, 1999.

Rambelli, Fabio. *Vegetal Buddhas: Ideological Effects of Japanese Buddhist Doctrines on the Salvation of Inanimate Beings*. Kyoto: Scuola Italiana di Studi sull' Asia Orientale, 2001.

Ramble, Charles. "The Politics of Sacred Space in Bon and Tibetan Popular Tradition." In *Sacred Spaces and Powerful Places in Tibetan Culture*, edited by Toni Huber, 3–33. Dharamsala: Library of Tibetan Works and Archives, 1999.

Ray, Reginald A. *Buddhist Saints in India*. New York: Oxford University Press, 1994.

Reynolds, Frank E., and Mani B. Reynolds, trans. *Three Worlds according to King Ruang: A Thai Buddhist Cosmology*. Berkeley, CA: Asian Humanities Press, 1982.

Rhum, Michael R. *The Ancestral Lords: Gender, Descent, and Spirits in a Northern Thai Village*. DeKalb: Northern Illinois University Press, 1994.

Rhys Davids, C. A. F., and K. R. Norman, trans. *Poems of Early Buddhist Nuns (Therīgāthā)*. Oxford: Pali Text Society, 2009.

Rhys Davids, T. W., trans. *Buddhist Birth-Stories*. London: George Routledge and Sons, 1878.

———, trans. *The Questions of King Milinda*. Vol. 1. Delhi: Motilal Banarsidass, 1988.

———, trans. *The Questions of King Milinda*. Vol. 2. Delhi: Motilal Banarsidass, 1993.

Ricard, Matthieu. *A Plea for the Animals: The Moral, Philosophical, and Evolutionary Imperative To Treat All Beings with Compassion*. Boulder, CO: Shambhala, 2016.

Robinson, James B., trans. *Buddha's Lions*. Berkeley, CA: Dharma, 1979.

Robson, James. *Power of Place: The Religious Landscape of the Southern Sacred Peak (Nanyue) in Medieval China*. Cambridge, MA: Harvard University Press, 2009.

Rockhill, William Woodville. *The Land of the Lamas*. Varanasi: Pilgrims, 2000.

Roetz, Heiner. "Chinese 'Unity of Man and Nature': Reality or Myth?" In Meinert, *Nature, Environment and Culture in East Asia*, 23–39.

Rolston, Holmes, III. *A New Environmental Ethics: The Next Millennium for Life on Earth*. New York: Routledge, 2012.

Rongxi, Li, trans. *The Great Tang Dynasty Record of the Western Regions*. Berkeley, CA: Numata Center for Buddhist Translation and Research, 1996.

Rotman, Andy, trans. *Divine Stories (Divyāvadāna, Part 1)*. Boston, MA: Wisdom Publications, 2008.

Rowell, Galen. "The Agony of Tibet." In Kaza and Kraft, *Dharma Rain*, 222–230.

Ruegg, D. Seyfort. "Ahiṃsā and Vegetarianism in the History of Buddhism." In *Buddhist Studies in Honor of Walpola Rahula*, edited by Somaratna Balasooriya, Andre Bareau, Richard Gombrich, Siri Gunasingha, Udaya Mallawarachchi, and Edmund Perry, 234–241. London: Gordon Fraser, 1980.

Ruiter, Dick de, trans. *Buddhist Folk Tales from Ancient Ceylon*. Havelte, Netherlands: Binkey Kok Publications, 2005.

Safina, Carl. *Beyond Words: What Animals Think and Feel*. New York: Henry Holt, 2015.

Sahni, Pragati. *Environmental Ethics in Buddhism: A Virtues Approach*. Abingdon: Routledge, 2008.

Sakamoto, Yukio. "On the 'Attainment of Buddhahood by Trees and Plants.'" In *Proceedings of the IXth International Congress for the History of Religions, Tokyo and Kyoto, 1958*, 415–422. Tokyo: Maruzen, 1960.

Samuel, Geoffrey. *Civilized Shamans*. Washington, DC: Smithsonian Institution Press, 1995.

San Francisco Zen Center. "Apprenticeship." Accessed February 27, 2017. http://sfzc.org/green-gulch/farm-garden/farm-and-garden-apprenticeship-program.

———. "Green Gulch." Accessed February 27, 2017. http://sfzc.org/green-gulch/green-gulch-watershed/watershed-work-party-days.

Śāntideva. *The Bodhicaryāvatāra*. Translated by Kate Crosby and Andrew Skilton. Oxford: Oxford University Press, 1995.

Schaefer, Donovan O. *Religious Affects: Animality, Evolution, and Power*. Durham, NC: Duke University Press, 2015.

Schaller, George B. *Wildlife of the Tibetan Steppe*. Chicago: University of Chicago Press, 1998.

Schmithausen, Lambert. "Buddhism and the Ethics of Nature—Some Remarks." *Eastern Buddhist* 32, no. 2 (2000): 26–78.

——. *Buddhism and Nature*. Tokyo: International Institute for Buddhist Studies, 1991.

——. "The Early Buddhist Tradition and Ecological Ethics." *Journal of Buddhist Ethics* 4 (1997): 1–74. http://dharmaflower.net/_collection/earlybuddhist.pdf.

——. *Fleischverzehr und Vegetarismus im indischen Buddhismus, Teil 1*. Bochum: Projekt Verlag, 2020.

——. *Plants in Early Buddhism and the Far Eastern Idea of the Buddha-Nature of Grasses and Trees*. Lumbini, Nepal: Lumbini International Research Institute, 2009.

——. *The Problem of the Sentience of Plants in Earliest Buddhism*. Tokyo: International Institute for Buddhist Studies, 1991.

Schumacher, E. F. *Small Is Beautiful: Economics as If People Mattered*. New York: Harper Perennial, 1973.

Seager, Richard Hughes. "American Buddhism in the Making." In *Westward Dharma: Buddhism beyond Asia*, edited by Charles S. Prebish and Martin Baumann, 106–119. Berkeley: University of California Press, 2002.

——. *Buddhism in America*. New York: Columbia University Press, 1999.

Seligmann, C. G., and Brenda Z. Seligmann. *The Veddas*. Cambridge: Cambridge University Press, 1911.

Seneviratne, H. L., and Swarna Wickremeratne. "*Bodhipuja*: Collective Representations of Sri Lanka Youth." *American Ethnologist* 7, no. 4 (1980): 734–743. https://doi.org/ae.1980.7.4.02a00080.

Shabkar Tsogdruk Rangdrol. *The Life of Shabkar*. Translated by Matthieu Ricard. Albany: State University of New York Press, 1994.

Shahar, Meir. *The Shaolin Monastery: History, Religion, and the Chinese Martial Arts*. Honolulu: University of Hawai'i Press, 2008.

Shaw, Sarah. *The Jātakas: Birth Stories of the Bodhisatta*. Gurgaon, India: Penguin Books, 2006.

Sheng-ji, Pei. "Some Effects of the Dai People's Cultural Beliefs and Practices upon the Plant Environment of Xishuangbanna, Yunnan Province, Southwest China." In *Cultural Values and Human Ecology in Southeast Asia*, edited by Karl L. Hutterer, A. Terry Rambo, and George Lovelace, 321–339. Ann Arbor: Center for South and Southeast Asian Studies, University of Michigan, 1985.

Shiu, Henry, and Leah Stokes. "Buddhist Animal Release Practices: Historic, Environmental, Public Health and Economic Concerns." *Contemporary Buddhism* 9, no. 2 (2008): 181–196. https://doi.org/10.1080/14639940802556529.

Smith, Joanna F. Handlin. "Liberating Animals in Ming-Qing China: Buddhist Inspiration and Elite Imagination." *Journal of Asian Studies* 58, no. 1 (1999): 51–84. https://doi.org/10.2307/2658389.

Smuts, Barbara. "Encounters with Animal Minds." *Journal of Consciousness Studies* 8, nos. 5–7 (2001): 293–309. http://www.ingentaconnect.com/content/imp/jcs/2001/00000008/f0030005/1213.

Smyers, Karen A. *The Fox and the Jewel: Shared and Private Meanings in Contemporary Japanese Inari Worship.* Honolulu: University of Hawai'i Press, 1999.

Snellgrove, David L., ed. *The Nine Ways of Bon: Excerpts from gZi-brjid.* Boulder, CO: Prajna Press, 1980.

Snyder, Gary. *Back on the Fire: Essays.* Emeryville, CA: Shoemaker and Hoard, 2007.

———. *Nobody Home: Writing, Buddhism, and Living in Places.* San Antonio, TX: Trinity University Press, 2014.

———. *A Place in Space: Ethics, Aesthetics, and Watersheds.* Berkeley, CA: Counterpoint, 1995.

———. *The Practice of the Wild.* Berkeley, CA: Counterpoint, 1990.

———. *Turtle Island.* New York: New Directions Books, 1974.

Soeng, Mu, trans. *The Diamond Sutra: Transforming the Way We Perceive the World.* Boston, MA: Wisdom Publications, 2000.

Somasekaram, T., M. P. Perera, M. B. G. de Silva, and H. Godellawatta, eds. *Arjuna's Atlas of Sri Lanka.* Dehiwala, Sri Lanka: Arjuna Consulting, 1997.

Sørensen, Henrik H. "Of Eco-Buddhas and Dharma-Roots: Views from the East Asian Buddhist Tradition." In Meinert, *Nature, Environment and Culture in East Asia*, 83–104.

Spiro, Melford E. *Burmese Supernaturalism.* Englewood Cliffs, NJ: Prentice-Hall, 1967.

Sponsel, Leslie E., and Poranee Natadecha-Sponsel. "A Theoretical Analysis of the Potential Contribution of the Monastic Community in Promoting a Green Society in Thailand." In Tucker and Williams, *Buddhism and Ecology*, 45–68.

Sponsel, Leslie E., Poranee Natadecha Sponsel, and Nukul Ruttanadakul. "Coconut-Picking Macaques in Southern Thailand: Economic, Cultural, and Ecological Aspects." In Knight, *Wildlife in Asia*, 112–128.

Stace, W. T. *Mysticism and Philosophy.* Los Angeles: Jeremy P. Tarcher, 1960.

Stanley, John, David R. Loy, and Gyurme Dorje, eds. *A Buddhist Response to the Climate Emergency.* Boston, MA: Wisdom Publications, 2009.

Stein, R. A. *Tibetan Civilization.* Stanford, CA: Stanford University Press, 1972.

Sterckx, Roel. "Attitudes towards Wildlife and the Hunt in Pre-Buddhist China." In Knight, *Wildlife in Asia*, 15–35.

———. "'Of a Tawny Bull We Make Offering': Animals in Early Chinese Religion." In Waldau and Patton, *Communion of Subjects*, 259–272.

———, ed. *Of Tripod and Palate: Food, Politics, and Religion in Traditional China.* New York: Palgrave Macmillan, 2005.

———. "Transforming the Beasts: Animals and Music in Early China." *T'oung Pao* 86 (2000): 1–46. https://doi.org/10.1163/15685320051072672.

Stewart, James John. *Vegetarianism and Animal Ethics in Contemporary Buddhism.* London: Routledge, 2016.

Stone, Christopher D. "Should Trees Have Standing? Towards Legal Rights for Natural Objects." *Southern California Law Review* 45 (1972): 450–501. http://heinonline.org/HOL/LandingPage?handle=hein.journals/scal45&div=17&id=&page.

Strain, Charles R. "Reinventing Buddhist Practices to Meet the Challenge of Climate Change." *Contemporary Buddhism* 17, no. 1 (2016): 138–156. https://doi.org/10.1080/14639947.2016.1162976.

Strassberg, Richard E., trans. *A Chinese Bestiary: Strange Creatures from the Guideways through Mountains and Seas.* Berkeley: University of California Press, 2002.

Sulak, Sivaraksa. "The Religion of Consumerism." In Kaza and Kraft, *Dharma Rain*, 178–182.

Suzuki, Daisetz Teitaro, trans. *The Lankavatara Sutra: A Mahayana Text*. London: Routledge and Kegan Paul, 1973.

Swearer, Donald K., ed. *Me and Mine: Selected Essays of Bhikkhu Buddhadāsa*. Delhi: Sri Satguru Publications, 1991.

Swearer, Donald K., Sommai Premchit, and Phaithoon Dokbuakaew. *Sacred Mountains of Northern Thailand and Their Legends*. Chiang Mai, Thailand: Silkworm Books, 2004.

Tambiah, Stanley J. *Buddhism and the Spirit Cults in Northeast Thailand*. Cambridge: Cambridge University Press, 1970.

——. *The Buddhist Saints of the Forest and the Cult of the Amulets*. Cambridge: Cambridge University Press, 1984.

Tanahashi, Kazuaki, ed. *Treasury of the True Dharma Eye: Zen Master Dogen's Shobo Genzo*. Boulder, CO: Shambhala, 2012.

Taylor, J. L. *Forest Monks and the Nation-State: An Anthropological and Historical Study in Northeastern Thailand*. Singapore: Institute of Southeast Asian Studies, 1993.

Teiser, Stephen F. *Reinventing the Wheel: Paintings of Rebirth in Medieval Buddhist Temples*. Seattle: University of Washington Press, 2006.

Terwiel, Barend Jan. *Monks and Magic: Revisiting a Classic Study of Religious Ceremonies in Thailand*. Copenhagen: Nordic Institute of Asian Studies, 2012.

Ṭhānissaro Bhikkhu, trans. *Udāna: Exclamations*. Ṭhānissaro Bhikkhu, 2012.

Thargyal, Rinzin. *Nomads of Eastern Tibet: Social Organization and Economy of a Pastoral Estate in the Kingdom of Dege*. Edited by Toni Huber. Leiden: Brill, 2007.

Thich Nhat Hanh. *Love Letter to the Earth*. Berkeley, CA: Parallax Press, 2013.

——. "The Sun My Heart." In Kaza and Kraft, *Dharma Rain*, 83–91.

Thubten Jigme Norbu. *Tibet Is My Country*. New York: E. P. Dutton, 1961.

Tin, Pe Maung, and G. H. Luce, trans. *The Glass Palace Chronicle of the Kings of Burma*. London: Oxford University Press, 1921.

Totman, Conrad. *Japan: An Environmental History*. London: I. B. Tauris, 2016.

Tsangnyön Heruka. *The Hundred Thousand Songs of Milarepa*. Translated by Christopher Stagg. Boulder, CO: Shambhala, 2016.

——. *The Life of Milarepa*. Translated by Andrew Quintman. New York: Penguin Books, 2010.

Tsering, Dawa, and John D. Farrington. "Human-Wildlife Conflict, Conservation, and Nomadic Livelihoods in the Chang Tang." In *Tibetan Pastoralists and Development: Negotiating the Future of Grassland Livelihoods*, edited by Andreas Gruschke and Ingo Breuer, 141–156. Wiesbaden: Dr. Ludwig Reichert Verlag, 2017.

Tucker, Mary Evelyn, and Duncan Ryūken Williams, eds. *Buddhism and Ecology: The Interconnection of Dharma and Deeds*. Cambridge, MA: Harvard University Press, 1997.

Tuttle, Gray. "Tibetan Buddhism at Ri bo rtse lnga/Wutai shan in Modern Times." *Journal of the International Association of Tibetan Studies* 2 (2006): 1–35. http://www.thlib.org/static/reprints/jiats/02/pdfs/tuttleJIATS_02_2006.pdf.

Tylor, Edward B. *Primitive Culture*. Vol. 1. London: John Murray, 1871.

Uexküll, Jacob von. "A Stroll through the Worlds of Animals and Men." In *Instinctive Behavior: The Development of a Modern Concept*, edited by Claire H. Schiller, 5–80. New York: International Universities Press, 1957.

Wagner, Alan Gerard. "Dumb Animals? Comparing Chan and Tiantai Views of Animals' Abilities in Two Song Liturgies for Releasing Living Creatures." Paper presented at the annual meeting of the American Academy of Religion, San Diego, CA, November 23, 2019.

Waldau, Paul. *Animal Studies: An Introduction.* New York: Oxford University Press, 2013.

——. *The Specter of Speciesism: Buddhist and Christian Views of Animals.* Oxford: Oxford University Press, 2002.

Waldau, Paul, and Kimberly Patton, eds. *A Communion of Subjects: Animals in Religion, Science, and Ethics.* New York: Columbia University Press, 2006.

Walker, Brett L. *A Concise History of Japan.* Cambridge: Cambridge University Press, 2015.

——. *The Lost Wolves of Japan.* Seattle: University of Washington Press, 2005.

Walshe, Maurice, trans. *The Long Discourses of the Buddha.* Boston, MA: Wisdom Publications, 1995.

Walters, Kerry S., and Lisa Portmess, eds. *Religious Vegetarianism: From Hesiod to the Dalai Lama.* Albany: State University of New York Press, 2001.

Watanabe, Manabu. "Religious Symbolism in Saigyō's Verses: A Contribution to Discussions of His Views on Nature and Religion." *History of Religions* 26, no. 4 (1987): 382–400. https://doi.org/10.1086/463088.

Watson, Burton, trans. *The Lotus Sutra.* New York: Columbia University Press, 1993.

——, trans. *The Vimalakirti Sutra.* New York: Columbia University Press, 1997.

Webb, James L. A., Jr., *Tropical Pioneers: Human Agency and Ecological Change in the Highlands of Sri Lanka, 1800–1900.* Athens: Ohio University Press, 2002.

Wickremeratne, Swarna. *Buddha in Sri Lanka: Remembered Yesterdays.* Albany: State University of New York Press, 2006.

Williams, Duncan Ryūken. "Animal Liberation, Death, and the State: Rites to Release Animals in Medieval Japan." In Tucker and Williams, *Buddhism and Ecology,* 149–162.

Williams, Paul. *Mahāyāna Buddhism: The Doctrinal Foundations.* London: Routledge, 1989.

Wilson, Edward O. *Biophilia.* Cambridge, MA: Harvard University Press, 1984.

Winzeler, Robert L. *The Peoples of Southeast Asia Today.* Lanham, MD: Altamira Press, 2011.

Woodhouse, Emily, Martin A. Mills, Philip J. K. McGowan, and E. J. Milner-Gulland. "Religious Relationship to the Environment in a Tibetan Rural Community: Interactions and Contrasts with Popular Notions of Indigenous Environmentalism." *Human Ecology* 43 (2015): 295–307. https://doi.org/10.1007/s10745-015-9742-4.

Xu Yun. *Empty Cloud.* Translated by Charles Luk. Worcestor: Element Books, 1988.

Yale University Center for Environmental Law and Policy. "2020 Environmental Performance Index." Accessed June 4, 2020. http://epi.yale.edu.

Yalman, Nur. *Under the Bo Tree: Studies in Caste, Kinship, and Marriage in the Interior of Ceylon.* Berkeley: University of California Press, 1971.

Yamasaki, Taikō. *Shingon: Japanese Esoteric Buddhism*. Boston, MA: Shambhala, 1988.

Yang, Der-Ruey. "Animal Release: The Dharma Being Staged between Marketplace and Park." *Cultural Diversity in China* 1 (2015): 141–163. https://doi.org/10.1515/cdc-2015-0008.

Yang, Jwing-ming. *The Essence of Shaolin White Crane: Martial Power and Qigong*. Wolfeboro, NH: YMAA Publication Center, 1996.

——. *Qigong: The Secret of Youth*. Boston, MA: YMAA Publication Center, 2000.

Yu, Anthony C., trans. *The Monkey and the Monk*. Chicago: University of Chicago Press, 2006.

Zaehner, R. C. *Mysticism Sacred and Profane*. New York: Oxford University Press, 1961.

Index

CPSIA information can be obtained
at www.ICGtesting.com
Printed in the USA
LVHW020531090322
712938LV00010B/1433